AURAL DIVERSITY

Aural Diversity addresses a fundamental methodological challenge in music and soundscape research by considering the nature of hearing as a spectrum of diverse experiences.

Bringing together an interdisciplinary array of contributors from the arts, humanities, and sciences, it challenges the idea of a normative listening experience and envisions how awareness of aural diversity can transform sonic arts, environments, and design and generate new creative listening practices.

With contributors from a wide range of fields including sound studies, music, hearing sciences, disability studies, acoustics, media studies, and psychology, *Aural Diversity* introduces a new and much-needed paradigm that is relevant to scholars, students, and practitioners engaging with sound, music, and hearing across disciplines.

John L. Drever operates at the intersection of acoustics, audiology, urban design, sound art, soundscape studies, and experimental music. He is Professor of Acoustic Ecology and Sound Art at Goldsmiths, University of London, where he co-leads the Unit for Sound Practice Research (SPR). He has a special interest in soundscape methods, in particular field recording and soundwalking.

Andrew Hugill is Professor of Creative Computing at the University of Leicester. He is also a Professor of Music and his principal research areas are composition, musicology, and creative technologies. His publications include *The Digital Musician* (Routledge), now in its third edition. He founded the Aural Diversity project.

AURAL DIVERSITY

Edited by John L. Drever and Andrew Hugill

LONDON AND NEW YORK

Cover image: Sarah Owen

First published 2023
by Routledge
4 Park Square, Milton Park, Abingdon, Oxon OX14 4RN

and by Routledge
605 Third Avenue, New York, NY 10158

Routledge is an imprint of the Taylor & Francis Group, an informa business

© 2023 selection and editorial matter, John L. Drever and Andrew Hugill; individual chapters, the contributors

The right of John L. Drever and Andrew Hugill to be identified as the authors of the editorial material, and of the authors for their individual chapters, has been asserted in accordance with sections 77 and 78 of the Copyright, Designs and Patents Act 1988.

All rights reserved. No part of this book may be reprinted or reproduced or utilised in any form or by any electronic, mechanical, or other means, now known or hereafter invented, including photocopying and recording, or in any information storage or retrieval system, without permission in writing from the publishers.

Trademark notice: Product or corporate names may be trademarks or registered trademarks, and are used only for identification and explanation without intent to infringe.

British Library Cataloguing-in-Publication Data
A catalogue record for this book is available from the British Library

Library of Congress Cataloging-in-Publication Data
Names: Drever, John Levack, editor. | Hugill, Andrew, editor.
Title: Aural diversity / edited by John Levack, Drever and Andrew Hugill.
Description: Abingdon, Oxon; New York: Routledge, 2022. |
Includes bibliographical references and index. |
Identifiers: LCCN 2021055584 (print) | LCCN 2021055585 (ebook) |
ISBN 9781032025001 (hardback) | ISBN 9781032024998 (paperback) |
ISBN 9781003183624 (ebook)
Subjects: LCSH: Music and the Deaf. | Music for the hearing impaired. |
Deaf musicians. | Hearing impaired. | Hearing aids | Sound–Social aspects.
Classification: LCC ML3838 .A947 2022 (print) |
LCC ML3838 (ebook) | DDC 780.87/2–dc23
LC record available at https://lccn.loc.gov/2021055584
LC ebook record available at https://lccn.loc.gov/2021055585

ISBN: 978-1-032-02500-1 (hbk)
ISBN: 978-1-032-02499-8 (pbk)
ISBN: 978-1-003-18362-4 (ebk)

DOI: 10.4324/9781003183624

Typeset in Bembo
by Newgen Publishing UK

This book is dedicated to the late David Baguley,
who so sadly died while it was in preparation.

CONTENTS

List of Figures x
List of Tables xii
Acknowledgements xiii
List of Contributors xiv

1 Aural Diversity: General Introduction 1
  John L. Drever and Andrew Hugill

2 Aural Diversity: A Clinical Perspective 13
  David M. Baguley

PART I
Acoustic Environments and Soundscape 25

3 Sound Before Birth: Foetal Hearing and the Auditory Environment
  of the Womb 27
  Julian Henriques, Eric Jauniaux, Aude Thibaut de Maisieres, and Pierre Gélat

4 Phonating Hand Dryers: Exploits in Product and Environmental Acoustics,
  and Aural Diverse Composition and Co-Composition 42
  John L. Drever

5 The Auditory Normate: Engaging Critically with Sound, Social Inclusion
  and Design 55
  William Renel

6 Listening with Deafblindness 64
　 Matt Lewis

7 Soundscapes of Code: Cochlear Implant as Soundscape Arranger 73
　 Meri Kytö

8 ∼ 82
　 Patrick Farmer

9 Autistic Listening 90
　 William J. Davies

10 Fire, Drums and the Making of Place during a *Correfoc* 101
　 Karla Berrens

11 Alphabetula 112
　 Josephine Dickinson

12 Textual Hearing Aids: How Reading about Sound Can Modify Sonic Experience 115
　 Ed Garland

PART II
Music and Musicology   123

13 The Show Must Go On: Understanding the Effects of Musicianship, Noise Exposure, Cognition, and Ageing on Real-World Hearing Abilities 125
　 Samuel Couth

14 Diverse Music Listening Experiences: Insights from the Hearing Aids for Music Project 134
　 Alinka Greasley

15 Consequences of Ménière's Disease for Musicians, Their Music-Making, Hearing Care, and Technologies 143
　 Andrew Hugill

16 Socialising and Musicking with Mild Cognitive Impairment: A Case Study from Rural Cornwall 160
　 Chris J. H. Cook

17 Thomas Mace: A Hearing-Impaired Musician and Musical Thinker in the Seventeenth Century 168
　 Matthew Spring

18	Do You Hear What I Hear? Some Creative Approaches to Sharing and Simulating Diverse Hearing *John D'Arcy*	178
19	Sign in Human–Sound Interaction *Balandino Di Donato*	187
20	The Aural Diversity Concerts: Multimodal Performance to an Aurally Diverse Audience *Duncan Chapman*	193
21	Music-Making in Aurally Diverse Communities: An Artist Statement *Jay Afrisando*	203
22	Attention Reframed: A Personal Account of Hearing Loss as a Catalyst for Intermedia Practice *Simon Allen*	207
23	Lost and Found: A Pianist's Hearing Journey *David Holzman*	210
24	Composing with Hearing Differences *Andrew Hugill*	217
25	Composing 'Weird' Music *Anya Ustaszewski*	223

Index 226

FIGURES

2.1	The human ear	15
3.1a	Foetal ear on 3-D ultrasound imaging at 12 weeks	31
3.1b	Foetal ear on 3-D ultrasound imaging at 24 weeks	31
3.2	Comparison between external microphone on neck of sheep (lower line at the start) and hydrophone in the amniotic sac (higher line at the start) (Source: Scott, 'Variance in Frequency Response between External and Internal Sound Sources.')	34
3.3	Foetal filter derived from recordings in Figure 3.2 (Source: Scott, 'Variance in Frequency Response between External and Internal Sound Sources')	35
3.4	Julian Henriques, Aude Thibaut de Maisieres, and Eric Jauniaux (l to r) with Sonic Womb Orrb at Brain Forum, Lausanne, 2016	36
3.5	(a) 3D map of the acoustic attenuation inside the womb. (b) Slice of the acoustic attenuation map in the coronal transverse plane passing through the uterus. The patient was 37 weeks and 3 days pregnant at the time of the scan	38
4.1	Hand dryer in public toilet	45
4.2	Mobile Otohime	47
4.3	Another mobile Otohime	48
4.4	A hand dryer in the Building Research Establishments' anechoic chamber. Photograph by Tim Steiner, used with permission	49
7.1	Electrodogram of the word 'choice', *Clinical Guidance Manual* (2018, 32). © Cochlear Limited 2021. This material is reproduced here with kind permission of Cochlear Limited	78
9.1	A simple model of the auditory processing chain	91
9.2	Thematic map of autistic accounts of soundscape listening	95
10.1	La Vella de Gràcia devils at Gracia's annual celebration. Image from the Colla Vella de Gràcia (Photograph by Joanna Chichelnitzky. Used with permission)	103
10.2	La Vella De Gràcia Lucifer and diablessa. Image from the Colla Vella de Gràcia (Photograph by Joanna Chichelnitzky. Used with permission)	104

List of Figures **xi**

13.1	The complex interaction between musicianship, noise exposure, age and cognition on real-world hearing abilities, such as speech-in-noise processing. See numbers within the text for description of effects	127
15.1	Thematic map of coded interview responses	149
15.2	Comparative Word Frequency analysis	150
17.1	The Lute Dyphone from Thomas Mace's *Musick's Monument* (p. 32)	172
17.2	Thomas Mace's Table/Organ, *Musick's Monument* (p. 243)	174
17.3	Thomas Mace's Music Room, *Musick's Monument* (p. 239)	175
19.1	Eleonor Turner playing *The Wood and The Water* using MyoSpat	188
20.1	Listening outside with wireless headphones (Kelston Barn summer 2019) Photo: © Miguel Angel Aranda de Toro (used with permission)	194
20.2	Listening inside (Kelston Barn, summer 2019) Photo: © Miguel Angel Aranda de Toro (used with permission)	195
23.1	Part of the score of *Pianissimo* by Donald Martino, with David Holzman's markings. Reproduced with kind permission of Lora Martino	211
23.2	Arnold Schoenberg *Drei Klavierstücke,* Op. 11, Nr. 1. First page with David Holzman's annotations. Reproduced by arrangement with Universal Edition A. G. Wien	213
23.3	First page of *First Piece, Battle Piece* by Stefan Wolpe, with David Holzman's annotations. Reproduced by arrangement with Peer Music	214

TABLES

10.1	Senses working the hardest in a *Correfoc*	106
10.2	Temporality of sensuous shift	107
15.1	Ménière's Disease Group (MDG)	144
15.2	Other Hearing Difference Group (OHD)	147
15.3	Interview guide	148
24.1	Andrew Hugill's diplacusis	220

ACKNOWLEDGEMENTS

We gratefully acknowledge the support of GNResound Ltd and the personal contributions of Miguel Angel Aranda de Toro and Marie Schleimann Nordlund. We are grateful to Cochlear for permission to reproduce their copyrighted material in this book.

CONTRIBUTORS

Simon Allen is an experimental composer, new music interpreter, improvisor, educator and producer. See www.simonallen.co.uk

Jay Afrisando is an award-winning music composer and sound artist. Employing multisensory approaches, he shares awareness of diverse hearing profiles, acoustic ecology, and our everyday technological interactions. He is a Jerome Hill Artist Fellow 2021–22 and OneBeat 2015 Fellow. www.jayafrisando.com/

David Baguley is a clinical consultant and Professor of hearing sciences. He leads the Clinical Hearing Sciences team at the NIHR Biomedical Research Centre at University of Nottingham, researching hearing loss, tinnitus, hyperacusis, and ototoxicity. He has published over 200 academic papers and five books. He has been awarded the British Tinnitus Association Research Prize five times and prizes from the British Society of Audiology, the American Academy of Audiology, the Royal Society of Medicine Section of Otology.

Karla Berrens lectures in sociology at the University of Barcelona and is a researcher with TURBA group at UOC and CRIT group at UB. Her research field is the corporeal relationship we establish with space and the making of place through the senses, notably on the interplay between hearing, memory, and emotion. Her aural experience has been heightened after a traffic accident and she seeks to explore other ways of feeling sound and space.

Chris J. H. Cook is a PhD candidate at Goldsmiths, University of London, undertaking practice-based research and working collaboratively with people who have dementia. Although he does not identify as having any disabilities, he does have a bilateral, constant-tone tinnitus.

Duncan Chapman is a composer/musician based in Lincolnshire UK. Much of his work involves collaborations with a wide range of people creating performances, installations & recordings. Solo work is on Silent, Takuroku & Linear Obsessional labels & Dusk Notes (a collaboration with Supriya Nagarajan) was released in 2020.

List of Contributors   **xv**

Samuel Couth is a lecturer in Audiology/Hearing Sciences in the Division of Human Communication, Development and Hearing at the University of Manchester. His research explores the effects of noise exposure on hearing abilities in musicians, including subclinical hearing deficits known as 'hidden hearing loss'. He also investigates barriers to – and facilitators of – hearing protection use in musicians. Samuel's hearing profile is audiometrically 'normal', but he experiences permanent tinnitus in both ears, which is more pronounced in his left ear.

John D'Arcy is an artist and researcher based at the Sonic Arts Research Centre, Belfast. His work typically involved technology-mediated live performance, voice-based intermedia artwork, and participatory song-making.

William J. (Bill) Davies is Professor of Acoustics and Perception at the University of Salford. He has research interests in human perception and cognition in complex sound scenes, with applications in soundscapes, room acoustics, spatial audio, environmental noise, music and machine listening. He was diagnosed autistic as an adult and experiences the atypical attention and speech processing reported by many autistic people.

Josephine Dickinson studied composition with Michael Finnissy and Richard Barrett after an Oxford Classics degree. She has published four collections of poetry including *Silence Fell* (Houghton Mifflin) and *Night Journey* (Flambard), and has collaborated extensively with artists, musicians, film-makers, and writers. Her unique history of deafness profoundly informs her practice: https://aeon.co/essays/a-deaf-musician-and-poet-receives-a-cochlear-implant

Balandino Di Donato is a Lecturer in Interactive Audio at Edinburgh Napier University. He researches embodied human-computer interactions in music performance. He was previously a Lecturer in Creative Computing at University of Leicester and a Research Associate at Goldsmiths – University of London's Embodied AudioVisual Interaction Unit (EAVI) for the realisation of a wireless EMG board and AI-driven software for musical applications, as part of the ERC funded project BioMusic.

John L. Drever operates at the intersection of acoustics, audiology, urban design, sound art, soundscape studies, and experimental music. He is Professor of Acoustic Ecology and Sound Art at Goldsmiths, University of London, where he co-leads the Unit for Sound Practice Research (SPR). He has a special interest in soundscape methods, in particular field recording and soundwalking.

Patrick Farmer is a writer, lecturer, and curator. He teaches in Oxford and lives on the Malvern Hills. Farmer has published several books and written compositions for groups such as Apartment House and the Set Ensemble. He is currently working on a book of essays entitled *To Suckle a Field of Monsters*.

Ed Garland is the author of *Earwitness: A Search for Sonic Understanding in Stories* and is currently completing his PhD at Aberystwyth University. His thesis title is 'Sonic Experience in Contemporary Fiction: Sound in the Novels of Deborah Kay Davies, Mike McCormack, and Marlon James'. He acquired hearing loss by the very common method of listening to loud music from a young age and playing the drums in various bands.

Pierre Gélat is a Lecturer in Medical Innovation and Enterprise at the UCL Division of Surgery and Interventional Science (Faculty of Medical Sciences). Pierre is working on the clinical translation of emerging cancer therapies based on focused ultrasound. He has contributed to the development of a novel mathematical treatment planning framework for the non-invasive ablation of tumours of the abdomen.

Alinka Greasley is Associate Professor in Music Psychology in the School of Music, University of Leeds where she teaches music psychology at all levels, and leads the MA Applied Psychology of Music. Her expertise lies in social and applied music psychology and in studying musical preferences and listening behaviour. Her recent work has focused on how hearing loss affects music listening and she was PI of the AHRC-funded Hearing Aids for Music project.

Julian Henriques is convenor of the MA Scriptwriting and MA Cultural Studies programmes, director of the Topology Research Unit, co-founder of Sound System Outernational in the Department of Media, Communications and Cultural Studies, Goldsmiths, University of London. Prior to this, Julian ran the film and television department at CARIMAC at the University of the West Indies, Kingston, Jamaica. He is currently the PI on an ERC Consolidator research grant, Sonic Street Technologies: Culture, Diaspora, and Knowledge.

Pianist **David Holzman** has won international acclaim for his recitals, recordings and writings. He graduated from The Mannes College of Music in 1972, studying piano with Paul Jacobs. His reputation is based largely upon his championing of many of the twentieth century's most noted and challenging composers. He is currently working with Resound Hearing Aids and Cochlear to help them make their hearing devices more helpful for performing artists.

Andrew Hugill is Professor of Creative Computing at the University of Leicester. He is also a Professor of Music and his principal research areas are composition, musicology, and creative technologies. His publications include *The Digital Musician* (Routledge), now in its third edition. Ménière's Disease has left him with severe hearing loss. In 2018, he was diagnosed autistic and founded the Aural Diversity project.

Eric Jauniaux, MD, PhD, FRCOG is Professor in Obstetrics and Fetal Medicine, EGA Institute for Women Health, Faculty of Population Health Science, University College London, UK. Eric Jauniaux has worked for over 30 years on placental and foetal development and on the diagnosis and management of placental-related complications of pregnancy.

Meri Kytö is a senior researcher and adjunct Professor in auditory culture studies at the University of Eastern Finland, has mild tinnitus at 6000 Hz, and a bubbling barotrauma in her right ear. She works in the Academy of Finland funded research project *Auditory Cultures, Mediated Sounds and Constructed Spaces,* to understand experiences, perceptions and agency in urban, commercial, and working environments regarding background music. She has edited ten books and special issues on soundscape studies and ethnomusicology.

Matt Lewis is a sound artist and musician, his work focusses on the relationships between sound and the social. Recent commissions include Clandestine Airs with Resonance FM and VOID, *'no such thing as empty space'*, in collaboration with deafblind charity Sense, *Where Is the Rustling Wood?*, part of Metal Culture's Harvest 15 with Studio Orta, *Music for Hearing Aids* as part of Unannounced Acts of Publicness in Kings Cross and *Exploded Views* with Turner Contemporary.

Aude Thibaut de Maisieres is a co-founder of Sonic Womb Productions, a multidisciplinary collaboration between doctors, scientists, engineers and sound artists, that seeks to study the acoustic environment in utero in order to improve incubators for premature babies, raise awareness of noise impact in pregnancy and explore new auditory experiences for well-being.

William Renel (he/him) is a practice-led researcher based at the Helen Hamlyn Centre for Design at Royal College of Art and the Director of Research at community interest company Touretteshero. Renel's interdisciplinary research explores the intersections of sound studies, critical disability studies, and design with a focus on developing new ways of understanding and challenging how sound and hearing exclude d/Deaf and disabled people in society.

Matthew Spring studied lute with Diana Poulton and Jacob Lindberg at the RCM and has published both on lute music and British provincial music. He gained a first-class music and history BA from Keele University, an MMus in Ethnomusicology from Goldsmith's College London University, and a PhD from Magdalen College Oxford. He was a Reader in Music at Bath Spa University from 2004 and is now Visiting Fellow. Matthew's solo authored books include: *The Balcarres Manuscript* (2010 AHRC grant), and *The Lute in Britain* (2001).

Anya Ustaszewski is a composer and sonic artist, with particular interest in musique concrete, experimental sound art, sonic sculptures and portraiture, and modernist classical music. As a composer, musician, and performer, Anya works with a variety of sounds and instruments, including those taken from everyday objects and found sounds. She has particular interest in immersive and abstract narrative sound experiences, as well as altered sensory perceptions and innovative use of software and technology.

1
AURAL DIVERSITY
General Introduction

John L. Drever and Andrew Hugill

What is Aural Diversity?

'Aural Diversity' describes the plurality of senses of hearing, encompassing the whole of human and animal nature and extending to machine listening. Aural Diversity exists not as a set of textbook definitions stipulating metrics, but rather as an acknowledgment of the complexities of lived and embodied experience in all its diversity and fluctuation.

Animal hearing and machine listening strictly fall outside the scope of the book, although they do inform some of the discussions. Our focus is primarily upon human ears, with their many different shapes, sizes, and characteristics. Human hearing changes frequently and in ways which may be temporary or permanent. Most people will only experience 'normal' hearing for a relatively brief period in their lives. There is also an array of hearing conditions and auditory perceptual disorders that affect roughly one-sixth of the world's population (Vos et al. 2013). Put simply: everybody hears differently. If we are willing to embrace this wide diversity of human auditory perception, then the sense of hearing is best approached as a spectrum. But this is not a simple task, as *auraltypical* models are deeply ingrained in society and science (Drever 2019, 2021).

Just as acoustical engineering is reliant on scientific exactitude predicated on universally agreed formulae and precisely calibrated instruments, so there is an underlying expectation that our understanding of hearing, as expressed in the requisite standards, can offer equal rigour. The principles of acoustics (as in all science) demand repeatability and reproducibility. Compared with other engineering disciplines, however, acoustics is often regarded as out of kilter, and even referred to as a 'black art' (e.g. Brooks 2002, 1), due to its integration of industrial measurements with human response metrics. So, although acoustics acknowledges that noise is a 'perceived quantity' (ISO 532-2:2017(E): V) and thus subjective, the presumption is that, by rigorously adhering to scientific criteria informed by statistical models one can establish a set of acoustical principles that hold for most of the population.

Textbooks state that human auditory perception of frequency spans from 20 Hz to 20k Hz. 0 dB(A) (or 0.00002 Pascal) is prescribed as the threshold of audibility, with the threshold of discomfort at 110 dB(A) and pain at around 130/140 dB(A) (or 200 Pascal). This gamut is exemplified by the ear's ability to register a vast range of sounds, from a pin drop to the loudest sound pressures in human history (albeit at its peril), such as an erupting volcano. The logarithmic scale of the

DOI: 10.4324/9781003183624-1

decibel was selected as the primary unit in acoustics as it better mirrors the nature of the human hearing encompassing this massive range, compared to the linear Pascal scale. Human hearing does not provide a flat frequency response (i.e. how it responds to different frequencies of the same acoustic energy), a quality that we would demand of a measurement microphone: it is most acute around the frequency range of human speech between 200 Hz and 10k Hz, and at the far ends of the spectrum tail off. A-weighted decibels take account of this shifting frequency response and are therefore referred to in most of the acoustics regulations and practice. There are some variations to this shape, such as C-weighting, which is flatter, characterising how hearing responds to exposure to very loud sound (i.e. over 100 dB).

The 'one size fits all' acoustical metric is typified by ISO 226:2003 Normal Equal Loudness-Level Contours (also known as Fletcher–Munson curves), from which A-weighting is derived. In the test, originally devised by Harvey Fletcher in the Bell Labs in the 1930s, tones are presented in groups of two, an octave apart, projected directly in front of the listener in a free-field listening condition (i.e. an anechoic chamber (Drever 2017)). The levels are adjusted until the listener perceives both as equally loud. This is repeated with another pair of frequencies, until a frequency spectrum from 20 Hz to 12,500 Hz is mapped out. The register of those adjustments across this spectrum are plotted, providing an account of the listener's hearing acuity with regards to a given frequency and its perceived loudness related to its sound pressure level. But who are these listeners? Well, the chart presented in the standard is a statistical blend of data from 12 studies from 1983 to 2002, based on subjects aged around 18–25 years old and so this became the age group stipulated in the standard. Moreover, these listeners had to be 'otologically normal' (as they called it):

> [a] person in a normal state of health who is free from all signs or symptoms of ear disease and from obstructing wax in the ear canals, and who has no history of undue exposure to noise, exposure to potentially ototoxic drugs or familial hearing loss.
>
> *(BS ISO 226:2003)*

We could argue that this seven-year bracket, which has been selected to exclude the developmental stage of hearing and age-related hearing loss (i.e. their hearing is stable and optimal), is a surprisingly small subset to stand in for human auditory perception. True, the testing method could not be reliably carried out by children as it takes some skill to judge equal loudness, but consequently there is a major discrepancy here if we were to use this standard to represents children's hearing for example – a child's ear canals are much smaller and shorter than the average adult's and as a result it has been inferred that they could be experiencing the same sound as much as 20 decibels louder (Cohen 2010). Nevertheless, according to the *Springer Handbook of Auditory Research* edition on *Loudness*, 'there is a general consensus among psychoacousticians that equal-loudness measurements continue to be the "gold" standard to which results obtained by other methods must conform' (Florentine, Popper, & Fay 2011, 32). The pioneering otolaryngologist Alfred A. Tomatis cautioned us back in 1963, 'whenever we try to define physiological normality we are on shaky ground, all the more so because the unit we adopt is a unit of sensation' (Tomatis 1996, 49). He compared aural sensitivity to judging whether 'a cup of coffee is twice or three times as sweet as another?' (Tomatis 1996, 49).

Sound studies, experimental music, and sonic arts discourse is rich in the classification of ever more nuanced kinds of listening: Schaeffer's *quatre écoutes* (Schaeffer 1966); Smalley's nine *indicative listening fields* (Smalley 1993); Truax's *listening-in-search* and *listening-in-readiness* (Truax 2001); Clarke's ecological approach (Clarke 2005); Oliveros' *deep listening* (Oliveros 2005); Norman's *referential listening* (Norman 1996); Kassabian's *ubiquitous listening* (Kassabian 2013); Back's *sociological listening* (Back 2007); Mullender's elite-level listener of the hostage negotiator (Mullender 2012). These different modes of listening are demarcated and encouraged and presumed universally obtainable with the right attitude and training (Drever 2019, 2021). Moreover, the discourse in these fields glosses over of any hearing-type that does not accord with the otologically normal. Discourse, practice regulations, and societal attitudes are suffused with auraltypical tendencies. The listening subject's idealised hearing is taken as read, as Jonathan Sterne writes: 'sound studies has a creeping normalism to it that is, an epistemological and political bias towards an idealized, normal, nondisabled hearing subject' (Sterne in Novak & Sakakeeny 2015, 73). And this archetype of idealised hearing spills into society at large. Consider, for example, Tom Rice's medical anthropology field research enquiring into listening practices in hospital. While going into depth on the practice of auscultation in a culture where a stethoscope is 'fundamental to the construction and performance of a medical identity' (Rice 2013, 72), he encountered a third-year medic with hearing impairment. She discussed a wide range of challenges, and the strategies she has adopted to cope with them. She would avoid specific areas of medicine that she regarded as 'highly "auditory"', such as: general practice, paediatrics, respiratory medicine, and cardiology (Rice 2013, 111). Auscultation, for her, manifested particular anxieties. Despite using an amplified stethoscope, which was just as effective as an unamplified one, she needed to take more care than an otologically normal medic. Moreover, she had to remove her hearing aids to use the stethoscope, and she felt that although this may be satisfactory for her exams, 'in a normal medical setting the same procedure might undermine patients' confidence in her diagnostic abilities' (Rice 2013, 113).

Disability Studies, and in particular d/Deaf Studies, have already explored some of the social and cultural consequences of shifts in our understanding of the human trait of hearing. These are research fields that, in the main, are driven by notions of identity and culture (Bauman 2008; Ladd 2005; Obasi 2008). They also reflect on diversity: 'disability brings together people who may not agree on a common definition or on how the category applies to themselves and others' (Adams, Reiss, & Serlin 2015, 6). The relationship of d/Deaf culture to normalcy is a defining feature of a field which is characterised by its positive affirmation of difference:

> To many in the deaf community, being deaf has nothing to do with 'loss' but is, rather, a distinct way of being in the world, one that opens up perceptions, perspectives, and insights that are less common to the majority of hearing persons.
>
> *(Bauman & Murray 2014, 9)*

Acceptance of the insights of d/Deaf Studies, such as this 'opening up' of aural perception, is very important in relation to the themes of this book. However, the phrase 'aural diversity' denotes a general condition and therefore includes *all* forms of hearing. Like 'biodiversity', or indeed 'neurodiversity', it is not so much indicative of an individual divergence from a perceived norm, but rather a description of the reality that any group of people (and animals and machines) will exhibit a range of hearing characteristics. The terminologies associated with divergences will vary greatly from group to group, or from individual to individual, and are anyway in a state of continuous evolution. For example, the formulation 'd/Deaf' reflects a distinction between those who are Deaf (sign language users) and deaf (hard of hearing, but who have their native tongue as their first language and may lip-read and/or use hearing aids). Furthermore, many d/Deaf people prefer identity-first language (i.e. 'deaf person', rather than 'person with deafness'), whereas someone with an illness that affects their hearing may prefer to separate the condition from themselves (e.g. 'individual with otosclerosis', rather than 'otosclerosis individual'). Aural diversity, then, is about recognising and accepting that people hear in varied ways, rather than asserting one divergence over the rest. Understanding aural diversity will consequently involve exploring many different groups and individuals with distinctive hearing characteristics.

The book also explores prosthetic technologies (hearing aids, cochlear implants, etc.) as an extension and adaptation of human hearing in relation to soundscape and music. Once again, our focus is interdisciplinary and concerns itself with reflections on diversity rather than detailed examination of either the medical or engineering aspects of these devices. Their influence and consequences for music and soundscape simply cannot be ignored. The rapid development of cochlear implants (CI) has led to much research into their capacity for music (Dritsakis et al. 2017). Musicians such as the concert pianist David Holzman have described in detail the transformation in their musical abilities brought about by CI (Holzman 2019). Original works such as the *Tonotopia* installation by Tom Tlalim (2018) have presented CI listening to non-CI wearers. Research into the uses of CI for musical rehabilitation has also been conducted (Dritsakis et al. 2017). The same may be said of hearing aids. Alinka Greasley's chapter in this book draws on findings from the 'Hearing Aids for Music' project to explore how different levels of hearing and the use of hearing aid technology affect music listening behaviour. It also highlights the diversity in people's musical experiences, despite their apparently similar medical diagnoses.

Such technologies come close to machine listening, especially to the extent that AI processes are embedded. The transformation of hearing they bring about introduces a new kind of mediated diversity. Like many pervasive media today, they have become so intertwined with everyday existence that there is even discussion of them as 'transhuman ears' (Trippett 2017). Yet the fact remains that only 17% of people who could in theory benefit from wearing a hearing aid actually do so (WHO 2020). So, any discussion of these devices is seen within the wider audiery context – the everyday and specialist situations in which listening and consequently hearing come into play – in which actual aural diversity is barely acknowledged. This auditory context expands and connects multiple disciplines, including clinical, social, cultural, audiological, ecological, technological, artistic, environmental, and historical fields.

The Aural Diversity Project

The concept of *aural diversity* was first proposed by John Drever at the *Hearing Landscape Critically: Music, Place, and the Spaces of Sound* conference in 2015 (Drever 2015). The word itself was designed to echo 'neurodiversity' and so to raise awareness of the diversity of hearing. It was created in an attempt to square the incongruent combination of acoustic data and wide user feedback in his influential study into hand dryer noise, conducted between 2011 and 2014.

In 2018, Andrew Hugill worked with Drever to develop a project entitled 'Aural Diversity'. In his book *The Digital Musician,* first published in 2008, Hugill had described the consequences of tinnitus for hearing and listening (Hugill 2008, 30). In 2009, his own experience of severe hearing loss due to Ménière's Disease led him to re-think his whole approach to music (see his artist's statement in this volume).

The Aural Diversity project has engaged with a wide network of aurally divergent musicians, artists, and academics, as well as many organisations, groups, and companies. It has attracted funding from several sources, including GNResound Ltd (the hearing aid company), Arts Council England, and the UK Arts and Humanities Research Council. In 2019, it staged two pioneering concerts by and for aurally diverse people and featuring many different ways to listen and perform. These are discussed in this volume by Duncan Chapman. It also held an academic conference, which led directly to the writing of this book. Many of the contributors were actively involved with the project during those events.

The primary foci of the Aural Diversity project are music and soundscape. These are fields characterised by acute listening, in which hearing difference *might* be expected to be very important but, surprisingly, is in fact largely ignored. This book is therefore contributing to a change in cultural context. Our hope and expectation is that the world will adjust over time to become more aware and accepting of hearing differences. We hypothesise a culture in which aural diversity is the accepted norm and we can all develop the language and tools to share and talk about our hearing. We imagine how listening situations may adapt to the hearing needs of individuals, rather than the other way around.

To achieve this requires more perspectives than just those from music and soundscape, though. Fields such as hearing science, audiology, acoustics, psychology, engineering, and other humanities including media, the arts, history, literature, and philosophy, are all very relevant. We must take a cross-disciplinary approach to this challenge in order to explore how both science and art treat aural diversity and the ways in which they overlap and inform one another. This produces a set of lively interdisciplinary discussions which may be transformative for all the participating disciplines. The structure of this book sets out to reflect this wide range of perspectives in a way that seeks productive encounters rather than setting up stumbling-blocks and obstacles.

About This Book

The book is organised into two Parts, the first concerning **Acoustic Environments and Soundscape** and the second **Music and Musicology**. It is not the aim of the book to drive a wedge between music and soundscape, but nevertheless the chapters that make up those Parts do position themselves mainly within either field. Preceding all of this is a clinical perspective on aural diversity from **David Baguley**, a Professor of Hearing Sciences at the University of Nottingham with a background in Clinical Audiology. While welcoming the concept of aural diversity, Baguley raises a number of critical issues in relation to clinical understanding of hearing difference. As with the science of acoustics, audiology and otology commonly define normal hearing as a standard from which people may deviate. The language of those disciplines is one of 'impairment', 'dysfunction', and 'loss'. Baguley seeks to establish a more nuanced understanding of such language than is provided by many discussions of the medical and social models of disability. While acknowledging the pejorative tenor of such words, he emphasises the compassionate intentions of the audiology clinic and the very real, indeed life-changing, consequences of some of these symptoms. He reflects that previous generations might well have been less inclined to celebrate aural diversity, because of the poor outcomes and poorer support for those with hearing loss, tinnitus, etc. This situation still prevails to some extent, and to diminish the disabling effects of many of these conditions would be to misrepresent them, notwithstanding the problems created by such language. In discussing this, Baguley sets out a detailed survey of the main types of hearing differences and their implications in this new context. This critical reflection signals that aural diversity must work *with* the established clinical disciplines if it is to shift paradigms. It is not enough simply to set itself in opposition to prevailing orthodoxies. The beneficial changes in perspective that would ensue are enthusiastically delineated by Baguley.

Acoustic Environments and Soundscape

'Soundscape' is a circa 50-year-old subject area that has undergone perpetual development and revivification by allied disciplines such as anthropology, geography, ethnomusicology, and sociology. The concept of the soundscape was developed separately by Michael Southworth researching urban design and by R. Murray Schafer, initially within the field of music education. In his *Book of Noise* (1998, first published in 1968) Schafer describes the soundscape as 'the entire acoustic environment of our lives, wherever we may be, at home, at work, indoors' (Schafer 1998, 4). Music as a metaphor with accompanying behavioural attitudes tends to be close at hand in Schafer's thinking; in very much an enabling manner, the idea of soundscape is proposed as a symphony:

> And we are simultaneously the audience, the performers and the composers.
>
> *(Schafer 1998, 4)*

This powerful idea was refined by Barry Truax, in *Acoustic Communication*, first published in 1984 (Truax 2001) where soundscape is predicated on the act of auditory perception and the making sense of that perception, extending from subjective perception to a shared, collective reading:

> An environment of sound… with emphasis on the way it is perceived and understood by an individual, or by a society. It thus depends on the relationship between the individual and any such environment.
>
> *(Truax 1999)*

In her introduction to *The Soundscape of Modernity: Architectural Acoustics and the Culture of Listening in America, 1900–1933* (2002), Emily Thompson compares the concept of soundscape with the established concept of landscape:

> A soundscape's cultural aspects incorporate scientific and aesthetic ways of listening, a listener's relationship to their environment, and the social circumstances that dictate who gets to hear what. A soundscape, like a landscape, ultimately has more to do with civilization than with nature, and as such, it is constantly under construction and always undergoing change.
>
> *(Thompson 2004, 1–2)*

More recently, and most significantly in terms of actual application, soundscape studies are being shaped by the field of acoustics. As acoustics has gradually adopted the soundscape concept, it has become necessary to codify it into a shared understanding by a scientific community. This resulted in the following definition of soundscape as:

> an acoustic environment as perceived or experienced and/or understood by a person or people, in context.
>
> *(D ISO 12913-1:2014(E))*

Crucial to this definition is the question: what constitutes context? This has been broken down into three component areas:

(1) auditory sensation,
(2) interpretation of auditory sensation,
(3) responses to the acoustic environment. (BS ISO 12913-1:2014)

As auditory perception is the mechanism for listening, aural diversity has a crucial role to play in experiencing, defining, and analysing a soundscape. There are as many soundscapes of any given acoustic environment as there are hearers/listeners and, as hearing acuity fluctuates, so does the soundscape. Now, with its recent inclusion of 'hearing impairments and hearing aids' as factors that may 'influence auditory sensation', within the criteria of the new International Standard definition and conceptual framework of soundscape (BS ISO 12913-1:2014), we are witnessing a sea change in how hearing may be understood. Generalisable metrics predicated on the otologically normal (British Standard: International Organisation for Standardization 2003, 226) are no longer adequate, as hearing becomes a shifting, unsteady human trait that we individually, tacitly, know from day-to-day experience.

In this section of the book, we present research that explores the at times challenging and antagonistic interface between the soundscape (i.e. perceptual) and the acoustic environment (i.e. physical) encompassing specific and often intersecting groups: autism, d/Deaf and deafblind, cochlear implant user, foetal hearing from within the womb, and a personal account of tinnitus. We share a case study on a problematic acoustic environments and creative strategies to transcend it; learn about carnival-like cultural practices and the sensory experience of participants; and are drawn to listen to that interface through literature.

> **Julian Henriques** and his collaborators present the development of The Sonic Womb research project, which highlights the important of foetal hearing and explores the vital acoustical qualities of the acoustic environment of the womb form the perspective of the unborn child.
>
> **John Drever** presents an account of his study on high-speed hand dryers in public and workplace toilets. The study followed up with a social survey and found grievances among the wide range of users. The chapter concludes with a review on the attempts to address the findings through appropriate creative practice.
>
> **William Renel's** chapter focuses on the under researched area of accessibility, inclusion and social equity with regards to d/Deaf and disabled people in socially public spaces. With reference to disability studies and inclusive design he proposes the 'auditory normate' to describe the notion of an idealised sonic citizen around which the contemporary world is built.
>
> **Matt Lewis** approaches his study from the perspective of participative and creative research, working with hundreds of deafblind people, audiologists, and sound designers by listening with deafblindness.
>
> **Meri Kytö** presents her finding from a year-long ethnography of a cochlear implant user, as they adapt to and learn to listen and interpret the acoustic environment anew.
>
> Replacing tinnitus with a '∼' **Patrick Farmer** endeavours to describe and reflect on his own auditory experience, remembering that by simply thinking about it can intensifies the awareness of its presence.
>
> **William Davies** upends the extant research on autistic listening that has tended to emphasise differences as deficits. Speaking from the perspective as an autistic researcher, he outlines specific skills such as soundscape decomposition, awareness of detail and the ability of achieving a flow state.
>
> **Karla Berrens** presents a sensory ethnography from Barcelona of a practice that includes voluntary exposure to auditory extremes and impairment with fire and drums and its aftermath, in the *Correfoc*.
>
> **Josephine Dickinson**'s poem *Alphabetula* uses ancient place names to convey the sense in which ears have created the unmapped landscape of the high fells in Cumbria.
>
> With reference to novels such as Valeria Luiselli's *Lost Children Archive*, **Ed Garland** shows us how through literary methods and allusion we can learn to listen differently.

Music and Musicology

In John Blacking's classic text *How Musical is Man?* he makes the following observation about human musicality:

> [...] the nature from which man has selected his musical styles is not only external to him; it includes his own nature—his psychophysical capacities and the ways in which these have been structured by his experiences of interaction with people and things, which are part of the adaptive process of maturation in culture. We do not know which of these psychophysical capacities, apart from hearing, are essential for music making, or whether any of them are specific to music.
>
> (Blacking 1974, 25–6)

The apparently straightforward assertion that 'hearing [is] essential to music' raises many questions. What is meant by 'hearing'? Is someone who cannot hear (in the conventional sense) excluded from music altogether? When we speak of 'man', does that imply a universal human equipped with two perfectly balanced and functioning ears? And what other psychophysical capacities might be essential for music, but excluded by the term 'hearing'?

There is a pervasive lack of awareness of hearing differences in music. In some cases, this is quite intentional. Music is a profession in which having a 'good ear' is regarded as foundational. Indeed, musicians are generally assumed to have *better* hearing than non-musicians. This has even been objectively measured and verified in scientific research (Parbery-Clark et al. 2009). It is hardly surprising therefore that musicians, and especially professional musicians, are so often reluctant to admit to hearing impairments (Schink et al. 2014). Furthermore, there is a disturbing lack of awareness amongst musicians of the risks to hearing of their profession (Pouryaghoub et al. 2017; O'Brien et al. 2014; Pawlaczyk--Łuszczyńska et al. 2010). Perhaps this is a result of a culture which tries to ignore or suppress the problem and encourages a 'defiance' of hearing conditions (Hugill 2019). Many professions that are predicated on the assumption of an expert listener (not just musician, but also sound designer, studio engineer, piano tuner, etc.) have too much to lose if it were to become known that their key assets – their ears – are not performing adequately.

Musicians are almost four times more likely than non-musicians to develop hearing conditions or auditory perceptual disorders (Schink et al. 2014). Tinnitus is more than twice as prevalent among musicians as non-musicians, affecting two in eight of the musical population. Nor is this restricted to the effects of amplified music: classical musicians experience tinnitus just as much as rock and pop musicians (Luders et al. 2016). Hyperacusis is disproportionately common amongst musicians, regardless of genre. So, for example, of 241 symphony orchestra musicians surveyed, 79% experienced some kind of hyperacusis, and 10% of them severely so (Jansen et al. 2009), while 39% of 139 jazz/rock musicians had a similar experience (Kahari et al. 2003). Diplacusis is less well known than tinnitus or hyperacusis, but studies have consistently shown that musicians have a considerably higher risk of developing that condition too (Di Stadio et al. 2018; Hugill 2019). For many musicians, the onset of hearing loss signals the end of their career, or at least a diminished involvement in music. For those who remain, there is a process of developing strategies to enable them to continue to engage with music while accommodating their conditions. This often involves a process of learning to *stop* listening, or to become 'non-auditory attending' musicians (Fulford et al. 2011, 459).

Musicology is similarly underpinned by a set of normative assumptions that ignore differences in hearing. To take a single example, consider this elaboration of a theory of musical listening by the musicologist and conductor John Butt:

> To start with the most obvious level of truism: we can surely assume that virtually all music in the human world presupposes that someone will hear it – otherwise there would be no reason, unless very obscure, to create it.
>
> *(Butt 2010, 6)*

A later statement drives the point home:

> [...] all music is the product of a fundamental human capacity to hear [...]
>
> *(ibid. 17)*

There is no discussion of what it means to 'hear', which is not at all unusual because almost all of musicology emanates from this tacitly agreed premise. Where hearing difference *is* discussed, the discourse usually takes the form of a heroic narrative about deaf or hard-of-hearing people overcoming their deficits. The most celebrated example is, of course, Beethoven. There are myriad speculations about how he transcended his increasing hearing loss despite the evident distress it caused him, as described in his valedictory *Heiligenstadt Testament* of 1802. As Robin Wallace points out: 'The fact that Beethoven continued to compose music after he lost his hearing has been presented as an act of heroism or a miracle of ingenuity' (Wallace 2018, 1). These heroic narratives about Beethoven are just as prevalent in medical studies as they are in musicology. A recent article in a leading otology journal observed: 'in spite of his hearing loss, Beethoven never lost his love for music and continued composing music, at times using some of the acoustic hearing aids that were just being developed' (Perciaccante et al. 2020, 1305). The general position of all these accounts is one of amazement at Beethoven's defiance in refusing to allow his hearing loss to interfere with his musical activities. A rare example of an attempt to counteract such heroic narratives is Dame Evelyn Glennie's *Hearing Essay* (2015). Writing as a deaf percussionist she aimed 'to set the record straight and allow people to enjoy the experience of being entertained by an ever-evolving musician rather than some freak or miracle of nature' (Glennie in Cox & Warner 2017, 125). But this position is the exception rather than the rule in a field that is dominated by auraltypical thinking.

This section of the book examines the challenges facing musicians and the consequences of aural diversity for composition, performance, and musicology, as well as for listeners. A number of case studies are included that illustrate the range of resulting research questions that may arise.

Samuel Couth explores the impact of hearing problems on musicians and the phenomenon of 'hidden hearing loss', in which the effects of noise exposure may have been underestimated.

Alinka Greasley investigates the ways in which perception of music is transformed by hearing aids, reporting on the 'Hearing Aids for Music' project at University of Leeds.

Andrew Hugill researches the experiences of musicians with Ménière's Disease, a complex and unpredictably fluctuating condition that affects both the balance and hearing mechanisms.

Chris J. H. Cook discusses the place of sound and music in the life of Trevor, an amateur early musician who lives on the Westernmost tip of Cornwall and who also has mild cognitive impairment.

Matthew Spring appraises the work of Thomas Mace, a musician who was active mainly during the latter part of the seventeenth century, by discussing the ways that his hearing loss affected his thinking on music and the practical steps he took to continue his musical life.

John D'Arcy discusses a project he directed in 2018–20, entitled *Do You Hear What I Hear?*, which explored how aural diversity might be shared with the broader public through technology-assisted interactive experiences.

Balandino Di Donato examines the use of new musical technologies in aurally diverse situations, in particular the MyoSpat system, which translates physical gestures into audiovisual signals. He describes a case study project developed with harpist Eleonor Turner, which incorporates British Sign Language into the performance.

Duncan Chapman reflects on the Aural Diversity concerts of 2019, describing the issues raised by the different approaches to listening that were adopted and some of the listening technologies that were deployed.

Jay Afrisando describes his compositional work and the consequences of engaging with aurally diverse communities, arguing for a broader conception of sonic arts and listening.

Simon Allen discusses the impact of hearing loss on his musical career. He examines accessibility issues and how creativity may be changed by experimentation within a context of aural diversity.

David Holzman describes his severe and profound hearing loss and how he has subsequently tackled pianistic interpretation of some of the twentieth century's most challenging music. He talks about his adoption of hearing aids and cochlear implants as part of his musical progress.

Andrew Hugill describes the consequences of severe hearing loss, tinnitus, and diplacusis for his composition. He explores the creative challenges that arise when trying to deal with these changes as part of the compositional process.

Anya Ustaszewski describes her musical evolution with hyperacusis and misophonia resulting from autism and ADHD. She affirms her difference as a positive way to communicate and explore new creative possibilities.

Conclusion

This book shows how aural diversity may not be just a new theme but in many ways a paradigm shift. It sets out to initiate this new disciplinary area, by discussing aural diversity primarily in human experience from foetus to old age, including prosthetic extensions by devices such as hearing aids and cochlear implants. It concerns the transformation of everyday listening as a universal experience. Our central argument is that differences in hearing are typically framed as deviations from a tacitly agreed standard. This idealised and singular notion of hearing is embedded very deeply in our culture, to the extent that it is accepted without question. It leads to social and cultural exclusion of groups of people whose ears are incapable of meeting the tacitly agreed standard. We ask the central question: *whose* ear has primacy in disciplines that are built on an assumption of otological normalcy?

Many of the discussions are completely new when considered outside their home discipline. While our main focus is on music and soundscape, the multidisciplinary nature of the book is essential as we try to understand the rich complexity of aural diversity from a number of different viewpoints. In a wider sense, it is to be hoped that the scientific approach advanced here will encourage more inclusion of aurally divergent individuals and groups in artistic and cultural activities that are intended to enrich all of us.

References

Adams, R., Reiss, B., and Serlin, D. (2015) *Keywords for Disability Studies*. New York: New York University Press.
Back, L. (2007) *The Art of Listening*. London: Bloomsbury.
Bauman, H-D., L. ed. (2008) *Open Your Eyes: Deaf Studies Talking*. Minneapolis: University of Minnesota Press.
Bauman, H-D., L. and Murray, J. eds. (2014) *Deaf Gain: Raising the Stakes for Human Diversity*. Minneapolis: University of Minnesota Press.
Blacking, J. (1974) *How Musical is Man?* Seattle: University of Washington Press.
Brooks, C. (2002) *Architectural Acoustics*. Jefferson: McFarland and Co.
Butt, J. (2010) 'Do Musical Works Contain an Implied Listener? Towards a Theory of Musical Listening', *Journal of the Royal Musical Association*, 135(S1): 5–18, DOI: 10.1080/02690400903414780.
Clarke, E. (2005) *Ways of Listening: An Ecological Approach to the Perception of Musical Meaning*. Oxford: Oxford University Press.
Cohen, Joyce (2010) 'Want a Better Listener? Protect Those Ears', *The New York Times*, 1 March 2010. Available at www.nytimes.com/2010/03/02/health/02baby.html (accessed May 2021).
Cox, C. and Warner, D. (2017) *Audio Culture* (revised edition): Readings in Modern Music. London: Bloomsbury.
Di Stadio, A., Dipietro, L., Ricci, G., Della Volpe, A., Minni, A., Greco, A., De Vincentiis, M., and Ralli, M. (2018) 'Hearing Loss, Tinnitus, Hyperacusis, and Diplacusis in Professional Musicians: A Systematic Review', *Int. J. Environ. Res. Public Health*, 15, 2120.
Drever, J. L. (2015) *Topophonophobia – the Space and Place of Acute Hearing. Hearing Landscape Critically: Music, Place, and the Spaces of Sound*. Harvard University.
Drever, J. L. (2017) 'The Case for Auraldiversity in Acoustic Regulations and Practice: The Hand Dryer Noise Story'. *Proceedings of the 24th International Congress on Sound and Vibration (ICSV24)*, London.
Drever, J. L. (2019) '"Primacy of the Ear" – But Whose Ear?: The Case for Auraldiversity in Sonic Arts Practice and Discourse'. *Organised Sound*, 24(1): 85–95.
Drever, J. L. (2021) 'Sound Art: Hearing in Particular'. In: Jane Grant, John Matthias, and David Prior, eds. *The Oxford Handbook of Sound Art*. Oxford: Oxford University Press.
Dritsakis, G., van Besouw, R. M., Kitterick, P., and Verschur, C. (2017) 'A Music-Related Quality of Life Measure to Guide Music Rehabilitation for Adult Cochlear Implant Users', *Am J Audiol*. 2017 Sep. 18;26(3): 268–82.
Florentine, M., Popper, A. N., and Fay, R. R. eds. (2011) *Loudness*. New York: Springer-Verlag.
Fulford, R., Ginsborg, J., and Goldbart, J. (2011) 'Learning Not to Listen: The Experiences of Musicians with Hearing Impairments', *Music Education Research*, 13(4): 447–64. DOI: 10.1080/14613808.2011.632086
Glennie, E. (2015) *Hearing Essay*. Available at www.evelyn.co.uk/hearing-essay/
Holzman, D. (2019) 'Deep River: A Pianist's Encounter with Hearing Loss'. Available at http://auraldiversity.org/media/
Hugill, A. (2008) *The Digital Musician*. New York: Routledge.
Hugill, A. (2019) 'Aural Diversity', Paper given at *Equality, Diversity and Inclusion in Music in Higher Education*. City University, 24 January.
International Organization for Standardization (2003) 'ISO 226:2003 Acoustics: Normal Equal Loudness Level Contours'. Available at www.iso.org/standard/34222.html (accessed 7 August 2021).
International Organization for Standardization (2014) 'ISO 12913-1:2014 Acoustics – Soundscape: Part 1 Definition and Conceptual Framework'. Available at www.iso.org/standard/52161.html (accessed 7 August 2021).
Jansen, E. J., Hellman, H. W., Dreshler, W. A., and de Laat, J. A. (2009) 'Noise Induced Hearing Loss and Other Hearing Complaints among Musicians of Symphony Orchestras', *Int Arch Occup Environ Health*, 82(2): 153–64.
Kahari, K., Zachau, G., Eklof, M., Sandsjo, L., and Moller, C. (2003) 'Assessment of Hearing and Hearing Disorders in Rock/Jazz Musicians', *Int. J. Audiol.*, 42: 279–88.
Kassabian, A. (2013) *Ubiquitous Listening: Affect, Attention and Distributed Subjectivity*. Berkeley: University of California Press.
Ladd, P. (2005) 'Deafhood: A Concept Stressing Possibilities, Not Deficits', *Scand J Public Health Suppl.*, 66: 12–17. doi:10.1080/14034950510033318.

Luders, D., Goncalves, C., Lacerda, A., Silva, L., Marques, J., and Sperotto, V. (2016) 'Occurrence of Tinnitus and Other Auditory Symptoms among Musicians Playing Different Instruments', *Int Tinnitus J.*, 20(1): 48–53.

Mullender, R. (2012) *Dispelling the Myths and Rediscovering the Lost Art of Listening (Communication Secrets of a Hostage Negotiator)*. Belfast: Griffin.

Norman, K. (1996) 'Real-World Music as Composed Listening', *Contemporary Music Review*, 15(1): 1–27.

Obasi, C. (2008) 'Seeing the Deaf in "Deafness"', *The Journal of Deaf Studies and Deaf Education*, 13(4): 455–65, https://doi.org/10.1093/deafed/enn008

O'Brien, I., Ackermann, B. J., and Driscoll, T. (2014) 'Hearing and Hearing Conservation Practices among Australia's Professional Orchestral Musicians', *Noise Health* 16: 189–95.

Oliveros, P. (2005) *Deep Listening: A Composer's Sound Practice*. New York: iUniverse, Inc.

Parbery-Clark, A., Skoe, E., and Kraus, N. (2009) 'Musical Experience Limits the Degradative Effects of Background Noise on the Neural Processing of Sound', *Journal of Neuroscience*, 29(45): 14100–7.

Pawlaczyk-Łuszczyńska, M., Dudarewicz, A., Zamojska, M., and Sliwińska-Kowalska, M. (2010) Ocena ryzyka uszkodzenia słuchu u muzyków orkiestrowych [Risk assessment of hearing loss in orchestral musicians]. *Med Pr.* 61(5): 493–511. Polish. PMID: 21341518.

Perciaccante, A., Coralli, A., and Bauman, N. (2020) 'Beethoven: His Hearing Loss and His Hearing Aids', *Otology & Neurotology*, 41(9): 1305–8.

Pouryaghoub, G., Mehrdad, R., and Pourhosein, S. (2017) 'Noise-Induced hearing Loss among Professional Musicians', *Journal of Occupational Health*, 59(1): 33–7. doi:10.1539/joh.16-0217-OA

Rice, T. (2013) *Hearing the Hospital: Sound, Listening, Knowledge and Experience*. Canon Pyon: Sean Kingston Press.

Schaeffer, P. (1966) *Traité Des Objets Musicaux: Essai Interdisciplines*. Paris: Éditions du Seuil.

Schafer, R.M. (1998) *The Book of Noise*. Ontario: Arcana Editions.

Schink, T., Kreutz, G., Busch, V., Pigeot, I., and Ahrens, W. (2014) 'Incidence and Relative Risk of Hearing Disorders in Professional Musicians', *Occupational and Environmental Medicine*, 71(7): 472–76. doi: 10.1136/oemed-2014-102172.

Smalley, D. (1993) 'The Listening Imagination: Listening in the Electroacoustic Era', in Paynter, J. et al., *Companion to Contemporary Musical Thought Vol 1*. London, Routledge, pp. 514–54.

Sterne, J. (2015) 'Hearing'. In: David Novak and Matt Sakakeeny, eds. *Keywords in Sound*. Durham, NC: Duke University Press.

Thompson, E. (2004) *The Soundscape of Modernity: Architectural Acoustics and the Culture of Listening in America, 1900–1933*. Cambridge, MA: MIT Press.

Tlalim, T. (2018) 'Tonotopia: Listening through Cochlear Implants'. Installation piece and exhibition. London: V&A Museum.

Trippett, D. (2017) 'Music and the Transhuman Ear: Ultrasonics, Material Bodies, and the Limits of Sensation', *The Musical Quarterly*, 100(2): 199–261.

Truax, B. (1999) *Handbook for Acoustic Ecology*. Vancouver: World Soundscape Project. Available at www.sfu.ca/sonic-studio-webdav/handbook (accessed 23 August 2021).

Truax, B. (2001) *Acoustic Communication* (2nd edition). Westport: Greenwood Press.

Vos et al. (2013) 'Global, Regional, and National Incidence, Prevalence, and Years Lived with Disability for 301 Acute and Chronic Diseases and Injuries in 188 Countries, 1990–2013: A Systematic Analysis for the Global Burden of Disease Study', *The Lancet*, 386 (9995): 743–800.

Wallace, R. (2018) *Hearing Beethoven: A Story of Musical Loss and Discovery*. Chicago: University of Chicago Press.

World Health Organization (2020) 'World Report on Hearing'. Geneva: WHO. Available at www.who.int/publications/i/item/world-report-on-hearing

2
AURAL DIVERSITY
A Clinical Perspective

David M. Baguley

Introduction

Clinical perspectives on hearing are based on the premise that any divergence from 'normal' leads to impairment and thence disability. Clinical diagnostic workups are performed to determine the extent of auditory threshold alteration, of auditory discrimination abilities, and to identify the site of lesion (e.g. the element of the human hearing system that is dysfunctional or broken). Interventions and treatments may then be planned, and these may involve drugs, surgery, or technology (hearing aids or cochlear implants). The outcomes of such therapy are increasingly being assessed by symptom specific Patient Reported Outcome Measures (PROMS), which are developed in partnership with patients in order to capture the most important and salient aspects of their particular disorder.

It is acknowledged that this clinical perspective thus, at first glance, seems diametrically at odds with that of aural diversity (as defined in the General Introduction). However, a more nuanced consideration of this issue may glean some important insights.

Firstly, let us note that some diseases that have hearing loss as a symptom can be life altering and in some cases, life threatening. Cholesteatoma is an ear disease involving an accumulation of epidermoid cells, congenital or acquired, and can present with conductive hearing loss (see below) (Nadol 2010). If untreated the tumour can erode the bone within the middle ear that protects the brain, and meningitis (and risk of death) can ensue. A vestibular schwannoma is a slow growing benign tumour arising from the nerves of hearing and balance (Merchant and McKenna 2010). If it grows, it can compress the vital structures within the brainstem of the brain that control many automatic features of the human body, including breathing, balance, and mobility, and major disability can ensue. Whilst these diseases are rare, the common sense implication is that an aural diversity perspective should not preclude medical examination and investigation of the aetiology of hearing problems.

Second, the seemingly pejorative vocabulary of Audiology (hearing loss, impairment, disability) is based on compassion rather than criticism. Many audiologists and otologists came into the field because of family experience of hearing issues, and are highly motivated to improve the life experience of those affected. Whilst a 'rescuer' model was sometimes evident in the early days of cochlear

DOI: 10.4324/9781003183624-2

implantation (CI) of the congenitally deaf, this is now rare. On the contrary, models of shared decision making (Pryce et al. 2018), and patient led setting of treatment outcome goals are increasingly common, as are the uses in Audiology of strategies like mindfulness (Marks et al. 2020), based on self-compassion. Additionally, a community of audiologists and otologists who are content to be identified or self-identify as aural diverse themselves is growing.

Finally, one might reflect whether whilst the concept of aural diversity is both welcome, and positive and affirming, but could also be viewed as something that previous generations of aural diverse individuals would not have seen as such. Until the advent of the use of CI in the congenitally deaf became widespread, outcomes for those individuals were poor in terms of cognitive and emotional development, risk of abuse, risk of mental health issues, and professional opportunities – and some of these issues have not disappeared. People with tinnitus have, until recently, been very badly served by medical health systems, and there have been well documented situations of crisis and calamity. In previous times it would have been fraught with risk to describe the personal experience of musical hallucination, which might have led to forceable mental health intervention. Let us celebrate aural diversity by all means: but let us not lose track of the fact that support and help is available (and needed) by many people with such experiences.

Hearing: Anatomy, Physiology, Functionality

Human hearing is remarkable. It allows the detection and recognition of sound, placed in time and space in the auditory scene around us, and the discrimination and analysis of patterns of sound that underpin vocal communication and music. The sense of hearing is interwoven with systems of reaction and alarm – and this is possibly a driver of the development of hearing in an evolutionary sense – but also with emotion and learning, in both simple and complex aspects. Pavlov (b.1844–d.1936) conditioned his dogs using a sound stimulus, giving an indication of sound perception leading to learning and response, but if we were to observe an audience at a Chamber music recital we would potentially notice awe, and a numinous sense of beauty. Sound detection and recognition are rapid, occurring at various points within the central auditory system, but the neural networks that respond to sound on the basis of previous experience, meaning, and salience are widely distributed throughout the brain and understanding of these processes is emergent, supported by new developments in neuroimaging.

For a detailed description of human auditory anatomy and physiology the reader is directed elsewhere (Fuchs 2010), but for the purposes of the present volume there are some important points to be made. Figure 2.1 illustrates the intricate and deeply involved structure of the human ear. The external ear canal (technically the External Auditory Meatus – EAM) draws sound waves towards the Tympanic Membrane (TM) or eardrum. The EAM transforms the frequency distribution of sound, and modern hearing aid fitting techniques take account of this with measurements taken close to the TM. Sound energy is transmitted from the TM into the Middle Ear, which is bridged by the ossicular chain: a bridge of the smallest bones in the human body (Malleus, Incus, Stapes). The middle ear is ventilated by the Eustachian Tube (ET) which opens on swallowing every few minutes, but poor ET function is strongly implicated in childhood glue ear (Otitis Media with Effusion) and many other disorders of the middle ear.

The cochlea has traditionally been called the 'organ of hearing', though a modern understanding considers the ear and brain as a system working together rather than having a single 'organ' approach. However, effective cochlear function is essential for human hearing abilities, and cochlear dysfunction leads to reduction in hearing thresholds, and the ability to identify and discriminate sound,

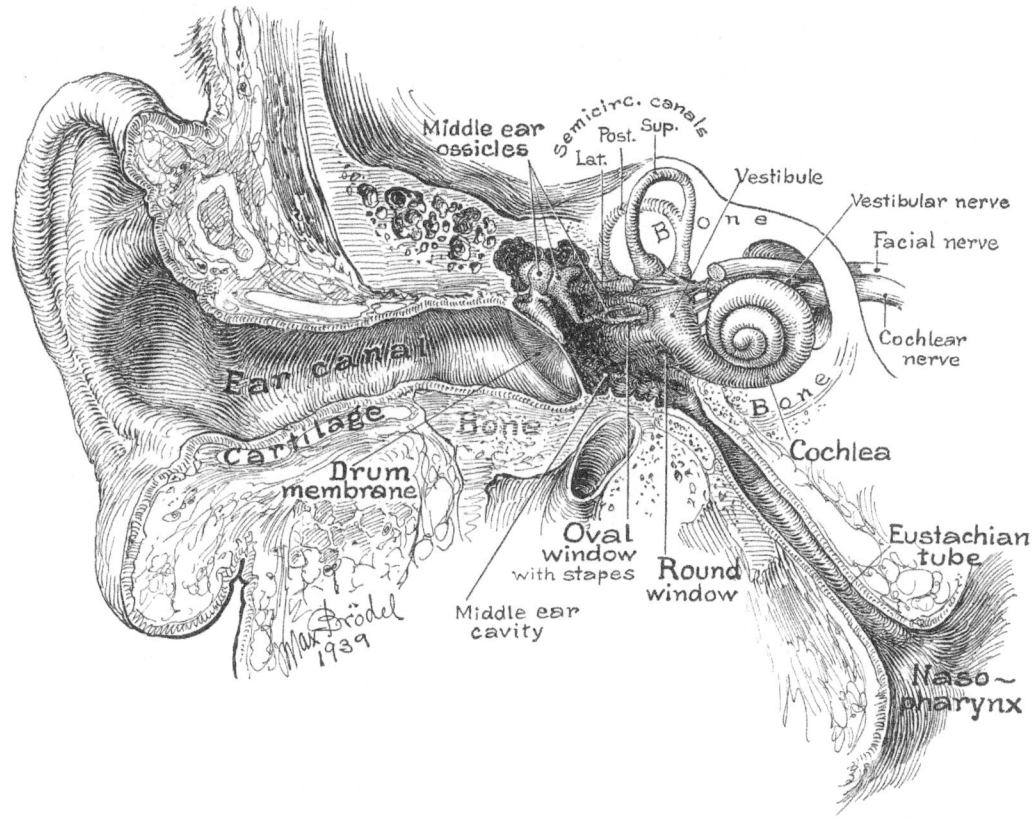

FIGURE 2.1 The human ear

and to locate sound in auditory space. Cochlear function degrades with age, and with exposure to noise and other insults such as ototoxic medication, immune disease, and reduction in the supply of nutrients and oxygenated blood. There is a substantial variation in vulnerability to age related hearing loss (ARHL) that is has been identified as genetic, though there is a complex interaction with social class and noise exposure.

The cochlea transduces sound via the Organ of Corti. This system has a metabolic engine (the Stria Vascularis) which underpins the effective function of the cochlea, but also gives opportunities for pathology and disease. The Basilar Membrane runs through the tubular structure of the Cochlea and vibrates with sound energy, with specific sound frequencies setting up patterns of of vibration (called standing waves). Within the Organ of Corti there are two types of hair cells. The Inner Hair Cells (IHC) number approximately 3000 in humans, and are organised by acoustic frequency along the length of the BM. When activated the IHC stimulate the synapses of the auditory nerve (which are themselves vulnerable to sound and other insults) and thence the auditory brain. The Outer Hair Cells (OHC) are quite different: paradoxically much larger in number (12,000 in humans), the OHC respond to signals downwards from the brain rather than transmitting upwards, and have a major function in the tuning and specificity of the BM. This is achieved due to the ability of OHC to change their shape in response to sound, and hence move, and in tandem to increase sound related movement on the BM.

Cochlear function is certainly essential for hearing, but the auditory brain provides the detection, analysis, and discrimination that are needed for hearing in its truest sense. Hearing function interweaves with systems of reaction, arousal, emotion, and learning, in complex and multidirectional aspects.

As such, issues with hearing are multidimensional and can be highly complex. A traditional view of 'deafness' would relate to the need for sound to be intense before it can be detected, but this does not consider the discrimination of sound, the recognition, and the reaction to sound that are all important aspects of human hearing.

Hearing Well

The concept that there is such as thing as 'normal hearing' is broadly accepted in the clinical community (WHO 2001) but this should be carefully and critically examined (see Kryter 1998, for review). There have been numerous surveys to determine the hearing thresholds of young individuals who did not report any hearing difficulties. These have resulted in definitions of 'otologically normal' (see Drever 2019, for critique of this concept). However these generally used small groups of subjects, and were not performed in well sound proofed environments. Additionally, the usual method of threshold determination has been Pure Tone Audiometry (PTA), which is a crude psychoacoustic test, though it does have a standardised procedure (BSA 2018). Frequencies commonly tested are pure tones at 250 Hz, 500 Hz, 1000 Hz, 2000 Hz, 4000 Hz, and 8000 Hz, the original intent being to survey the human speech frequencies. A pianist reader of this text will note that beginning at 250 Hz excludes the entire low frequency range of a piano keyboard (middle C is 256 Hz), and others will note that many humans have good hearing up to 16,000 Hz, this extended high frequency hearing being useful in speech discrimination in noise and music perception. The method of frequency estimation is also far from ideal: in standard techniques a tone is applied to one ear through headphones at 1000 Hz, 40 dB, and the subject is asked to respond by pressing a button if the tone is audible. Without being able to see the operator, the tone is then applied at 10 dB quieter, and repeatedly until the subject stops responding, at which point it is raised in 5 dB increments until the subject responds again, this being recorded as the threshold at that frequency. This is repeated for each threshold. Whilst this does glean audiometric thresholds for pure tone, albeit crudely with a test-retest variability of 5–10 dB, this does not capture any meaningful sense of 'hearing' in the real world.

Thus there are concerns to be raised about definitions of 'normal hearing' on the basis of audiometric testing. Other issues arise however when one considers variations in anatomy and physiology. Each person's external ear anatomy differs, including that of the pinna, and of the external ear canal. The way that one's distinctive anatomy transforms sound as it makes its way to the tympanic membrane contributes to sound localisation abilities, and in experimental settings persons trying to localise sound that has been transformed by another person's pinna have substantial difficulties. The transformation of sound in the external ear canal contributes to hearing aid performance, and modern hearing aid fitting protocols insist that the output of the device is verified by measures taken close to the tympanic membrane rather than externally as was traditionally the case.

The cochlear too has individual variability, not just in threshold, but in the manner in which sound is processed in a non-linear manner, and in differences in thresholds between the octave audiometric thresholds. The extent of these individual variations became apparent with the introduction of otoacoustic emissions (OAE): these are sounds emitted by the cochlear in response to external sound stimulation.

The existence of Auditory Processing Disorders (APD – see below), in which individuals with little or no reduction in PTA have severe difficulty discriminating sound, especially in background noise, is indicative that there are variations in these abilities. Rather than just pathological/non-pathological it is more reasonable to assume a range of abilities, and that these may change with mood and concentration.

Thus the concept of an immutable standard of 'normal hearing' has substantial flaws on a number of counts.

Hearing Disorders

In this section we will review the major types of aural diversity, giving the clinical names, and in each case reviewing the epidemiology, mechanisms, lived experience, and treatment. The intent is not to pigeonhole people: rather to reflect on the rainbow diversity of aural experience in present day humanity.

Deafness from birth or early infancy still affects approximately 1/1000 live births (Lieu et al. 2020). This can be genetic in nature, or due to birth difficulties or early infection and treatment. The vast majority of cases are detected in the neonatal period using OAE testing, and whilst the shock to new parents can be intense, the benefits in terms of early intervention (rehabilitation, hearing aids, cochlear implants) are usually very substantial indeed. The majority of the congenitally deaf can converse almost as well with spoken language within a few years of their hearing peers, and as such are less likely to fluently use sign language (Yoshinaga-Itano et al. 2021). The community who do use sign language as their major form of communication often prefer to be identified as Deaf rather than deaf, and within Deaf culture there are vibrant themes of spirituality, community, poetry, and comedy.

Age related hearing loss (ARHL) is the process by which cochlear function deteriorates with increasing age (Chueng et al. 2018). It is also known as presbyacusis, and initially affects high frequencies and progresses into mid and eventually low frequencies. Various mechanisms and causes have been identified, including the cumulative effects of noise, metabolic degeneration, and loss of cochlear hair cells. The impact is more complex than one might initially imagine: auditory thresholds increase so that quiet sound is inaudible, and the high frequency nature of this means that important high frequency sounds in speech are lost (such as the high frequency consonant sounds t, c, f, s). The dysfunction of cochlear hair cells means that the inner ear is no longer able to encode small changes in the frequency and timing of sound, and the impact of this is that the ability to discriminate sound, especially speech, is reduced: this can be described as a *smearing* of sound. Lastly, the dynamic range of hearing is reduced, in that not only does sound have to be louder to be detected, but also that the ability to tolerate louder sounds is reduced. This phenomenon is known as recruitment, and can be severe.

The prevalence of ARHL is high, affecting >50% of individuals aged 70 years and above (Chueng et al. 2018) and it essentially a normal part of ageing. As such there have been advocates for hearing screening of all UK adults at age 50 or 60 years: however, where this has been undertaken uptake of testing is low, and of those suitable for hearing aids, device uptake, and sustained use, vanishingly low. The reflection may be that a person with ARHL does not perceive themselves to have a problem: the TV volume can be increased, and they are unaware of the birdsong and other sounds that they are missing – it is their communication partners that have the issue, and it is only when pressure from them (especially for men) becomes intense that they will countenance hearing aids.

Usual treatment for ARHL is indeed with digital hearing aids (usually fitted binaurally to maximise benefit) and care has to be taken to programme the devices to the frequency pattern of the audiogram, and to avoid exceeding the dynamic range of hearing. Different programmes may be used for hearing speech in quiet, speech in noise, and for music listening. In cases of severe/profound ARHL, a cochlear implant may be utilised.

Noise can be a major problem for hearing, and noise induced hearing loss (NIHL) is a common injury in combat troops, musicians, those who work in noise, and people exposed to intense leisure noise (McCombe and Baguley 2018). Due to the resonance of the external ear canal the audiometric change is seen as a notch with a peak at 4–6 k Hz. After brief or limited exposure to noise the change in hearing thresholds can be temporary (known as temporary threshold shift -TTS) but repeated or hyper-intense noise exposure leads to permanent threshold shift (PTS). The mechanism is injury to the cochlear hair cells, and specifically the outer hair cells are more vulnerable due to their active motile contribution to cochlear sensitivity. As with ARHL the change in audiometric thresholds is accompanied by reduced discrimination abilities, reduced loudness tolerance, and often by tinnitus (see below). In a substantial proportion of cases NIHL is associated by recrimination or blame (self or to others seen as causative), and in some situations, particularly NIHL associated with occupational noise, compensation may be sought and awarded.

One group of people that have certainly been poorly served in the past is people with single-sided deafness (SSD), also called unilateral hearing loss (Lucas et al. 2018). This often occurs suddenly, as one cochlea catastrophically fails due to viral attack, ischaemia (reduction of blood supply), or an immune disorder. A person with SSD is typically unable to localise sound, and hence feels unsafe in many everyday situations, such as walking a child to school. Additionally the ability to distinguish speech in noise can be very markedly reduced. Such a person can become isolated and stressed, and this may be compounded by the common presence of severe tinnitus (see below). These experiences are surprisingly common: it has been estimated that 10,000 individuals in the UK develop SSD each year. Treatment has traditionally been hearing aids, either standard acoustic, Contralateral Routing of Sound (CROS) devices, or bone conduction hearing aid devices: however cochlear implants are increasingly being used as they deliver true binaurality of hearing.

The term tinnitus refers to the experience of sound when there is no external source (McFerran et al. 2019). Some frameworks distinguish between *objective* and *subjective* tinnitus: *objective* where a bodily source can be identified, such as turbulent cranial arterial or venous flow, or a spontaneous cochlear otoacoustic emission, and *subjective* where no such mechanism can be found, but this classification is not absolute and brings more problems than benefits. The experience of tinnitus can be very varied, including whistling, hissing, screeching, screaming sounds. It can be very variable, changing on the basis of mood, external sound, or spontaneously. Additionally it can be very complex: whilst many people just experience one relentless sound, it others there can be multiple and complex sounds. Broadly speaking the distribution of left eared, right eared, and central tinnitus is equal, and sex distribution is also equal. The prevalence of tinnitus rises with age, and in association with ARHL, though there is a well established prevalence in children. Prevalence data varies substantially with the index questions that are asked: if the enquiry is about spontaneous sounds with no external source that last for more than five minutes then the first world prevalence approximates 5% – adding enquiry about severity, in particular affecting sleep, and the prevalence is circa 1%. The impacts can include insomnia, poor concentration, anxiety, and depression. There is conflicting evidence whether tinnitus can adversely affect hearing abilities: the possibilities include attentional distraction as well as interference with the detection and discrimination of sound. Mechanisms of tinnitus are a source of contention in the field. Animal models of tinnitus exist, but they generally seek to initiate tinnitus using insults that are not generally seen in human populations, such as hyper-intense noise, or extreme high doses of salycilate based drugs (such as aspirin) which are not in use in people. In general one can consider tinnitus to arise from abnormal spontaneous activity in the central auditory system, which can be ignited by a cochlear lesion, or disinhibited by cochlear hearing loss. Once present in the system it can become self correlated (synchronous) and hence detected as a signal of importance. This then activates systems of reaction to threat and danger, and the tinnitus acquires emotional salience. In turn this leads to agitation, irritation, and increased arousal, with negative impact upon the ability to sleep and concentrate, which can lead to emotional exhaustion. Treatment is also contentious, but there is a consensus that combining informational counselling, sound therapy (including hearing aids where indicated), and psychological techniques deriving from cognitive behavioural therapy (CBT) is presently associated with reduced tinnitus awareness and impact.

In general, aural diversities consist of hearing less sound, but hyperacusis (Fagelson and Baguley 2018 for review) is an exception. Also described as reduced, decreased, or collapsed, sound tolerance, the experience of a person with hyperacusis is of their sound environment being intensely and/or painfully loud even when in the presence of mild or moderately intense sound. This can occur in people with either no raised audiometric thresholds, or with cochlear dysfunction. It is a challenge to determine a consistent estimate of prevalence, but an approximation of 2% in both child and adult populations seems reasonable. Detail investigations are underway but the mechanism of hyperacusis appears to be dysfunction of the system of auditory gain within the human central nervous system that allows an individual to range between straining to hear quiet sound, and reducing (compressing) the loudness of intense sound. As a neural mechanism this is substantially different to the cochlear phenomenon of recruitment as described in the context of ARHL above. A framework to understand the lived experience of hyperacusis has been proposed, with categories of loudness, fear, annoyance, and pain hyperacusis. Critics have noted that these categories are not mutually exclusive, and do not allow for movement within and between these categories. This framework did however draw attention to the experience of pain hyperacusis, when sound sensation is accompanied by sharp and deep otalgia (ear pain). This was hard to understand until auditory physiologists identified fibres within the cochlear nerve which are associated with pain experience, and which are linked with the cochlear hair cells – this appears to be a mechanism of loud sound causing pain, which would cause an individual to withdraw from the source. Dysfunction or potentiation of such a system could lead to pain hyperacusis and this is under urgent investigation. Present treatment of hyperacusis includes (as with tinnitus) explanation and informational counselling, sound therapy (but here to attempt to recalibrate the system of auditory gain by using quiet and consistent sound stimulation), and elements of CBT.

A further subtype of sound tolerance disorders is misophonia, wherein an individual experiences a strong adverse reaction to specific sounds (McFerran, 2016). These are usually human created, and the most usual are breathing, eating, or coughing: there is often one particular source person that is the trigger, and this is most commonly a close family member. The reaction of the affected individual has been described as rage, or disgust: clinically speaking the response appears to be so deep and powerful that it defies specific definition. The behavioural outworking of this can be calamitous for family relationships, where family members are no longer able to share mealtimes or other leisure activities, and descriptions of isolation and recrimination abound. The prevalence of misophonia in the general population has yet to be robustly determined: the majority of the cases seen clinically are adolescents, which raises a question of whether the natural history of the condition is improvement into adulthood (or being able to more closely control one's auditory environment). It also seems that some features of misophonia are common in the general population - being close to a messy eater on a crowded train can be enraging, but it is the development of a sensitivity to a particular person that is distinctive in severe misophonia. Work into mechanisms is ongoing: functional imaging studies indicate abnormally strong connections between the auditory emotion/reaction systems in the brain of people with misophonia, but how and why these develop is unknown. Present treatment is essentially psychotherapy based: whilst many people with misophonia develop auditory strategies to mask (with music for example) or reduce (with hearing protection) the trigger sounds, the effectiveness of these seems to be limited.

Diplacusis refers to a particular situation where a single sound can either be heard as multiple sounds in the same ear (diplacusis monoralis) or in each ear (diplacusis dysharmonia) (Fagelson 2018). This is a cochlear phenomenon, and essentially arises from dysfunction of systems of pitch perception. This is especially prevalent in musicians, and exposure to noise has been identified as a risk factor, but it may also be the case that musicians are more inclined to notice this as a serious problem (and potential impediment to their performance) than the general population. Information about the natural history of diplacusis is sparse, and formal treatment strategies do not exist.

Within the middle ear there are two muscles. The stapedius muscle is connected to the stapedius bone, and the function is to reduce the sound of one's own voice as it contracts with vocalisation, and to reduce the loudness of intense external sounds, though whether it can effectively do that for abrupt digital sound is debateable. It is much less clear what the function of the tensor tympani muscle may be. It is innervated (controlled) by systems of reaction and arousal, contracting rapidly when a person is shocked, and contracting persistently and continuously when a person is stressed. Either or both muscles can go into spontaneous spasm – similar to the eyelid muscle which can flutter in blepharospasm. The spasm of the middle ear muscles is called middle ear myoclonus (MEM) and can lead to an intermittent or continual fluttering which can be extremely annoying (Wescott, 2016). Either or both of the muscles can be involved, but it is more common for the tensor tympani to spasm, and so the condition is sometimes called Tensor Tympani Syndrome. It is hard for those undergoing this experience to describe it, alternating between vocabulary of sound or sensation. In some people this is worsened or triggered by stress: in some it is improved by a slight positive pressure on the tragus of the ear with a finger or earplug. In severe cases a specialist otologist can section either or both of the muscles, but often there is a strong reluctance to undertake this as no repair is possible, and each of the muscles has function that is lost with such surgery (though in the case of the tensor tympani this is somewhat unclear).

Auditory processing disorders (APD) have been mentioned above, and the characteristic issue of being unable to discriminate speech, especially in background noise, has been described (see Wilson 2018 for review). There are many subtypes, each of which has physiological mechanisms, ranging from the cochlear nerve being unable to preserve the synchrony of sound, so that signal becomes noise, to auditory brainstem structures being unable to encode the frequency and temporal characteristics of sound, to the two hemispheres of the brain being unable to work in tandem to process and localise sound in auditory space. The existence of APD was controversial at first, but there is now a consensus that when a person complains of such difficulties, they should be taken seriously and offered diagnostic testing, often only available at specialist audiology centres. The prevalence of such problems in the general population is essentially unknown: rehabilitation consists of auditory training, and in some cases hearing aids or cochlear implants.

Many people have the experience of hearing a catchy song on breakfast radio, and it playing in their head through the morning: this phenomenon is entitled 'ear worms' and is normal, though it certainly can be annoying. A different experience, however, is when internal music perception arises unbidden, with a fierce intensity and intrusion, and this is entitled musical hallucination (Cope et al. 2016). The music may be familiar, but often from childhood or early memory, and may be music that has never had pleasure or attraction. The phenomenon is more common in older people, in females, and in persons with a cochlear hearing loss. Proposals of mechanisms include deafferentation (e.g. lack of cochlear input to the auditory brain allows a musical memory to range unchecked), social isolation, and some medications have been implicated. A medical check is indicated to exclude the possibility of transient ischaemic attack underlying the experience. If the hallucinations are verbal rather than musical the psychiatric input is required to exclude incipient psychosis.

A new subtype of aural diversity arising from sound exposure has been entitled acoustic shock (McFerran and Baguley 2007; McFerran 2016). Following exposure to a sudden, abrupt, unexpected sound, often from a digital source such as headphones or an alarm, a person may experience a constellation of reduced hearing, tinnitus, hyperacusis, and sharp and persistent ear pain (otalgia). This can be extremely distressing and debilitating, and as with NIHL the psychological impact may be compounded by blame – though usually of the instigator rather than self. A high prevalence of acoustic shock has been noted in call-centre workers, where use of digital telephony is ubiquitous, and when many workers are pressured and stressed, and it has been proposed that these psycho-social factors may increase the risk of developing the condition. Interestingly. Cochlear function as determined by PTA is often normal or only mildly affected. Mechanisms of acoustic shock remain unclear, though there is one specific proposal of tonic contraction of the tensor tympani muscle in the middle ear (also implicated in middle ear myoclonus as discussed above), but this hypothesis is as yet unproven. Treatment of acoustic shock is very problematic and challenging, and standard techniques for improving tinnitus and hyperacusis appear to have little traction.

There are a group of people with complaint of hearing loss in whom no physiological abnormality can be found. A small number of them may be feigning the hearing loss, to claim compensation, avoid military service, or to achieve some psycho-social benefit (disability pension for example). This has traditionally been called 'malingering' and there are well established audiology protocols to identify these situations. In others however a diagnosis of Functional Hearing Loss needs to be considered (Baguley et al. 2016). This is a category of Functional Neurological Disorder (FND), wherein a symptom is genuinely being experienced, such as a tremor, paresis, or seizure, but in whom no neurological physiological lesion can be identified. The mindset to adopt is that such disorders are problems with the brain's software rather than the hardware. The majority of people with FND deeply desire to be well, including those with hearing loss variants, and there is no element of feigning. Unfortunately recognition of FND in Audiology and Otology services is only now emerging, so some substantial change of perspective is slowly underway.

Diversity, Impairment, or Loss?

At this point let us pause and reflect. There are a number of perspectives on hearing that are valid and part of the lived experience of human beings, and each may bring a glimpse of insight when one adopts an aural diversity mindset. The first is the use of the term '*loss*'. There are two situations that come to mind. A person who used to be able to hear without any challenges, but now, through age, noise, or ototoxic medication, finds this extremely difficult, can authentically and legitimately speak of their 'loss', and their family and communication partners may speak of this also. A hearing couple with a newborn child that they have been informed is severely deaf will also speak of loss: of a readjustment of hope and aspiration. In my career I have lived through (and been closely involved in) the development of cochlear implants, but before these were available for those people with congenital deafness I recall the pain of a young father, informed by me of his child's deafness, saying 'but I hoped he would go to university' – and at the time that would probably not have been likely. But, I also recall the joy of two young Deaf parents, delighted to be told that their child had cochleas that were not able to perceive sound – should the appropriate vocabulary be *loss*?

A second perspective is that of hearing in the built environment. The review above of the various challenges that can occur with loudness perception and impaired discrimination of sound are significant when assessed in sound-proofed rooms: but are substantially more troublesome in auditory environments such as supermarkets, railways stations, and hospitals. The attention paid to the visual aesthetics of these environments (such as that is) does not seem mirrored by the auditory experience.

As things stand, there are several paradoxes. As an audiologist by background, my hope is that the people I encounter in clinic will benefit from our interaction, and whether through discussion/counselling, or the use of technology, their hearing related burden may reduce. But also, I acknowledge that my vocabulary of *loss, impairment, dysfunction* is pejoratively laden, and speaks of disability and brokenness rather than diversity.

As a hearing scientist I seek to discover how nerve cells in the cochlea and the cochlear nerve might recover from insult or injury: for example how might I and colleagues protect children with brain tumours needing chemotherapy that will most likely reduce their hearing abilities from that life altering consequence?

Additionally, the vocabulary of *aural diversity* is vitally important. Each of us hears differently: clinicians may try and categorise such experiences by site of lesion, or by cochlear dysfunction, and whilst this might be useful for intervention, and technology, the wide experience of human hearing may be best expressed by a vocabulary of diversity.

Acknowledgement

David Baguley is supported by the UK National Institute of Hearing Research (NIHR), but his views are his own and do not represent those of NIHR nor the UK Department of Health and Social Care.

References

Baguley, D.M., Cope, T.E., & McFerran, D.J. (2016) Functional auditory disorders. *Handb Clin Neurol.*, 139: 367–78. doi: 10.1016/B978-0-12-801772-2.00032-1.

British Society of Audiology (2018) Recommended procedure: Pure-tone air-conduction and boneconduction threshold audiometry with and without masking. www.thebsa.org.uk/wp-content/uploads/2018/11/OD104-32-Recommended-Procedure-Pure-Tone-Audiometry-August-2018-FINAL.pdf

Chueng, L., Baguley, D.M., & McCombe, A. (2018) Age related sensorineural hearing impairment. In Watkinson, J.C. & Clarke, R.W. (eds), *Scott Browns Otolaryngology*, Volume 2, 8th Edition. CRC Press, Boca Raton, FL, USA, 685–92.

Cope, T.E, Sedley, W., & Kumar, S. (2016) Musical hallucinations. In Baguley, D.M. & Fagleson, M. (eds), *Tinnitus: Clinical and Research Perspectives*. Plural, San Diego, USA, 261–70.

Drever, J.L. (2019) 'Primacy of the ear' – but whose ear?: the case for auraldiversity in sonic arts practice and discourse. *Organised Sound*, 24(1): 85–95.

Fagelson, M. (2018) Diplausis. In Fagelson, M. & Baguley, D.M. (eds), *Hyperacusis and Disorders of Sound Intolerance*. Plural, San Diego, USA, 191–206.

Fagelson, M. & Baguley, D.M. (eds) (2018) *Hyperacusis and Disorders of Sound Intolerance*. Plural, San Diego, USA.

Fuchs, P.A. (2010) Introduction and overview. In Fuchs, P.A. (ed.), *The Ear: Oxford Handbook of Auditory Science*, Volume 1. Oxford University Press, Oxford, UK, 1–14.

Kryter, K.D. (1998) Evaluation of hearing handicap. *J Am Acad Audiol.*, 9: 141–6.

Lucas, L., Katiri, R., & Kitterick, P.T. (2018) The psychological and social consequences of single-sided deafness in adulthood. *Int J Audiol.*, Jan. 57(1): 21–30. doi:10.1080/14992027.2017.1398420.

Lieu, J.E.C., Kenna, M., Anne, S., & Davidson, L (2020) Hearing loss in children: A review. *JAMA*, 324(21): 2195–2205.

McCombe, A. & Baguley, D.M. (2018) Noise induced hearing loss and related conditions. In Watkinson, J.C. & Clarke, R.W. (eds), *Scott Browns Otolaryngology*, Volume 2, 8th Edition. CRC Press, Boca Raton, FL, USA, 693–700.

McFerran, D.J. (2016) Acoustic shock. In Baguley, D.M. & Fagleson, M. (eds), *Tinnitus: Clinical and Research Perspectives*. Plural, San Diego, USA, 181–96.

McFerran, D.J. (2016) Misophonia and phonophobia. In Baguley, D.M. & Fagleson, M. (eds), *Tinnitus: Clinical and Research Perspectives*. Plural, San Diego, USA, 245–60.

McFerran, D.J. & Baguley, D.M. (2007) Acoustic shock. *J Laryngol Otol.*, 121(4): 301–5. doi: 10.1017/S0022215107006111.

McFerran, D.J., Stockdale, D., Holme, R., Large, C.H., & Baguley, D.M. (2019) Why is there no cure for tinnitus? *Front Neurosci.*, 13: 802. doi: 10.3389/fnins.2019.00802.

Marks, E, Smith, P., & McKenna, L. (2020) I wasn't at war with the noise: How mindfulness based cognitive therapy changes patients' experiences of tinnitus. *Front Psychol.* 17 Apr, 11: 483. doi: 10.3389/fpsyg.2020.00483.

Merchant, S.M. & McKenna, M.J. (2010) Neoplastic growth. In Merchant, S.M. & Nadol, J.R. (eds), *Schucknecht's Pathology of the Ear*, 3rd Edition. People's Medical Publishing House, Shelton USA, 477–536.

Nadol, J.R. (2010) Infections. In Merchant, S.M. & Nadol, J.R. (eds), *Schucknecht's Pathology of the Ear*, 3rd Edition. People's Medical Publishing House, Shelton, USA, 279–352.

Pryce, H., Durand, M.A., Hall, A., Shaw, R., Culhane, B.A., Swift, S., Straus, J., Marks, E., Ward, M., & Chilvers, K. (2018) The development of a decision aid for tinnitus. *Int J Audiol.*, 57(9): 714–19. doi: 10.1080/14992027.2018.1468093.

Wescott, M. (2016) Middle ear myoclonus and tonic tensor tympani syndrome. In Baguley, D.M. & Fagleson, M. (eds), *Tinnitus: Clinical and Research Perspectives*. Plural, San Diego, USA, 145–62.

Wilson, W.J. (2018) Evolving the concept of APD. *Int J Audiol.*, 57(4): 240–48. doi: 10.1080/14992027.2017.1409438.

World Health Organization (WHO) (2001) International classification of functioning, disability, and health. https://apps.who.int/iris/bitstream/handle/10665/42407/9241545429.pdf

Yoshinaga-Itano, C., Manchaiah, V., & Hunnicutt, C.J. (2021) Outcomes of universal newborn screening programs: Systematic review. *Clin Med.*, 10(13): 2784.

PART I
Acoustic Environments and Soundscape

3
SOUND BEFORE BIRTH

Foetal Hearing and the Auditory Environment of the Womb

Julian Henriques, Eric Jauniaux, Aude Thibaut de Maisieres, and Pierre Gélat

Aural diversity means not only do each of us hear differently, but also that our hearing changes radically throughout our lifetime. Nowhere is this auditory range greater than between the hearing we do before we are born and thereafter, as infants, children, and adults. The Sonic Womb research project has been exploring foetal hearing for over a decade; its aims are two-fold. One is to draw attention to the importance of foetal hearing – or indeed that there is such a thing – by demonstrating to medical professionals and the public alike what and how a baby hears inside the womb. The other aim of the Sonic Womb project is to research the amplifying and attenuating effects of the mother's body on the auditory environment available to her unborn child. Such biomedical evidence will help us achieve the objective of the project. This is to modify the incubators for premature babies in such a way as to avoid the auditory stress to which they are currently inadvertently exposed in neonatal wards.

The womb is a liminal place, a threshold between conception and birth, and according to some traditions between our former life and a new one. It is also a neglected place, a nether zone, where we are an unseparated part of another (our mother) prior to our entry into the world at birth as an 'individual' albeit a highly dependent one. In fact, our uterine environment has significant effects on the baby's development, not only on account of the nutrients (and possibly toxins) it receives via the placenta, but also on account of the auditory environment to which it is exposed from the mother's daily life. It is not commonly appreciated that the baby's faculty of hearing is fully formed and functional from the end of the second trimester of pregnancy.

While the unborn baby's hearing is very different to that capacity after birth, the fact that an unborn baby is sensitive to sound raises some important questions. For the Sonic Womb research project our most important task is to give an accurate account of the auditory environment available to the unborn baby. Finding answers to this has clinical implications, such as, what influences or effects does foetal hearing have on life after birth? Also, especially if audition is the *only* source of sensory stimulation before birth, what effects does this have on the physiological development of the foetus?

If the unborn baby can hear from inside the womb this also raises substantial philosophical questions. How is our consciousness after birth affected by its presumed origins in an entirely auditory world? If life begins *before* birth rather than *at* birth, as is conventionally assumed, might this change who we think we are? While any attempt to answer these broader questions is well beyond the scope of this chapter, they are part of the setting for the Sonic Womb project, one of whose origins was an interest in the effects and affects of intense auditory environments, such as the Jamaican reggae sound system dancehall session (Henriques 2011).

Evidence of the effects of uterine hearing comes from one study whose striking findings were that the cry melody of a new-born baby is shaped by their language environment before birth. Mampe and her team found that a newborn's cry mimicked the intonation contours of their mother's speech and was therefore significantly different for French and German babies (Mampe et al. 2009). This is also true of French and English babies (Madaule 1994). Prior to contemporary medical science, historically, there has been interest in what the baby hears before birth. In the ancient Indian Sanskrit epic of the *Mahabharata* the hero Abhimanyu overhears his father Arjuna discussing a battle plan that many years later afford him victory in the decisive battle. More recently Ian McEwan has explored this theme of foetal hearing in his novel *Nutshell* as a contemporary retelling of *Hamlet*.

Auditory Stress in Neonatal Wards

The Sonic Womb project has quite immediate practical concerns over the lack of medical interest or understanding of the importance of foetal hearing.[1] Specifically, premature babies surviving in incubators – but without the protective auditory environment of their mother's womb – are exposed to auditory stress. This finding has been a major stimulus for the project's objective to establish the parameters of the typical uterine auditory environment in order to simulate this for premature babies and thereby to improve the clinical outcomes for premature babies.

Over the years medical science has advanced to the extent that foetuses born as early as 22 weeks of gestation can survive. Around 15 million babies are born prematurely worldwide each year and children born very preterm, in turn, have an increased likelihood of sensory, cognitive, and motor deficits. Prematurity mainly affects the newborn early cortical auditory encoding, whereas immaturity of the brain and secondary damage linked to prematurity additionally influence higher cortical functions of auditory perception and distraction (Hovel et al. 2015). At school age, children born prematurely experience more problems across most educational domains than children born at term. In particular, they have a higher incidence of speech delay, learning disorders, attention-deficit hyperactivity, and developmental co-ordination. These findings suggest that the perinatal auditory environment may play a role in development of auditory processing. Despite improving rates of survival for very premature newborns over the last 20 years, the rate of disabilities has remained relatively constant. The children who have been the most premature are not necessarily those with the lowest scores, suggesting that other factors than those associated directly with the complications of prematurity are at play.

In the neonatal intensive care unit (NICU), the premature newborn will be exposed for weeks, sometimes months, to a non-physiological but very carefully controlled environment until its lungs and digestive tube have developed sufficiently to keep the baby alive without medical support. Incubators for premature newborns can control temperature, air quality, nutrition, and lighting, but ventilators and incubator fans generate low-frequency band sound pressure levels and when all equipment are switched on, the sound pressure levels increased to 68 dB(A) (Marik et al. 2012). Hearing loss and sleep disturbances have been documented in children previously hospitalised in NICU with continuous exposure to sound levels > 60 dB. In addition, the absence of physiological auditory stimulation, mainly the maternal voice, as well additional artificial noises, such as monitoring alarms, are known to have adverse effects.

The evidence to support the use of sound devices such as music players with recorded maternal sound placed inside the incubator of premature newborn is limited and heterogenous. This is particularly the case for very premature newborns who are exposed the most from noise stress of prolonged hospitalisation inside NICU. An experiment based on maternal sound stimulation using maternal voice and heartbeat sounds recorded individually for premature (at 26–32 weeks) neonates lowers the frequency of cardiorespiratory events in neonates born at ≥ 33 weeks of gestation compared to routine hospital sounds (Doheny et al. 2012). Similarly, newborns born at ≥ 35 weeks' gestation but not at 33 to 34 weeks' gestation show increasing wakefulness in response to their mother's voice (Shellhaas et al. 2019). These finding also suggest that exposure to the mother's voice might protect newborns from awakening after bursts of loud hospital noise when their mother is at home. A more robust pattern of evidence has been found with feeding behaviours, as well as cognitive and neurobehavioral development (Provenzi et al. 2018). Overall, the maternal voice appears to be a non-noxious intervention which should be embedded in future research protocols developmental care strategies for newborns admitted to both intensive care and special care.

Current Interest in the Womb as Auditory Environment

The issue of auditory stress is also a matter of concern outside the medical profession. What and when can my baby hear in the womb? These are some of the commonest questions asked by expectant parents during pregnancy, worried that attending a rock concert, for example, might be damaging to their baby's hearing and which their obstetric team will have difficulty answering as the scientific evidence is limited. These questions were taken up by the American Academy of Paediatrics, when in 1997 they expressed concern about the effect of high noise levels on the foetus and newborn and recommended further research. Indeed, half of human beings now live in cities with a cacophonous urban soundscape far in excess of our ancestors' auditory environment. It has been found that high levels of occupational and environmental noise can raise blood pressure (Penney and Earl 2004) and thus will directly impact the wellbeing of pregnant mothers and indirectly their foetus.

Interest in the womb as an auditory environment also goes beyond medical concerns. Ever since ultrasound technology became widely available to reveal the foetal heartbeat in the 1970s, there has been a curiosity in the womb as a soundscape. It is interesting to remember that we first meet our baby sonically. The ultrasound scan image giving parents the first 'sight' of their unborn is only a visualisation of the sound reflection of the foetus. The general public's curiosity about the foetal sound world has generated a market of technological gadgets that attempts to satisfy it. A cursory search on the App Store reveals many apps of 'womb sounds' purporting to replicate the acoustic environment in utero.

In February 2021, an American musician couple, Elizabeth Hart and Ivan Diaz Mathe, announced the upcoming release of *Sounds of the Unborn*, an album of songs by their yet unborn daughter Yupanqui. This was produced using 'biosonic MIDI technology' hooked to Hart's stomach which recorded the vibrations of the in-utero movements of Yupanqui and translated them into sound. Hart and Mathé then edited and mixed the results 'while trying to respect Yupanqui's musical autonomy so as to allow her message to exist in its raw form' (Beaumont-Thomas 2021). The foetus, since then born, is claimed as sole artist of the album.

This technological interest goes beyond the womb as soundscape to listen to, or even to create artistically from. Since the late 1980s, audio devices have been marketed claiming to stimulate foetal hearing inside the womb as a benefit to the child once born. Without any scientific evidence, it is claimed that playing music to your unborn foetus accelerates foetal 'learning' and cognitive development. The desire to transmit sound as closely as possible to the foetus in utero has even led a company to develop a vaginal speaker, the 'Babypod'. The founder, Dr Marisa Lopez-Teijon, recognising that placing speakers on maternal abdomens elicited no responses from the foetuses, explained: 'We decided that we had to bring closer to them the source of sound' (Lopez-Teijon 2021). Lopez-Teijon solution to this problem was to design a speaker to be inserted in the vagina of pregnant women. The Babypod is marketed without medical advice on it as a source of potentially dangerous bacterial infection.

This technological invasion of the womb is not a neutral matter. Marie Thompson evaluating the interest in the Babypod alongside other reproductive sound technologies, describes this as 'uterine audiophilia'. She argues that 'by treating the womb as "the perfect classroom", prenatal sound systems imply an intense maternal obligation to invest in and impress upon the future-child' (Thompson 2021, 1). This becomes yet another responsibility outsourced to the individual. Thompson continues that by constituting 'the pregnant person's body as an occupied, resonant space… as passive container and a source of noise that is to be overcome, uterine audiophilia relies upon politically regressive conceptualisations of pregnancy' (ibid.). Thompson argues 'that these devices mark the hitherto under-theorised convergence of auditory culture, technology and reproductive politics' (ibid.). Clearly such intimate interventions require further consideration on political as well as medical grounds.

Women artists have also taken up this critical approach. Discussing her 2016 performance piece *Intimate Karaoke, Live at Uterine Concert Hall*, the Montreal artist Dayna McLeod, remarked on how much the shape of the uterus lends itself to a concert hall (McLeod 2021). McLeod explained how she proposed her uterus as a queer performance site in order to draw attention to the often heteronormative and reproductive expectations aimed at women's bodies (ibid.). She also wanted to question why we feel entitled to make demands on these bodies in the first place and assigning a new kind of value to her middle-ageing, queer, female body.

The Foetal Auditory Environment

With these considerations as a background the Sonic Womb project began to explore the foetal auditory environment. Our knowledge of the development of the human hearing before birth derives from embryology and anatomical studies and neurophysiology clinical studies in premature newborns. Comparative anatomy has shown that for most mammals, like all other organisms, organs associated with specific senses in humans develop during the first half of pregnancy and mature during the second half. The cochlea and peripheral sensory end-auditory organs of the human foetus are fully formed by 24 weeks (Birnholz et al. 1983). From around 28 weeks, at the start of the third trimester of pregnancy, the auditory pathways of the central nervous system develop as shown by a significant activation to sound detected in the left temporal lobe of the foetal brain, confirming that sound processing occurs beyond the reflexive sub-cortical level (Jardi et al. 2008). Using ultrasound imaging it is now possible to detect in-utero from 24 weeks the blink-startle responses to vibroacoustic stimulation and this response is consistently present after 28 weeks (Figures 3.1a and 3.1b) (Birnholz et al. 1983).

There is also evidence that the foetus recognises the voice of its mother from around 33–34 weeks of gestation (Jardri et al. 2012). The ability of the foetus to detect changes in sounds is a prerequisite to normal development for cognitive function and it can be related to language learning and clinical aspects of auditory disorders (Partanen et al. 2013). Interpretation of acoustic and linguistic information on intrauterine recordings suggests that the prosodic features of speech (pitch

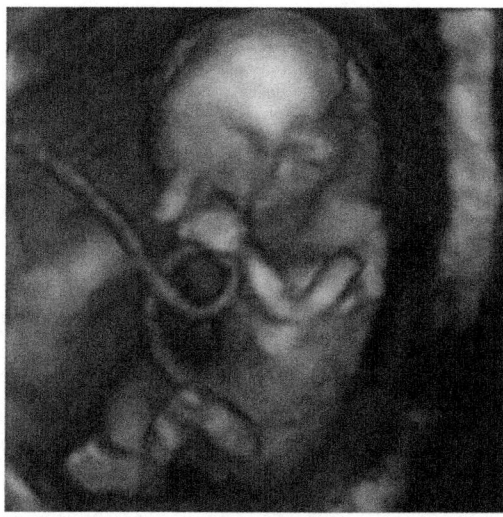

FIGURE 3.1A Foetal ear on 3-D ultrasound imaging at 12 weeks

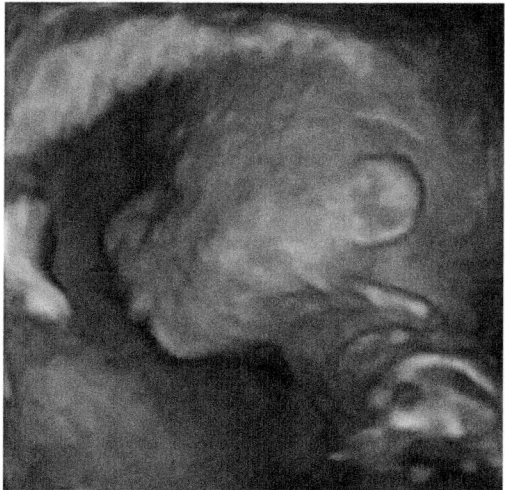

FIGURE 3.1B Foetal ear on 3-D ultrasound imaging at 24 weeks

contours, rhythm, and stress) are detectable by the foetus. Extensive prenatal exposure to a melody or to specific human speech induces neural representations that last for several months and may contribute to language acquisition during the first year after birth.

The foetus in utero is exposed to three sources of sounds: (1) the maternal physiological internal sound from her heartbeat and digestive system; (2) the maternal voice generated by her vocal cord and transmitted through her spine; and (3) external sound from the surrounding environment. Sound waves reach the cochlea by quite different pathways: through the middle ear to the vestibular (oval) window in air, and through the skull bone in water. The vibration of the cochlea then sends auditory signals to the brain. The hearing threshold or intensity at which premature neonates born at 27–29 weeks of gestation perceive sound is approximately 40 dB, decreasing to a nearly adult level of 13.5 dB by 40–42 weeks of gestation (Lary et al. 1985). These findings support the concept of a continuing postnatal maturation of acoustic neural pathways from the beginning of the third trimester of pregnancy. Low-frequency sound energy easily penetrates to the foetal head, with less than 5 dB attenuation for frequencies below 0.5k Hz, whereas higher frequencies are attenuated by up to 20–30 dB.

The auditory energy in amniotic fluid stimulates foetal hearing through a bone conduction route rather than through the external and middle ear systems. Intrauterine sound recording in humans during labour after membrane rupture showed that low-frequency sounds (0.125k Hz) generated outside the mother were enhanced by an average of 3.7 dB.

Environmental noise is becoming of increasing public health concerns before and after birth and chronic high noise levels affect all life on earth (Osbrink et al. 2021). Sources of high sound levels for foetuses include industrial, leisure, and environmental noise and foetal stimulation devices.

A systematic review based on the World Health Organization (WHO) environmental noise guidelines for the European region found weak associations between environmental noise, specifically aircraft and road traffic noise and adverse birth outcomes including preterm birth and low birth weight (Selander et al. 2016). In utero, the foetus has some protection from high-frequency sounds (> 250 Hz) through attenuation by maternal tissues. However, long-term exposure to high sound pressure levels (> 85 dBA) of occupational noise during pregnancy is associated with slightly reduced foetal growth but not with premature birth (Selander et al. 2019) supporting the evidence for a link between noise exposure during pregnancy and both maternal and foetal complications.

The Foetal Filter

On the basis of our knowledge of the foetal auditory environment as significantly different from postnatal hearing the next step for the project was to emulate the filtering effects of the mother's body. We called this the foetal filter – amplifying some frequencies and attenuating others. At this point in 2013 Dan Scott a sound artist and acoustician joined the team tasked with designing the filter. The parameters of the filter were rendered simply as the particular settings of a graphic equaliser (EQ). These settings were derived on the basis of the scientific literature available and on some initial experiments we conducted to measure the sound transfer function of a pregnant yew's abdomen and uterine wall. The experimental design was in principle straightforward, that is, to record a single source with a microphone on the yew's neck and a hydrophone in its uterus and measure the difference. Scott states that the results are consistent with what has been reported in the experimental literature, such as, Lecanuet 1998. As Scott states, our study supports:

> … previous evidence of a general attenuation from around 500 Hz to 1 kHz up to 10 kHz and beyond. In this study attenuation ranges from 0 – 10 dB at around 1 kHz to up to 30 dB at 15 kHz. Some of the frequency charts also display an increase in frequency at around 15 kHz… (Scott 2016).

Scott continues, 'However this study also suggests that below 500 Hz there is actually an increase in frequency response, creating an audible and recorded bass-heavy sound environment within the womb.' Scott summarises the findings as follows:

a) There is an attenuation of frequencies within the womb from around 1 kHz declining on an even curve down to around -30 dB at 16 kHz.

b) There is an increase in spectral content below 500 Hz. Again, on an even curve and rising to around 25 dB.
c) There is some evidence that beyond 16 kHz the frequency response increases again to around 5–10 dB higher than the external sound source.
d) There appears to be a kind of 'limiting' effect in the womb. Levels rarely, if ever, rise above a certain level (c. -90 dB on the Adobe Audition test), however loud, or quiet, the external sound is.

One example can serve to illustrate the amplifying and attenuating effects of the filter as derived from the difference between external and internal sound recordings (Figures 3.2 and 3.3).

One of the shortcomings of our first study was that although we could measure accurately the differences between the recordings, without calibrated microphones and hydrophones it was not possible to measure the absolute sound levels. Another issue, more difficult to address is the fact that whatever the foetus can hear it is via the aquatic medium of the amniotic fluid, rather than the gaseous air, and this hearing is directly via the skull to the middle ear, rather than the outer ear. As adults we can get quite an accurate impression of this aquatic listening experience: one only has to remember how it sounds listening underwater when swimming. Indeed, the organisation Wet Sounds organises swimming pool concerts where audience float on their backs, heads back, ears below the surface, or dive deeper for complete submersion (Wet Sounds 2021). Musicians play on the poolside with mics feeding through to amps and underwater transducers.

Underwater listening provides some approximation of foetal hearing in that the amniotic fluid surrounds the foetus. With both swimmer and baby, the entire skull serves as a transducer. Rather than the stereo images provided by our two ears, there is very little directionality to sound – it appears to be coming from every directions. Also due to the similar density of water and body tissue it is difficult to differentiate between a sound source as external or internal to the body; in short, there is no separation between inside and outside. These factors are pertinent for considering the epistemological and ontological nature of our auditory identity, as briefly discussed in the conclusion, but rather difficult to simulate for listening to sounds via the foetal filter.

Despite this challenge we did need to find a listening environment, platform or installation that allowed adults to get as clear as possible experience of the foetal filter sound. The key point is to hear the comparative difference between filtered and unfiltered sound sources, as the attenuation and amplification is not that noticeable for the average person. Also, we quite quickly habituate to a distorted sound source – especially when it is a familiar to us, that is, we hear what we would expect to hear from a doorbell ring, once we recognise that's what it is, even though the actual sound available might be quite heavily filtered. Notwithstanding this, we decided the best way to demonstrate the effect of the foetal filter was to show its effects on everyday sounds. So, Scott built a soundtrack of everyday sounds in an urban environment – a bus ride, a tube journey, heels on the pavement, a jackhammer on the street, a noisy restaurant, domestic hoovering and a lavatory flush, as well as classical and pop music sounds. A filtered version of this 'sound walk' was then recorded on one stereo channel and an unfiltered version on the other, the toggle between them was played on a normal domestic stereo system. Sadly, the results were not that impressive, that is to say, the filtered version did not appear to be dramatically different from the normal one. While it is important to note how much is available for the foetus to hear, this setup did not demonstrate the value of understanding how different this in fact was.

We decided the fault was not with our foetal filter, but with the listening environment. At this point we were fortunate enough to come across an MA Design alumnus of Goldsmiths, where Julian Henriques worked, who had been spent several years since graduating developing

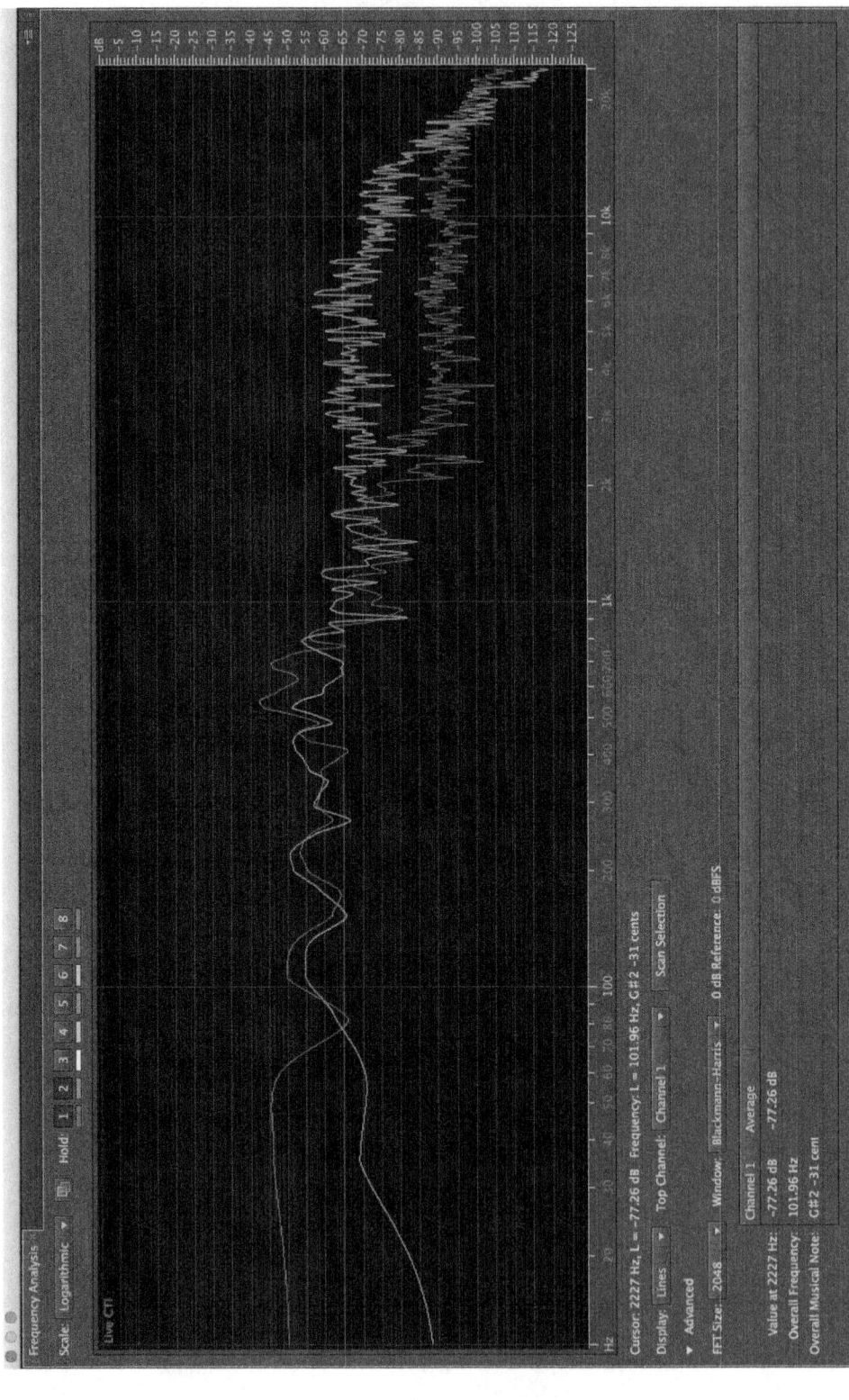

FIGURE 3.2 Comparison between external microphone on neck of sheep (lower line at the start) and hydrophone in the amniotic sac (higher line at the start). (Source: Scott, 'Variance in Frequency Response between External and Internal Sound Sources.')

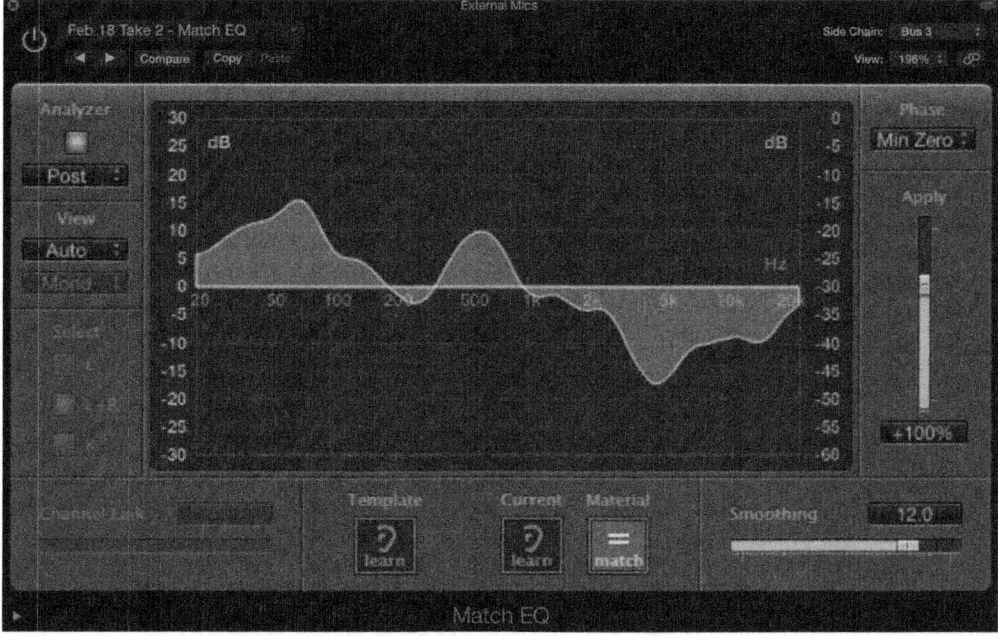

FIGURE 3.3 Foetal filter derived from recordings in Figure 3.2 (Source: Scott, 'Variance in Frequency Response between External and Internal Sound Sources.')

a multi-media viewing and listening pod. Designer Lee McCormack had named this an Orrb (McCormack 2021). For us it made an ideal sound pod, where the listener would be sealed off from the rest of the world, reclining on a comfortable chair in a darkened well-ventilated space. The visual appearance of the Orrb, with its rounded egg shape, was perfect for setting up womb-like expectations (Figure 3.4).

Joined by sound artist and engineer Aurelie Mermod, we set about converting the Orrb into the Sonic Womb Orrb. This entailed making the listening environment as immersive as it could be. We installed four transducers to vibrate the inner shell of the pod to emulate the non-directionality of foetal listening. In addition, we mounted a standard domestic quality stereo pair of speakers in front of the seat. This was equipped with a subwoofer to achieve bone conduction of sound to the lower back and calves. The next step was, of course, to test it with a substantial number of listeners.

Demonstrating Foetal Hearing with the Sonic Womb Orrb

The opportunity to demonstrate the Sonic Womb Orrb came with the kind invitation of Jamil and Whalid Juffali to bring our Sonic Womb Orrb to the Brain Forum exhibition and conference in Lausanne, Switzerland, in May 2016.[2] As a collaboration with Lee McCormack's Orrb Technologies the Sonic Womb Orrb we installed our listening environment in the exhibition hall as the demonstration of the first dedicated platform to reproduce hearing as in utero in the last trimester of pregnancy.

We rebuilt the sound walk as a track than began with unfiltered normal sounds via the stereo speakers, but quickly dived into the filtered sound environment via the transducers, to emerge back into unfiltered auditory environment at the end. The filtered track also included internal bodily

FIGURE 3.4 Julian Henriques, Aude Thibaut de Maisieres, and Eric Jauniaux (l to r) with Sonic Womb Orrb at Brain Forum, Lausanne, 2016

sounds (heartbeat, stomach and bowels) and most intriguingly, a mother's voice, which was partly filtered as being heard and an external sound and partly not filtered as an unique internal transmitted from the mother's vocal chords via her spine chord directly behind the uterus.

Before entering the Sonic Womb Orrb, as they waited in the queue, listeners were invited to watch a short slide show presentation about sound in utero, including, for example such inducements as:

> Who wouldn't want to return to the origins of perception in the foetal state where hearing (from the 24th week of conception) is the only sense connecting consciousness to the outside world, a place long forgotten but eagerly rediscovered…

The slide show also included some of the key points on the bioscience of foetal hearing discussed above. They were then escorted to recline inside, hydraulic door closed, for their own private immersive experience.

On emerging from the Sonic Womb Orrb we had 127 listeners respond to our request to fill in a questionnaire, 57% female, 43% male, between 18 and 75 years old. For many the perception of bone conduction and the amniotic environment seemed convincing: '(It was) amazing to hear the sound and "feel" it at the same time as a vibration.' Another: 'I felt like I was actually immersed in a liquid, focused on the sounds as I didn't see anything.' The experience elicited a very wide range of emotional responses, from 'relaxing' (the most common), and 'meditative, calming' to 'revealing' and even 'shocking', and went in strength from 'comforting' to 'really emotional and amazingly intense'. One participant said: 'I felt extremely safe and protected. I didn't expect that.'

Some participants commented on an ambiguous sensation of familiarity: '(It is like) being put into a new experience and at the same time experiencing something quite familiar.' 'Unusual but familiar.' Only four out of all the participants said they hadn't enjoyed the experience, including one who found it 'weird and frightening'. Some participants translated their experience almost philosophically, going as far as saying it was 'like being reborn'. In sum, although all participants were exposed to exactly the same immersive experience, there was a huge range of responses that also came up in the conversations we had with participants. It was as if they were being confronted with a new experience and were therefore free of any assumptions about what it 'should' sound like.

Experimentation

The Sonic Womb Orrb trial was most valuable for demonstrating the powerful affective impact of a womb-like foetal filtered sound environment. This is important for drawing attention to the need for more research on this topic, without in itself bringing us any closer to an accurate bioscientific understanding knowing of the actual uterine auditory environment. To do this our research effort took off in a new direction. Pierre Gélat, a specialist in acoustics at UCL, joined the team initially to devise an experimental protocol by which sound transmission into the womb could be measured and quantified. Using calibrated sensors, the acoustic transfer characteristics between the external environment and the womb were measured in three pregnant sheep at frequencies between 100 Hz and 20 kHz, i.e. across most of the human audio range. A studio monitor emitted bursts of broad spectrum noise and acoustic signals were measured at locations close to the sheep using microphones, and inside the amniotic sac using a hydrophone. By comparing the output of the hydrophone with that of the microphones, the attenuation at a given frequency was inferred.

These measurements of acoustic transmission through the maternal abdominal and uterine walls indicated that frequency content is transmitted to the foetus throughout the audio range and that some frequencies are attenuated by as little as 3 dB. This study provided fresh data about in utero sound transmission of external noise sources beyond physiological noise (cardiovascular, respiratory, and intestinal sounds). This may help quantity the potential for foetal physiological damage resulting from exposure to high levels of noise during pregnancy. It could also play a vital role in informing standards and clinical recommendations on exposure of pregnant women to noise.

Computational Modelling

The above experiments extended our knowledge of the abundance of sound transmission into the foetal environment. To further explore the intricacies and complexities of the sonic space inside the womb, Pierre Gélat led the development of a computational modelling platform capable of simulating the acoustic transmission of generalised sound sources inside the maternal abdomen. At the heart of this platform lies the open-source software OptimUS, which was originally conceived as a focused ultrasound treatment planning tool for cancers of the lower abdomen (Haqshenas et al. 2021).[3] OptimUS employs state-of-the-art algorithms developed by mathematicians, which have the advantage of being both efficient and accurate relative to other schemes. This is because the computational domain is only required to be defined by surfaces enclosing a volume. A full volumetric mesh is thus avoided thereby reducing the problem size.

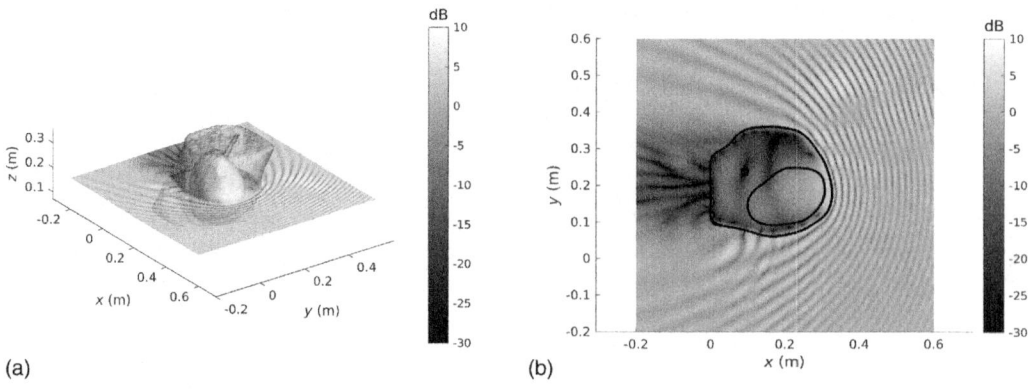

FIGURE 3.5 (a) 3D map of the acoustic attenuation inside the womb. (b) Slice of the acoustic attenuation map in the coronal transverse plane passing through the uterus. The patient was 37 weeks and 3 days pregnant at the time of the scan

Anatomical scans of pregnant woman were obtained using magnetic resonance imaging. The scans were provided by kind permission of Andrew Melbourne,[4] Nada Mufti[5] and Anna L David[6] of the GIFT-Surg team.[7] Through a knowledge of soft tissue and bone acoustic properties, the response of the human maternal abdomen to an external sound source was for the first time predicted across the full 20 Hz–20 kHz audio range. Furthermore, the complex effects of scattering and multiple reflections through different tissue domains could be observed. Figure 3.5 shows acoustic attenuation maps in decibels (dB), relative to the magnitude of the incident wave, throughout a pregnant abdomen's abdomen, including the uterus and the spine, at a frequency of 10 kHz. Where the incident sound (travelling here in the positive x-direction) interacts with the reflected sound, the attenuation can at some locations be positive thus resulting in sound amplification. At this frequency, significant sound transmission inside the uterus is observed, according to the model. The patient was 37 weeks and 3 days pregnant at the time of the scan (see Figure 3.5b).

This computational work serves two fundamental purposes. First, it enables us to form a literal picture of the sound field transmitted at multiple locations inside the abdomen, which would not be possible through measurement alone. Second, it reduces the need for in vivo experiments. This model serves as a stepping-stone towards a more comprehensive understanding of the foetal auditory environment and could in the future include the effects of physiological noise sources and their interactions with exterior sounds. It could also help to quantify mechanical stresses which arise in foetal tissue due to sound, since the latter produces localised compression and rarefaction of the medium through which it propagates.

Conclusion: Auditory Philosophy

Our research is still work in progress for achieving our ambition of the clinical outcome of a sonically friendly neonatal incubator. Exploring aural diversity identifies the womb as an important and barely explored site for investigation. In addition, the confined space of the womb offers vast scope for speculation as to our human origins, on which we can make only a few remarks here, by way of conclusion. The association of womb and cave has often been remarked upon. For Plato it features as a founding image for western philosophy as we are compelled to view only the shadows on the cave wall, never the reality from which they originate. The cave is also the skull by which the unborn hear, though in the visually dominated philosophy of the west Plato never mentions the echo, considerably more noticeable than a cave's shadows.

The cave of the womb is most obviously gendered, with the uterus giving its name to the 'condition' of hysteria to which women are said to be particularly subject. As Luce Irigaray remarks: 'The cave is the representation of something always already there, of the original matrix/womb which these men cannot represent since they are held down by chains that prevent them from turning their heads or the genitals toward daylight' (Irigaray 1985, 244). The auditory experience of the unborn is certainly beyond – or rather before – any representation. Peter Sloterdijk describes this as an 'intimate Atlantis' where we experience a 'conceptual helplessness' such that 'we traverse landscapes of pre-objective existence and prior relationships' (Sloterdijk 2011, 62). The womb's lack of visual reference and thereby any conceptual orientation suggests the idea of a sonic consciousness particularly in relation to the crucial role of the maternal voice, as Alfred Tomatis has long researched (Tomatis 1997. It must be assumed that our auditory identity necessarily proceeds any other layers of our being as we are born into a sonic world three months before the visual one. This overturns our conventionally assumed visual sensory point of origin as well its timing well before birth.

With sound the only possible reflections are echoic, but these as discussed above do not offer any opportunity to differentiate self from other as the fundamental western epistemological and ontological binary. Most significantly our birth of consciousness is precipitated from a state of co-existence with our mothers. This quite radical approach has been developed by leading feminist philosophers. Bracha Ettinger: 'The womb/matrix is conceived of here not primarily as an organ of receptivity or "origin" but as the human potentiality for differentiation-in-co-emergence. Its space is not a maternal "container", its time is not the inaccessible chronological past. It is the space and time of subjectivization in co-emergence' (Ettinger 2006, 220). Elselijn Kingma takes up this theme of our original connectedness: 'The "coming into existence" of humans and other mammals... occurs in what, for now, we shall call *intimate intertwinement* with another organism: the maternal organism... foetuses are, literally, Lady-Parts... either human organisms begin at birth, *or human organisms can be part of other human organisms*' (Kingma 2018, 166).[7,8] The importance of this female relational approach is how completely it undermines not only the conventional idea of the rational individual, as with the Cartesian *cogito*, but also the concept of individual as such. This is the unexpected outcome of our research journey into the sonic womb – beyond the kind of environment normally considered as being audible.

Notes

1 The Sonic Womb research project acknowledges the generous support of Nathalie and Charles-Henri Samani.
2 The Brain Forum was founded by the late Dr. Walid Juffali as part of the W Science initiative to to contribute to the progression of brain research and encourage global collaboration.
3 EPSRC grant EP/P012434/1.
4 Department of medical physics and biomedical engineering, University College London.
5 EGA Institute for Women Health, University College London.
6 University College Hospital.
7 Emphasis added. See also Kingma (2019), 'Were You a Part of Your Mother?'
8 Wellcome EPSRC Centre for Surgical and Interventional Sciences NS/A000050/1; www.gift-surg.ac.uk.

References

Beaumont-Thomas, B. (2021) 'US toddler to release debut album recorded in the womb'. *The Guardian*, 3 February.

Birnholz, J.C., & Benacerraf, B.R. (1983) 'The development of human fetal hearing', *Science*, 222: 516–18.

Doheny, L, Hurwitz, S, Insoft, R., Ringer, S., & Lahav, A. (2012) 'Exposure to biological maternal sounds improves cardiorespiratory regulation in extremely preterm infants', *J Matern Fetal Neonatal Med.*, 25: 1591–4.

Ettinger, Bracha L. (2006) 'Matrixial trans-subjectivity', *Theory, Culture & Society*, 23(2–3): 218–22.

Henriques, J. (2011) *Sonic Bodies: Reggae Sound Systems, Performance Techniques and Ways of Knowing*. London: Continuum.

Haqshenas, S.R., Gélat, P., van't Wout, E., Betcke, T., & Saffari, N. (2021) 'A fast full-wave solver for calculating ultrasound propagation in the body', *Ultrasonics*, 110: 106240.

Hövel, H., Partanen, E., Tideman, E., Stjernqvist, K., Hellström-Westas, L., Huotilainen, M., & Fellman, V. (2015) 'Auditory event-related potentials are related to cognition at preschool age after very preterm birth', *Pediatr Res.*, 77: 570–8.

Irigaray, L. (1985) *Speculum of the Other Woman*. Trans. Gillian C. Gill. New York: Cornell University Press.

Irigaray, Luce (2017) *To Be Born: Genesis of a New Human Being*. London: Palgrave Macmillan.

Jardri, R., Pins, D., Houfflin-Debarge, V., et al. (2008) 'Fetal cortical activation to sound at 33 weeks of gestation: a functional MRI study', *Neuroimage*, 42: 10–18.

Jardri, R., Houfflin-Debarge, V., Delion, P., Pruvo, J.P., Thomas, P., & Pins, D. (2012) 'Assessing fetal response to maternal speech using a noninvasive functional brain imaging technique', *Int J Dev Neurosci.*, 30: 159–61.

Kingma, E. (2018) 'Lady parts: The metaphysics of pregnancy', *Royal Institute of Philosophy Supplements*, 82 (Metaphysics): 165–87.

Kingma, E. (2019) 'Were You a Part of Your Mother?' *Mind*, 128(511): 609–46.

Lary, S., Briassoulis, G, de Vries, L., Dubowitz, L.M., & Dubowitz, V. (1985) 'Hearing threshold in preterm and term infants by auditory brainstem response'. *J Pediatr.* 107: 593–9.

Lopez-Teijon, M. (2021) 'BabyPod'. https://babypod.net/

Mampe, B., Friederici, A.D., Christophe, A., & Wermke, K. (2009) 'Newborn's cry melody is shaped by their native language', *Current Biology*, 19: 1994–7.

Marik, P.E., Fuller, C., Levitov, A., & Moll, E. (2012) 'Neonatal incubators: a toxic sound environment for the preterm infant?', *Pediatr Crit Care Med.*, 13: 685–9.

Madaule, P. (1994) *When Listening Comes Alive: A Guide to Effective Learning and Communication*. Norval: Moulin Publications.

McLeod, D. (2021) 'This Is What It Sounds Like: Intimate Karaoke, Live at Uterine Concert Hall'. *Canadian Theatre Review*, 184: 33–8.

McCormack, L. (2021) 'Designing user experience'. Available at www.leemccormack.co.uk/ (accessed 20 September 2021).

Osbrink, A., Meatte, M.A., Tran, A., Herranen, K.K., Meek, L., Murakami-Smith, M., Ito, J., Bhadra, S., Nunnenkamp, C., & Templeton, C.N. (2021) 'Traffic noise inhibits cognitive performance in a songbird', *Proc Biol Sci.*, 288: 20202851.

Partanen, E., Kujala, T., Näätänen, R., Liitola, A., Sambeth, A., & Huotilainen, M. (2013) 'Learning-induced neural plasticity of speech processing before birth', *Proc Natl Acad Sci U S A*, 110: 15145–50.

Penney, P.J., & Earl, C.E. (2004) 'Occupational noise and effects on blood pressure: Exploring the relationship of hypertension and noise exposure in workers', *Workplace Health & Safety*, 1 November.

Provenzi, L., Broso, S., & Montirosso, R. (2018) 'Do mothers sound good? A systematic review of the effects of maternal voice exposure on preterm infants' development', *Neurosci Biobehav Rev.*, 88: 42–50.

Scott, D. (2016) 'Variance in frequency response between external and internal sound sources in the womb of the pregnant ewe', *Sonic Womb Productions Ltd* (unpublished).

Selander, J., Albin, M., Rosenhall, U., Rylander, L., Lewné, M., & Gustavsson, P. (2016) 'Maternal occupational exposure to noise during pregnancy and hearing dysfunction in children: A nationwide prospective cohort study in Sweden', *Environ Health Perspect*, 124: 855–60.

Selander, J., Rylander, L., Albin, M., Rosenhall, U., Lewné, M., & Gustavsson, P. (2019) 'Full-time exposure to occupational noise during pregnancy was associated with reduced birth weight in a nationwide cohort study of Swedish women', *Sci Total Environ.*, 651: 1137–43.

Shellhaas, R.A., Burns, J.W., Barks, J.D.E., Hassan, F., & Chervin, R.D. (2019) 'Maternal voice and infant sleep in the Neonatal Intensive Care Unit', *Pediatrics*, 144: e20190288.

Sloterdijk, Peter (2011) *Spheres volume 1: Bubbles Microspherology*, trans. Wieland Hoban. Cambridge: Semiotext(e).

Thompson, M. (2021) '"Your womb, the perfect classroom": prenatal sound systems and uterine audiophilia', *Feminist Review*, 127: 1–17.

Tomatis, A. (1997) *The Ear and the Language*, trans. Billie M. Thompson. Norval: Moulin Publishing.

Wet Sounds (2021) 'Wet Sounds'. www.wetsounds.co.uk

4

PHONATING HAND DRYERS

Exploits in Product and Environmental Acoustics, and Aural Diverse Composition and Co-Composition

John L. Drever

Introduction

In this chapter I will share and reflect on the salient issues for aural diversity from an acoustic and environmental noise study of high-speed hand dryers in public and workplace toilets carried out between 2011 and 2014. Initially a student project for a Diploma in Acoustics and Noise Control with the Institute of Acoustics, I increasingly learnt of the wide range of users that were being adversely affected and the subject matter spread from acoustics to include sociocultural factors, its scale and scope snowballed. The findings evidenced a social situation so pressing and immediately acknowledged by the individuals who were affected by it and their carers, and yet at the time, underreported and hence unregistered by the public sector, that I decided to strategically switch roles: from the gathering and analysing of data to artistic activism. Reverting to my customary role as composer / sound artist, I sought appropriate modes to *affectively* communicate the findings beyond the customary empirical journal/conference academic paper output. So, in addition, I will chart out the evolution of my attempts to relate the project's findings through creative practice – most successfully through the method of phonating – feeling my way around what I hope may be regarded as somewhere on the way to realising aurally diverse practice.

An Auraltypical World

The prevailing sociocultural context that the study was situated is characterised by a deeply engrained normativity, namely, an *auraltypical* world – an all-pervasive framework that informs, and at time dictates, how we think about (both ontologically and epistemologically) and practice the soundscape, albeit unwittingly. The term, auraltypical (Drever 2015, 2017), takes its lead from a provocative concept coined from within the autistic community, a subset of society accustomed to being pigeon-holed by others, now turning the tables, categorising people who are not on 'the spectrum' as *neurotypical*. Thus, neurotypical refers to non-autistic people's normality and implies their tendency to impose their understanding of normality on everyone else as correct and natural (Silberman 2015). The exception to this pervasive understanding, a norm which is treated as a given by most of society, is neurodiversity (coined by Judy Singer in the 1990s).

Neurodiversity advocates propose that instead of viewing this gift as an error of nature […] society should regard it as a valuable part of humanity's genetic legacy while ameliorating the aspects of autism that can be profoundly disabling without adequate forms of support.

(Silberman 2015, 470)

Significantly, neurodiversity has also been related more widely to include all people with specific learning differences many off which co-occur or overlap such as dyslexia, dyspraxia, and attention deficit (hyperactivity) disorder (British Dyslexia Association 2021).

With the concept of auraltypical – which could of course intersect with neurodiversity vis-à-vis hyper/hypo-acute hearing – and its corollary *aural diversity* (Drever 2017), on articulating the divergent findings from this study I was propelled to question the validity of the dominant episteme of the 'normal hearer' and all that entails, and through creative practice, finding strategies to transcend it. In fact, it was on mulling over the vast diversity of experience (predominantly negative) from exposure to high-speed hand dryer sound that I had garnered, and the, at times, extremes of that experience, that the concept of the auraltypical crystallised.

Important Subgroups in Toilet Research

Clara Greed, a pioneer of accessible urban design and toilet provision, recognises the fundamental need for toilet access that works on the level of participation in society and the workplace: 'Public toilets are a necessary component for users of the built environment in enabling user-friendly, sustainable, safe, equitable and accessible cities' (Greed, 2003, 3). But as Barbara Penner refers to them as '[t]his humble yet complex space' (Penner, 2013, 9), there is a lot to consider including a range of social attitudes: I'm reminded of the amazing expert spitting sounds emanating from toilet cubicles in men's toilets in Hong Kong where spitting in public is an offence (Coomber, Moyle, & Pavlidis 2018). As the need for sanitary provision is universal, facilitating a basic physiological process, the study encompassed the full spectrum of society, and, as the UK government are beginning to slowly recognise, provision is particularly important for, 'women, those with children, older people and disabled people' (Ministry of Housing, 2021).

Hand Washing Practice

Toilets offer a range of sanitary needs for all ages and abilities including designated nappy changing space for infants and most importantly considering the COVID-19 pandemic, hand washing. In no way a new proposition, in 1860 Florence Nightingale stressed the importance of hand washing with hot water and soap: 'Every nurse ought to be careful to wash her hands very frequently during the day' (Nightingale 2017, 122). Today we have plenty of data to evidence that good hand hygiene, especially after using the toilet or before handling food greatly helps reduce the transmission of respiratory and gastrointestinal viral infections and pathogenic bacteria (see Centers for Disease Control and Prevention 2021). The epidemiological importance of hand drying within hand hygiene should not be underestimated, and is regarded as an important component of the handwashing process, as this advice to parents from The Bog Standard, a campaign to promote better toilets for pupils, warns: 'Warm, moist hands are a haven for bacteria….Wet hands can pick up and transfer much more bacteria than dry hands or even hands not washed at all' (The Bog Standard 2013).

High-Speed Hand Dryers

Since 2009 in the UK, hand drying facilities must be included with sanitary provision (BS6465-3). Several drying options are on offer: paper or cloth towels, warm air hand dryers and/or high-speed cold air dryers. The high-speed dryer first appeared on the market in 1993 with the Mitsubishi Jet Towel. In contrast to the extant warm air dryer that evaporates moisture, the high-speed dryer uses the force of cold air at extraordinarily high speeds (c. 400 mph), to strip off moisture from the hands and fingers. With its competitive claims of superior efficiency, hygiene, and speed (Snelling et al. 2011), the high-speed dryer rapidly became the drying option of choice. Comparative sound pressure levels were not regarded as a critical criterion in this mix which prioritised above all speed. The race was on to make the fastest drying cycle, with scant attention to the rule of thumb: the faster the hand drying cycle the louder the sound. In fact marketing material actively capitalised on the primordial equation of 'noise equals power' (Schafer 1994, 74); the high sound levels apparently evidencing its effectiveness in its task. The product names of the first generation of dryers were a veritable celebration of 'belliphonic' (Daughtry 2020) prowess – Airblade, Airforce, Air Fury, G-Force, Hurricane, Rafale, Jet Towel, Tornado, Typhoon – names rife with muscularity, anger, violence, extreme weather, and militarisation. And to be fair, there are many people with sensory seeking behaviour who relish the combined aural, visceral, and tactile power related to high-speed hand drying. Writing on sound, music, and trauma in wartime Iraq, Martin Daughtry recognises the double-edged nature of intense sonic experience:

> The co-vibration of resonance can be a deep-seated source of joy, and a visceral reminder of our fundamental interconnectedness, as choral singers the world over know in their bones. [...] But far less attention has been paid to its corollary, that acoustic interconnectedness increases our ability to be affected by others and by our environment in negative ways as well.[....] Because of this fact, a full or exhaustive consideration of sound cannot be undertaken without a consideration of the potential for violation and violence that sound constantly affords.
>
> *(Daughtry 2020, 165)*

Infant Hearing

The impetus for focusing on hand dryers was closely linked to becoming a father and the realisation that my child's hearing was considerably more sensitive than mine, counterposed with the instinct of caring for that sensitivity within loud and acoustically complex urban environments. It was on encountering high-speed hand dryers in 2007, located by the baby changing facility in a crowded male toilet in a popular amusement park in Hong Kong, that the incongruity between extreme sound levels and sensitive hearing, was thrown into sharp relief. The space that had been designed for this task was positioned between two high-speed Panasonic hand dryers which were in continual use. Inevitably, when the baby lay down, which is a necessary part of the nappy changing process, their ears were in close proximity to the dryers' loudest emission point. Even for my adult hearing, the sound levels were excruciating. I felt helpless as I could not mitigate the situation. The outcome was the task took longer to complete as the infant was in distress throughout, and quite understandably was inconsolable for some time after.

Several years later, as high-speed hand dryers became increasingly popular in the UK, another experience that motivated my study was a hand dryer I encountered in a cramped individual toilet in a small café in South London. The makeshift handwritten label stuck onto the dryer

FIGURE 4.1 Hand dryer in public toilet

stated: 'Caution Loud When in Use!' and below, an additional message possibly added by s customer: 'Known to Startle Children'.

Again, to my ears, the sound was harsh: the boxy reflective acoustic contributing to the sound level and quality. The sound levels and frequency content of the hand dryer felt out of kilter with the acuity of most children's hearing. As a caring parent, one of the roles is to instil confident and hygienic toilet practice, and yet here was an everyday scenario where noise-induced fight, flight, or freeze response, with the concomitant potential for ensuing phobias and related health effects, were being inadvertently provoked.

As high-speed hand drying became the standard hand dryer option, I began to witness parents forcing the hands of distraught children towards dryers, and I read in parent chat rooms, tips on habituating children to hand dryer noise, in particular autistic children. The underlying thinking here is that the hearing is at fault – it is too sensitive and must be recalibrated in line with contemporary efficient product design – rather than considering that the method and means of hand drying is simply too loud!

Noise Equals Power

The trope of noise equals power is well-rehearsed. Murray Schafer asserted, 'the association of noise and power has never really been broken in the human imagination' (Schafer 1994: 76). In the potted history within his classic tome, *The Soundscape: Our Sonic Environment and the Tuning of the World* (1994), we segue from the *sacred noise* of natural sounds such as thunder and volcanos, the sounds of church bells and organ to the untrammelled noises of the industrial revolution. In each case, it is 'having the authority to make [the biggest noise] without censure' (Schafer 1994, 76).

On responding to a customer comment online regarding his vacuum cleaner design – his first major industrial success – James Dyson (responsible for the multiple accolade and industry award winner hand dryer, Dyson Airblade) picked up on the relationship between noise and speed. He weighed up the speed of the fan with the consequential noise by-product, beguilingly comparing it to a Formula One vehicle:

> You'll find that noise does emanate from all different areas of the machine, but we do put a huge amount of work into getting this as balanced to ensure it is as quiet as possible. Remember that the fan rotates at 35,000rpm (Schumacher's Ferrari does 19,000) – so it creates a loud noise to silence… People care more about the machine's cleaning performance than they do about the noise though.
>
> *(Ehow UK, 2013)*

Revealingly, on chatting with a toilet attendant in a large busy shared toilet provision in 2012 in a major London train station, on asking if he was worried about hearing loss from the continuous hand dryer sound, he responded: 'Listen! It is so ecological!' For him, the noise equated to sound ecological design, trumping any personal auditory health concerns.

Cynically, I learnt of managers who promoted the use of high-speed dryers in toilet provision in the workspace as it reduced the time spent by staff on toilet breaks by impeding washroom chat; speech transmission being another important accessibility issue.

Acoustic Privacy

Toilets are one of those spaces of *sociofugality* where 'we feel the need to have a place of our own where environmental stimuli can be reduced and privacy assured', where there is a desire to preserve 'the individual's personal space' (Porteous 1977, 48–9). Toilets should offer an accessible, clean, private, safe, and conformable space; an environment where all people can feel confident, however, for many, toilets remain an awkward, potentially vulnerable space, cutting across sense modalities of sight, touch, smell, and hearing, where the private and public interfold. In this regard I learnt that background sound levels that are too quiet are also problematic; some people were grateful for the opportune role of the hand dryer as a white noise generator, offering some level of acoustic privacy. Inhibited urination or defecation in public bathrooms due to lack of privacy including acoustic privacy, due to anxiety or fear of being judged is very common (Haslam 2012, 39). For some this can be a severe inhibition, such as paruresis (shy bladder) and parcopresis (shy bowel), impacting their participation in society. Gender can play a role here, as a study by Weinberg and Williams (2005) found: '… heterosexual women were substantially more bothered than men by using public restrooms and more likely to think that having their faecal noises overheard would imply that they were not meeting a gender ideal' (Haslam 2012, 65); for a comprehensive discussion on toilets and gender see Gershenson and Penner 2009. In women's toilets in Japan, it is common etiquette to use water flushing sounds from a small audio playback device introduced by Toto, called an Otohime, to mask those involuntary personal sounds. This practice dates to the Edo period when aristocratic women used an *Otokeshi-no Tsubo*, a kind of urn that water was channelled through to generate appropriate masking sounds. (Yamaji 1991, 16). Figures 4.2 and 4.3 are examples of more recent mobile Otohimes.

With a concern for 'what kind of sounds [people] want and don't want to be exposed to', demonstrating a speculative fiction turn, composer Karlheinz Stockhausen imagined a noise cancellation device to 'clean the air to make people become aware of the sounds they produce'. *The Sound Swallower*, he proposed could be installed in toilets so: 'People could acoustically piss and shit in special acoustical toilets, but they wouldn't be bothering anyone else with their acoustic garbage' (Cott, 1974, 77).

FIGURE 4.2 Mobile Otohime

Acoustic Testing of High-Speed Hand Dryers

The first stage of my acoustical study was a comparative sound power test following BS EN ISO 3744:2010, of a wide range of hand dryers on the market including warm air dryers, provided by Intelligent Facility Solutions and carried out in BRE's anechoic chamber (Figure 4.4). A summary of the data can be found at Intelligent Hand Dryers, 2014 (www.intelligenthanddryers.com/blog/dr-drevers-hand-dryer-study). FFT analysis was made to offer a closer look at the spectral quality of the sounds. This was followed up with in-situ, gorilla-like measurements of hand dryers with sound pressure levels taken in unoccupied toilets in a wide range of contexts, including the measuring of reverberation times by popping balloons. I could then compare the levels of the same models, independent of the acoustic environment (i.e. sound power) with installed devices in a highly reverberant toilet. This was very revealing: a hand dryer in a self-contained individual toilet that had sound levels of 98 dB L_{Aeq} (set to 10 seconds which is the stated drying duration) was the equivalent to 11 hand dryers of the same model with no acoustics (Drever 2013).

FIGURE 4.3 Another mobile Otohime

Although they use the same unit (i.e. the decibel), sound power should not be confused with sound pressure; yet, in product marketing material you can often find them being used in interchangeably and we can witness the adoption of new, ambiguous terms such as *noise power*. It is also important to remember that the decibel scale is logarithmic, not linear.

Toilet Acoustics

Toilets can offer a relatively quiet zone within the urban setting (with sound levels as low as 45 dB L_{Aeq}), so the accidental triggering of a high-speed hand dryer, which is easily done by some brands in cramped conditions, marks an immediate shift in the room's sound pressure (80 to 98 dB L_{Aeq}), filling the whole space (Drever 2017). Developing his argument on 'noise equating power', Schafer goes beyond loudness *per se,* pointing out the acoustic profile: 'A man with a shovel is not imperialistic,

FIGURE 4.4 A hand dryer in the Building Research Establishments' anechoic chamber. Photograph by Tim Steiner, used with permission

but a man with a jackhammer is because he has the power to interrupt and dominate more acoustic space' (Schafer 1994, 77). Beyond loudness, high-speed hand dryers share that capacity to instantaneously 'interrupt and dominate' all available acoustic space of a shared toilet provision.

The acoustical standards and regulations related to toilet acoustics are highly limited. They are primarily concerned with noise transmission with adjacent rooms and have not yet addressed the introduction of highspeed hand dryers into this space. The modern toilet can be very small (e.g. 20m^3), you can even find converted broom cupboards being used as toilets. They are often rectangular, surrounded by hard, smooth surfaces with very low absorption coefficients across the spectrum, resulting in an ultra-reflective space with high-frequency room modes. Acoustically speaking, they are the most problematic space in which to install a powerful sound generating device such as a high-speed hand dryer.

Social Survey

The next stage was to survey users and carers from across the whole of society. I found grievances among the following groups – visually impaired due to the masking of spatial cues; hearing aid users; Alzheimer's disease; Ménière's disease; PTSD; cerebral palsy and, most significantly, hyperacusis sufferers, and autistic people with hyperacute hearing. Anya Ustaszewski helped me collect fascinating but worrying feedback from ASC chat rooms. This is a typical response:

> I can't stand those hand dryers and it amazes me whenever I see people nonchalantly using them like the sound is nothing. It's very painful for me. I won't go in restrooms that have

them unless it's absolutely necessary and if someone uses the dryer while I'm in there, I plug my ears. I don't care if I look like an idiot.

As autism represents a spectrum of experiencing and of sensing of the world, we also had comments from people who were drawn to the intensity of the sound, or who have specific issues regarding other toilets sounds:

> I am sorry for anyone who finds those sounds trigger them. Oddly, I have the reverse problem. I look forward to loud hand-dryer sounds in public toilets because they block out many other sounds that I do react to.

Echoing Greed, I was finding that hand dryer sound levels were adding another obstacle to toilet accessibility (Knight & Bichard 2011) and thus contributing to making cities, including the workplace and education, inaccessible for many vulnerable members of society.

The plethora of issues arising from the hand dryer study represented a microcosm for soundscape design and accessibility in the built environment. Following various features of my research in the Media I also started to receive directed correspondence from users who were really struggling with these, and related accessibility and domestic issues related to hearing, and were searching for advice and reassurance.

Sharing the Findings

The first tentative airing of my research on this topic was at the *3rd International Ambiance Network Conference* (Drever 2011), when high-speed hand dryers were still somewhat of a novelty. I was perturbed that what I found as troubling findings were met by antagonism from a handful of male delegates. I was told that they would queue up to use high-speed hand dryers as it was a thrilling experience and thus effective in drying hands. It's as if the loudness was an indicator of its effectiveness, and this experience of power was an act of visceral participation in industrial success. Very much in continuity with an earlier era – researching the history of work-related hearing loss, Allard Dembe suggests 'that the association of noise-as-loud-sound with power-as-strength-and-signifying is an important attraction of some technologies' (quoted in Bijsteveld 2008, 36).

Composer and acoustic ecologist Hildegard Westerkamp, who evocatively blends activism with composition in such work as *Kit Beach Sound Walk* (Westerkamp 1989) reminds us that through composition and co-composition human agency can be regained, as the concluding words from her voice-over articulates:

> As soon as I make space to hear sounds like this, or to dream them, then I feel the strength to face the city again, or even to be playful with it. Play with the monster then I can face the monster!
>
> *(Westerkamp 1989)*

Thanks to this kind of artistic inspiration, I returned to my compositional practice to not only affectively impart the sentiments of the study but to present work that takes a position vis-à-vis aural diversity at each stage of the chain from composer, performer to audience (Drever 2019).

Sanitary Tones: Ayre #1 [Airblade]

I initially endeavoured to address the findings of the research with a hermitic-like compositional approach. In *Sanitary Tones: Ayre #1 [Airblade]* (2013), a surround sound drone-based work that spectrally unfolds over an hour, I meticulously teased out the inherent musical potential of an anechoic recording I made of a Dyson Airblade. I presented the work in HAB Galerie, Nantes in 2013 with dozens of speakers spread around the whole gallery, creating somewhat of a sonic cyclone in the large open space. This might have been stimulating for some, but I had fundamentally failed to address the possible aural diversity of the audience and on reflection felt that I was tending on perpetuating a 'noise equals power' attituded, which is the common ground for much electronic music.

Litany of the Hand Dryers

Subsequently, in *Litany of the Hand Dryers* (2013), my son, now seven years old, gently sung the names in a quasi-Anglican chant style, interposed with the harsh recordings of those models. The work effectively exhibited the sentiment of the out-of-kilter brutal nature of the hand dryer sound when heard in juxtaposition with a voice of a typical yet unconsidered user, but it was still not a fundamentally an aurally diverse practice.

Sanitary Tones: Ayre #2 [Dan Dryer]

Sanitary Tones: Ayre #2 [Dan Dryer] (2016) was a site-specific installation presented in the cloakroom and washrooms in *Radar*, a music venue in Godsbanen, Aarhus, as part of *Sound Art Matters* (Aarhus University). Opening up my creative practice I recorded 98 different people from the full spectrum of ages from infants to older people in their 80s, phonating the sound of the popular Danish hand dryer brand, the Dan Dryer Turbo Design model. Their task was to reproduce the sound as best they could with their voices. The Dan Dryer logo is a Viking with sword and shield, sporting the classic horned Viking hat in the colour of the Danish Flag. One of the recordings I shared with the participants was a faulty Dan Dryer which made a bellowing Viking warrior-like cry. The voices were played back through a 16-speaker sound system based on Unity, developed by CAVI (Aarhus University) in a generative manner with regards to the choice of voice to play, the speaker selection, and the spatial trajectory of each voice.

Sanitary Tones: Ayre #3 [Kelston]

The learning from the previous works came together in *Sanitary Tones: Ayre #3 [Kelston]*, conducted under the auspices of Aural Diversity Old Barn in Kelston on 6 July 2019, which aimed at embracing aural diverse composers, performers, and audience alike by adhering to a set of conventions developed by Andrew Hugill, described in Duncan Chapman's chapter in this volume. Leaning even more towards co-composition, in preparation for the performance, I worked separately with each of the six performers. I invited them to listen to recordings of the sonic emission of 12 different models from the leading brands of hand dryers in the UK that I had recorded with a measurement microphone in the anechoic chamber in BRE with Intelligent Facility Solutions. I kept the sound levels at a comfortable level for each of the performers. I firstly asked them to mimic the sounds with their voices as best they can, and consequently asked them to valorise specific qualities of the sounds that they appreciated, proposing new speculative sound design. In the performance with radio mics, they reproduced the task, whilst also listening and copying the other performers' phonation as they moved slowly around the performance venue and audience. (For Drever's listening account of the performance see Chapman p. 198–9)

The idea of using voice came from two sources, product sound design and Alfred Tomatis' concept of audio-phonation.

Product Sound Design

I attended a workshop in 1999 by the product design group at Philips Design led by Heleen Engelen. They were working on, 'Changing present sounds or adding extra sounds to create appropriate auditive feedback for the different products' (Engelen, 1999) They presented three sounds of a woman's electric shaver for legs: the actual sound, which sounded harsh and rough; a slightly filtered smoother versions; and a more 'creative' version, with a low pitched male human vocalic quality. The design of the third version had a novel quality to it, by replacing the mechanical sound with a human voice added an auditory personification that was more pleasant to the ear, albeit unnerving and regarded as inappropriate by some I could imagine.

Audio-Phonation

The pioneering otolaryngologist, Alfred Tomatis was curious about the circuit between voice and audition (i.e. audio-phonation), including the consequence of hearing that diverged from the norm on phonation. On comparing the harmonics of held tones of singers with hearing loss, with their audiograms, he observed matching gaps in the frequency spectrum. From many similar studies, he surmised: 'we sing with our ears' (Tomatis 1996, 85). This resulted in the famous maxim: 'the voice reproduces only what the ear hears' (Tomatis 1996, 87) Or put in a more considered manner, audition 'adjusts, governs, and steers phonation' (Tomatis 1996, 72). Of course, the voice can make all kind of sounds devoid of effective audition and each voice has a limit on its faculty of sound reproduction, but a person 'can only enact with certainty what [they are] able to control' (Tomatis 1996, 87).

Embracing aural diversity with each performer's unique audio-phonation circuit, where everyone is a 'suitably equipped receptor' (Babbitt 1998; see Drever 2019 for a discussion on Babbitt and audition) afforded a richer soundscape, savouring the grain of each voice (Barthes 1987). Their particular hearing, and each other's hearing, became central and contingent on the spectrum of their phonating. Unlike the customary relationship with hand dryer noise, through phonation they had become responsible for their sound production, what Michel Chion calls *ergo-audition*: 'when an auditor is at the same time, completely or partially, answerable for, consciously or not, a sound that is heard' (Chion 2016, 91–2), such as footsteps, playing an instrument, or speaking and singing.

Positioning each performer's audio-phonation at the centre of the process and further passing that sounding around the group helped to open the compositional process – moving from my hearing and its unique vicissitudes to a community of diverse hearers; and replacing direct recordings of hand dryers with a personification of the dryers, intrinsically working on a human scale.

Conclusion

Reflecting on my journey, I am acutely aware of my shifting attitudes to sound and hearing as the study progressed: from a starting point of what I can now clearly see as naivety – I had not heard of hyperacusis nor misophonia, and my hearing loss and unilateral tinnitus was yet to come to the fore – towards an ever-increasing awareness of feeling ill-equipped with the training, tools, and discourse of the disciplines I was assiduously following. Crucially yet unwittingly, that gap was limiting the reach, even applicability of much of my practice, as I had failed to address: 'whose hearing and for whom'. Succinctly put by the Tomatis: 'No judge is worse than the musician who cannot conceive that others may not have and benefit from perceptive abilities like [their] own' (Tomatis 1996, 22). And it is telling that the most significant subsequent real world hand dryer noise study was carried out by a school pupil (Keegan 2020).

Ultimately what I was learning was the need to move from 'self-absorbed individualism' and nurture aural diversity through 'affective empathy': 'Our wellbeing depends on us stepping out of our own egos and into the lives of others, both people close to us and distant strangers' (Krznaric 2014).

References

Babbitt, M. (1998). Who cares if you listen? In R.P. Morgan (ed.), *Strunk's Source Readings in Music History. Vol. 7: The Twentieth Century*. New York: W.W. Norton.

Barthes, R. (1987). *Image, Music, Text*. London: Fontana Press.

Bijsterveld, K. (2008). Mechanical Sound: Technology, Culture, and Public Problems of Noise in the Twentieth Century. Cambridge, Massachusetts: The MIT Press.

British Dyslexia Association. Accessed July 2021. www.bdadyslexia.org.uk/dyslexia/neurodiversity-and-co-occurring-differences/attention-deficit-disorder

BS EN ISO 3744:2010Acoustics. Determination of sound power levels and sound energy levels of noise sources using sound pressure. Engineering methods for an essentially free field over a reflecting plane.

Centers for Disease Control and Prevention. Accessed May 2021. www.cdc.gov/healthywater/hygiene/fast_facts.html

Chion, M. (2016). *Sound: An Acoulogical Treatise*. Durham and London: Duke University Press.

Cott, J. (1974). *Stockhausen: Conversations with the Composer*. London: Picador

Coomber, R., Moyle, L., & Pavlidis, A. (2018). Public spitting in 'developing' nations of the Global South: Harmless embedded practice or disgusting, harmful and deviant? In: Carrington, K., Hogg, R., Scott, J., & Sozzo, M. (eds), *The Palgrave Handbook of Criminology and the Global South*. Cham: Palgrave Macmillan.

Daughtry, J.M. (2020) *Listening to War: Sound, Music, Trauma, and Survival in Wartime Iraq*. New York: Oxford University Press.

Drever, J.L. (2011). Sanitary ambiance: a study of current auditory ambiances of public toilets in England. *Urban Design and Urban Society, 3rd International Ambiance Network Conference*, The Ludwig Maximilian University of Munich.

Drever, J.L. (2013). 'Sanitary soundscapes: the noise effects from ultra-rapid "ecological" hand dryers on vulnerable subgroups in publicly accessible toilets'. *AIA-DAGA 2013*, Marano, Italy

Drever, J.L. (2015). Topophonophobia – the space and place of acute hearing. In *Hearing Landscape Critically: Music, Place, and the Spaces of Sound*, Harvard University.

Drever, J.L. (2017). 'The case for auraldiversity in acoustic regulations and practice: The hand dryer noise story'. *ICSV24*, Westminster, London, July 2017.

Drever, J.L. (2019). 'Primacy of the ear' – but whose ear?: The case for auraldiversity in sonic arts practice and discourse. *Organised Sound*, 24(1): 85–95.

Engelen, H. (1999). Sound design for consumer electronics. Soundscape before 2000, Amsterdam. Accessed May 2021. https://archief.ntr.nl/supplement/supplement_archief/radio/supplement/99/soundscapes/engelen.html

Ehow, UK. Accessed April 2013. www.ehow.co.uk/info_12011624_dyson-vacuum-noise.html

Gershenson, O. & Penner, B. (2009). *Ladies and Gents: Public Toilets and Gender*. Philadelphia: Temple University Press.

Greed, C. (2003). *Inclusive Urban Design: Public Toilets*. Oxford: Architectural Press, Elsevier.

Haslam, N. (2012). *Psychology in the Bathroom*. Basingstoke, Hampshire: Palgrave Macmillan.

Intelligent Hand Dryers (2014). Comparative hand dryer noise levels provided by Dr Drever. Accessed May 2021. www.intelligenthanddryers.com/blog/dr-drevers-hand-dryer-study

Keegan, N.L. (2020). Children who say hand dryers 'hurt my ears' are correct: A real-world study examining the loudness of automated hand dryers in public places. *Paediatrics & Child Health*, 25(4), June: 216–21.

Knight, G. & Bichard, J.-A. (2011). *Publicly Accessible Toilets: An Inclusive Design Guide*. London: Royal College of Art, Helen Hamlyn Centre for Design.

Krznaric, R. (2014). *Empathy: Why It Matters, and How to Get It*. Penguin Random House.

Ministry of Housing, Communities & Local Government (2021). Toilet provision for men and women: call for evidence. Accessed May 2021. www.gov.uk/government/consultations/toilet-provision-for-men-and-women-call-for-evidence/toilet-provision-for-men-and-women-call-for-evidence

Nightingale, F. (2017). *Notes on Nursing – What It Is, and What It Is Not*. CreateSpace Independent Publishing Platform. Kindle Edition.

Penner, B. (2013). *Bathroom*. London: Reaktion Books.

Porteous, J.D. (1977). *Environment & Behavior: Planning and Everyday Urban Life*. Reading, MA: Addison-Wesley Publishing Company Inc.

Schafer, R.M. (1994). *The Soundscape: Our Sonic Environment and the Tuning of the World*. Rochester, VT: Destiny Books.

Silberman, S. (2015). *NeuroTribes: The Legacy of Autism and How to Think Smarter about People Who Think Differently*. Crows Nest, Australia: Allen & Unwin.

Snelling, A., Saville, T., Stevens, D., & Beggs, C. (2011). Comparative evaluation of the hygienic efficacy of an ultra-rapid hand dryer vs conventional warm air hand dryers. *Journal of Applied Microbiology*, 110: 19–26.

The Bog Standard: Better Toilets for Pupils. Accessed April 2013 www.bog-standard.org/

Tomatis, A. (1996). *The Ear and Language*. Norval, Ontario: Moulin Publishing.

Weinberg, M.S. & Williams, C.J. (2005). Fecal matters: Habitus, embodiment, and deviance. *Social Problems*, 52: 315–36.

Westerkamp, H. (1989). 'Kits Beach Soundwalk'. In *Transformations*. empreintes DIGITALes (IMED 9631).

Yamaji, S. (1991). *Toile Kogengaku* [Modernology of Toilet]. Tokyo: Keibun.

5
THE AUDITORY NORMATE

Engaging Critically with Sound, Social Inclusion and Design

William Renel

Introduction: An Idealised Sonic Citizen

The diverse ways we communicate and listen and the divergent affects that sound has on us as we move through space are socially, politically, and culturally informed and play a vital role in defining our place in society. How we hear, and hear others, influences our experiences of the world. For many the realities of sound and hearing and attitudes towards these things dictate whether a public space is accessible or non-accessible. Sonic experiences are also shaped by what Steve Goodman terms 'audiosocial predeterminations' (Goodman 2010, 191) such as class, gender, and race, and by what Jennifer Lynn Stoever describes as the 'listening ear' – a socially constructed ideological system producing but also regulating cultural ideas about hearing and sound (Stoever 2016, 13). Historical auditory explorations within the fields of acoustic ecology, sonic ethnography, aural phenomenology, sonic anthropology and aural architecture, collectively point to the fundamental idea that sound impacts on our individual and collective experiences. However, it is notable that the experiences of d/Deaf and disabled people, and the notion of auraldiversity, are consistently underrepresented within these existing lines of auditory inquiry. Such perspectives are vital in understanding the ways in which people continue to negotiate auditory hierarchies through their everyday experiences of hearing and sound. This chapter aims to broaden the academic conversation about how the concept of auraldiversity shapes and is shaped by design by exploring the notion of the 'auditory normate' – an idealised sonic citizen around which the contemporary world is built. The chapter builds on existing understandings of the normate and normate template from the fields of disability studies and inclusive design to propose four pillars around which the auditory normate is constructed. These pillars reveal a politics of hearing in which the prioritisation of idealised sonic citizens who conform to the auditory mould of designed objects, systems, and services, developed without the inherent diversity of the population in mind, leads to exclusionary public spaces. Such spaces are initiated by designers whose understandings of disability and difference are anchored in the ableist inner workings of guidelines, regulation, and legislation (Boys 2017; Coleman et al. 2016).

A Note on Lived Experiences

This chapter aims to construct the notion of the auditory normate by foregrounding the lived experiences of d/Deaf and disabled people, in their own words and on their own terms. Direct quotes from interviews with d/Deaf and disabled research participants appear throughout the chapter. The interviews were undertaken by the author during an inclusive design research project at the Royal College of Art titled *Sonic Inclusion,* funded by the Arts and Humanities Research Council from 2015 to 2019.

The (Auditory) Normate Template

Normalcy is a central theme in disability studies, art, and activism. Disability studies as an academic field is an explicit attempt to 'reverse the hegemony of the normal and to institute alternative ways of thinking about the abnormal' (Davis 2006, 15). The term 'normate' was established by Rosemarie Garland-Thomson to refer to 'the constructed identity of those who, by way of the bodily configurations and cultural capital they assume, can step into a position of authority and wield the power it grants them' (Garland-Thomas 1997, 8). Aimi Hamraie suggests that the normate represents the unmarked privilege of majority embodiments and has situated the term within design discourse through the notion of the 'normate template'. Hamraie describes the normate template as a 'useful abbreviation for the complex, critical notion that the world was designed with normative inhabitants in mind' (Hamraie 2017, 20). The normate template begins with a concern that knowledge and ideologies privileging the normative are always present in design and aims to create a simple and useable word to classify the normative values distributed across design policy, planning, and development. The normate template suggests that design operates as the functional and communicative vessel of normalcy within the public sphere. By bringing these existing understandings of the normate and normate template to issues of sound and auraldiversity, we can start to investigate how the design and management of objects, environments, and services produce auditory hierarchies where access and status are distributed in relation to the everyday realities and diversity of human hearing. It is important to understand the politics of auraldiversity and hearing within the wider in/exclusionary potential of sound and space. For example, in 2018, Tamsin Parker – a disabled woman with learning disabilities – was forcefully removed from the British Film Institute on her birthday for laughing loudly at the film. Here, it was the auditory experience of other cinema-goers, who heckled and applauded as Tamsin was removed, that were prioritised in the way the sonic environment was socially produced and maintained. Tamsin's laughter and subsequent crying can be understood as a socio-political sounding of oppression, 'an acoustic politics of the voice' (Kanngieser 2011, 2). The applause and laughter of other cinema-goers are disabling utterances and those audience members who subsequently complained about the injustice of the event provide earwitness accounts that detail how sonic inequality continues to be produced and contested in the public sphere.

The following sections of the chapter detail four pillars around which the notion of the auditory normate can begin to be constructed: a social relational model of sonic exclusion, design, and systematically distorted communication, legislating the 'normal' ear and the social (re)production of auditory norms.

A Social Relational Model of Sonic Exclusion

A social relational model of disability contends that people are excluded by two forms of oppression: structural and psycho-emotional. A deep understanding of structural oppression is present within the foundations of disability studies and is central to the social model of disability which states that people are not excluded because of their impairments (the facts about their bodies and minds) but by a societal failure to consider difference in the way the world is designed and maintained. The social relational model of disability builds on this to theorise psycho-emotional disablism as barriers which impact the emotional well-being of disabled people (Reeve 2012). The social relational model of disability enables us to consider experiences of sonic in/exclusion as a form of social oppression that operates through structural and psycho-emotional barriers grounded in the exclusionary currency of auditory values and norms. Consider the following examples from research participants A, B, and C.

PARTICIPANT A: I've had a stammer since I was really young but it's only in the last few years that it's felt like an issue … there are so many automated phone lines now and they aren't setup for stammers … machines don't listen like people listen. Calling the bank or the council or whoever fills me with dread because I know it's probably going to take ages and make me feel rubbish. To be honest I just don't use phone services at all.

PARTICIPANT B: I got my 'severely sight impaired' certificate when I was a kid so have spent more than 30 years using my hearing and the sound world to know where I am. Across the road from us they built this massive tower block out of metal and glass that makes the sound of the road we live on bounce all over the place. My world has completely changed and I have lost loads of independence crossing the road and going to the shops … people talk about how the city is changing visually but they should have planning permission for changing the sound of the city, it's a social inclusion issue.

PARTICIPANT C: I missed a flight last year because they only told passengers that the terminal had changed via a tannoy announcement. It happens at train stations as well and I never really use the tube because most of the information when you are underground is given out as an announcement that I can't access. As well as being profoundly Deaf I have bi-polar and social anxiety so when these things happen, I think about them for weeks and months afterwards.

In these examples, exclusion is initiated by the structural auditory barrier created by an environment or service and is confounded by the undermining of the individual's emotional well-being. Such entanglements of structural and psycho-emotional oppression are further accentuated by the repetition and regularity in which such barriers are experienced. The social relational model of sonic exclusion is the first pillar around which the template of the auditory normate is constructed and held by society.

Design and Systematically Distorted Communication

Jurgen Habermas coined the term 'systematic distortion of communication' to describe the negation of open exchange and communication through the influence of socio-structural factors such as social class and status (Habermas 1971). Goodman uses this phenomenon to explore 'audiosocial predeterminations' – examining how factors relating to identity that are products of social processes and practices (such as sexuality, ethnicity, or disability) inform how hearing and listening function within human interactions (Goodman 2010, 191). In short, a middle-class accent will be experienced and responded to differently to a working-class accent in different contexts. This auditory behaviour generates hierarchies of sounding and listening practices informed by different socio-cultural contexts. The discriminatory potential of systematic distortion of communication is discussed in relation to gender, race, and disability (Young 1990; Stoever 2016; Paterson

2016), contending that human interactions are enclosed in socially coded and embodied markers grounded in white, middle class, non-disabled, male hearing practices. Better understanding how design might systematically distort communication is important in our exploration of the auditory normate and raises a critical question: how does the design of an object, environment, or service define who has access to what types of communication and on what terms? The following sections consider this question in relation to artificial intelligence, interior design, and temporal norms.

The Artificially Intelligent Idealised Ear

The 'voice revolution' and the turn to 'voice-first computing' is compounded by digital assistive systems such as Apple's Siri and Amazon's Alexa, the emergence of voice-controlled wearables, and the development of voice control systems within vehicle design and the built environment. But which hearing profiles are reflected in such technologies and whose voices are used in training the algorithms to listen? Voice-first computing utilises voice-recognition algorithms to classify voices within databases of dialects and accents; however, they have been heavily critiqued for privileging certain accents and failing to understand others (Cox 2019; Ouzounian 2020; Harwell 2018; Feild et al. 2018). This is evident in the following extract from an interview with research participant D.

> PARTICIPANT D: We don't use Siri or anything like that in our house. I've got aphasia and a brain injury which just sort of slows my speech down … both my daughters have learning disabilities which affect their speech sometimes and on top of that we are all originally from Tehran! So there is no way Siri understands what we are saying. I think [designers] need to think a lot more about how the computers can listen to different people because at the minute it's not working, they won't hear us.

Clearly, the design of the contemporary sonic world (be it spatial, technological or otherwise) serves as a container for the ideologies and priorities of those who made it. Overcoming the exclusionary potential of sound is therefore not only a matter of better understanding the diversity of human hearing, but also the auraldiversity of devices and technology.

The Auditory Implications of the Built Environment

Analysing the interior design of a space reveals a web of structural and visual concerns such as form, materiality, and layout. But it also highlights the assumptions about who the space is designed for. As Hamraie notes, from a 'doorframe's negative space to the height of shelves and cabinets, inhabitants' bodies are simultaneously imagined, hidden, and produced by the design of built worlds' (Hamraie 2017, 19). The service counter is an exemplar of how physical design parameters (such as height) might support or neglect different forms of communication within the built environment. Below are two interview extracts relating to the interplay between interior design and sonic exclusion.

> PARTICIPANT E: I'm profoundly deaf in my right ear but the hearing in my left ear isn't too bad. At work I have to press a buzzer and speak to someone to be let in … the intercom is way off to the right on a wall rather than just straight ahead next to the door. This means I have to face backwards away from the door to be able to hear the intercom … I always feel really stupid facing randomly away from the door, none of my colleagues have to do this and sometimes the automatic doors crash into the back of my head.

PARTICIPANT F: My local bar recently had a refurb and now it has no lowered counter, and all the tables are really tall with stools. As a wheelchair user that place is now completely inaccessible to me and I've stopped going there. I think they reckon it looks better, and they can fit more people in, but now I can't hear anyone or even really see anyone.

In these examples, the design of the environment is grounded in a series of normative assumptions that dictate where and how communication can take place. This leads to participant E feeling humiliated and separate from their colleagues and participant F being excluded because of a 'failure' to conform to the auditory expectations embedded in the design of the space.

Temporal Norms

'Autism Hour' is a scheme developed by the National Autistic Society (autism.org.uk) where shops and businesses adjust the sensory profile of their environment for an hour per week in areas such as reducing background music and avoiding tannoy announcements. Although such initiatives might increase the accessibility of public spaces for specific individuals at specific times, they fail to address the central issue that these spaces are non-accessible the rest of the time. Autism hour was discussed in interviews with research participants D, G, and H.

PARTICIPANT G: I have used the autism hour thing before and less sound is quite good but really I would rather just be able to go to the shops whenever.
PARTICIPANT H: My ears are sensitive to stuff like loud announcements, and I hate the check-out beep at the supermarket, but making it different for an hour first thing on a Sunday morning doesn't work for me … it would be good to be allowed to have sensitive hearing and have a lie-in.
PARTICIPANT D: My daughters don't really like big supermarkets because they sometimes overreact or get over stimulated by sudden noises … I wish [the supermarkets] were a bit more predictable sound-wise but I am not sure about the message it sends out when they do autism hour or a quiet hour … can't we have more than one day or more than one hour?

By dedicating a specific time in which a public environment meets the needs of a disabled person the supermarket is also acknowledging that the environment is non-accessible the rest of the time. Although schemes such as autism hour will work for some people, they also further the oppressive temporal norms that position d/Deaf and disabled people as welcome and included in society only at specific times or specific locations.

From these discussions of artificial intelligence, interior design, and temporal norms, we can understand how systematic distorted communication is created and reenforced by design. As Paterson and Hughes note, the contemporary world is a verbal world structured around a society where the 'norms of communication and norms of intercorporeal interaction reflect the carnal needs of non-disabled actors' (Paterson and Hughes 1999, 604). Systematic distortion of communication through design is the second pillar around which the template of the auditory normate is constructed.

Legislating the 'Normal' Ear

Sound and acoustics hold great potential to counteract the visual dominance that has driven western architecture historically (Herssens et al. 2011). Though inclusive design strives towards the design and management of environments that respond to the diversity of human interests and needs (Keates and Clarkson 2004), there is an observed lack of consideration for sound and auraldiversity within inclusive design research and practice (Heylighen et al. 2008, 2009; Renel 2018). One of the drivers in contemporary inclusive design is to influence governments and public policy through participatory methods (Balka 2013). However, existing considerations of sound and hearing within legislation and policy frame auditory design through the binary juxtaposition of 'special' and 'normal' hearing. Rychtáriková et al. propose that most research that informs acoustics legislation assumes an average person with 'good' hearing therefore disconnecting the aims of acousticians with those of inclusive designers (Rychtáriková et al. 2012). The statistical measure of absolute hearing threshold, which highlights the threshold of audibility by identifying the smallest level of auditory stimulus that a person can detect (Howard and Angus 2017), is a common reference in acoustics legislation, described as 'the best hearing level of younger people with undamaged hearing' (Truax 2001, 16). However, research since the 1960s has suggested that differences in human hearing thresholds are log-normal (consistently random) with differences as large as 25–30 db between 'best' and average hearing thresholds (Herman and Holzman 1967). The acoustic standard for normal equal-loudness-level contour (BS ISO 226 2003) has been described as the 'gold standard' of acoustics to which other standards must conform (Florentine et al. 2011) and is another exemplar of how the auditory normate has been constructed by legislation. The standard is grounded in the perspective of an 'otologically normal person' (Drever 2017). Average hearing thresholds (AHT) also propagate notions of auditory normativity in legislation by using the binary separation of 'good' and 'bad'. AHT are gathered using large data sets tested under optimal sound-field conditions and are used clinically to ascertain a 'reasonable estimate of what is "normal" with which what is "abnormal" may be contrasted' (Sahley and Musiek 2015).

Away from the acoustic measures detailed above, acoustics in schools has emerged as key area in which the socio-emotional implications of hearing and sound are being examined. In 2001 acoustics in schools became a priority area for built environment policy leading to an abundance of acoustic standards and regulations including:

- The Department for Education and Skills – Building Bulletin 93: The Acoustic Design of Schools (DfE 2003)
- Education Funding Agency – Acoustic Performance Standards for the Priority Schools Building Programme (EFA 2012)
- The Department for Education – Building Bulletin 93: Acoustic Design of Schools: Performance Standards (DfE 2015)
- Association of Noise Consultants and the Institute of Acoustics – Acoustics of Schools: A Design Guide (ANC/IOC 2015)

By examining these documents, we can better understand the role that legislation has played in the construction of the idealised sonic citizen. DfE 2015 groups people with visual impairment, hearing impairment, attention deficit hyperactivity disorders, auditory processing disorder, and autistic spectrum disorder together as a homogenised group of pupils with 'special hearing'. ANC/IOC 2015 also uses the term 'special hearing' to categorise a similarly diverse group of d/Deaf and disabled people. Both these documents and the EFA 2012 regularly compare people with hearing impairments to those with 'normal hearing'.

Each of these acoustic measurements, legislative documents, and standards are important. They are the communicative artefacts of design knowledge that bridge the gap between designed and lived experiences of a public space and will ultimately shape how hearing differences are framed in the design of the built environment. The documents contribute to the othering of d/Deaf and disabled people by polarising 'normal' and 'special' hearing in which 'special' is used to flatten the divergent sonic experiences of a diverse group of people into a homogenised group. The notion of legislating the normative ear is the third pillar around which the template of the auditory normate is constructed.

The Social (Re)Production of Auditory Normalism

The visual (re)production of disability is at the heart of several critically engaged discourses in design. Particularly in relation to the dominant iconographies of disability such as the International Symbol of Access which despite continuous campaigns to reimagine the symbol continues to reinforce a limited visual perception and understanding of disability in the cultural imaginary (Guffey and Williamson 2020). However, there is a lack of discourse relating to the (re)production of disability though sonic phenomena. When a sonic custom governs an environment the opportunity for auditory normalism to be (re)produced is established. Consider the following example in which disabled artist, writer, and activist Jess Thom describes the experience of attending a theatre performance of 'Extreme Rambling' by Mark Thomas. Jess has Tourette's Syndrome, a neurological condition that means she makes involuntary movements and noises called tics:

> During the interval I was asked if I'd move and sit in the production booth at the side of the stage because some members of the audience couldn't tolerate the noise of my tics.
>
> I'd made sure the theatre and Mark knew I had Tourette's before I arrived. The staff were welcoming and Mark came to meet me before the show. With my permission, he'd explained to the audience at the beginning that I would be making some unusual noises. When the theatre manager asked me if I'd move, he made it clear that I didn't have to. But inevitably, when I heard people around me had complained and didn't want me to be there, I felt extremely uncomfortable and I agreed to move.
>
> Once in the booth I was hit by a wave of humiliation and sadness. I started to cry. Part of me wanted to leave and never go to the theatre again.
>
> *(posted on touretteshero.com, blog, 26 May 2011)*

Here auditory normalism is socially produced by the inhabitants of the theatre and theatre manager, (re)produced in the prioritisation of audience members that fit the sonic customs of that space, and leads to Thom, as a member of the public that diverges from the template of the auditory normate, being discriminated against. Many people with impairments such as Tourette's that can be audible, or have the capacity to affect what is audible, have the common lived experience of being excluded because of a 'failure' to conform to the auditory norms of a space. These experiences may be heightened in environments that are governed by particular sonic rules such as lifts, cinemas, theatres, galleries, libraries, and museums, many of which prioritise the normative perspective of the silent or quiet person (Sedgman 2018; Whitfield and Fels 2013; Kitchin 1998; McGrath 1996). The social (re)production of auditory normalism discussed above is the fourth and final pillar around which the template of the auditory normate is constructed.

Conclusion

This chapter has aimed to broaden the academic conversation about how the concept of auraldiversity shapes and is shaped by design. The chapter initiates an auditory turn within existing understandings of the normate and normate template to propose the 'auditory normate' as a useful term describing the complex notion of an idealised sonic citizen around which the contemporary world is built. The examples of sonic exclusion shared by d/Deaf and disabled research participants highlight the critical role that lived experiences of hearing, sound, and auraldiversity play in constructing and contesting the concept of the auditory normate. The examples sound a call to action for sustained investigation and critique of the socially produced rules and auditory norms solidified in design. Clearly, the deconstruction of auditory normalism begins by identifying and removing structural and emotional barriers posed by design. But it also requires designers to engage critically with a politics of hearing in which the auditory mould of designed objects, systems, and services gives priority and status to an idealised sonic citizen. By acknowledging the importance of d/Deaf and disability embodiment and centring this in critiques of normalism and design, we begin to imagine auditory futures where a diversity of ears, bodies, and minds can meaningfully take up space together.

References

ANC/IOC (2015) 'Acoustics of Schools: A Design Guide'. Association of Noise Consultants and the Institute of Acoustics.

Balka, E. (2013) 'Action for health: Influencing technology design, practice and policy through participatory design', in *Routledge International Handbook of Participatory Design*. Abingdon: Routledge.

Boys, J. (ed.) (2017) *Disability, Space, Architecture: A Reader*. Abingdon: Routledge.

BS ISO 226. (2003) *Acoustics – Normal Equal-Loudness-Level Contours*. London: BSI.

Coleman, R., Clarkson, J., Dong, H., & Cassim, J. (2016) *Design for Inclusivity: A Practical Guide to Accessible, Innovative and User-Centred Design*. Abingdon: Routledge.

Cox, T. (2019) *Now You're Talking: Human Conversation from the Neanderthals to Artificial Intelligence*. London: Penguin Vintage.

Davis, L.J. (ed.) (2006) *The Disability Studies Reader*, 2nd ed. Abingdon: Routledge.

DfE (2003) 'The Acoustic Design of Schools'. The Department for Education and Skills – Building Bulletin, 93.

DfE (2015) 'Acoustic Design of Schools: Performance Standards'. The Department for Education and Skills – Building Bulletin, 93.

Drever, J.L. (2017) 'The case for auraldiversity in acoustic regulations and practice: The hand dryer noise story', presented at the *24th International Congress on Sound and Vibration*, London.

EFA (2012) 'Acoustic Performance Standards for the Priority Schools Building Programme', London: Education Funding Agency.

Field, M., Mills, E., & Fuller, G. (2018) 'Smart digital assistants threaten regional accents, research says'. *The Telegraph*. Available at www.telegraph.co.uk/technology/2018/08/15/smart-digital-assistants-threaten-regional-accents-research (accessed 14 July 2021).

Florentine, M., Popper, A.N., & Fay, R.R. (eds) (2011) *Loudness*. New York: Springer-Verlag.

Garland-Thomson, R. (1997) *Extraordinary Bodies: Figuring Disability in American Culture and Literature*. New York: Columbia University Press.

Goodman, S. (2010) *Sonic Warfare: Sound, Affect, and, the Ecology of Fear*. Cambridge: MIT Press.

Guffey, E., & Williamson, B. (2020) *Making Disability Modern: Design Histories*. New York: Bloomsbury.

Habermas, J. (1971) *Knowledge and Human Interests*. (Jeremy J. Shapiro Trans). Boston: Beacon Press.

Hamraie, A. (2017) *Building Access: Universal Design and the Politics of Disability*. Minneapolis: University of Minnesota Press.

Harwell, D. (2018) 'The accent gap'. *The Washington Post*, 19 July. Available at www.washingtonpost.com/graphics/2018/business/alexa-does-not-understand-your-accent/ (accessed 14 July 2021).

Hermann, E.R., & Holzman, B.R. (1967) 'Absolute thresholds of human hearing', *American Industrial Hygiene Association Journal*, 28(1): 13–20.

Herssens, J., Heylighen, A., Roelants, L., & Rychtáriková, M. (2011) 'Listening in the absence of sight: The sound of inclusive environments'. Presented at *Include*, London.

Heylighen, A., Rychtáriková, M., & Vermeir, G. (2008) 'The sound of inclusion: A case study on acoustic comfort for all', in *Designing Inclusive Futures*. London: Springer.

Heylighen, A., Rychtáriková, M., & Vermeir, G. (2009) 'Designing for every listener', *Universal Access in the Information Society*, 9(3): 283–92.

Howard, D.M., & Angus, J. (2017) *Acoustics and Psychoacoustics*. Abingdon: Routledge.

Kanngieser, A. (2011) 'A sonic geography of voice: Towards an affective politics', *Progress in Human Geography*, 36(3): 336–53.

Keates, S., & Clarkson, J. (2004) *Countering Design Exclusion: An Introduction to Inclusive Design*. London: Springer.

Kitchin, R. (1998) '"Out of place", "Knowing one's place": Space, power and the exclusion of disabled people', *Disability & Society*, 13(3): 343–56.

McGrath, J. (1996) *A Good Night Out: Popular Theatre: Audience, Class, and Form*. London: Nick Hern Books.

Ouzounian, G. (2020) *Stereophonica: Sound and Space in Science, Technology, and the Arts*. Cambridge: MIT Press.

Paterson, K. (2012) 'It's about time! Understanding the experience of speech impairment', in *Routledge Handbook of Disability Studies*, N. Watson, A. Roulstone, & C. Thomas, eds. London: Routledge, 165–177.

Paterson, K., & Hughes, B. (1999) 'Disability studies and phenomenology: The carnal politics of everyday life', *Disability and Society*, 14(5): 597–610.

Reeve, D. (2012) 'Psycho-emotional disablism', in *The Routledge Handbook of Disability Studies*, N. Watson, A. Roulstone, & C. Thomas, eds. London: Routledge, 78–92.

Renel, W. (2018) 'Auraldiversity: Defining a hearing-centred approach to socially equitable design of the built environment', *Built Environment*, 44(1): 36–51.

Rychtáriková, R., Herssens, J., & Heylighen, A. (2012) 'Towards more inclusive approaches in soundscape research: The soundscape of blind people', presented at *Inter-Noise*, New York, 19–22 Aug.

Sahley, T.L., & Musiek, F.E. (2015) *Basic Fundamentals in Hearing Science*. San Diego: Plural Publishing.

Sedgman, K. (2018) *The Reasonable Audience Theatre Etiquette, Behaviour Policing, and the Live Performance Experience*. London: Palgrave.

Stoever, J.L. (2016) *The Sonic Color Line: Race and the Cultural Politics of Listening*. New York: New York University Press.

Truax, B. (2001) *Acoustic Communication*. Westport: Ablex Publishing.

Whitfield, M., & Fels, D.I. (2013) 'Inclusive design, audio description and diversity of theatre experiences', *The Design Journal*, 16(2): 219–38.

Young, I. (1990) *Justice and the Politics of Difference*. Princeton: Princeton University Press.

6
LISTENING WITH DEAFBLINDNESS

Matt Lewis

Introduction

This chapter acts as a set of provocations and reflections on creative activities aimed at informing more inclusive approaches to the production, and participation in sound and music activities within deafblind culture and beyond. The discussion draws directly on an extensive body of creative and critical work that originated and developed between 2014 and 2020 with the deafblind charity Sense. The research involved collaborating with hundreds of the charity's users to collectively investigate and raise awareness of issues relating to listening and sensory loss. The project explored different aspects of human perception, through investigating a variety of listening and sound-making approaches. These approaches were aimed at enabling participants and audience members to come together to collectively share aspects of deafblind culture through sound. An integral part of the work involved devising, testing, and informally evaluating different pedagogical and presentation models for participatory sound-based practice. These included new modes of production, exhibition, and performance for music and multi-sensory art intended to work with the needs of people often excluded by conventional arts practice. Consultation with specialists was an invaluable part of the process as it enabled me to draw on considerable expertise in developing the project and helped imbed a broad range of research into the project which informed the production of the public outcomes. The involvement of these individuals and organisations meant that aspects of art, science, and technology could be combined in a meaningful and coherent way. Besides asking how music-making and sound practice might lead to greater inclusivity, the project sought to critically engage with emerging technology in meaningful ways, hoping to include as many participants as possible whilst accepting the individual affordances of those involved. Significant contributions were made by Dr Donna Corrigan – Sense Technology Co-coordinator and qualified audiologist, Call & Response-independent sound art organisation; Dr Louise Fryer – neuropsychologist, audio describer, and BBC presenter; and Subpac – developers of sub-bass, wearable technology.

Listening Together

The term Deafblind encompasses a wide range of individual conditions, and the charity Sense describes deafblindness as such:

DOI: 10.4324/9781003183624-7

A person is regarded as deafblind if their combined sight and hearing impairment cause difficulties with communication, access to information, and mobility. A person does not have to be deaf and blind to be considered deafblind - indeed many deafblind people have some residual vision and/or hearing.

(Sense, n.d.)

Many deafblind people face barriers to participation in mainstream activities, and even within support services assumptions are made about the validity of individuals engaging in sound and music-making. Despite this, it was found that sound and in particular music play many crucial roles for individuals in a variety of contexts. The deafblind stereotype is that of an isolated figure or as Barnett (2013) describes 'an island' (Barnett 2002 in Barnett 2012), and while perceptual, physical, social, and geographical isolation are sometimes features of deafblind experience and culture, deafblindness also emphasises connectivity, coming together, and sharing. For many deafblind people, relationships with family, support workers, and guides are an integral element of activities such as listening to music where the experience is mediated, moderated, and enhanced through shared physical contact with another. Communal listening is a key feature of musical culture and coming together to listen in different ways emphasises the connective possibilities of listening as a social practice. Shared listening is also contrary to personalised listening that is a dominant feature of headphone culture; in shared listening, narratives become intertwined, and a conglomeration of perceptual coming-togethers go to form an interfaced acoustic imagination. Shared listening also acknowledges the ecology of actions, individuals, and apparatus that make up the experience, such an ecology is articulated by Julian Henriques (2011) in what he calls 'sounding', 'which encompasses everything, everyone, and all the activities that go into the making of sound' (Henriques 2011, xxix). In Sonic Bodies, Henriques (2011), proposes an auditory epistemology that challenges established ideas related to knowledge, dominant ideas that privilege the mind and language. Henriques' proposition, of 'sounding', draws on sound system and dancehall culture and applies to deafblind listening as it encourages a way of knowing through sound that goes far beyond the act of listening itself. The affective coming together in deafblind listening to experience sound, no matter the perceived affordances for the listener, supports an inclusive knowledge system concerning music and sound which breaks down traditional distinctions and dominant ideas around listening practice. Just as Henriques' 'sounding' challenges assumptions that 'knowledge resides in "the mind" – as if this could be separate from its body' (Henriques 2011, xxviii). Deafblind listening challenges assumptions that listening is located in the ear or indeed only in the body at all.

In recording sessions, group improvisations, performances, and installations with Sense, sound became a conduit for connectivity that allowed participants, staff, and audiences to interact without the pressure of communication barriers. Recording and improvisation sessions, where, for example, participants partnered with communication staff also helped to establish a different dynamic that broke down the binary relationship where the primary purpose of the staff member is to communicate semantic information about the world. Through listening, making, and recording sounds together, a sense of collectivism and connectivity developed out of the project. For example, participants in the first phase of the project were proud that they had put their contribution on the aural equivalent of the display. One participant said, 'It was nice to recognise samples of sound we were part of' (Lewis 2015, 14). Participants and staff could also meet others from different centres around the country and beyond, demonstrating the importance of opportunities for physical connection as well as a creative endeavour. Also meaningful was that sound-making activities, which broke participants out of routine scheduled activities, enabled new dynamics to emerge.

Many staff commented that the project helped them to strengthen their relationships with individuals as they got to know them better by interacting with them in a unique setting and in a different way. Staff also spoke of returning to some of the sites visited during the gathering sessions and or initiating their own field-recording trips to new sites.

The experiences above highlight the efficacy of creative engagement with sound, or to use Henriques' term 'sounding', through listening, recording, and music-making, as a communal activity, and a way of establishing new relationships between individuals, each other and the world. In practical terms important questions were raised regarding presentation formats; during the earlier stages of the project, performances and installations took place in conventional venues such as theatres and arts centres and to relatively large groups of people. What developed throughout the project was the need for expediency and flexibility and in the later stages of the project, whilst working in Birmingham, new performance formats were explored that ranged from one-to-one performances in people's homes to an audio-tour in a department store. These allowed us to explore different modes of reception that considered individual needs and took the project out of traditional venues.

Imagination

Listening modes and categories theorised by Pierre Schaeffer (2007) and Michel Chion (1982) and developed upon by composers including Barry Truax (1984) and Dennis Smalley (1996), though sometimes hierarchical, all emphasise the shifting nature of listening. More recent discourse by Salomé Voegelin (2017), which also draws on phenomenology, champions listening as an embodied, multi-modal activity, where listening is a way of participating in the flux of the world. For Voegelin, the emphasis is on fluidity and connectivity through the whole body, not just the ears, whereby activities such as writing, music-making, and sound recording trigger 'auditory imagination' (Voegelin 2017, 36). For Voegelin, listening offers many possibilities that go far beyond the identification of the source of sounds or sounds as objects and is an embodied process that can unlock a myriad of possible connections and narratives. Marc Leman (2008), takes an ecological approach that also regards music-making and listening as embodied, multi-modal activity. Leman's work on embodied musical cognition links listening to human gesture and again places the body and imagination at the centre of our interactions with sound. For composer Pauline Oliveros (2005), triggering imagination was a key aim of the practice of 'deep listening', which is defined as listening which 'digs below the surface of what is heard …unlocking layer after layer of imagination, meaning, and memory down to the cellular level of human experience' (Oliveros 2005, cited in Pavlicevic & Impey 2013, 238). For Mercédès Pavlicevic & Angela Impey (2013), who employ deep listening as part of health and wellbeing practice, as well as activating imagination, is also a means of exploring and promoting diversity, and can help creatively acknowledge differences and divisions:

> Like jazz improvisation, we have argued that the deep listening stance holds diversity and seeks to balance the familiar with the unfamiliar, holding tensions and frictions rather than 'resolving' and creating 'inauthentic homogeneity, for the sake of imposed health and wellbeing currencies.
>
> *(Pavlicevic & Impey 2013, 249)*

The recognition of differences and tensions is important here as it allows for any response or level of engagement in creative activity to be accepted.

For Kyle and Barnett (2012), in one of the few comprehensive publications on deafblind experience, imagination is identified as the fulcrum of deafblind experience. 'Deafblind people use information obtained through the senses and from past experience to make sense of their environment and to provide a context into which they place themselves' (Kyle & Barnett 2012, 13). The embodied, multi-sensory approach to listening and sound-related activities as a way of triggering imagination promoted by Voegelin and the non-goal orientated philosophy of deep listening are ways of approaching more inclusive and open approaches to creative activities that acknowledge the agency of sound to connect whilst at the same time allowing for difference and possible strains and conflict.

It is important to remember that for many deafblind people, imagination is also closely linked to the communication and reception of practical information needed to support navigation, reassure and enhance a sense of presence during mediated experiences, Kyle and Barnett are keen to point out these links:

> Imagination is the process which drives this and is a crucial process to give meaning to the experience (and to prevent deafblind people from living in a void). The practical implications of this included the need to have internal creative descriptions of their surroundings. Communication aids can provide environmental detail such as locations of furniture, the size of the room, the weather, or sources of sound.
>
> *(Kyle & Barnett 2012, 13)*

Informal listening sessions alongside formal communication methods during the project helped participants with reflection on everyday experiences, through associating unfamiliar sounds with specific environments and emotional responses. One significant impact of the project was in supporting learners to respond to these environments, and as a result, extending their affordance of possibilities when it comes to navigating environments. As one of the support staff commented:

> The project has improved awareness of place-related sounds and helped students relate sounds to environments.
>
> *(Lewis 2015b, 14)*

A key part of the process was also the inclusion of staff and participants in the decisions over places to visit for field recording sessions. This enabled participants to exercise significant decision-making in choosing new activities that reflected their interests. Some participants had, for example, not travelled on a train before and so negotiating a busy station and travelling onboard a train was for many both scary and exhilarating. The recording sessions also supported learners in responding to these environments, and as a result extended their affordance of possibilities in navigating environments.

What emerged through the work with Sense was the importance of balancing opportunities for speculative, embodied listening which might trigger 'acoustic imagination', alongside communication through or about sound that could be functional. Examples of the latter being live or recorded audio description to describe a performance space or hand signing to communicate sonic aspects of a field recording trip. Louise Fryer who created audio-description for *No Such Thing as Empty Space* (Lewis 2015a), an installation created with project participants, reflected on the importance of taking time to communicate aspects of an environment before public exhibitions and performances:

> The final lesson stemmed from the fact that visitors wanted information about what the installation held in store. Sensory loss leaves you vulnerable; it is hard to extract yourself quickly from a space if it turns out to be not empty but threatening in some way. Advanced reassurance about the facilities available, the layout and the availability of people to help, allows people with sensory loss to fully engage with immersive installations.
>
> *(Lewis 2015b, 16)*

Rhythms

The daily rhythms of some deafblind people sometimes oppose normative modes of participation in arts activities. In 2013 at the early stages of the project, myself and around 20 deafblind people formed an ensemble that came together regularly at Park Theatre in London to make music and perform to others as part of *How in the World Do We Know?* (Lewis 2013). During the rehearsals before the first set of public performances I became increasingly frustrated and anxious that sessions never started on time because, for example, some band members took considerable time to reacclimatise themselves to the space or needed the toilet just as we were about to begin. Some members also slept during parts of the rehearsals so support workers had to fill in key roles such as bass guitar. Eventually, I gave in and accepted the situation, realising the creative potential of working together with the rhythms of others rather than against them. I now realise that as a non-deafblind person, I was stuck in what Rosmarie Garland Thomson (2002) calls 'normate-time'. Normate-time emphasises productivity and embodies the values of neo-liberalism. For Thomson, disability time or what Alison Kafer (2013) calls 'Crip Time', opposes normate-time and is deeply political but as Petra Kuppers (2014) reminds us shouldn't be fetishised or glamourised:

> These moments out of time, out of productive, forward-leaning, exciting time, can become moments of disability culture politics…these time experiences might be born out of pain and frustration, and these moments shouldn't be romanticized.
>
> *(Kuppers 2014, 29)*

Attention to the rhythms of all those involved in the creation and experience of art and music were key to the development of the project. These experiences led to scheduling public performances that were less fixed and traditional than those previously planned so that concerts occurred multiple times throughout the day and were focused on the daily rhythms of the performers. These formats also allowed for the fluidity of musical roles, for example, performers could sit out or leave during performances and other members would take over, sleep was also accommodated for, both for audience and performers.

Some deafblind people sleep a lot and, or during times that many of us are awake or indeed asleep. This predilection towards daytime sleep and or sleeping through group activities only amplifies the image of the isolated, non-productive, non-receptive deafblind person. Both Matt Fuller (2018), and Jonathan Crary (2013), in their recent work on sleep point out that assumptions about sleep as a non-productive activity, are firmly rooted in Western philosophy and culture. Crary highlights these links to consciousness and knowledge:

> Descartes, Hume, and Locke were only a few of the philosophers who disparaged sleep for its irrelevance to the operation of the mind or the pursuit of knowledge. It became devalued

in the face of a privileging of consciousness and volition, of notions of utility, objectivity, and self-interested agency.

(Crary 2013, 12)

As Crary (2013), points out, these attitudes, though still popular, are contrary to contemporary scientific discourse and there is growing evidence of the importance of sleep on a wide range of factors, evidence points towards sleep as a highly productive crucial activity, one at the centre of health, happiness, wellbeing, and indeed a success. Sleeping in public or particularly during concerts might be seen as an inappropriate response to the productive efforts of the musicians involved but if we are to embrace a more accepting and accessible culture around listening, we might need to accept the possibility that an audience or performers might sleep during live performances.

Ways of Listening

For Jonathan Sterne (2012) and Steve Goodman (2012) frequencies speak of socio-political issues and concerns. In his work on the MP3, Sterne asks us to consider what we lose in compression formats which are predicated towards the communication of semantic information, or the speedy consumption of music. For Goodman, frequencies, particularly infra and ultrasonic frequencies can be tools of resistance and containers for identity politics. Much of the work during the project with Sense involved exploring the affordances of frequencies outside the audible range and in particular of the range of human speech. One musical process experimented with at Park Theatre can be described as de-audification or haptification, where we pitched down musical vocal phrases formerly within the range of human hearing to those within the unsound register. The transformed voice was then experienced through haptic vests, transducers placed on drums and the floor or simply by sitting on speaker monitors; this allowed performers and later audience members to focus on the haptic experience of vocal communication. Haptic and tactile experience and communication are a major feature of deafblind culture, with for example hand-signing and sometimes Tadoma, common forms of communication. Other, contingent, individual methods are also common, such as used by artist and musician Marcus, one of the Park Theatre band members, who explained to me how he sometimes places his hand on the speaker on the ceiling of tube carriage to feel the vibration of the station announcement to help identify which stop the tube train is at. Using haptic experience was also a major feature of the touring installation *No Such Thing as Empty Space*. In the installation, haptic vests, vibrating, and tactile signage allowed visitors to focus on and experience lower register frequencies with greater intensity. As one audience member reflected:

> I liked the range and quality of sounds and that they were experienced in a tactile as well as an auditory way – combined together it gave and an unusual experience.
>
> *(Lewis 2015, 15)*

Using such approaches aimed at increasing inclusivity, was also a way of challenging hierarchies of modes of communication. Much of the discourse within sound studies challenges notions of visual common-sense, and within communication, I argue that tactile and haptic common-sense and experience, are also marginalised and given less validity than speech or written language. For Terra Edwards (2012, 41) the dominance of visual translation over tactile is also problematic and 'Visual common sense will always, in the interpreting frame, trump the common sense of a tactile world' (Edwards 2012, 41). The focus on haptic and tactile experience is therefore not just practical but highly political.

A major part of the creation of the immersive installations in the project involved the collecting of material through field-recording sessions, during these sessions further issues relating to perceived disability and sound were revealed. Assumptions are sometimes made around the level of engagement of individuals and what they may or may not respond to because of their perceived disability, and a common experience during field-recording sessions was that when presenting a set of headphones and microphone to an individual with a hearing impairment I was told by staff that the recordist wouldn't be able to hear anything. Not uncommon results however were smiles and giggles from the person wearing the headphones. I do not know what the listener may or may not be perceiving, but it goes to show the importance of not taking anything for granted and that recording is an embodied activity and not just about collecting sound or augmentation of hearing. Findlay-Walsh (2019) sees field recording as a multi-sensory act that allows the participant 'an access point for embodying and inhabiting alternative spaces, experiences and perspectives' (Findlay-Walsh 2019, 33). For Findlay-Walsh, who also draws on the ideas of Voegelin, field-recording has efficacy way beyond the capture of sound, where the act of recording connects the body with the environment and gives access to memory and imagination.

There are intimate links between technologies informed and designed for those with sensory loss and pervasive media consumed more widely. From gaming to personal sports audio to voice assistants and online meeting platforms, there are connections to sensory loss. Unfortunately, we often see reductive, solutionist, or one-size-fits-all approaches to media-tools promoted in the accessibility market. For example, musical interfaces or communication tools are all too often marketed with over-inflated claims and hype. What the project with Sense highlighted more than anything concerning media tools, such as vibrating-vests, midi-controllers, specialist microphones and bone conductors, was the often massive difference in affordances that a situation, interface, or device might offer to one individual compared to another. Sasha Costanza-Chock (2020), in their work on Design Justice, argues that we replicate social inequalities in designed objects:

> currently, the values of white supremacist heteropatriarchy, capitalism, ableism, and settler colonialism are too often reproduced in the affordances and disaffordances of the objects, processes, and systems that we design.
>
> *(Costanza-Chock 2020, 20)*

Costanza-Chock's work on Design Justice is highly relevant to deafblindness as throughout the project I experienced assumptions being made about the affordance of media tools marketed to groups of people blanketed together because of perceived disability. The one-size-fits-all approach marketing media tools driven by a financial imperative often increases marginalisation rather than leading to greater inclusivity. Similar affordances and dissaffordances offered by media objects used in the project were also present for audiences for the immersive installations, as Louise Fryer reflects:

> While some people found this space disturbing and claustrophobic, others thought it was fun, happy, sunny and peaceful and returned multiple times. Some of the audience found the work 'disorientating' and 'scary', while others found the same moments 'blissful' and 'exciting'.
>
> *(Lewis 2015, 15)*

These reactions emphasise that an experience affords all of us a unique set of possibilities and the extent to which we all experience the world in very different ways. Most importantly, it shows the impossibility of creating a broadly pleasing artistic experience or one that is ever truly accessible and the need to test and be experimental limits but within safely held boundaries.

One final unexpected but important finding of the project was that creative sessions provided an opportunity for informal assessment of the recognition skills of individuals and shed light on the hearing impairments experienced by some individuals, which were not always picked up upon when speech recognition was focused on. For example, it was noticed by Donna Corrigan that one student was exhibiting much less recognition of sounds in one ear over the other, and also the false recognition of musical sounds by another student might be evidence of loss at particular frequency ranges. The use of creative sessions for informal assessment is now an aspect that Sense has expressed interest in including in activities, by having audiologists present in creative sessions.

Despite a problematising of conventional formats for music performance, participation in sound-based practice and the use of media-tools, the intention is not to propose that any of the methodologies or modes of production discussed above solve problems for those with sensory loss. It is simply to suggest that sonic culture has much to gain from further including those often marginalised by sensory impairment, especially when so much of our understanding of listening owes a debt to sensory loss. I hope the work acknowledges the efforts we have to make in order to move from a marketised personalisation of listening experience towards approaches that allow all of us to both participate on an individual level and connect to each other, our imagination, and the world.

Acknowledgements

The work above emerged out of a creative project with many different individuals with sensory loss from across the UK, primarily from the community of the charity Sense. The project also included communication and support staff, teachers, consultants and senior management. I'd like to thank everyone involved for their support, trust, enthusiasm, and individual contributions to the creative work discussed. The project was also kindly support by Islington Council, Arts Council England, Metal Culture, MK Gallery, Park Theatre, and AIR.

References

Barnett, S. and Kyle, J. (2012) 'Deafblind Worlds', Report for Deafblind Studies Trust.
Chion, M. (1982) *Audio-Vision: Sound on Screen* (Trans. Gorbman, Claudia). New York: Columbia University Press.
Costanza-Chock, S. (2020) *Design Justice*. Cambridge, MA: The MIT Press.
Crary, J. (2013) *24/7: Terminal Capitalism and the Ends of Sleep*. New York: Verso.
Edwards, T. (2012) 'Sensing the rhythms of everyday life: Temporal integration and tactile translation in the Seattle Deaf-Blind community', *Language in Society*, 41(1): 29–71.
Findlay-Walsh, I. (2019) 'Hearing how it feels to listen: Perception, embodiment and first-person field recording', *Organised Sound*, 24(1): 30–40.
Fuller, M. (2018) *How to Sleep. The Art, Biology and Culture of Unconsciousness*. London: Bloomsbury Academic.
Garland-Thomson, R. (2002) 'Integrating disability, transforming feminist theory', *NWSA Journal*, 14(3): 1–32.
Goodman, S. (2012) *Sonic Warfare: Sound, Affect, and the Ecology of Fear*. Cambridge, MA: MIT Press.
Henriques, J. (2011) *Sonic Bodies: Reggae Sound Systems, Performance Techniques, and Ways of Knowing*. New York: Continuum.
Kafer, A. (2013) *Feminist Queer Crip*. Bloomington: Indiana University Press.
Kuppers, P. (2014) 'Crip time', *Tikkun*, 29(4): 29–30.
Leman, M. (2008) *Embodied Music Cognition & Mediation Technology*. Cambridge, MA: MIT Press.

Lewis, M. (2013) 'How in the world do we know?', *Immersive Installation*. Available at www.mattlewis.info/how-in-the-world-do-we-know [Accessed 1 Apr. 2021].

Lewis, M. (2015a) 'No such thing as empty space'. Available at: www.mattlewis.info/no-such-thing-as-empty-space [Accessed 1 Apr. 2021].

Lewis, M. (2015b) 'No Such Thing as Empty Space Sound Project Report'. London: Sense.

Mercédès, P. and Impey, A. (2013) 'Deeplistening: Towards an imaginative reframing of health and well-being practices in international development', *Arts & Health*, 5(3): 238–52.

Mills, M. (2010) 'Deaf jam', *Social Text*, 28(1): 35–58.

Oliveros, P. (2005) *Deep Listening: A Composer's Sound Practice*. Lincoln, NE: Deep Listening Publications.

Schaeffer, P., in Kane, B. (2007) 'L'Objet Sonore Maintenant: Pierre Schaeffer, sound objects and phenomenological reduction', *Organised Sound*, 12(1). London: Cambridge University Press.

Smalley, D. (1996) 'The listening imagination: Listening in the electronic era', *Contemporary Music Review*, 13(2): 77–107.

Sterne, J. (2003) *The Audible Past*. Durham: Duke University Press.

Sterne, J. (2012) *The Meaning of a Format: MP3*. Durham: Duke University Press.

Truax, B. (1984) *Acoustic Communication*. Norwood, NJ: Ablex Publishing Corporation.

Voegelin, S. (2017) *Sonic possible worlds: hearing the continuum of sound*. New York: Bloomsbury.

7
SOUNDSCAPES OF CODE
Cochlear Implant as Soundscape Arranger

Meri Kytö

Our relationship with the sensory environment is becoming more and more technologically mediated. Environments are mediated for us or by us every day, often by infrastructures sustained by pervasive technology. The compressed signal of the human voice on the telephone, filtered background-noiseless Zoom meetings, stereo sound radio broadcasts, surround sound movies, and noise-cancelling technology in headphones are all part of everyday listening, rendering the soundscape with layers upon layers of sonic materials. Some layers are more treated or mangled with signal processing and amplification systems, some more with the reverberations of the physical acoustic spaces we are in.

For many, the sonic environment is enhanced and processed by a sound processor located in their listening device, be it an external hearing aid or a neuroprosthetic device like a cochlear implant. A cochlear implant or a CI is an electric hearing aid, a neuroprosthetic in three parts. It is for people with severe hearing loss, one part of which is implanted behind the ear under the skin onto the skull with electrodes curling inside the cochlea. The second part, called the transmitter, is positioned on top of this implant with a magnet, and the third part, a sound processor, on the auricle. The miniscule microphones in the sound processor pick up sounds for the processor to filter according to its algorithmic programmes and the customised calibrations for the individual user. Then, the digital signal is guided through the transmitter to a string of 22 electrodes positioned in the cochlea which stimulate the cells in a way that the auditory nerve is able to transmit this stimulation to the brain. The outcome is a sensation, a perception of sound: hearing. Unlike the external hearing aid, a CI does not reproduce sound waves that have travelled through the sound processor. It skips the parts of the ear that reacts to sound waves and stimulates the cells near the auditory nerve directly.

The history of neuroprosthetic digital hearing aids dates back to early experiments in the 1960s (Mudry & Mills 2013) leading to further development in the 1970s, and finally as wearable technologies entering the consumer market in the 1980s (Levitt 2007). There are about 600,000 people using CIs worldwide (Dietz et al 2018, 574.) Valued at nearly $1,2 bn in 2018, the market for CIs is growing at a healthy pace, with the Australian firm Cochlear Limited dominating this market (Research & Markets 2018).

DOI: 10.4324/9781003183624-8

CIs are prosthetic technologies that extend what the body can do. As Tia DeNora writes, through the creation and use of such technologies, actors and their bodies are enabled and empowered, their capacities are enhanced: 'they are capacitated in and through their ability to appropriate what such technologies afford' (DeNora 2000, 103). I am interested in what these affordances offered by CI technology are. People living with cochlear implants hear their environment primarily through microphones and code. These acoustic spaces can be understood as what Rob Kitchin and Martin Dodge call *code/spaces*, environments that are shaped by and made possible by computer code in many complicated and often invisible ways, which only become noted when the code stops working or a machine breaks down (Kitchin & Dodge 2011). In this chapter I examine these embodied human–technology relationships by asking what kind of listening agency is given to the implant and how a coded soundscape can shape understandings of space and place, that is, our understanding of acoustemology (Feld 2015). These questions are approached with an empirical study: a one-year ethnography with an adult informant adapting and learning to listen with two cochlear implants.

Walking with Helinä – Methodological Background

In 2017, I received an email from an acquaintance who, knowing I worked as a soundscape scholar, asked me for information on CI use. She was asking these questions because her sister Helinä had just been implanted with a CI. The sister was going through a lot of 'hearing for the first time experiences' with the implant, sounds and acoustic phenomena she hadn't realised were part of her everyday environment: a visit to a public indoor swimming pool (full of echo), to a supermarket (with background music), to a railway station (with voices over the Tannoy), washing dishes (with the water dripping), and to a coffee shop (where you can hear people sitting in the table next to you, talking). It was clear from the email that the whole family was astonished, excited, and overwhelmed by this novel situation, and wanted to understand it better.

Helinä is an office worker in her 40s, a mother of three adult children. She was born with severe hearing loss to a hearing family, has used hearing aids from the age of four, and is a stellar lipreader. Six years back when her left ear started to be of no use even when using an external hearing aid, she requested an implant. After two years of appealing to the local healthcare authority, her request was accepted and eventually, she got two CIs.

I suggested to Helinä that we could do a study together. We had mutual interests in that we realised that we both wanted to learn from each other. I had been interested in situated knowledges (Haraway 1988) in studying soundscapes, and Helinä was curious about communicating with sound. Eventually we ended up working together for one year while she was adapting and learning to listen with the CIs. We did various listening walks in different environments; I accompanied her to the doctors, and she also kept a sound diary which I could then read. We talked regularly, together and with family members and exchanged correspondences. This cooperation resulted in a rich ethnographic body of material of which this chapter presents only a few glimpses at what I learned during the year. To protect her privacy in this study we decided to pseudonymise her name to Helinä. Helinä is an old-fashioned Finnish women's name, meaning the sound of chiming and tinkling. We thought this would be symbolic and descriptive of her newly augmented ability to hear high-pitched sounds.

This study attempts to fill some of the gaps between soundscape studies and technologically mediated listening. When R. Murray Schafer's classic book *The Tuning of the World* (1977) was re-released in 1994, the name of the book was substantially altered to *The Soundscape: Our Sonic Environment and the Tuning of the World*. Soundscape is often understood as 'our soundscape', which appears to be constructed of public sonic space, shared listening experience, often surprisingly in open-air space, the outdoors, or in urban settings ('the street'). According to Barry Truax, the model of the acoustic community is one of the main results of the *Five Village Soundscapes* project, carried out by the World Soundscape Project group in the 1970s (Truax 2009, 286). The model emphasises and is predicated on conscious listening, vast amounts of shared sonic information (the basis of acoustic communication), locality, stability, and balance in the acoustic environment.

The choice of perspective, or rather the rhetoric of the books written during the era of awakening of environmental and social consciousness, has affected the emphasis of soundscape research during the last 50 years. This has meant that the mainstream of soundscape research still often focuses on a presumption that soundscape is something shared and in common. The 'shared' includes cultural understandings of sonic environments and social memory, often represented in a national or geographically local context. The 'common' includes the mundane and material environment to which the inhabitants or citizens have a responsibility for, or – in the light of today's global climate – even an obligation. This pedagogical and political stance is laudable until we realise that the so-called shared experience of the soundscape might not be that shared after all, or at least it can't be said that there is a sonic environment that all would perceive in the same way. This leaves the shared understanding of soundscapes with a wobbly perceptual grounding which should be considered carefully when making generalisations of how soundscapes are understood.

Sensory perception is in itself methodologically challenging to study, and hearing through CIs raises even more questions of origins or sources of sound, of knowledge and experience, for both people using them and to people who do not. The presence of a machine should not complicate the issue though; in fact, quite the opposite. As Jonathan Sterne states, everything that is known about the so-called natural state of hearing in itself is a product of an interaction between technology, sound and the ear (Sterne 2015, 116). The presence of this listening technology gives an opportunity to question the very 'commonness' of hearing and think of it as a boundary project for knowledge production, to use the term of Donna Haraway. For Haraway, bodies as objects of knowledge are 'material-semiotic nodes', the boundaries of which materialise in social interaction. Boundaries of objects are drawn by mapping practices (Haraway 1988, 595). From the very start of our work together, Helinä expressed a need to learn culturally contextual pieces of knowledge concerning sound and spatiality. For this reason, listening walks, walking with a focus on sensing the sonic environment, proved to be the most fruitful method for us to be in dialogue about sound and listening. While moving, we could observe each other's listening while interacting with our surroundings, mapping our understanding in social interaction.

A Sense of Code/Space

During our first walk together, Helinä had been using one CI for a few months. This machine was a so-called hybrid, an implant combined with an electroacoustic hearing aid that enhances lower frequencies acoustically, in her case sounds below 400 Hz, while higher frequencies were generated by the CI. While out and about she would keep me walking on the 'CI-side' of her (left) so that we could talk. On her right ear which had been 'the better one' before the operation she was wearing a hearing aid. The right ear was also to be operated with an implant later in the autumn. During this walk I would ask her to tell me what she hears. She would indicate an acoustic phenomenon, I would listen for it and try to locate it in space, and then we would discuss the possible sound sources and their various meanings and ways to describe them. For example, we would discuss airplanes flying by. She would first say 'okay, now I hear a faint rumble descending in pitch… it is not a car… it might be an airplane, as I know there is an airfield near by'. She would then look up and try to locate the airplane, and as she didn't in this moment have any spatial hearing (as she would later), she would turn until she saw one. Then, as the plane disappeared, asked if an airplane makes a different kind of noise when it flies in a cloud, if that would be the reason for the descending pitch. We then discussed acoustics of different spaces, of how far sound moves in spaces, how it changes in volume, what reverberation feels like, and how it sometimes defines how people use their voices, talking softly or loudly. She would also search for descriptive words imitative of high-pitched sounds, asking me if I would use the same, for example: 'the light switch clicks up, paper rustles, trousers swish, brakes of buses screech, knitting needles click', this all in Finnish of course. Finnish being an onomatopoetically flexible language, these descriptions of qualia would sound like *naksuu, rapina, kahina, vinkuu, kilinä*, respectively. The outcome of the discussions was never very clear; mostly tentative thoughts, doubt, and above all, wonder.

The CIs have changed Helinä's relationship to her sonic environment in various ways. But one of the more drastic changes seems to be the sense of space gained with the second implant. Helinä described the difference between the external hearing aids and the implants as being enormous, like between black and white and colour. She writes in her sound diary:

> There's depth. Before, [the soundscape] was flat and dull, now there are all kinds of elements. Before, everything was the same volume: steps, talking, everything was the same volume. Now I can differentiate between what is near and what is far. First, I need to learn to recognise the source, but after that I know. And directions; I couldn't tell if [a sound was] coming from behind me or where, but now I can.

As Don Ihde states, people invent technologies but while using them technologies re-invent people (Ihde 2007, 243). From the very beginning Helinä has wanted an embodied relation to the machine, in Ihde's words the CI should become 'incorporated' as Helinä's medium of perception, become parts of her very self. She often noted how exhausting attentive listening was, writing in her sound diary that, 'I'm going to work on Monday [the first time after the second surgery], and we'll see how tired I will be after the working week or if I feel the need to switch the implant off.' At the same time she explained how she felt dependent on the CIs and feared she would some day lose them, saying, 'at the moment I'm actually quite horrified about the thought that I couldn't hear anymore. That's why I say that if go unconscious I want my implant to stay turned on.'

It is evident that for Helinä learning to listen with the CI is both arduous and rewarding as sensory labour, that is, recognising, interpreting, enduring, handling, and responding to different sensations carrying information and mediating affect. But this process has also changed her perception of self. She can't hear her own voice without a device, and ever since the age of four she has had to get used to hearing her voice differently every time the hearing aid was updated, every four years or so. For her the microphone and the code render an interface of self. Before the CIs, she heard her voice with the external hearing aids as if 'from the bottom of a well'. Now the voice is much more clear, present, and closer, and it has done a great deal for her self-confidence in social situations.

The listening technology transforms Helinä's bodily human experience of the sonic environment into a code/space she both depends on and needs to manage by occasionally turning it off. She feels the machine demands a lot from her but her expectations for it, for medicine and the science behind it are also very high. The difference between the external hearing aids she had before and the CI sound processors are in the complexity of its automated algorithms and how they produce a sense of space. Using tools and machines to accompany the external hearing aids have been part of her everyday life, like audio induction loops, FM devices, wireless microphones

(Roger Pen), and alarm clocks, doorbells, fire alarms, and baby monitors with lights or vibration, not to mention sign language as a tool; even after the CIs they are useful. But the CI sound processor is more comprehensive in its scope, more incorporated in her body, and producing soundscapes of code, that is, heard 'landscapes of code', to use the term of Minna Saariketo (Saariketo 2020). This opens up the question of what is meant by listening and learning to listen in situations where the sonic environment is technologically generated by a CI. Or, to be more precise, does the machine have listening agency? What kind of agency? Given by whom?

The Sound Processor as a Listening Machine

In the social sciences, interest in code and algorithms is based on their abilities to make things happen and produce ways to see, know, and do. In critical studies of algorithms and software the focus is often on the performativity of the code and algorithms, the choices, values, and intentions that are inscribed in them. The premise is that programmes are born in political, technical, cultural, and social constellations and are thus saturated with disputes, emotions, intensities, meanings, power formations, and imaginaries (Saariketo 2020, 29. See also Mackenzie 2006, 19, Kitchin and Dodge 2011, 37). In her study on the technological history of the CI sound processor, Mara Mills states with unquestionable clarity, that:

> CI signal processors embody a range of cultural and economic values, some of which are deliberately 'scripted' into design, others of which accrete inadvertently. These scripts include the privileging of speech over music, direct speech over telecommunication, nontonal languages over tonal ones, quiet 'listening situations' over noisy environments, and black-boxed over user-customizable technology.
>
> *(Mills 2013, 323)*

The complexity of algorithmic programmes often mythologises data technology making it unobtainable for people living with them. To prevent this kind of interpretation and give the machine no more algorithmic power (Bucher 2018) than necessary, I will describe briefly how the sound processor works.

The processor in Helinä's CI model Cochlear CP910 is called SmartSound iQ. For the signal to be optimal for the electrical stimulation of her cochlear nerve the processor uses dozens of algorithms to filter and denoise digital information. The basic sound processing algorithms of the processor deal with wind noise reduction, compression, adjustment of the directional microphones' sensitivity, and volume control. The device uses 22 channels to create stimulating pulses. The input of these channels is individually processed with several algorithms and when combined they can be used as selectable programmes, although most of the time the machine does this detection automatically. These automated processes are also called adaptive processes, a choice of words that emphasises the machine's ability to respond to changes in input, not only react to them. The complexity and meticulousness of the pulses generated can be visualised with an electrodogram. Here is a graph depicting a timeline of a half-second, the word 'choice' under one algorithmic strategy (electrode 1 is the highest pitch-wise, 22 the lowest).

The main challenge for the designers of processors is to get a good signal-to-noise ratio, or to get speech and other desired signals clearly audible and to tone down noise. The Cochlear Clinical Guidance Manual describes the main data programmes (Clinical Guidance Document 2017, 13–14). These include the *ADRO* – Adaptive Dynamic Range Optimisation (a digital preprocessing signal algorithm designed to improve audibility of low-level sounds and reduce the

78 Meri Kytö

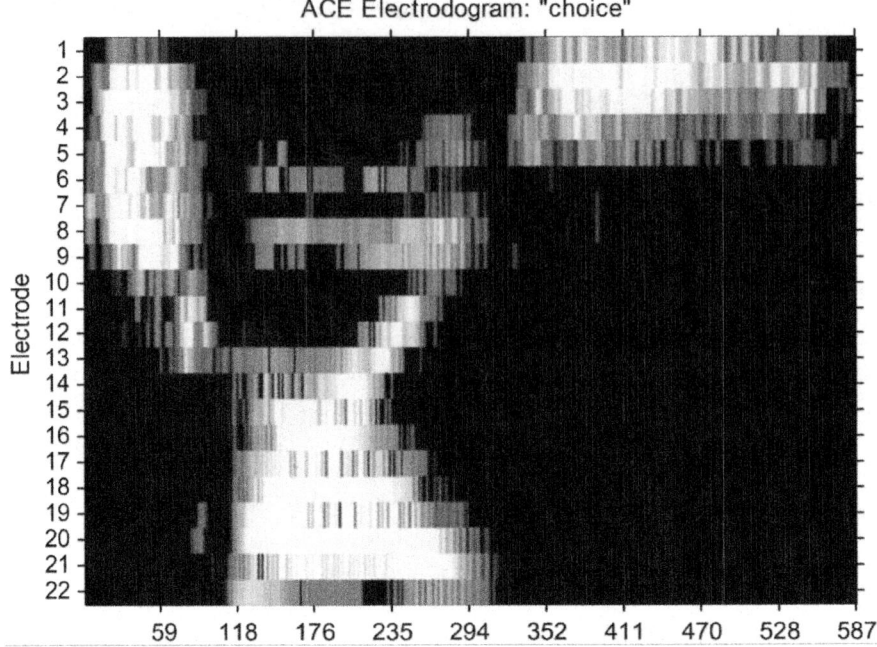

FIGURE 7.1 Electrodogram of the word 'choice', *Clinical Guidance Manual* (2018, 32). © Cochlear Limited 2021. This material is reproduced here with kind permission of Cochlear Limited

gain on higher-level sounds to keep the signal level at the desired point), the *Whisper* (a fast-acting compression circuit that makes soft sounds easier to hear), and the *Beam* (a beamforming algorithm that uses spatial input processing and intelligent noise cancelling to automatically adjust microphone directionality depending on the presence and type of noise sources), just to mention a few.

Combination programmes can be selected using a personal remote control (and in the newer processor model, with a mobile app). When activating the second implant, Helinä's doctor took up the use of the remote control and emphasised the good qualities of the available programmes, demonstrating that they are helpful for those who just want to pop the gadgets on to their ears and take them off, that is, people who strive for an embodied relationship with their implant. The default combination programme in SmartSound iQ for everyday use is SCAN, which classifies incoming signals into six 'scenes': quiet, speech, speech in noise, music, noise and wind. Based on these classifications, the SCAN programme automatically selects and turns on the most appropriate input processing algorithms. During the appointment the doctor added the SCAN programme to the programme slot 4:

> DOCTOR: The scanner is a programme that– what it does is that it sniffs around your sonic environment and tries with the help of its artificial intelligence to find the best operating settings for that situation, and I think then… like, if you are a normal person you really should try it because it's this kind of 'switch on and forget it' system. The only problem is that it pumps the sound a bit
>
> HELINÄ: Yeah, and then, I think it has, there is a delay
>
> DOCRTOR: Yes yes
>
> HELINÄ: So, I kind of feel that I miss something

DOCTOR: Yes, in a way, it is a problem, or it is a disadvantage, the pumping, but you just need to know it does that
HELINÄ: Yeah, I guess
DOCTOR: [- -] With the other programme you can decide for yourself but with the adaptive programme you won't know because it can skip a bit, like when two people are talking and the other is louder than the other, it will jump to listen to the louder one even though you would like to listen to the more quiet one but then if a motorcycle buzzes behind you it will try to cut it off. So that's why programme number three is 'outdoor' and number four the scanner, okay?
HELINÄ: Yeah

As the implant bypasses most of the hearing organ's abilities to react to loud noises from the environment, this needs to be done automatically by the machine. This results in a 'pumping' that is heard in the volume of the sound. In describing how the processor 'pumps', delays and goes quiet between changing programmes, Helinä voices a concern of the machine being too noticeable. The doctor is trying to help her adapt to the workings of the machine by explaining its internal logic in choosing foci for Helinä to hear, and at the same time participating in legitimising and sustaining its configurations.

Helinä longed for a background relation with the CI, for it to fade into the background of conscious experience. She wanted the machine to be as easy to use as possible. That is why she also shunned using a remote control. Her aim was to learn to focus beyond the machine, which of course demanded quite a lot of upkeep and calibration in the beginning. For her the device needed to be fully domesticated; she spent a lot of time describing to me how she understands what is 'real' (what others without hearing-impairment hear) and what is machine interface. She didn't trust the adaptive programme because it felt fake, compared to what she felt was a neutral default setting. In a way, it was important for her that there would be a 'neutral' setting for her to choose and learn to predict so that the ability to choose the levels and foci of attention would be more hers than the machine's.

Arranging the Soundscapes of Code

This interface between the audio signal and the self bring forward the challenges of regularising sonic phenomena to signal-to-noise automation. Regularising phenomena for the purposes of automation is in the core of data practices. This regularisation automatically drops out features that are not contributing to data class predictions. Regularisation changes the object, sometimes radically, and should thus be confronted as a technique of disciplinary power (MacKenzie 2017).

The secondary agency given to the CI – by Helinä, the doctors, the developers, the health care services – resembles that of a mediator. According to Bruno Latour, a mediator has the power to transform and translate meanings, whereas an intermediary merely transfers meanings without transformation (Latour 2005, 39). It is obvious that the CI is not merely an intermediary but an arranger of soundscape, arranging sound in order and, as such, working on a model that is both communicatively relevant and culturally situated. As with machine seeing, machine listening is a similar a type of automation that is integrated into the everyday lives of their users, but recedes into a 'technological unconscious' (Thrift 2004). In the background of mundane practices there are complex programmes and certain representations to which people do not cognitively invest in, the taken-for-granted processes that keep the corporeal body in the recursive loop of code-based technological infrastructure (Parviainen and Ridell 2021).

The agency of the CI sound processor extends its physical presence and the closed calculations of the individual processor in a similar fashion to other wearable tech like smartphones and fitness trackers that generate, collect, and circulate relational data. While being experienced as intimate technologies, these wearables at the same time render corporeality into an external object to be (self-)surveilled, and the data generated delivered to global technology companies for analysis and profit. CI users participate in the generation of big data, thereby assisting in cybernetic feedback mechanisms (see Parviainen & Ridell 2021), in Cochlear Ltd's case at least in maintenance and the development of future products. It should be noted that there is a difference between wearables and neuroprostheses. The sense of body-ownership, the desired feeling that the prosthesis is a part of the body, something belonging to the beholder, makes the issue of data generation and surveillance more complicated in the broader socio-technological frame.

Laura Mauldin claims that with the emergence of CIs, deafness has been redefined from a sensory (hearing) loss to a neurological (processing) 'problem'; the CI is recast as a device that merely provides access to the brain. Mauldin sees this redefinition shifting responsibility from the device to the individual, subsequently displacing 'failure' in habilitation from the device onto the individual's ability to train their brain (Mauldin 2014, 131–2). This pressure and weight of a successful domestication of the CIs is also present in Helinä's experience although her take on the machine is very pragmatic overall. During the long and ongoing process, different emerging agencies are weighted, contested, and questioned. The combined programmes have eventually proved useful in extreme situations. The doctor has hinted that she could in the future calibrate the processors herself through bespoke software. The idea that the implant would categorically not be turned off has turned into an empowering choice. One year after the second implant was activated Helinä wrote to me: 'At night I rest. Before, I seldom was alone at night. Now I don't feel the need to have a hearing person nearby. I feel it's more of an advantage that I can take these off. I don't need to hear anything at night.'

References

Bucher, Taina (2018) *If… Then: Algorithmic power and politics*. New York: Oxford University Press.
Clinical Guidance Document (2017), Cochlear Limited.
DeNora, Tia (2000) *Music in Everyday Life*. Cambridge: Cambridge University Press. https://doi.org/10.1017/CBO9780511489433.
Dietz, Aarno, Tytti Willberg, Ville Sivonen, and Antti A. Aarnisalo (2018) 'Sisäkorvaistute – kokeellisesta hoidosta arkipäivän kuntoutukseksi', *Lääkärilehti*, 73(9): 570–5.
Feld, Steven (2015) 'Acoustemology', in *Keywords in Sound*, David Novak and Matt Sakakeeny (eds). Durham: Duke University Press.
Haraway, Donna (1988) 'Situated knowledges: The science question in feminism and the privilege of partial perspective', *Feminist Studies*, 14(3): 575–99.
Ihde, Don (2007) *Listening and Voice: Phenomenologies of Sound*. New York: State University of New York Press.
Kitchin, Rob and Martin Dodge (2011) *Code/Space: Software and Everyday Life*. Cambridge, MA: MIT Press.
Latour, Bruno (2005) *Reassembling the Social: An Introduction to Actor-Network-Theory*. New York: Oxford University Press.
Levitt, Harry (2007) 'A historical perspective on digital hearing aids: How digital technology has changed modern hearing', *Trends in Amplification*, 11(1): 7–24. https://doi.org/10.1177/1084713806298000.
MacKenzie, Adrian (2017) *Machine Learners: Archaeology of a Data Practice*. Cambridge, MA: MIT Press.
Mauldin, Laura (2014) 'Precarious plasticity neuropolitics, cochlear implants, and the redefinition of deafness', *Science, Technology & Human* Values, 39(1): 130–53. doi:10.1177/0162243913512538.
Mills, Mara (2013) 'Do signals have politics?', in *The Oxford Handbook of Sound Studies*, Trevor Pinch and Karin Bijsterveld (eds), pp. 320–46. New York: Oxford University Press.

Mudry, Albert and Mara Mills (2013) 'The early history of the cochlear implant: A retrospective', *JAMA Otolaryngol Head Neck Surg*, 139(5): 446–53. doi: 10.1001/jamaoto.2013.293.

Parviainen, Jaana and Seija Ridell (2021) 'Infrastructuring bodies: Choreographies of power in the computational city', in M. Nagenborg, T. Stone, M. González Woge and P.E. Vermaas (eds), *Technology and the City*, pp. 137–55. Berlin: Springer. https://doi.org/10.1007/978-3-030-52313-8_8.

Research and Markets (2018) 'Cochlear implants market'. Available at www.researchandmarkets.com/reports/4846722/cochlear-implants-market (accessed 15 July 2021)

Saariketo, Minna (2020) *Kuvitelmia toimijuudesta koodin maisemassa*. Tampere: Tampere University. http://urn.fi/URN:ISBN:978-952-03-1531-3.

Sterne, Jonathan (2015) 'Compression: A loose history', in Lisa Parks and Nicole Starosielski (eds), *Signal Traffic: Critical Studies of Media Infrastructures*, pp. 31–52. Champaign, IL: University of Illinois Press.

Thrift, Nigel (2004) 'Remembering the technological unconscious by foregrounding knowledges of position', *Society and* Space, 22(1): 175–90.

Truax, Barry (2009) 'Introduction to five village soundscapes (1977)', in Helmi Järviluoma, Meri Kytö, Barry Truax, Heikki Uimonen and Noora Vikman (eds), *Acoustic Environments in Chance & Five Village Soundscapes,* pp. 286–9. Tampere: TAMK.

8

∼

Patrick Farmer

1

For me, writing an essay in a book concerned with 'Aural Diversity' requires writing about my hearing. In this regard I'd like to begin with an apology, particularly to those who live with tinnitus, as I'll be mentioning it throughout. This last year I've been undergoing research as part of a funded AHRC project, with Dr. Marie Thompson, concerned with 'Tinnitus, Auditory Knowledge and the Arts' (Farmer and Thompson), and as such, when I need to write the word tinnitus, I have started to replace it with the symbol of a wave (∼),[1] representing what I tentatively call 'wave signification'. This is concerned with phenomena, such as tinnitus, that once you hear and/or think about them, seem to shift in perception, whether in terms of signification, location, volume, intensity, or otherwise…

My experience of ∼ rarely understands or keeps to boundaries, and as such, this chapter takes place in-between fields and subjects, concerning itself with the scholar Lisa Blackman's call for the humanities to take the sciences more seriously, and of course for a reciprocal response. Separate subjects are seen as, to quote Blackman, 'critical friends', rather than opponents or antagonistic partners (Blackman 2019, xvii).

It follows that this chapter is also concerned with the difficulty of directly and indirectly writing and communicating the diversity of ∼ experience. Where possible, ∼ will 'write' for itself, acting as its own duration, a method of coexistence often made apparent by its referential absence. I will attempt to enfold these positions by drawing on my own experiences of living with ∼[2] and by following Blackman's call, emphasising the 'complex, processual, indeterminate, contingent, non-linear, relation nature of phenomena constantly open to effects from contiguous processes' (ibid., p. xviii).

I draw on my own experiences of ∼, in the wake of its highly individual and fluctuating nature, to avoid treating it as an object and to foster a dynamic space of empathy and interdependence. This has led me to realise that I can't write about ∼ without writing about other hearing 'conditions' of mine; about my 'deaf' right ear that is nevertheless possessed of as much sound as my left (which I've been told by various audiologists is in 'perfect working order'), about autophony and superior semicircular canal dehiscence.

These mixed up natures become particularly apparent when I have written about walking. ∼ can make ordering my thoughts while writing so difficult that walking often serves as something of an antidote, allowing me, among other things, to dictate thoughts into my phone. However, as with so many antidotes there is often an obverse, as both autophony and superior semicircular canal dehiscence can make walking as difficult as ∾ makes writing. Walking, then, is a practice in unto itself that in this essay I write about primarily in relation to ∾ and the above-mentioned hearing 'conditions', but also Gertrude Stein and Leo Solomons' experiments with automatic writing, what scholar Barbara Will has called Stein's 'attentive inattentiveness' (Will 2001, 5), and the anthropologist Anna Lowenhaupt Tsing's notion of 'disturbance based ecologies' (Tsing 2015, 5).

Gertrude Stein and Leo Solomons' experiments with automatic writing were in part an attempt to abstract states of reflection from what Stein called 'the sound-hum of the human motor' (Will 2001, 170), and such an approach has helped me to think about both the implications of ∾ bereft of association, and the phenomenological ways in which this might be possible. Thinking with Stein's theory of the human motor and the subsequent practice of attentive inattentiveness, I have also considered if thinking with ∾ as a model might in turn be beneficial for its communication. Ultimately, I believe it is. ∾ is that which requires clarity and specificity of expression, but also, in its potential to block and obfuscate, can create a semblance of communicative possibility among the difficulties. ∾ teaches me about both the permeable and specious natures of separation through the heightened sense of isolation that is so common among those who live with ∾.

It is this line, specious and otherwise, that I think with through the work of Anna Lowenhaupt Tsing, a line that, like the wave symbol, quavers unpredictably between states, between what Tsing classifies as 'harmony and conflict' (Tsing 2015, 5) never fully settling on either side for long, or indeed, not recognising them as polar and unreconcilable opposites. Tsing's disturbance-based ecology is a model upon which I base my relationship with ∾, interpreting the notion of disturbance in relation to ∾ as a method of communicative collaboration, full of potential contradictions.

2

I consider ∾ to be akin to both a rock in the bed of a river and the river itself, a phenomenon, for example, in which matter and meaning both interpenetrate and live apart. Trying to 'learn' from ∾ necessitates a cultivation of models that can help me think about it in ways that trying to simply ignore it cannot. In this light I have adopted what quantum physicist David Bohm imagines as the 'transitory subsistence of a flowing stream' (Bohm 2006, 62), the ever fluctuating states of matter whose substance is never quite the same. Thinking with Bohm, I imagine that such a body of water subsists among ever-changing cymatic patterns, vortices, ripples, and waves, which have no independent existence as such, abstracted as they are from the rising and falling of the flow.

In my reading of Bohm the noise of a river is largely dependent on the material and consistency of its bed, and this helps me think about ∾ as that which overflows from self and environment, as both the separation and confluence of a river and its vibrating rocks, where what 'is' is the process of becoming itself, a kind of 'non-Newtonian' nature, which is to say, a 'flow' that both quavers and solidifies under pressure. Such inevitability, as if ∾ were in multiplicitous dimensions that can only be avoided for so long before having to go through and in them, rings true to a corollary that for many, myself included, is comparable to its coming and going, its rising and falling. Even if ∾ is constant, there can still be moments of bittersweet and indeterminate reprieve.

I have often been unsuccessful in my attempts to write about ∾ indirectly, however, such an endeavour continues to remind me to pay attention inattentively, to attempt when possible to remove or soften association from the experience. Thinking about ∾ during unspecified moments of its absence can inevitably 'call it back again', and yet for me such moments are some of the times when I can think about it 'clearly'.

To write indirectly is to try and hold ∽ back, though I know of no sure-fire way that this can be done, ∽ is such a part of me that I can change with it as it changes with me. If I try to think or write about ∽ whilst I am, quite literally, in the mist of it, my ability to compose, to even hear myself, is greatly reduced, and as such, each section of this chapter represents a time in which I was somehow able to think and write about ∽ without being overly affected by it.

Approached through a myriad of fields, ∽ is the loud among the quiet, the signal among the noise, the audible among the inaudible, it is that which both softens and hardens. Such an entangled, indeterminate and processual basis of relation requires a number of different experiences, fields, and environments to open to one another, to allow each other in and to let each other out, fostering a place where lines of knowledge and experience can crumple and fold. As they fall together, the convergence of fields can create what Blackman calls 'threshold experiences', revealing the 'indeterminacy of the human' (Blackman 2017), or in this case, the variability of ∽.

3

My ∽ can be an immense distraction, fatiguing, painful, a well of anxiety that often stops me sleeping, particularly when new sinusoidal (chemical?) rhythms 'appear' in my left ear – in my right ear I live with four different tones that are like standing waves made of the skull, an intensity both solid and fluid. And yet, the experiences I've had of living with ∽ have taught me so much and led me to so many places that I can't say with any degree of certainty that I would have found otherwise. I don't wish for this to come across as some kind of neo-liberal dogma however, I'm very aware of how problematic it can be to impress your own methods of coping, of living with, a 'condition', onto another, and yet I can think of no other way of living with ∽ other than trying to learn from it.

Sometimes I have a lot to say about ∽, and sometimes absolutely nothing (not through disinterest, but rather inability). Like so many, I can get very tired of the rigid segregation of dichotomies, such as internal/external – loud/quiet – subjective/objective – phantom/real (this last one in particular, being as I grew up with a father who heard voices), that can often be found among ∽ discourse.[3]

4

I speak and think about ∽ with the most clarity whilst I'm walking. When I'm sat down I often feel blocked, as if it were an intervening screen, this is something I've found particularly difficult this year of prolonged lockdowns. Of course, walking isn't a guarantee of emptying, just as being sat down isn't always a still road to vacuity, but generally speaking, walking acts as a kind kinetic mediation, almost vaporising ∽ and its effects.

I can't write about ∽ and its relationship to walking without mentioning vertigo, a state of destabilisation that rises and falls due to, in my case, what's called superior semicircular canal dehiscence. This is a hole or opening in the bone that overlies the superior layer of said canal, which is part of the vestibular labyrinth of the inner ear. It is a hole, the size of the tip of a ballpoint pen, between the inner ear and the brain cavity that makes such things as moving my head, walking, or even standing up, a decidedly difficult kind of making, the cautious yet often unavoidable splitting and remaking of one thing from and with another. With regard to my ∽ during the lockdowns of 2020, it has been frustratingly obvious how dependent my tacit coping was on motion and movement (by which I mean my somewhat egoistical belief that due to an earlier career in music I was able to adjust to the presence of several sine tones in my right ear primarily because those sounds were so familiar to me anyway), where now, in spite of my efforts, I have slowly lost or misplaced this ability and have delved from sensation into psychology where I can't often tell if I am making it worse than it actually is… I can't help but picture patterns of labyrinthine movement twinned with stasis, a blurring mixture of the inability to do anything other than obliterate differences and a sort of urgency to become what the poet Fanny Howe calls a 'spiral-walker', which is to say, learning how to make useful distinctions amidst the twists and turn-agains of bewilderment (Howe 2003, 9).

As I walk, in part to try and mitigate the intensity of ∼, it often feels like my body is being mixed up and displaced. I can feel the environment that would otherwise pass through my body unnoticed, or inaudibly, as my feet touch the ground they rattle my right ear, I can hear my eyes moving in their sockets, my tongue in my mouth. At times it can feel like I no longer 'actually' hear. I imagine my voice, I remember walking. My voice breaks open and falls out of itself. If I look up whilst walking I have to stop, and right myself, my vision swims and my heartbeat rises into my right ear. Such things are those which enmesh self with environment. Even if my ∼ is the product of an over-active auditory cortex, its resonant precarity with environment, sonic and otherwise, is evidence as to their interrelated and overlapping nature.

Instead of spiralling through the cochlea, some of the vibration that passes into the inner ear is ejected out of (and indeed into) this hole in the canal. This means that when subsequent fluid moves in the balance organs, the brain receives signals that the head is moving when it's not. Vibration spins the senses, like walking in a straight line whilst turning around, both still and relentlessly vertiginous.

But sound is in my bones, it's not as if vibration only enters through the ear. My body is in so many ways the sound of its own participation. Pulse, heart, feet, the hiss and static of muscles, billions upon billions of biochemical responses… These things can all get into the balance organ of the inner ear through the hole, and cause havoc.

At the life of this hole, vibration is, in essence, bifurcating; peeling apart in much the same way as the brain can pull apart and remake a hydrogen atom. If I think of my voice as it travels out of my mouth and around to the ear, it also travels through the jaw bone and passes into the hole, disturbing the balance organs, aggravating my voice as if a number people were speaking instead of one.

During such moments, the sounds I experience are an internal echo of the body, as I don't think they pass along the cochlea nerve, but rather reflect and ricochet around the bone of the canal and the brain cavity. What I hear during such moments feels like the sound of vibration itself.

5

The poet Gertrude Stein began a series of experiments in automatic writing in the late 1890s whilst still a psychology student at Harvard University. She, along with her colleague Leo Solomons, hoped to discover the limits of 'motor automatism', and in the process, to show such limits to be equal to the explanation of the 'second personality'.[4] or in other words, 'to study as carefully as possible the process by which a reaction becomes automatic'. Is it possible that the subjective can be ejected from the subject?

Scholar Barbara Will writes that 'unlike the Surrealists, Stein saw automaticity not as a "vehicle […] of revelation", but as the ground-zero murmur of the psyche, the sound-hum of the human motor' (Will 2001, 70). Stein and Solomons explored motor-reactions 'unaccompanied by consciousness' in the exploratory hope that they could be divorced from such actions as reflection, judgement, and will. They moved among what 20 years later would become the prototypical Surrealist lacunae of murmurs, seeking to directly inscribe the rumble of affect in a navigation and negation of intentionality.

By testing their ability to 'become automatic' Stein and Solomons constructed a number of acts of distraction, such as moving a pencil over paper (as though writing) whilst being engaged in reading a story and writing at dictation (in which the experimenters say that the constant repetition of one word was of great value for overcoming 'this habit of attention'). Stein and Solomons tried to develop a mode of writing divorced from conscious intention, from the event of meaning formation, going so far as to refer to automatism as 'a general background of sound, not belonging to anything in particular'.

Part of why Stein was so interested in divorcing language from the hum of the human motor was in order to access it in its singularity, pointing towards language as if it were its own reality, as if there were nothing behind or beyond it. My ongoing experience of ∼, thought of through the lens of wave signification (a site of infinitesimal exchange and process that we recall is concerned with such phenomena that, once heard or thought, shift in perception, avoiding fixed signification), bears witness to a self-same desire to slough off associated meaning, to become what I might call disenchanted. This arises, at least in part, from my experience with recording sound beyond the threshold of human hearing, certainly beyond the threshold of mine anyway, sound that is bereft of association and thus orbits the apperceptive space of preconceived ideas and previous perceptions.

The idea of 'positive' distraction for me relates to the notion that attention and inattention can cohabit ∼, that one might be temporarily diverted from the other, only to rejoin, affected or changed, at a later date. The metaphoric implications of such 'in' contiguity are too broad to explore here, but it's worth mentioning the inherent difficulty of paying attention to ∼ without associating, to attend in ways that Stein framed as attentively inattentive, without reflecting, intentionally or otherwise, something that many people who experience ∼ (and indeed do not) will surely understand. This bears witness to the difficulty of 'unhearing' ∼ once I am conscious of it, or indeed, the unavoidable fact that no single method of mitigation seems to work for long.

In Stein's book, *Everybody's Autobiography*, she writes of her interest in a group of reporters, telling us that a photographer is the only one among them who looks intelligent and is listening, 'Of course I do he said you see I can listen to what you say because I don't have to remember what you are saying, they can't listen because they have got to remember' (Stein 2014, 244). To which Stein appends, 'of course nobody can listen if they have to remember what they are hearing…' (ibid., p. 225).

This seems to be an extension of Stein's interest in automaticity, in divorcing 'the sound-hum of the human motor' not only from reflection, judgement and will, but from recollection, and indeed representation. In Stein's portrait, titled *Henry James,* she asks and answers, 'What is a sound. A sound is two things heard at one and the same time but not together' (Stein 1998, 157). I feel like the attention Stein paid to the almost metabolic nature of audition (Stein defined 'genius' as talking and listening at the same time and was said to have a 'strong auditory consciousness') often emerges through the rhythms of habitual actions that, as they emerge, slowly hollow themselves out.

If a sound is 'two things heard at one and the same time but not together', I imagine that said two things might be the thing that makes the sound and the sound that propagates from said thing; it could be the sound and its potential meaning, heard as conscious intention, in other words the sound and what the listener thinks with and through as they listen to the sound; it could even be the sound and the sound-hum of the human motor… It might be all of these things, it might be none of them. Imagining, for a moment, it's the second possibility, 'the sound and what the listener thinks of as they listen to the sound', that which Stein was often at pains to keep separate in her work, we remember that the only reporter Stein deemed 'intelligent' was the one who could listen because he did not have to remember.

In this sense we might be well served to look at the state of consciousness that Stein and Solomons say can accompany automatism, one that is purely cognitive, not controlling, but passive, or watchful, an attentive inattentiveness. For Stein and Solomons, their 'problem was to get sufficient control of the attention to effect a removal of attention' (ibid., p. 511), which, in my own experience, can manifest through walking, cultivating, often through a number of indeterminate factors, a sufficient lack of attention, in order to affect the transitory subsistence of ∼.

Whilst reading through Stein and Solomons' paper I realised that my previous thoughts on walking and its relationship with ∼ were somewhat misguided. I had believed that I was able to think, in other words, to hear myself think, unencumbered by the relentless presence of ∼, by 'arriving' at an unplanned and undetermined point in the walk, as if a location. I now think that it is more likely that said state is facilitated by becoming so engrained in the walk, which can happen at any time and anywhere, that I am not wholly aware that I am walking.

Stein's notion of attentive inattentiveness is a highly generative way of thinking and living with ∼, it paradoxically reminds me to remain open to change, to indeterminacy, to the obverse of gestures, actions, and dispositions. An ear (as more often than not ∼ is 'located' in the space just above my right ear, as if it were pulling at the helix to let more air pressure in) emptied of its habits, becomes strangely indifferent, disenchanted, hosting whatever aural field happens upon it. This may seem like an overly negative disposition, but the use of such terms for me points towards a sense of possibility in which I am able to hear with the least possible interference.

6

In *The Mushroom at the End of the World…*, Anna Lowenhaupt Tsing asks: 'What do you do when your world starts to fall apart?', to which she responds, 'I go for a walk, and if I'm really lucky, I find mushrooms' (Tsing 2015, 1). On a number of occasions in her book, Tsing beautifully explicates what a disturbance based ecology might consist of, particularly in relation to the cultivation of the matsutake mushroom in Japan. We are introduced to the patterned notion that, 'if you want matsutake in Japan, you must have pine, and if you want pine, you must have human disturbance' (ibid., p. 151). We learn that, according to Tsing's forest-research interlocutor, Kato-San, 'erosion is good', and that pine flourishes on mineral soils and that erosion uncovers them. The forest is not a garden, says Tsing, it has to grow itself, and yet Kato-San helps it along by creating a 'certain kind of mess', one that would advantage pine.

In my experience walking is neither a stilling nor masking of ∼, but a means of deliberate cultivation, a fostering of 'intentional' absence that nevertheless retains its indeterminacy. In the introduction to this chapter I wrote that I believe thinking with ∼ can be beneficial for its communication, that it contains within itself a need for clarity of expression and yet, obversely, the very fact that it can so often block attempts at communication means that it can potentially provide new ways of thinking about communicating, about such things as proximity and the temporary nature of binary relationality. Placing such a contention alongside Tsing's experiences of the role of disturbance in forests, that 'pines, matsutake, and humans all cultivate each other unintentionally', leads me to develop a walking practice as a kind of phenomenological intuiting, one that doesn't stop or start with the self alone, but is a way of concentrating on, or thinking with, ∼, without becoming absorbed entirely.[5]

I have no good explanation as to what happens to ∼ when I walk, sometimes it is simply drowned out, or absorbed, by my dehiscence, which has the decidedly unpleasant effect of making the latter all the more present. Of course ∼ doesn't disappear entirely, if I really try and listen I can hear it, but as I walk it's not an obstacle, perhaps due to the metabolic nature of exertion, an ever-changing environment that I continue to pass through as it passes through me, a disturbance based ecology in which I am neither in harmony or conflict with myself and my surroundings, but aurally indifferent, disenchanted, 'realigning possibilities for transformative encounters' (Tsing 2015, 152).

Clearly this dynamic is rarely simple, if I listen too hard or for too long to ∼, I can disappear into it. Living with it can necessitate both a need to be with and to do something else, whether walking, speaking, listening… One part is so often found in another, in the transitory subsistence of vortices, ripples and waves, arising and vanishing in the total process of the flow. To live in the midst of such vertiginous life is to become with transitory phenomena, finding ways to speak about ∼ as and when, crossing the waters with 'critical friends'.

What do I do when I can no longer hear myself think, when my ∼ becomes deafening? I go for a walk, and if I'm really lucky, I hear myself listening.

Notes

1 This is an attempt to acknowledge the different experiences and definitions of tinnitus, incorporating them into the life of this essay in a way that is neither loud nor quiet. It's my hope that the nature of this symbol, as a mode of unsaying or even pointing, will be beneficial to readers as they attempt to navigate the vagaries of tinnitus in ways particular to them. I'm not saying that replacing the term with the symbol is a guarantee of avoiding aggravation, but it is nevertheless an attempt at an ethics, a linguistic equivalent we might say, of thinking about alternatives before using a sinetone to audibly represent tinnitus.
2 I hope the reader will forgive my insistently writing about myself in this regard. As difficult as I find doing so, it is preferable to generalising about ∼, an experience so diverse that to try and claim it 'is' something is to do the people who live with it a great disservice. Writing about my own experiences at the same time enables me to be a little more specific about the ways in which ∼ can transversally dissolve into a singular experience before resuming its nebulous diversity. Personal experience in this sense is not synonymous with uniqueness. Shared experience radiates spectrally from the personal in having to constantly relearn and react to the multiplicitous facets and churning contingencies of ∼.
3 The loud /quiet dichotomy is something that each person who experiences ∼ need make their own by necessity. This is an immanent kind of making, the cautious yet often unavoidable splitting and remaking of one thing from and with another.
4 Stein writes that 'it is well known that many 'hysterical' subjects exhibit a remarkable development of the subconscious life… It has often been argued that the performances of these 'second personalities' are essentially different from the merely automatic movements of people…' (Solomons and Stein 1896, 492). Stein hoped to close the gap between these states of being in her experiments.
5 For an interesting take on such a practice in relation to bodies of water, see: (Neimanis 2017).

References

Blackman, L. (2019) *Haunted Data, Affect, Transmedia, Weird Science*. London: Bloomsbury Academic.
Blackman, L. (2017) 'Keynote presentation', *CARPA*, 01/09/2017. Available at https://nivel.teak.fi/carpa5/lisa-blackman-speculative-science-thresholdexperiences-and-transsubjectivities/ (accessed 01.04.21).
Bohm, D. (2006) *Wholeness and the Implicate Order*. New York: Routledge.
Hagood, M. (2019) *Hush; Media and Sonic Self-Control*. Durham: Duke University Press.
Howe, F. (2003) *The Wedding Dress, Meditations on Word and Life*. Berkeley: University of California Press.
Neimanis, A. (2017) *Bodies of Water, Posthuman Feminist Phenomenology*. London: Bloomsbury.

Solomons, L., & Stein, G. (1896) 'Normal motor automatism', *Psychological Review*, 3(5): 492.
Stein, G. (2014) *Everybody's Autobiography*. Cambridge, MA: Exact Change.
Stein, G. (1998) *Writings, 1932–1946*. Library of America.
Tsing, A.L. (2015) *The Mushroom at the End of the World, On the Possibility of Life in Capitalist Ruins*. Princeton: Princeton University Press.
Will, B. (2001) 'Gertrude Stein, Automatic writing and the mechanics of genius', *Forum for Modern Language Studies*, 37(2): 173.

9
AUTISTIC LISTENING

William J. Davies

Introduction

Autism is a lifelong neurodevelopmental condition diagnosed by differences in social interaction (e.g., conversation style), social communication (e.g., eye contact) and social imagination (e.g., restricted interests). Incidence rates have risen substantially over the last 50 years, alongside increased availability of diagnosis and changes to diagnostic criteria (Matson & Kozlowski 2011). The current NHS prevalence is 1.1% for the UK. I use the term autism here in the same way as the current diagnostic manuals, to include all autistic spectrum conditions, such as Asperger Syndrome (American Psychiatric Association 2013). Autism may be accompanied by a learning disability, but in the current diagnostic guidelines autism and learning disability are two independent diagnoses. It is notable that, although the basis of autism is neural (autistic brains seem to process information differently), it is diagnosed by observation of behaviour.

The majority of autistic people experience atypical sensory processing, for example a heightened sensitivity to sound or texture (Crane, Goddard, & Pring 2009). These sensory differences were noticed from the earliest identifications of autism (Kanner 1943) although they have only recently been included as a diagnostic feature. Response to sound is probably the most obvious of the sensory differences, so early autism literature often features accounts of children upset by loud sounds in experiments (Hermelin & O'Connor 1970) or covering their ears when they hear a vacuum cleaner or a washing machine (Frith & Baron-Cohen 1987).

The research priorities of autism researchers are not, on the whole, well aligned to those of autistic people (Fletcher-Watson et al. 2018). Hearing differences may be an exception to this. Understanding sensory differences appears in the top ten research topics of the autistic community (Autistica 2015). And there is a large and rapidly growing body of research on hearing in autistic people, especially on auditory processing differences (O'Connor 2012). However, this chapter will argue that this literature provides an incomplete and one-sided picture of autistic auditory experience. This is because almost all of it is conducted by non-autistic researchers looking from the outside, onto an autistic experience they do not share.

DOI: 10.4324/9781003183624-10

Autistic Listening **91**

A Model of Auditory Processing

Before looking at accounts of how autistic people respond to sound, it will be helpful to review a standard model of auditory processing. Figure 9.1 illustrates an overview of the chain of auditory processing that applies to all humans. Auditory perception is represented as blocks, each performing a function or set of functions and passing output information on to the next block. This functional representation is an abstraction from the biological reality: the blocks do not map exactly onto identifiable anatomical structures. In this section, the function(s) of each block are described as they are thought to occur in an auraltypical person; the many aural divergences described in this book will be reflected in a difference within one or more block in Figure 9.1.

The first stage of auditory processing is hearing. Hearing describes the processing of sound in the ear. The inner ear (the cochlea) is responsible for turning the acoustic signal into neural data that are interpreted by the brain. This first stage is signal detection. The ear also performs low-level processing of the sound to code information such as pitch and loudness into the neural data stream (Fastl and Zwicker 2007). Subsequent stages take place in the brain.

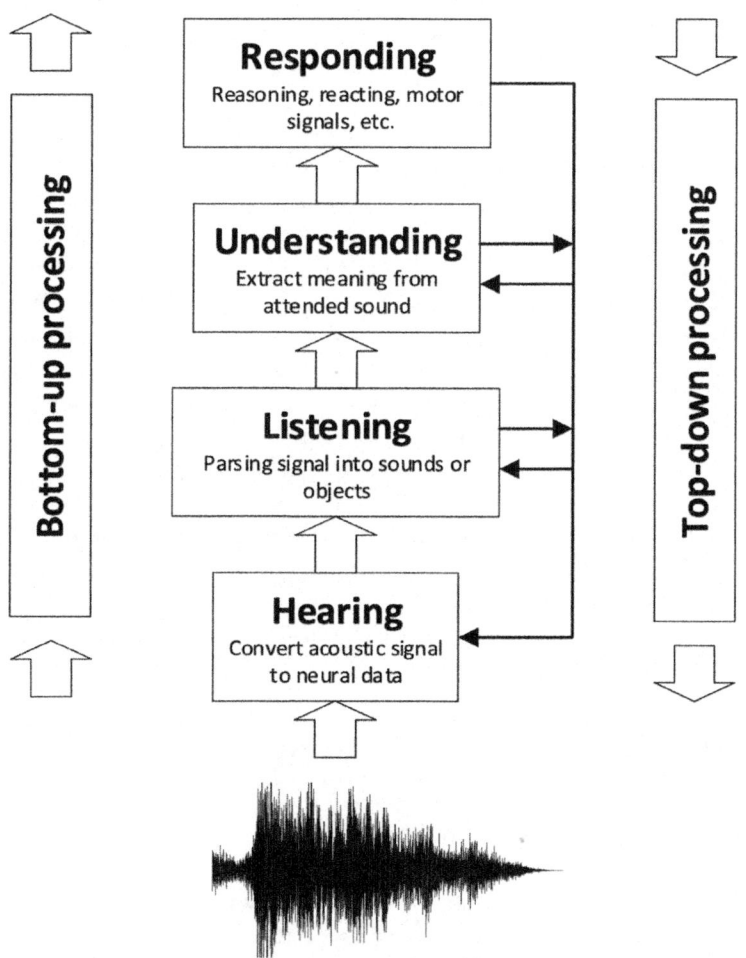

FIGURE 9.1 A simple model of the auditory processing chain

The second stage is labelled listening. Here the incoming signal is parsed into meaningful sound objects. This part of listening is called auditory scene analysis (Bregman 1994). It allows us to take the soundscape around us and separate out the combined sound into separate parts. Often, this is primarily done at the level of sound sources. For example, we are exposed to an indoor soundscape consisting of someone speaking, room reverberation, ventilation noise, and traffic noise through the window. Our brain performs auditory scene analysis to integrate the reverb with the speech and separate the ventilation and traffic noise into separate signals. Our attention mechanism selects one of these sounds for further, more detailed processing (Spence & Santangelo 2010).

In this example, we probably selected the speech signal. Speech is a very rich signal containing linguistic information but also many contextual indicators of the person speaking (age, emotional state, education, etc.) The higher processing of these happens in the box labelled 'Understanding'. If we selected a different sound, perhaps the traffic noise, different processing would be applied to extract information about the context of that sound (such as speeds, distance, and so on).

The top of our chain of auditory processing is labelled Responding. This is where conscious processing begins, and we react to the rich sound information in a useful way. If we are listening to speech we are probably now reasoning and perhaps formulating our own verbal response. If we detected a car coming towards us, we are now building motor signals to move out of the way.

The auditory processing chain is often represented as a one-way system only, from the sound at the ear (bottom) to the conscious response (top). But in fact, there are several pathways from upper layers to lower ones. Two are important to mention here. The first is attention. Attention is often modelled as two competing processes (Shinn-Cunningham 2008). Top-down attention is where we select a sound to listen to. We might choose to pay attention to the speech rather than the ventilation noise (assuming the speaker is interesting enough). But our awareness can be captured by bottom-up attention. This happens when a sound is salient enough. Examples are a sudden bang, or someone speaking our name. Typically-functioning attention is usually modelled as a system in which these competing processes provide a tight focus on one sound only at any one time. When we attend to the speech, we no longer notice the traffic noise.

The second top-down pathway is provided by the brain's predictive model of the world. Sensing the world around us at maximum detail from moment to moment is wasteful of the brain's resources, given that the world does not change very rapidly, most of the time. A more efficient strategy is to build an initial model of our surroundings and then predict the near future. Sensory input can then be mainly used to update the prediction (Clark 2013). In this model, bottom-up attention capture happens when the world deviates from our prediction. This frees up more cognitive resources for planning and reasoning.

Autistic Auditory Processing in the Literature

Notable differences between autistic and typical people have been found at all stages of the auditory processing chain in Figure 9.1. The view of the autism research literature is almost wholly negative. Researchers have found evidence of several types of difference between autistic and non-autistic people's processing of sound. Autistic listening is almost always labelled as impaired, based on the differences found, even when the deficit could be seen as partly or entirely a value judgement. The literature contains evidence on loudness and pitch perception, orientation to sounds, prosody perception, understanding speech in noise, and auditory attention.

Loudness Perception

Loudness and pitch belong in the 'Hearing' block in Figure 9.1, being extracted from sound by the inner ear. The aversion to loud sounds found throughout the history of writing on autism is now usually discussed in the literature using the framework of hyperacusis. Hyperacusis is a medical diagnosis that simply means an 'unusual tolerance to ordinary environmental sounds' (Baguley 2003). Given the large number of clinical observations and first-person accounts, it is surprising that there have been very few good-quality measurements of hyperacusis in autism. Perhaps the best data are provided by Khalfa et al. (2004). They measured the auditory threshold (the quietest sound that can be detected) and the loudness discomfort level (at which sound is perceived as very uncomfortable) in both autistic and typical teenagers. The autistic participants had the same threshold, but a significantly lower loudness discomfort level. The relationship between objective sound intensity and perceived loudness was also different between the two groups. More research is needed, but this different loudness-intensity function seems to be the basis for the reported hyperacusis.

Pitch Perception

The literature is clear that some autistic people are better at judging (relative) pitch changes (Bonnel et al. 2003) and are more likely to have absolute ('perfect') pitch judgement. It has been estimated that 5% of autistic people exhibit absolute pitch vs 0.05% of the general population (Rimland and Fein 1988). Reading this literature as an autistic researcher, it is striking that the authors who report these results often frame them in a negative light. Suggestions include that superior pitch perception might lead autistics to focus on irrelevant stimuli, that it could be responsible for poorer performance at speech decoding or associated with worse social integration generally. Mottron et al. (1999) are one of the few groups to make the obvious observation that superior pitch perception in a child might indicate a future in music.

Speech in Noise

Listening to speech in background noise is a key task for most people. Humans with unimpaired hearing typically perform this task very well, with enough intelligibility for conversation achieved when the speech is only a few decibels above the background noise level. Because speech and many background noises are dynamic signals, changing all the time, good performance in a speech-in-noise task depends on being able to extract information from brief glimpses of the speech when it emerges above the background. Several results suggest that autistic people perform more poorly on this task (for example, Alcántara et al. 2004) perhaps due to less complete separation of the speech and noise objects in the Listening stage of Figure 9.1.

Speech Prosody

Prosody refers to the elements of speech additional to the 'words', such as changes in intonation, stress, rhythm, etc. These convey a variety of social cues including turn-taking and emotion. Some researchers have reported that autistic people perform more poorly at perceiving affective prosody – detecting the emotional state of the speaker. This is usually interpreted using the theory that autistic people have impaired theory of mind (Baron-Cohen 2000). A more sophisticated experiment was performed by Chevallier et al. (2011). They gave participants a demanding cognitive task to perform in addition to evaluating the emotional state of the speaker. Results showed that autistic participants performed more poorly than typical participants on the affective prosody task, but only when the additional cognitive load was high. These results are inconsistent with a pervasive deficit in theory of mind. Instead, the results are consistent with a situation in which an autistic listener must do additional cognitive work to consciously process non-verbal cues embedded in the speech of a non-autistic speaker, as predicted by the double empathy theory of Milton (2012). A recent experiment by Crompton et al. (2020) investigated this directly and found that autistic-with-autistic and non-autistic-with-non-autistic speech communication was equally effective, while autistic-with-non-autistic communication was significantly less effective.

Perceptual Capacity

The perceptual capacity of a person is a measure of their ability to process sensory information. It can be measured by loading a person with several simultaneous stimuli while asking them to perform a task (such as detect one target stimulus within the mixture). Remington and Fairnie (2017) found that autistic adults could cope with a higher load (in terms of number of distractor sounds) while remaining accurate. This is one of very few results in the literature which explicitly conclude that autistic auditory processing can be superior. One might hypothesise that this superiority might be the result of some autistic adults having many years' training at performing the additional cognitive tasks involved in consciously processing the social cues embedded in the speech of non-autistic interlocutors.

Auditory Attention

There is a large body of autism research that identifies differences in what autistic people attend to and how fast they attend to it. Most of this is in the visual domain, however, and there remain significant gaps in the auditory literature. Visual results show better performance at processing local detail with either worse or equivalent performance on the global whole, depending on the study (Mottron et al. 2006). Auditory results are more mixed, and differences seem smaller. One significant group of auditory attention studies measure automatic orientation towards sound. Here the researcher emits a sound in the presence of a child and then measures the extent or speed with which the child turns towards the sound. Sometimes the stimulus is speech, sometimes a click or tone. A typical result is provided by Dawson et al. (2004) who report that autistic toddlers are significantly less likely to interrupt their play and turn towards a 'social stimulus' such as snapping fingers or humming. An alternative explanation – that the autistic toddler has a better focus on her rewarding play task – is not discussed by the researchers.

Van de Cruys et al. (2014) have proposed that differences in autistic attention (and other perceptual features) could be accounted for by a brain that ignores fewer of its own top-down prediction errors. This could potentially explain why small, local changes are more noticeable to autistic people and perhaps also why responses to large-scale change arrive more slowly.

Anecdotal Reports

If mainstream autism research tends to see autistic differences (and even superiorities) as deficits, how do autistic people see themselves? A simple way to access autistic views is to look online. There have been several generations of autistic discussion forums, autistic blogs and, more recently, autistic use of social media. A convenience sample of this material was surveyed for accounts of auditory processing experiences by autistic people. Sources providing significant data were the web forums Wrong Planet, Reddit, and AutismForums, individual blogs (especially those linked from

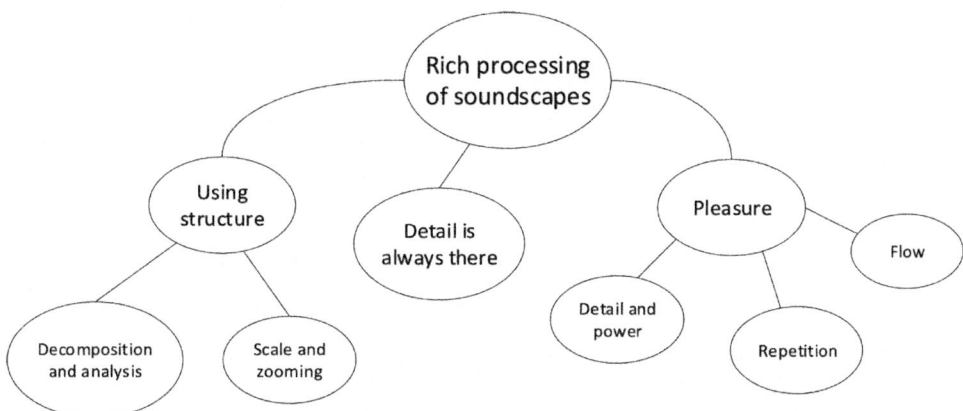

FIGURE 9.2 Thematic map of autistic accounts of soundscape listening

the large Actually Autistic Blogs List) and Twitter. All the material examined was written by people presenting as autistic themselves. The material was subjected to thematic analysis (Braun & Clarke 2006) from the standpoint of an autistic researcher with a good knowledge of auditory perception concepts. I was particularly interested in accounts of autistic listening experience from the inside out, in contrast to most of the published literature (Davies 2019).

Three main themes emerged: hyperacusis and being overwhelmed by sound, difficulty processing a target sound (especially speech) in the presence of noise, and rich processing of soundscapes. The first two themes have been studied in the autism research literature, as summarised above. The third has not and so will be the focus here. The theme of rich processing of soundscapes emerged as a way of describing the active, sometimes playful way in which autistic people spoke of using the sound environment around them. Several times I was struck by similarities with the kind of analytical listening that trained musicians employ, especially conductors or bandleaders, or by the acquired familiarity a mechanic might use to diagnose a fault. The soundscape theme has three sub-themes, as illustrated in Figure 9.2.

Using Structure

In several accounts autistic people reported being aware of a structure in the soundscape and sometimes not just perceiving the structure but using it, either as a way to extract meaning or as a form of play. This may be discussed in terms of how individual sounds relate to each other or more abstracted patterns are noticed and valued:

> the possibility of engaging with layers of relatively gentle sound, thinking about different elements of it & identifying sounds seems to satisfy my brain in the same way as a flow state.

One way of engaging with structure is to perform a decomposition, to use top-down attention to break the soundscape into smaller parts. Some people enjoy this kind of analysis with music:

> I also escape into layers of music. I have a good musical memory and can replay songs in my head as if I were dropping a needle on a record. I can zero in on the different melodies, rhythms, timbre. I can bring the bass section forward and back.

Others describe doing this decomposition with everyday soundscapes:

> If I'm alone in the house, I sometimes 'unpick' everything I can hear, to relax. So, that's the fridge, that's the road outside, that's bird song, that's the electricity in the walls, that's the lamp' etc. The world is noisy, but easier when I've noticed how/why noisy.

This kind of exercise can be pleasurable for its own sake, or it might be used as a relaxation technique. It is notable that some respondents explicitly made connections between musical and non-musical sounds:

> When in natural surroundings. Woods, beach etc. I can separate and rejoin sounds into individual music type notes then back into symphonies.

The phrase 'zooming in' is quite often used when autistic people discuss listening. It suggests using top-down attention to traverse the structure of a soundscape by focussing on more and more detailed levels:

> When I listen to music I can 'zoom in' on different parts of it. I can find the structure of different parts and split it up.
> I do that too! I guess it's one of our superpower. For me it's a positive trait. For all the artist friends I met, it's a positive trait to have someone that can somehow "really" listen and understand their creations.

In a previous paper, I described using my own experience of using my attention to zoom in on an outdoor soundscape to examine it at smaller and smaller scales, down to attributes of the initial attack of a car exhaust impulse, for example (Davies 2015). When I presented this at a conference (before my autism diagnosis), my fellow acousticians met me with polite bemusement. I was also surprised that in my experiments, my (presumed) neurotypical participants did not seem to do this either, tending instead to group lots of sounds in a complex soundscape into 'background' (Woodcock et al. 2017). For autistic people, there is almost always something to be noticed in the background.

Pleasure

In many accounts, autistic people expressed pleasure from listening in several ways. Sometimes this was taking pleasure in the exercise of an ability or power, perhaps one they knew to be unusual. At other times, it is pleasure to be gained from revealing hidden small sounds, or from experiences that come gradually, after time is invested. This autistic person gains pleasure in methodically examining a rich soundscape in detail. There's a hint here that there's a lot going on in what could be lumped together in 'background' sound:

> Tiny nature sounds. When I tune in there is so much going on, even in a 'quiet' place. One of my favourite sound experiences was hearing people whispering together in a foreign language in a hushed library (probably for more ASMR-like reasons). Calming, deepening, 'flow' for sure.

Single sound objects can also reward detailed, patient examination:

> My mum had a ceiling extractor fan in the bathroom. I swear I could listen to that thing for hours. The complexity of different oscillations beating against each other, and the patterns/non-patterns that would create, was beautiful to get lost in.

While repetitive behaviour is heavily stigmatised in most of the literature (and also often in society) it is interesting to read autistic people's accounts of repeated listening to a song or sound. Sometimes this seems to be a form of play in itself:

> I fixate on songs and would replay one over and over again (even in my head) & would constantly 'dissect' it by tuning out certain parts (ie. 1 replay I'd only listen to the guitar & drown out other parts).

Many accounts mention the idea of detailed listening engendering a flow state. Flow is a term coined by Csikszentmihalyi to describe 'the experience of complete absorption in the present moment' (Nakamura & Csikszentmihalyi 2009). It is widely viewed as highly positive and many texts advise readers on how to attain it when performing tasks. Autistic people are sometimes puzzled that flow seems to be regarded as somewhat elusive and difficult to experience, since the common autistic experience of complete engagement with an interest fits the definition of flow well (McDonnell & Milton 2014). Thus, it is not hard to find accounts of autistic detailed listening that seem to describe a flow state:

> When I work on my musical projects, I tend to hear the whole score in my head and piece every instrument loop detail where they fit. It relaxes me and makes me extremely aware of what I'm doing to the point that I lose track of time.

Detail Is Always There

Several autistic people note that they seem to be continually aware of a high level of detail in the soundscape around them, suggesting the atypical attention mechanism reported in the literature. If the background always has something going on, it can be hard to ignore. For some this leads to their being overwhelmed. For others, the continual detail is sometimes annoying, while perhaps also useful:

> I'm in a choir. I am not diagnosed as autistic but have been diagnosed with hyperacusis is, and have my suspicions. I focus on each singer's voice. I can tell you who can't hit the high G, who keeps breathing in the middle of a phrase, etc. It is bothersome but I can't stop.
> I can pick out individual bird song and locate the bird. However in a restaurant or cafe I can't filter the background, I can hear everyone's conversations which can be interesting or very annoying.

Discussion

It is clear from the literature that many autistic people process sound differently to non-autistic people, in several respects. Differences are seen at all levels of auditory processing, from low-level attributes like pitch and loudness, to higher-level features such as extracting information from speech. Almost all of the autism literature frames these differences as deficits. It is hard not to think that the overwhelmingly negative account in the literature is at least partly due to researchers starting out with a view that autistic people are inferior and looking for evidence to support this. This impedes progress in autism research for four reasons. The first is simply that it prevents straightforward recognition of autistic superiority where it exists. Better pitch perception should probably not be viewed as a deficit. Secondly, deficit framing distorts a balanced evaluation of existing results. For example, a recent meta-analysis of the literature on affective speech prosody perception in autistic people found the differences between autistic and typical listeners was 'likely due to the tendency of the existing research to overly focus on deficits in autism' (Zhang et al. 2021). Thirdly, where there are problems that really affect autistic people, as in hyperacusis, deficit research usually stops at identifying the flawed humans or perhaps goes on to suggests a remedy at the level of the individual. Adopting a more equal standpoint can change conclusions significantly. For example, a difference in the function connecting sound intensity to loudness could be seen as a neutral difference. The distress of hyperacusis then comes from environments which are not adapted to someone with a steeper intensity-loudness function. Perhaps hyperacusis will eventually be a problem of disabled accessibility. Finally, the deficit researcher does not set out to look for positive aspects of autistic experience and so misses the potentially novel, such as the rich processing of soundscapes described above.

Some of the accounts of autistic soundscape listening can be related to findings in the auditory perception literature. The awareness of detail might be explained by differences in auditory attention, and perhaps ultimately by differences in the brain's predictions about the environment. The spontaneous soundscape decomposition and zooming across scale seem novel, however, and potentially in contrast with poorer performance at separating speech from noise. This deserves further qualitative and quantitative investigation. Hyperacusis in autistic people needs a more comprehensive study and perhaps warrants the attention of acoustic engineers to help design more accessible everyday acoustic environments. Finally, the pleasure of autistic listening, especially when achieving a flow state, should be more widely known and celebrated.

References

Alcántara, José I., Emma J.L. Weisblatt, Brian C.J. Moore, and Patrick F. Bolton (2004) 'Speech-in-noise perception in high-functioning individuals with autism or Asperger's syndrome', *Journal of Child Psychology and* Psychiatry, 45(6): 1107–14.

American Psychiatric Association (2013) 'Diagnostic and statistical manual of mental disorders' (DSM-5®). *American Psychiatric Pub.*

Autistica (2015) *Your Questions: Shaping Future Autism Research*. Available at www.autistica.org.uk/downloads/files/Autism-Top-10-Your-Priorities-for-Autism-Research.pdf (accessed 9 April 2021).

Baguley, David M. (2003) 'Hyperacusis', *Journal of the Royal Society of* Medicine, 96(12): 582–5.

Baron-Cohen, Simon (2000) 'Theory of mind and autism: A review', *International Review of Research in Mental Retardation*, 23: 169–84.

Bonnel, Anna, Laurent Mottron, Isabelle Peretz, Manon Trudel, Erick Gallun, and Anne-Marie Bonnel (2003) 'Enhanced pitch sensitivity in individuals with autism: a signal detection analysis', *Journal of Cognitive Neuroscience*, 15(2): 226–35.

Braun, Virginia, and Victoria Clarke (2006) 'Using thematic analysis in psychology', *Qualitative Research in Psychology*, 3(2): 77–101.

Bregman, Albert S. (1994) *Auditory Scene Analysis: The Perceptual Organization of Sound*. Cambridge, MA: MIT Press.

Chevallier, Coralie, Ira Noveck, Francesca Happé, and Deirdre Wilson (2011) 'What's in a voice? Prosody as a test case for the Theory of Mind account of autism', *Neuropsychologia*, 49(3): 507–17.

Clark, Andy (2013) 'Whatever next? Predictive brains, situated agents, and the future of cognitive science', *Behavioral and Brain* Sciences, 36(3): 181–204.

Crane, Laura, Lorna Goddard, and Linda Pring (2009) 'Sensory processing in adults with autism spectrum disorders', *Autism*, 13(3): 215–28.

Crompton, Catherine J., Danielle Ropar, Claire V.M. Evans-Williams, Emma G. Flynn, and Sue Fletcher-Watson (2020) 'Autistic peer-to-peer information transfer is highly effective', *Autism*, 24(7): 1704–12.

Davies, William J. (2015) 'Cognition of soundscapes and other complex acoustic scenes.' *Internoise 2015*, 9–12 August 2015, San Francisco. Available at http://usir.salford.ac.uk/id/eprint/36148/1/Davies%20Soundscape%20Cognition%20Internoise%202015%20submitted.pdf (accessed 23 May 2022).

Davies, William J. (2019) 'Autistic listening', *Aural Diversity Conference*, Leicester, UK, 30 Nov.–1 Dec. Available at http://usir.salford.ac.uk/id/eprint/56380/ (accessed 9 April 2021).

Dawson, Geraldine, Karen Toth, Robert Abbott, Julie Osterling, Jeff Munson, Annette Estes, and Jane Liaw (2004) 'Early social attention impairments in autism: social orienting, joint attention, and attention to distress', *Developmental* Psychology, 40(2): 271.

Fastl, H., and E. Zwicker (2007) 'Information Processing in the Auditory System', *Psychoacoustics: Facts and Models*, T.S. Huang, T. Kohonen, and M.R. Schroeder (eds), p. 58. Berlin: Springer.

Fletcher-Watson, Sue, Jon Adams, Kabie Brook, Tony Charman, Laura Crane, James Cusack, Susan Leekam, Damian Milton, Jeremy R. Parr, and Elizabeth Pellicano (2018) 'Making the future together: Shaping autism research through meaningful participation', *Autism*, 23(4): 943–53.

Frith, U., and S. Baron-Cohen (1987) 'Perception in autistic children' In *Handbook of Autism and Pervasive Development Disorders*, edited by D.J. Cohen and A.M. Donnelan, 85–102. Wiley.

Hermelin, Beate, and Neil O'Connor. 1970. *Psychological Experiments with Autistic Children*. Oxford: Pergamon.

Kanner, Leo. 1943. 'Autistic disturbances of affective contact', *Nervous* Child, 2(3): 217–50.

Khalfa, Stéphanie, Nicole Bruneau, Bernadette Rogé, Nicolas Georgieff, Evelyne Veuillet, Jean-Louis Adrien, Catherine Barthélémy, and Lionel Collet (2004) 'Increased perception of loudness in autism', *Hearing Research*, 198(1–2): 87–92.

Matson, Johnny L., and Alison M. Kozlowski (2011) 'The increasing prevalence of autism spectrum disorders', *Research in Autism Spectrum* Disorders, 5(1): 418–25.

McDonnell, Andy, and Damian Milton (2014) 'Going with the flow: reconsidering "repetitive behaviour" through the concept of 'flow states', in *Good Autism Practice: Autism, Happiness and Wellbeing*, G. Jones and E. Hurle (eds), pp. 58–63. Edgbaston: British Institute of Learning Disabilities.

Milton, Damian E.M. (2012) 'On the ontological status of autism: the "double empathy problem"', *Disability & Society*, 27(6): 883–7.

Mottron, Laurent, Michelle Dawson, Isabelle Soulieres, Benedicte Hubert, and Jake Burack (2006) 'Enhanced perceptual functioning in autism: an update, and eight principles of autistic perception', *Journal of Autism and Developmental Disorders*, 36(1): 27–43.

Mottron, Laurent, Isabelle Peretz, Sylvie Belleville, and N. Rouleau (1999) 'Absolute pitch in autism: A case study', *Neurocase*, 5(6): 485–501.

Nakamura, Jeanne, and Mihaly Csikszentmihalyi (2009) 'Flow theory and research', in *Handbook of Positive Psychology*, C.R. Snyder, and S.J. Lopez (eds), pp. 195–206.

O'Connor, K (2012) 'Auditory processing in autism spectrum disorder: a review', *Neuroscience & Biobehavioral Reviews,* 36(2): 836–54.

Remington, Anna, and Jake Fairnie (2017) 'A sound advantage: Increased auditory capacity in autism', *Cognition*, 166: 459–65.

Rimland, B., and D. Fein (1988) 'Special talents of autistic savants', in *The Exceptional Brain: Neuropsychology of Talent and Special Abilities*, Loraine Kobler and Deborah Fein (eds), pp. 472–92. New York, NY: Guilford Press.

Shinn-Cunningham, B.G. (2008) 'Object-based auditory and visual attention', *Trends in Cognitive Sciences*, 12: 182–6.

Spence, Charles, and Valerio Santangelo (2010) 'Auditory attention', in *Oxford Handbook of Auditory Science: Hearing*, C.J. Plack (ed.), pp. 249–70. Oxford: Oxford University Press.

Van de Cruys, Sander, Kris Evers, Ruth Van der Hallen, Lien Van Eylen, Bart Boets, Lee de-Wit, and Johan Wagemans (2014) 'Precise minds in uncertain worlds: predictive coding in autism', *Psychological Review*, 121(4): 649–75.
Woodcock, J., Davies, W.J., and Cox, T.J. (2017) 'A cognitive framework for the categorisation of auditory objects in urban soundscapes', *Applied Acoustics,* 121: 56–64.
Zhang, Minyue, Suyun Xu, Yu Chen, Yi Lin, Hongwei Ding, and Yang Zhang (2021) 'Recognition of affective prosody in autism spectrum conditions: A systematic review and meta-analysis', *Autism*: 1362361321995725.

10
FIRE, DRUMS AND THE MAKING OF PLACE DURING A *CORREFOC*

Karla Berrens

Place, Senses and *Correfoc*

When we move through a space, we are in constant dialogue with it, making sense of it through our bodies. This tacit conversation between our corporeal experience of space and our memories, emotions, gender, sensory functionality, sensibilities, and affects are pillars in the making of place (Ahmed 2008a, 2008b; Agnew 2011; Johnson 2011; Low 2014; Burkitt 2014; Jones 2014; Berrens 2017, 2019). The latter is strongly influenced by the manner we understand the senses. If we work with the typically Western five-fold division of the senses, we may find we are short of perceptions to describe our corporeal relationship to space. For example in events with a strong sense of temperature, such as a fire performance, thermoception is relevant. In this chapter I'm expanding beyond this division to embrace other bodily reactions that condition our ways of relating to our surrounding (Latour 2004; Howes 2009; Paterson 2009; Bates 2011; Rhys-Taylor 2010), notably crossing over to explore feelings/perceptions of pleasure and pain through auditory stimuli.

When we attend to the richness of perception that our bodies offer, we attune ourselves to the gates separating interior from exterior, as if we were tuning an instrument. But what happens to our sensorium when the environment generates short and strong stimuli? In a *Correfoc* (I will explain this in detail in the following sections), where there are almost constant fire, whistling, and crackling sounds, accompanied by the Tabalers' incessant drumming, our sensory perception of the surroundings is strongly impacted. We are electively in an aurally diverse experience of our surroundings (Drever 2019). The soundscape is above the sonic threshold of pain for an aurally typical person (between 115 and 140 dB) yet this is one of the most popular events in Catalan popular culture (Drever 2019). Hence this is an aurally overwhelming activity where the continuity between hearing and environment is overridden and at times, broken. This chapter seeks to examine some aspects of this shift in perceptual experience when exposed to an intense sensory stimuli and the temporality of that sense of place (Lopez 2005; Horowitz 2013; Berrens 2019).

Methodology

This research was originally thought of as a combination between quantitative and qualitative methodologies, having the qualitative part of the research bear most of the data gathering.

DOI: 10.4324/9781003183624-11

However the Covid-19 pandemic has affected the research and, besides a reflective street ethnography from the previous *Correfoc*s, I have only been able to use online methods, so far this chapter presents the first part of what was intended as methodological bricolage (Kusenbach 2003; Murthy 2008; Yardley 2008). Therefore, to date, the research articulates around a survey and five follow up interviews. This survey had a quantitative section with multiple-choice questions and a qualitative one with open questions. The second part of the methodology had to be articulated around ethnography, interviews, and focus groups. This second part will be undertaken after the pandemic. Hence, the research is ongoing.

The survey has been distributed remotely to four devils' groups in Barcelona. From these groups, the survey was passed to all sections, indiscriminately of age or role within the group (even though it was only passed to minors where at least one of the parents was active in another section of the group, hence minors are not comprehensibly represented). To date, there have been 64 replies to the survey, but replies keep coming in. Taking into account the number of people in each group, this is a significant number, representing 70% of the overall active members over 18.

The quantitative questions results are presented as percentages. The survey's open questions and the five interviews have been analysed using thematic analysis and grounded theory seeking to understand the way space is perceived bodily whilst on a *Correfoc* and the temporality of this perception (Wetherell 1998; Liu 2016).

Correfoc: History and Name

Catalunya has a longstanding tradition of integrating fire into popular culture, from throwing fireworks on 23 June, to the running under umbrellas of fire sparks and being chased by devils' burning firecrackers. Fire is deeply embedded in our popular culture, being Catalan myself, I have always enjoyed watching *Correfocs,* but it wasn't until 2017 that I decided to join one of the Colles, 'La Vella de Gràcia'. *Correfocs* are the most striking example, literally meaning 'fire run'. It refers to running under the fire produced by a group of people dressed as 'devils', called devils or fire devils. This tradition derives from the twelfth century's Devils' Dances. Those were performed in religious festivities' context and were a 'spoken dance', mixing a theatre play and a dance between Lucifer's devils and Archangel Saint Michael.

From these static representations, an event with fireworks emerged, still keeping the idea of Lucifer's devils. It would take place at the end of the spoken dance. Contemporary devils are equipped with fireproof clothing, evoking Hell in different ways by having representations of fire, dragons, skulls, and/or charcoal. They carry a long wooden or metal stick at the end of which there is a small metallic spike where a firework is attached, this is called a '*maça*'. Some devils' groups have a *maça* with space for more than one spike to fit several firecrackers simultaneously. When lit, the firework turns on itself around the spike, thus producing an umbrella of sparks. This can be accompanied by a whistling sound or vary in colours, depending on the kind of firework. At the end, the firework explodes with a loud 'boom', the *thunder.* The devil removes its remains from the spike and attaches another one, restarting the process. Most groups (*colles*) have 'figures', one, two or sometimes even three main characters. The most usual are Lucifer, normally having a distinctive costume, and a bigger *maça* called *ceptrot* with lots of spikes. Then there is a '*Diablessa*' meaning female devil. Having a distinctive costume, *Diablessa* carries a specific *maça*, sometimes called *ceptrot* too. Finally, there sometimes is the figure of Archangel Saint Michael, but this is more usual with the *colles* still practising the spoken dance. In the latter's contemporary version, devils compose '*versots*', ironical verses as a cheeky dialogue between Lucifer and his devils. Saint Michael comes to slay them all.

FIGURE 10.1 La Vella de Gràcia devils at Gracia's annual celebration

Image from the Colla Vella de Gràcia. (Photograph by Joanna Chichelnitzky. Used with permission.)

The groups of devils started incorporating Beasts, fiery representations of animals with special attachments to fix fireworks onto them. One or several people are used to make the animal dance. With time, there was a separation in the *colles* in sections, minors' section (under 18 years old), beast's section (beast operators) and devils. Each section could be accompanied by a group of *tabalers* or not.

Fast forward to 1979 in Barcelona, for la Mercè, the city's main festivity (24/09). As per tradition, several *colles* were performing their static fire events in the middle of the city; we say 'devils were burning'. To everybody's surprise, including the police force, several participants started engaging with the devils while they were burning. Instead of watching from afar, they got close and started dancing under the umbrella of sparks. This led the devils to engage in a cheeky game, chasing spectators around the streets. From this moment on, where fire was literally running after participants, the events were renamed *Correfocs*. Normally, *Correfocs* take place in two ways. The first

FIGURE 10.2 La Vella De Gràcia Lucifer and diablessa

Image from the Colla Vella de Gràcia. (Photograph by Joanna Chichelnitzky. Used with permission.)

one is called a *cercavila*, Devils and *Tabalers* go around the streets of the city or the village burning and drumming all along. There are departure and arrival points set beforehand doing a *tabalada*, a drumming route. (In fact, organising a *cercavila* requires a lot of permissions from the council and health and safety controls.) The other format is called a *carretillada*. Even being a static performance, there is a lot more firepower used at once. *Carretillades* consist of a *Colla* taking over one square. They may hang fireworks through the square so there is a roof of fire, then they will adopt a circular shape, and dance in circles, sometimes having special figures or special *maces* inside (held by a devil). The aim is to generate an aesthetic and sonic fire composition that can last from a few to around twenty minutes. During a *cercavila* there can be moments where all devils cease dancing alone, get together in a circular shape and ignite their fireworks simultaneously, generating a circle of fire.

Fire, Devils, and Clothing

For this chapter it is relevant to note the health and safety regulations that have an effect on the sensuous body. It is standard for devils to wear fireproof jackets, *cassaques*, having a hood, often with horns. Jackets and hood are made from heavy cotton fabric, then fireproofed using a spray-on product, making them stiff. Devils also wear trousers made of the same fabric. Traditionally the shoes meant to be worn are not fireproof nor offer full feet coverage. They are called *espardenyes* and are a traditional Catalan shoe used in popular culture. For the lack of full foot coverage, there is an increasing number of *colles* that have swapped them for boots. Those offer full foot coverage and are not flammable.

Two protective elements are common to most devils: protective gloves and protective glasses. The gloves are fireproof and thick or leather; they prevent burns when changing the firework from the spike or sparks. The glasses are normally standard protective eye gear used by construction workers. They add protection behind the hood, which is sometimes not large enough to shield the eyes from the sparks. Protective glasses are a controversial topic. On one hand, they offer a layer of protection both from the fire, sparks, and any part of the firework that may head towards the eye area when exploding. However, the hood and the heat from being under the fire make protective glasses prone to becoming steamed, thus hindering the devils' capacity to see what is in front of them. We will see more about the effect this has later on.

The following two items of protective gear are not compulsory though recommended. Those are a buff or foulard to cover the nose and mouth area, and another one to cover the hair. Both need to be made out of cotton or fireproofed material, as otherwise they are very dangerous. Not all devils use hair foulards but there is an increasing number of devils that use one to cover the mouth and nose area. The reasons for this are two-fold, firstly in order to protect against the fire sparks and bits of the firecrackers that are projected when the latter explodes at the end. Secondly, in order to reduce the amount of smoke inhaled at *Correfocs*. Let's imagine the smoke there can be at a *Correfoc*. Imagine a narrow street with high buildings on each side. This architecture creates the sensation of being in a long and high corridor, like a tunnel. Then add a group of 25 devils burning, dancing/jumping, organised in two parallel lines, a devil every 12 metres, generating a constant umbrella of fire with two axes. Now imagine the smoke each firework is making whilst lid and the smoke when it explodes, one every 10 seconds on average. In the long narrow streets of Barcelona, the smoke becomes trapped between the buildings and does not disperse fast. This smoke is gunpowder related, it is very common for devils to finish a *Correfoc* with their faces smeared in a dark powder that smells like sulphur when you wash it out. With this scene in mind, covering the mouth and nose area, albeit not fully effective to completely eliminate the smoke residue from the devils' faces, does help.

Last but not least there is a protective gear element gaining popularity within devils and also *tabalers*. Those are earplugs. Go back to the scene described above. The street layout and building configuration makes the sound reverberate along the street and the buildings. The *Correfoc* soundscape is constructed from the addition of exploding fireworks – either a few at a time or many simultaneously if there is a joint burn – and incessant drumming. From this we can gather that a *Correfoc* is indeed a very loud performance, normally above the 130 dB, reaching 175 dB at some points.

From here we can go on to explore the survey's results and examine in which ways the protective gear is felt to diminish the sensory experience produced by the *Correfoc*.

The Senses and Protective Gear

In the section above we have explained the protective gear used by Fire Devils and *Tabalers*. Here we are going to examine in which ways they influence the sensuous relationships during the *Correfoc*. A 96.9% of participants affirm they wear protective gear, from which 82.5% wear fireproof clothing (whether that be the full suit or just the trousers – *tabalers* only wear the lower part of the suit with a thick cotton t-shirt and a thick cotton jumper). An 87.4% use further protection, from those 78.5% use glasses, 66.7% use a foulard for hair, 60.8% foulard for nose and mouth, and 58.9% use gloves. It is striking to see that only 35% use earplugs.

TABLE 10.1 Senses working the hardest in a *Correfoc*

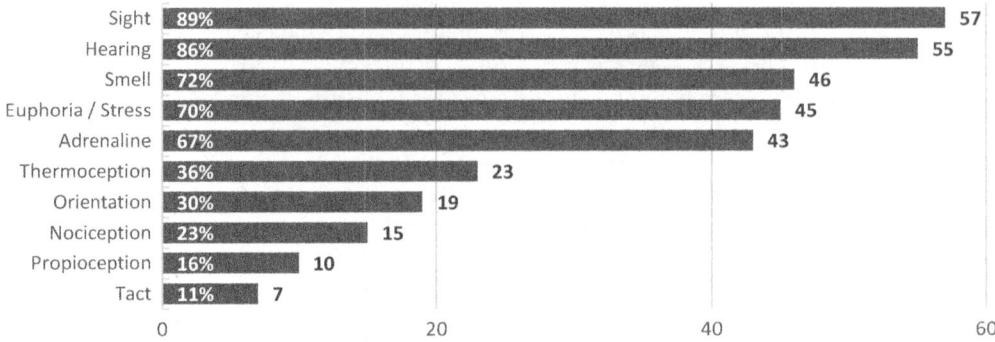

From the protective gear, 34.6% use it in order to reduce the senses, while for 65.4% this reduction is a collateral effect, using it primarily for safety. From this reduction, participants estimate that hearing and touch are the two most affected senses, followed by sight. The latter is the sense that is reduced willingly in spite of the issues this may produce (less accurate vision) because safety is deemed more important. Taste is the sense deemed less reduced, followed by smell.

98.3% of participants agree that a *Correfoc* entails the interplay of various senses. I asked them which senses they thought are working harder during the *Correfoc*. For this question I did not use the Western five-fold division of the senses but rather moved towards a more contemporary conception of the sensuous body, bodily sensations. I divided the latter by 10. Table 10.1 presents the findings for this ten-fold division: hearing, smell, sight, tact, orientation, adrenaline, euphoria/stress, proprioception, thermoception and nociception. This division was done taking into account preliminary conversations and the auto-ethnographical part of the previous research (Berrens 2019).

We can see that sight (89%), hearing (86%) and smell (72%) are the three senses deemed to work the hardest by participants, followed by euphoria/stress and adrenaline. Nociception (23%) is the third to last sense, which raises the question of how participants react to the extreme sonic levels that impact and permeate the body in a *Correfoc*. We will see in the discussions how it can influence the relationship we establish with a given activity and space.

We can see in Table 10.2 that 78.1% of participants agreed there was a shift in the sensorium but mostly during the *Correfoc*. Hearing and smell were the two senses where there were a 45% of participants affirming they remained affected after the duration of the *Correfoc*.

We will explore in the discussion the relationship of the sensory stimulation with our perception of space, and the role of the sensory dynamics in the making of place.

Fire, Drums, Feelings, and Space

Emotions in Fire and Drums

This chapter dwells on the feelings that arise during a *Correfoc* and then examines their interplay with the multisensory dimension of the perception of space (Helmreich 2010; Ingold 2011). In this part of the project, the questions about the feelings during a *Correfoc* were divided in three groups. Either one replied as a devil (including Beast carriers), or as a *tabaler*.

TABLE 10.2 Temporality of sensuous shift

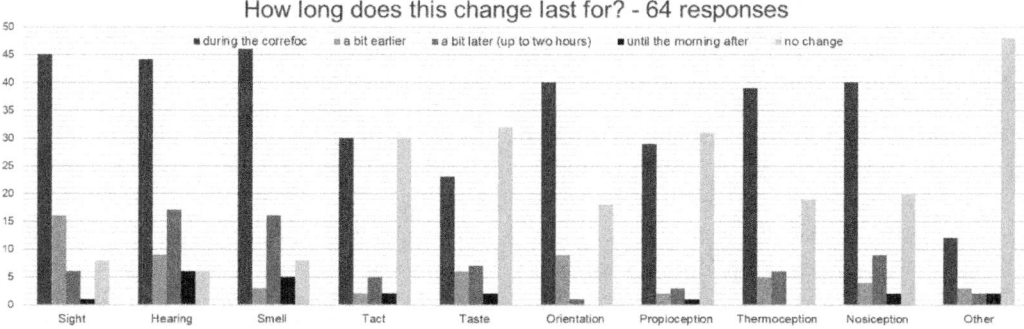

Getting into a *Colla* in Barcelona is not a straightforward process. There are many but normally already at full capacity. Being part of a *Colla* in Catalunya is embracing a core aspect of Catalan popular culture, Fire festivities. The *Colla* does more than just *Correfocs*, it has social activity beyond fire, fostering a sense of belonging to the *Colla* itself and also to a wider Catalan popular culture network. There is a sense of duty when being a member of a *Colla*, making sure Catalan popular culture does not disappear.

When asked how they felt during *a Correfoc* there was a positive response from both devils and *tabalers*. Devils talked about a feeling of euphoria, energy, powerfulness, and adrenaline (together with accelerated pulse) as bodily feelings. Then they also remarked the positive feelings that arose from a sense of belonging. There was a common sense of pride in belonging to the group and to Catalan popular culture, which was also manifested by *tabalers* and I will dwell on this later. There was also a positive feeling associated with friendship, company, and pride of the *Colla*'s performance.

The negative aspects were feelings of vulnerability, stress, and feeling lost in space. Then, associated with an extreme use of the senses, was the feeling of being overwhelmed, of being too hot and very alert. There is a disconnection happening between the aurality of space and the environment that I will elaborate on later.

Tabalers valued as positive their happiness about the *mise-en-scène*, feeling the soul of the party, being the ones marking the rhythm. They felt bubbly and being the centre of attention. There were also positive feelings like feeling young, happy, and full of adrenaline. The negative feelings were because of the ears' suffering or feeling scared if they were too close to fire or felt too observed.

We can see that one of the main positive aspects is feeling part of something bigger than just a *Colla* per se. For the devils there is a direct reference to Catalan popular culture. For *tabalers* it is on the change of dynamics their passage on the streets generates. When a *Correfoc* traverses the neighbourhood, the streets are closed to the traffic so the participants can use both the pedestrian and the road to move around. Therefore the normality of the city layout is temporally challenged in a new configuration.

Burning, Drumming, and Relating to Space

When asked about their relationship to space, 84.4% of participants knew the spaces they were going to transit before the *Correfoc*. For many of them, these are the spaces of everyday life; it is their neighbourhood or parts of the city that are heavily transited. There are several *Colles* in Barcelona and they tend to do all their local *Correfocs*. Barcelona is divided in districts, so each *Colla* will normally do their district's *Correfocs*, the one for the City's patron and then can be invited to other districts or villages around Catalunya to do *Correfocs*. In this chapter, because of Covid's limitations, I worked with *Gracia's Colles* (one of the districts).

For devils, the positive aspects were finding a balance in the relationship with space; feeling respected and having a sense of spatial domination as they made the streets theirs through the howling of the firecrackers, they felt everything was smaller. Knowing the space previously was important in order to have spatial references: once you start burning, unless you have them, every street feels the same.

The negative emotions and feelings brought forward by the devils were a sense of danger, reduced visibility, and thus a feeling of isolation sometimes. Also, they did not enjoy the loss of references and felt claustrophobic at some points. For a few individuals, however, having reduced visibility encouraged a different hearing. Albeit brutally high and intense, the buzzing of the firecrackers, in addition to being a colonising sound, becomes a guide to orientating in space (Berrens 2019).

The *tabalers* liked the sense of magic, feeling they were respected while drumming, the sensation of the space opening up while they were invading it with their drumming sound, they felt were making the space theirs and noted an increase in their vitality. They did not enjoy feelings of being overwhelmed by either a space too packed with people or the fact they felt in the loudest possible place between their drumming and the constant fireworks' explosions and whistling.

Knowing the space proved to be an asset among the participants since it meant there was less of a possibility of feeling isolated (Hall 2009). Nevertheless, as noted in the introduction, a *Correfoc* is a space where aurality becomes diverse. People partaking in *Correfocs*, whether they be as assistants or performers, enter a temporary space of an uncommon sensory relationship to the environment. Even if one knows the street layout beforehand, the *Correfoc* changes the perception of it, disassociating our sensory memory of the space from the perception at the time of the *Correfoc*. It is worth noting that both fire devils and *tabalers* felt the space was theirs while they were performing. Therefore we can argue that the colonisation of space that *Correfocs* impose makes place in a temporary manner for devils and *tabalers*. During that timespan the space where the spectacle takes place, is theirs, subverting the mainstream uses of streets, annihilating the imbalance between pedestrian and car space there is in most of Barcelona. The space is not only fully pedestrian it is fully festive.

Discussion

As seen above, only a 35.6% of the participants use earplugs. Considering the decibels in a *Correfoc*, this is an extremely low percentage. In addition, we have seen nociception is the third to last sense in action while in a *Correfoc*. When asked in subsequent interviews, devils and *tabalers* argued that although the volume was very loud, the *Correfoc*'s sounds were pleasant for them. They could feel their eardrums pulsate, and there was a clear perception of pain but the sense of belonging to the group and to the spectacle coupled with the adrenaline of being under the sparks made this a pleasant perception.

In addition, devils and *tabalers* require to feel oriented in space; blocking this aural sense has an impact on their making of place through a sense of isolation and not knowing where the rest of the group is. For many of them, using earplugs generates a sense of alienation as they already don't see clearly between the heat, the steamed glasses, and the smoke. Thus, as mentioned earlier, aurality becomes a main source to understand space and what is going on. At a *Correfoc* the devils need to hear the instructions of the head of Fire, the *tabalers* those of the head of Music, earplugs can become a nuisance. The devils are in constant movement, *tabalers* are dancing, the street is full of smoke and sparks, aurality is key in making sense of the place one is alongside the rest of the performers and spectators.

The decibels at which *Correfocs* happen are deafening, and can be very painful to undefended ears; we see that 18% of participants affirm their hearing remains altered for up to two hours and a further 5% until the day after the *Correfoc*. Sound's pain threshold is normally around 140 dB, I argue aurality, even if painful, is key in feeling connected with the space around and with the *Colla* (Berrens 2019; Imrie 1996; Schartwz 2003, 2011).

Adrenaline and euphoria/stress were also highlighted (by 67% and 70% of participants respectively) as main corporeal perceptions, the question then is to what extent does this induced state change the way we feel in space during that timespan, hence asking whether there was a shift in spatial perception during the *Correfoc*, which was largely acknowledged (78%). Therefore, during the *Correfoc* there is a heightened expression of our corporeal relationship to space, heavily influenced by euphoria/stress and adrenaline and by losing vision as a sense-anchor, a sense around which we are often reliant on our relationship to space (Berrens 2015; Latour 2004). These are temporal sensations that influence the way we make place.

Thus, in this chapter nociception becomes a pleasant perception, even if its physicality is uncomfortable. The intensity of the sound, the buzzing in the ears coupled with the smell of sulphur, the rush of adrenaline, and euphoria bring forward positive memories that shift the perception from pain to pleasure. The emotional attachment to the *Correfoc's* embodied temporal experience also provokes this shift in aural sensibility. For some people, whether or not aurally typical, the *Correfoc* can become too much and be limiting aurally (Drever 2019; Berrens 2019). In fact, as a result of repeated participation at *Correfocs* without the appropriate hearing protection, some research participants suffer from hearing loss and different forms of tinnitus. This aural diversity is self-inflicted. Interestingly, these participants did not self-identify as aurally diverse but thought it was part of the ritual of being in a *Colla*. Their hearing has diminished and aspects of their daily life have been affected but somehow it is part of their image of being a devil/*tabaler*. There is a sense of pride in the hearing loss and/or the tinnitus. As if it was a badge of honour. Even when the tinnitus is temporary (lasting less than 24 hours after the *Correfoc*) it strengthens the sense of belonging, a long-standing commitment to one of the most important spectacles of Catalan culture, and more specifically a deep commitment and belonging to a *Colla*.

In addition, drawing a relation between the emotions and feelings *tabalers* and devils highlighted, notably belonging and the subversion of space's dynamics, we see those two aspects were a key influence in their making of a temporal place (Jones 2014). Summing up, I argue the sensuous spectacle created during a *Correfoc* both changes the way the participants relate to space and their own sensorium, generating a '*Correfoc place*'. It may change their hearing, worsening it gradually from the exposure to loud sound. It does not, however, at this stage of the research, change their relationship to those spaces permanently or their sense of place.

To conclude this discussion, I argue the temporality of the spectacle, the sense of belonging and heightened sensorium accounts for the feeling of owning the space and turns nociception into a pleasant feeling. The loudness, the drumming, the collective performance of a dance with fire and beats creates a sensation of collective binding. This is what makes the exposure to such a loud spectacle become pleasant and why nociception was not relevant in the survey and only appeared in the interviews when the participants spoke about a degree of hearing loss and tinnitus. This comes into sharp contrast with my previous research exploring nociception amongst spectators during *Correfocs* where I explored how the loudness could completely block a person's sensorium, effectively making them shut down (Berrens 2019). Hence, here we have the same decibel's levels but the opposite result. Thus, the *Colla's* sense of belonging, pride and the rush of adrenaline and euphoria generates positive memories that overwrite the painful aural sensation provoked by the *Correfoc*'s soundscape and reinforce a positive and ephemeral making of place for its duration.

Acknowledgements

I would like to thank Andrew Hugill and John Drever for their thoughtful edits and comments. I would like to thank la *Colla Vella de Gràcia* for all their time and help. All images are from the *Colla Vella de Gràcia*.

References

A.a.v.v. (2020) *Foc, Foc, Correfoc*. Rustega: Barcelona.
Agnew, J. (2011) 'Space and place', in Agnew, J., & Livingstone, D.N. (eds), *The Sage Handbook of Geographical Knowledge*, pp. 316–30. London: Sage.
Ahmed, S. (2008a) *The Cultural Politics of Emotion*. Edinburgh: Edinburgh University Press.
Ahmed, S. (2008b) *Queer Phenomenology: Orientations, Objects, Others*. Durham: Duke University Press Books.
Bates, C. (2011) *Vital Bodies: A Visual Sociology of Health and Illness in Everyday Life*, PhD diss., University of London.
Berrens, K. (2015) *Ensounded Bodies: Making Place in London's East End*. PhD diss. Universitat Oberta de Barcelona.
Berrens, K., & Calvet-Mir, L. (2016) 'Urban garden's ambiances as a key to understand urban space', in N. Rémy & N. Tixier (eds), *Ambiances Tomorrow, 3rd International Congress on Ambiances*, Volós: University of Thessaly, pp. 587–92.
Berrens, K., & Cereceda, M. (2017) 'Listening bodies: tact, pain and urban accessibility', paper presented to *Invisible Places*, Sao Miguel Island, Portugal, 7–9 April.
Berrens, K. (2019) 'Sonic and tactile bodies: sound, haptic space and accessibility', in Doughty, K., Duffy, M., & Harada, T. (eds), *Sounding Places: More-Than-Representational Geographies of Sound and Music*, edited by Edward Elgar Publishing: Cheltenham.
Burkitt, I. (2014) *Emotions and Social Relations*. Thousand Oaks, CA: Sage.
Drever, J. (2019) '"Primacy of the ear"– but whose ear?: The case for auraldiversity in sonic arts practice and discourse', *Organised Sound*, 24(1): 85–95.
Hall, T. (2009) 'Footwork: Moving and knowing in local space(s)', *Qualitative Research*, 9(5): 571–85.
Helmreich, S. (2010) 'Listening against Soundscapes', *Anthropology News*, 51(9): 10.
Horowitz, S. (2013) *The Universal Sense: How Hearing Shapes the Mind*, Reprint edition. New York: Bloomsbury USA.
Howes, D. (2009) *The Sixth Sense Reader*. London: Bloomsbury.
Imrie, R. (1996) *Disability and the city: International Perspectives*. London: Sage.
Ingold, T. (2011) 'Worlds of sense and sensing the world: A response to Sarah Pink and David Howes', *Social Anthropology*, 19 (3): 313–17.
Johnson, J.L. (2011) 'Non-representational theory: Space, politics, affect', *Emotion, Space and Society*, 4(3): 195–6.
Jones, H. (2014) *Stories of Cosmopolitan Belonging: Emotion and Location*. London: Routledge.
Kusenbach, M. (2003) 'Street phenomenology the go-along as ethnographic research tool', *Ethnography*, 4(3): 455–85.
Latour, B. (2004) 'How to talk about the body? The normative dimension of science studies', *Body & Society*, 10(2–3): 205–29.
Liu F., & Kang, J. (2016) 'A grounded theory approach to the subjective understanding of urban soundscape in Sheffield', *Cities*, 50: 28–39.
López, N.G. (2005) 'Alarmas y sirenas: sonotopías de la conmoción cotidiana', *Quaderns-e de l'Institut Català d'Antropologia*, 5.
Low, S.M. (2014) 'Placemaking and embodied space', in Sen, A. & Silverman, L.B. (eds), *Making Place, Space and Embodiment in the City*. Indiana: Indiana University Press.

Murthy, D. (2008) 'Digital Ethnography: An Examination of the Use of New Technologies for Social Research', *Sociology*, 4(5), pp. 837–55.

Paterson, M. (2009) 'Haptic geographies: Ethnography, haptic knowledges and sensuous dispositions', *Progress in Human Geography,* 33(6): 766–88.

Rhys-Taylor, A. (2010) *Coming to Our Senses: A Multi-Sensory Ethnography of Class and Multiculture in East London*. PhD diss. University of London.

Schwartz, H. (2003) 'The indefensible ear: A history', in Bull, M. and Back, L. (eds), *The Auditory Culture Reader*. Oxford: Berg.

Schwartz, H. (2011) *Making Noise - From Babel to the Big Bang and Beyond*. Cambridge, MA: MIT Press.

Wetherell, M. (1998) 'Positioning and interpretative repertoires: Conversation analysis and post-structuralism in dialogue', *Discourse & Society*, 9(3): 387–412.

Yardley, A. (2008) 'Piecing together—a methodological bricolage', *Forum Qualitative Sozialforschung / Forum: Qualitative Social Research*, 9(2), n.p.

11
ALPHABETULA

Josephine Dickinson

Asecretplacemadeofwordsancaorananaerobicā
cBughaburnthillbierceblābēambeonetbreathingb
larmònachbogachbaitineachblàrbruachbrugbái
sínboglachbogletbrochanbreunlochCurhaghc
rageecealdcūcilcaochcarcaircanachcorrachcr
aiccmircokelaykDidderdyandedwfrdeepdubEros
ioneanachFlassflassheflossheflotfugolfyrhthef
eithfriddfianachfizmerfogaggeyfoggitfraochfl
owGrugogglistegolagottygadsHassockhaggy
harphaugrhewhrīsheawanhogghussockhaeghūsI
ceJuniperusKiarrkringlaLāwercelownlònlèigch
ruthaichMossFlatsmandalamōrmosimyrrmignma
wnmòinedhubhmòinteachmossmotemumpNether
hearthsikenautnearuOglenorganicoxaPhloemp
ollpeatpiprakeiceplumpeplompepotpwllpaethpeewi
tlandplimpyllauQuackyquagmirequickfreshque
rcusRūhsicrionnachmaoimmackerelriotráreikri
velingrosrùsgraonrossSundorseljascēapstubbst
ratigraphicspongesskarthsealhsauthrsefsīcsíksío
nsískógrsuntswangsīdestuggedskallislackslunk
TiteitotttruntufttusktimbrtrodteinebiorachU
ppeunconsciousuferaVeggsvondrviddavráWaef
rewaeterwatterweligwentwithigwuduwiellewy
rmwhamwindwaleeXylemYarfyarphaZamzody

Notes on the poem *Alphabetula*
© **Magma Poetry, 2017 (reproduced with permission).**

As a totally d/Deaf poet/artist/composer I experience the visual presence of a poem on the page at one end of a continuum of which the other end is the proprioceptive nature of the poem as gesture.

The poem 'Alphabetula' came about during a collaboration with artist Laura Harrington (for her book *Haggs and High Places*, Harrington 2015) in the setting of an area of eroded blanket peat high up on the fells ten miles south of where I live in Alston, Cumbria. This is a place to which there are no footpaths. It is not on the map. In order to reach it you follow the course of a sike or stream near the source of the River Tees to a place where peat haggs stand in a circle around an area, roughly the size of a football pitch, scattered with the remains of 7,000 year-old birch trees. On all sides it is surrounded by the high fells, including Cross Fell and Dufton Fell. Here the cotton grass and sphagnum moss, the various species of hydrophilic, peat-creating vegetation, are slowly repopulating the surface. Here scientists study the processes involved in this natural restoration and healing of peatland, with the intention of encouraging it in other areas of blanket bog throughout the North Pennines.

The only sound up here seems to be the wind, blustering through the cotton grass and the many voices of water.

In a place like Moss Flats it is possible to feel those 'words that print cannot touch' of which Walt Whitman writes (Whitman 1891–92, 179). The scattered birch twigs form alphabet-like shapes dating from an era which pre-exists all known human alphabets.

Alphabetula is made up of place names, local dialect words, and names for meteorological phenomena that typically occur here piled up in anaerobic lines like the millimetre by millimetre yearly layers of detritus of sphagnum moss and whatever sinks into the surface. It is an ecosystem that is present all over the fells and moorlands of the northern Pennines.

Here, the place names and place name elements of which they are composed are a living record and map of the numerous incursions of peoples, the Welsh, the Romans, the Nordics, the Picts, and the Celts which have laid down their layers and seams in the physical, cultural, aural landscape, and stamp the inflections, colours, and shapings of the various local dialects and speech-forms.

It is in a very real sense that ears have created this landscape. This valley, raised high amongst the highest point of the northern Pennine fells, easily cut off in winter, is itself like the embodiment of an ear. Here the tensions between proximity and distance, between body and mind, between observation and habitation, sensuous immersion and detached observation, between culture and nature, are enacted in every moment of daily life for those who live there. In the summer the revving of the bikers' machines echoes across the valley. In the winter the barking of dogs resonates from a distance with a non-linearity of spatial position that confounds. The cracking of air rifles peppers the night as locals seek out rabbits. Every Sunday morning the ringing of church bells bathes the town and the surrounding land in tunes, from the most ancient Seikilos Epitaph to contemporary film scores and beyond. In spring the fluting of curlews, the bubbling voices of lambs provide a subtle counterpoint to this multi-attack soundscape which yet bridges all these tensions with the give-less breath of a melodic line, a harmonic entity made up of opposites and unisons. In summer the fields ring with the bands and crowds assembled for Alston Live. And underpinning it all is the ever-present sound of water in all its forms.

Aaron M. Moe writes: 'The origin of a word lies not in a Greek or Latin root: rather, it lies within the elemental forces of the Earth and in the elemental forces of a body' (Moe 2019, 123). A word is made of the body's response to such stimuli as the texture of surfaces, to heat and cold, to velvet, to barbed wire, to gestures both in parallel with and reaching the mouth such as 'yumm'. A word is made of the biting wind, of freezing water chasing one's ankles, of the presence of a robin come down to feed, of the hocketing of geese in the yard, and the distant skein of wild geese creating formations in the sky. It is made of maps, of diagrams drawn out to postpone the dangerous moment when words and poems must be committed to the linearity of writing. And writing is an extension of the body. It hurts. It is dangerous. It is the other side of the coin to listening and attentiveness, which are also an extension of the body. As Moe also wrote: '… attentiveness is prior to Aristostle's "impulse to imitate"' (Moe 2014, 24). In a very real sense the 'poem on the page' is not the same as the 'written poem'. For the latter is an internalised entity. The former is, in the words of Jonathan Skinner: 'itself physiological, an appendage of the body' (Skinner 2018, 75).

In writing poems, even as part of a collaborative project, there is a risk that the linearity of the alphabetic drawing involved in inscribing them on paper will form a solipsistic barrier. How to overcome this? Does the poet create a literal currency out of poems, as I did in my bank note poems Bolt, Ginnell, and Snicket, written for a separate, community project, or turn them into quasi-lithic monuments? A simpler, more effective strategy is suggested by thinking of the geological term witness, which is an eroded fragment of a former more extensive stratum, such as the scattered 7,000 year-old birch of Moss Flats. Etymologically, to witness means to know a place. And to live in a place such as Alston Moor, in the shadow of Cross Fell, connected to the land, to the seasons, to the animals, to the people, to the culture in ever widening tentacles (to use a word given a special resonance by Donna Haraway) is profoundly an act of witness which is itself a poem (Haraway 2016). To be a witness is very different from being a detached observer. It is to be connected on many levels and in many ways. It is to encompass and attempt to resolve dichotomies and tensions such as those described by John Wylie: the culture/nature and other dualities of conventional thinking (Wylie 2007). It is to be the poem I live, rather than writing poems about the place I live. It is to live the poem I am.

References

Haraway, D. (2016) *Staying with the Trouble, Making Kin in the Chthulucene*. Durham: Duke University Press.
Harrington, L. (2015) *Haggs and High Places*. Durham: Durham Book Festival and University of Durham.
Moe, A. (2019) *Ecocriticism and the Poiesis of Form: Holding on to Proteus*. New York: Routledge.
Moe, A. (2014) *Zoopoetics*. Lanham, MD: Lexington Books.
Skinner, J. (2018) 'Visceral Ecopoetics', in Olson, C. and McClure, M. eds, *Proprioception, Biology and the Writing Body, Ecopoetics, Essays in the Field*. Iowa City: University of Iowa Press.
Whitman, W. (1891–92) *A Song of the Rolling Earth, Leaves of Grass*. Philadelphia: David McKay.
Wylie, J. (2007) *Landscape*. New York: Routledge.

12

TEXTUAL HEARING AIDS

How Reading about Sound Can Modify Sonic Experience

Ed Garland

Textual Hearing Aids

The narrator of Stevie Davies' story 'Backpack' overhears her neighbours, the Wilsons, 'whining at one another' (Davies 2018, 95–106). She does not hear any words, but describes the overall tone: 'the Wilsons converse in voices resembling the song of weeping strimmers on doleful summer afternoons' (Davies 2018, 97). I enjoy the sardonic wit of this comparison, and its image of melancholy gardening equipment. But when I first read it, I thought that the sentence's comparison was inaccurate, despite my enjoyment of its imagery. Voices do not sound like strimmers, I told myself, no matter the strimmer's mood. Then I was walking around Aberystwyth at lunchtime, and I heard two men talking loudly to each other inside a nearby house. The house was empty of furniture, and the men were in separate rooms, working on a renovation. Their voices resonated against the bare walls and floorboards and spilled out of the open windows. I could not make out their words, but their tone was unmistakeably the same as the tone in Davies' story. I suddenly found myself listening to weeping strimmers, a call-and-response between diesel-powered rotary laments, a mopey whirr that mowed the air.

In that moment, a remembered phrase from a book enabled me to hear something that I had never heard outside of a book before. It was a moment that confirmed what Kate Lacey points out: the written word was 'the first media technology to affect the listening experience' (Lacey 2013, 26). One reason this is true is that text encodes sound. Therefore, 'reading *included* listening' (Lacey 2013, 45). That is, words have a sonic dimension even when we read in silence. While this sonic dimension includes the sounds of the words themselves, it also includes the sounds to which those words may refer. When I heard the men inside the house, something in their tone activated Davies' phrase in my memory, and I heard my world differently because of what I had read. The difference was that I could suddenly perceive a similarity between specific mechanical processes and particular vocal expressions. I realised that Davies' fiction contained a tiny sonic truth that I no longer doubted. The printed book is a technology that affected my listening experience.

In this chapter, I argue that reading fiction can enrich our relationship with sound. I support this argument by analysing excerpts from Valeria Luiselli's 2019 novel *Lost Children Archive*. This highly acclaimed and formally inventive fiction offers us many representations of sound and shows us how written narratives can encourage us to diversify our listening practices.

DOI: 10.4324/9781003183624-13

I am interested in the relationship between reading and sound because of my permanent tinnitus and hearing loss. According to the audiologist, the hearing loss is a moderate to severe kind common in people of my age (37) who have spent most of their lives listening to loud music. The tinnitus consists of ringing sounds in both ears. The tone and pitch of the ringing are the same in each ear, but their intensities fluctuate independently, as if they are processed through separate filters whose parameters constantly change. Sometimes they resemble tiny bells, and sometimes they resemble the songs of a pair of drunken nightingales. I do not wear electronic hearing aids: I have been considering them for about seven years, but still do not feel like taking on the challenges of wearing them.

I believe that one way reading can modify our listening is by enlivening the connections between imagination and perception. This kind of modification is not measurable with the traditional methods of the audiologist, in which you sit in a booth and listen to sounds that test your speech comprehension, or establish the lowest amplitude at which you can hear a prerecorded beep. As Mara Mills argues, such tests form part of a tradition in which 'a person's hearing is routinely judged relative to a norm rather than to an environmental setting, a profession, or a preference' (Mills 2020, 23–48). Tests for speech comprehension, for example, may use a 'norm' – a standard – established by telephone companies, and thus ignore or devalue our ability to hear frequencies above 3,000 Hz, since such frequencies are less important to the technological infrastructures of telephone networks (Mills 2020, 42). An aura of objectivity surrounds these norms, against which the severity of our loss is judged. But as Mills shows, these norms emerge from the socioeconomic priorities of telecommunication companies, public education institutions, and military health screening assessments. The numbers and graphs we receive after being tested against these norms are, of course, extremely useful, but we don't need to make them into the only means by which we assess our hearing. They are a part of what Mills calls 'the historical-industrial context of quality control: the transfer of tools and concepts from medical diagnosis to machine calibration and back again' (Mills 2020, 43). They allow us to assess our hearing from a certain perspective, and to contribute to the ongoing refinement of machine-aided hearing technologies, but they do not tell us everything that can be known about how we respond to sound.

D/deaf writers often show us how we may encounter sound through organs besides the ear. As the poet David Wright writes: 'I see a visionary noise of wind in a disturbance of foliage', reminding us that visual events may have sonic aspects, and that there is a profound interrelationship between all of our senses (Wright 1993, 13). Fiction attends to these sensory interrelationships within dramatised social contexts. Thus, novels and stories can tell us a great deal about what Mills calls our 'environmental setting … and preference[s]' relative to sound (Mills 2020, 42). Sonic moments in written fiction, in which a character's preferences influence how they respond to what they hear, can enrich our consideration of how sounds carry meanings between ourselves and our surroundings. This enriched consideration is the kind of modification that high-street hearing aid shops cannot provide.

The concept of 'sonic experience' can help us to analyse what happens between fictional characters and the sounds they encounter. This term comes from the work of Jean-François Augoyard and Henry Torgue, who state that 'there is no universal approach to listening: every individual, every group, every culture, listens in its own way' (Augoyard and Torgue 2005, 4). The emphasis is on the action of listening, in which we apply some degree of our attention to what we hear. But we should also remember that, as Jean-Luc Nancy points out, to hear means not only to apprehend a sound but also 'to understand the sense' of something (Nancy 2007, 6). The idea of sonic experience, then, modifies hearing-as-understanding by encouraging us to listen differently.

We listen differently when we attend to the social, psychological, and political aspects of the interrelated processes of listening and hearing: as well as having physical and cognitive differences in their auditory systems, people will assign different values, descriptions, and emotions to the same sounds. Moreover, the fact that everybody listens in their own way reminds us that everybody also responds to the physiological facts of hearing loss and tinnitus in their own way. Some people choose to wear hearing aids, for example, while others do not. Some people experience high levels of distress because of their tinnitus while some are only intermittently or not at all bothered by it. We might describe these differences in practical and emotional response as differences in sonic experience.

I should note that what I present here under the term 'sonic experience' is my own modification of the original conceptual framework. While Augoyard and Torgue remind us that every sound occurs within a social and historical context, and that no sound 'can be isolated from the spatial and temporal conditions of its physical signal propagation', they pay little, if any, attention to aural diversity (Augoyard and Torgue 2005, 4). That is, their research implicitly assumes that, even if we all listen in our own way, we do so through ears that offer more or less the same standards of auditory perception. We can easily expand the parameters of sonic experience to include an attention to differences in auditory perception, at the same time as we ask how we develop our habitual responses to, and preferences for, certain sounds and sonic conditions. Valeria Luiselli's *Lost Children Archive*, as I will now demonstrate, dramatises these concepts of sonic relationships and preferences.

Sonic Experience of the Family

Luiselli's novel follows the final months of a marriage between two unnamed audio documentary makers as they drive from New York to the Mexican border with their children. The mother is working on a project about unaccompanied child migrants, while the father is exploring Apache history. Most of the novel is narrated by the mother, but towards the end, the boy takes over the narration, as he and his sister become lost in the desert and encounter a group of migrant children, while searching for a place called Echo Canyon. The novel repeatedly uses the act of recording sound to consider the relationships between character, setting, and sonic experience.

A particularly effective example of such explorations comes early in the story. The narrator describes a long project that she and her husband worked on together, in which they tried to record a sample of every language spoken in New York. At the end of this project, she says, 'we had an archive full of fragments of strangers' lives but had close to nothing of our own lives together' (Luiselli 2020, 30). What follows is a written list of those sounds they failed to record with their devices. The list of sounds offers an exploration of what Julie Beth Napolin calls 'the shared psychic and social life of listening and reading' (Napolin 2020, 5). As we read, we also listen, in our imaginations, to this collection of sounds recorded in text. They are social sounds: they emerge from the daily interactions between the members of the family. The length of this list reminds us that we may hear an enormous number of sounds in any given day, any of which may carry a psychological significance, even if we don't realise this as we hear it. Since the list is too long to reproduce in full, I present a partial and fragmented excerpt:

> [T]he radio in the early morning, and the last reverberations of our dreams merging with news of crises, discoveries, epidemics, inclement weather; the coffee grinder, hard beans becoming powder … the hum of crowded streets where my husband fished for stray sounds with his boom while I approached strangers with my handheld recorder, and the stream of

all their voices, their accents and stories … the strange white noise that children produce in playgrounds – a vortex of hysteria, swarming cries – and the perfectly distinct voices of our two children amongst them … the friction of our coats against the northern gusts come winter; the effort of our feet pedalling rusty bicycles along the river path come spring … the sound of everything and everyone that once surrounded us, the noise we contributed, and the silence we leave behind.

(Luiselli 2020, 30–1)

The list starts by describing the state of consciousness in which the narrator's family hears the morning radio: while their dreams still linger in their minds. This lingering quality is compared to a particular sonic phenomenon: reverberation. Augoyard and Torgue define reverberation as what we hear when 'a sound continues after the cessation of its emission' (Augoyard and Torgue 2005, 116). For example, when a choir in a cathedral stops singing, but their voices still linger in the air. Every sound possesses some degree of reverberation, but it is most obvious in large, open-plan buildings. Luiselli's narrator uses the idea of reverberation to describe how the family's dreams form part of the psychological context in which they hear the news on the radio. She thereby makes a link between hearing and feeling in which reverberation becomes an auditory metaphor for the way narratives (such as dreams) influence experience. We might then consider the diversity of ways in which people encounter reverberation. To return to the example of a choir in a cathedral: even if we do not auditorily perceive all of the 'emission' or 'cessation' of the voices, we nevertheless encounter the choir as a sonic experience through its visual, somatic, and affective dimensions, which may reverberate in our minds long after the singing has ended.

While they hear the news, the family also hears the coffee grinder. Instead of describing the grinder's tone or amplitude, the narrator simply observes what happens to the beans in the grinder. The matter-of-fact description reflects what the critic Clare Messud writes in her review of *Lost Children Archive*: 'the mother's narrative voice, in its varying registers, sounds as natural as is possible' (Messud 2019). One of the grammatical features of this natural, plain-speaking style is a lack of similes. Unlike the narrator in Stevie Davies' story, Luiselli's narrator rarely if ever compares one sound to another. Sometimes, as with the coffee grinder, those elements that we might think of as obviously sonic, like whirring or buzzing, are not described at all. Instead, the narrator attends to the process – 'beans becoming powder' – that is the source of the sound. Her attention to sounds as processes is different from that of her husband, who 'fishes' for sounds with his boom (a microphone attached to the end of a handheld pole). Her husband, that is, approaches sounds as objects, and I will discuss the philosophy of sonic objects below. For now, note that the narrator also emphasises the idea of process in many of the other sounds in her list: she appreciates the variety of 'accents and stories' in the overall 'stream' of sound on the street. She notes that her own children's cries remain perfectly discernible within the 'vortex' of children's voices in the playground, and there is a kind of audible foreshadowing of later events here: the children are not yet 'lost', as they will be by the end of the novel. In the 'friction' of the coats in the wind, and the 'effort' of pedalling bicycles, the narrator again attends to processes and avoids describing overt sonic characteristics. Directing our attention to the action of wind on the surface of a winter coat, and the experience of pushing down on the pedals of a bicycle, we imagine the associated sounds without hearing them named as, for example, 'swishing' and 'panting'. The emphasis is on the experience of sonic production, rather than auditory perception. Moreover, all of these processes relate to the narrator's experience of her family. They are physical and mechanical phenomena that metaphorically echo common aspects of interpersonal relationships, like the friction between people, or the effort associated with emotional bonds. At the end of the list, the narrator describes the end of her relationship with her husband as a kind of sonic experience: 'the silence we leave behind'. In other words, the 'silence' is the sonic dimension of the marriage's disintegration, rooted in the fact that neither the narrator nor her husband has ever recorded the sounds of their family.

As the novel develops, the narrator describes the large-scale processes of political decisions that have led to the deaths and/or imprisonment of unaccompanied migrant children at the US border with Mexico. The sonic features of these processes are most evident in the novel's final section.

Grains of Sound

At the end of the story, the narrator's ten-year-old stepson speaks into a recorder as he and his five-year-old step-sister wander through the desert near the Mexican border. In the recording, he explicitly addresses his words to his stepsister, making it clear that he is telling their story so that she will have a record of it when she grows old enough to understand it. Nearly the whole of the boy's speech is written without full stops, which recalls other novels that employ the same technique – for example, Beckett's *The Unnameable,* and the final chapter of Joyce's *Ulysses,* as well as contemporary works like Mike McCormack's single-sentence novel *Solar Bones*. Such texts often attract the label 'stream of consciousness', but this section of *Lost Children Archive* uses its lack of full stops to probe the relationship between reading, recording, and voice. The section's title is 'Echo Canyon', which is the name of the place in the desert the two children try to reach while they are lost. Within his speech, the boy sometimes echoes things his stepmother has said, and thus that we have read, earlier in the novel. Through its textual arrangement, then, the novel now begins to behave like a kind of recording technology, in which one character replays snippets or samples of another character's speech. These textual echoes happen within a narrative that describes the sounds that occur while being lost in the desert. One of the key features of being lost, according to the boy, is the way the harsh desert light affects his sonic experience:

> everything invisible in that light … if light had been useful, we wouldn't have got lost inside of it … and for a moment [the world] did disappear completely and all that was there was the sound of our mouths breathing thin air, in and out, and the sound of our feet, on and on, and the heat on our foreheads burning out our last good thoughts.
>
> *(Luiselli 2020, 320)*

The light is no longer 'useful' because it is too bright to illuminate the world. When the exhausted children become delirious, their sensory experience is reduced to sound and temperature. In his delirium, the boy 'echoes' his stepmother's habit of describing sounds by attending to their underlying processes: the breathing is 'in and out', the feet go 'on and on', but he names no explicit sounds like 'panting' or 'thudding'. Instead, the boy describes the sources of these sounds, which are the specific movements he makes with his body. The emotional result of this physical intensity is that 'good thoughts' vanish from his mind. He has to keep walking 'on and on' in the same way he has to keep speaking his story, and in the same way we keep reading the endless sentence.

After a long time of exhausted wandering, during which the boy and his sister spend some time with a group of children who are fleeing violence in Latin America, they come upon the office of a border official. The boy's description of this office probes the physical, emotional, and political aspects of sonic experience. The hut is

> nothing but a small rectangle walled off from that disgusting desert by just a meager adobe wall and a thin, single-leaf aluminium door, under the crevice of which the hot, relentless

wind drags the last notes of all the desert worldsounds disseminated across the barrenlands outside.

(Luiselli 2020, 323)

Here, the hut becomes a kind of institutional ear, into which the wind, 'relentless' as the endless sentence of the boy's narration, brings the sounds of the surrounding environment. The terms 'small rectangle' and 'single-leaf' describe the hut and its door while also hinting at the physical properties of the book we hold in our hands, and the pages between our fingers as we read, reminding us that the book, like the hut, is also a receptacle for the sounds of the desert. The action by which the wind carries these sounds is to 'drag', as if the sounds have been gathered up against their will to be detained, like the children from the other countries will be detained by the US immigration system to which the hut belongs. The boy's exhausted emotional condition is evident in his description of the desert as 'disgusting', and in the way he imagines that the dragged-in sounds are the 'last notes' of the 'desert worldsounds'. He then explains what he means by this portmanteau term with a list of sounds that begins with 'twigs snapping' and 'birds crying', continues with 'voices begging for water', and ends in the inaudible: 'bones eroding and disappearing into the sand' (Luiselli 2020, 324). The 'worldsounds', we then understand, are the sounds of everything that happens in the desert, whether we are there to hear them or not. The boy then implies that if we can't hear what happened in the desert, we can still feel it, in a very particular way. He describes 'a lady' who works in the hut. She hears 'none' of the worldsounds, but 'somehow she senses all of it, as if sound particles were stuck to the sand particles blown by the desert wind into ... her welcome mat' (Luiselli 2020, 324). In other words, the same sand particles that contributed to the unheard sounds of migrating people's bodies 'eroding and disappearing' will sooner or later arrive on the border official's welcome mat. The boy thus emphasises the political aspect of sonic experience: through the circulation of physical materials, we are linked to the political processes that cause unaccompanied children to beg for water in the desert. Pondering this link, the boy considers the existence of 'sound particles'. Like his father, who 'fishes' for sounds, he thinks of sounds as objects. He thereby challenges what Mandy-Suzanne Wong calls the 'prevailing ideologies that tout the fleeting intangibility and relativity of sound, and discourage or decry its thing-power: its physical impact and otherness' (Wong 2018). These 'prevailing ideologies' are the ones that argue, implicitly or explicitly, that the sound wave is the most important property of sound in general. Such ideologies disregard the stability and durability of sounds, emphasising 'transience and relativity by insisting that sounds are not objects but experiences or practices' (Wong 2018). I have, of course, been arguing in this chapter that sonic experience in *Lost Children Archive* is largely the experience of sound as a process. But what the boy shows us, I think, is that there is room within the idea of sonic experience to encounter sounds as objects. The boy's sand particles arrive on the welcome mat as avatars of the sounds in whose production they were involved on their journey across the desert. The sand particles are tiny objects whose symbolic resonance is rooted in their recent history as physical constituents of the sounds of eroding bones. This troubling quality mobilises what Wong calls the 'thing-power' of sound.

As David Wright saw a 'visionary noise of wind in a disturbance of foliage', the border official 'senses' the desert's 'worldsounds' in her welcome mat – a grimly ironic accessory for such a hostile institution. These sounds are then imagined blowing back out into the desert 'unregistered, unheard, unless by chance they happen to spiral into the small conch-shaped sockets of human ears, such as those of the lost children ... who now listen to them and try to name them in their minds but find no words, no meanings to hold on to' (Luiselli 2020, 324). The sounds do not dissipate as waves but persist as objects. But the children find 'no meanings' because they find 'no words' to name those sounds that have blown into their ears. They lack the language to sufficiently enhance their auditory attention. Thus they cannot hear the full scale of the suffering in which they are involved, as a small part of the more than 102,000 unaccompanied child migrants apprehended by US border officials between 2013 and 2015 (Pierce 2015). While I don't agree that the absence of words entails the absence of meaning, this passage emphasises how languages can enrich our perceptions and thus extend our understanding of sonic experience. We are encouraged to notice that written descriptions enable us to 'register' sounds, however small, that we did not have access to before we encountered a particular sentence or story. The grains of sound blowing into the children's ears reflect the process of reading the novel itself – all those granules of sonic experience blowing into a 'socket,' that object of reception: our mind's ear.

Reading Ears

I have only provided two brief sketches of the many ways in which *Lost Children Archive* attunes us to sonic experience by exploring interpersonal conflicts, recording methodologies, and the politics of national borders. This state of being attuned, I think, is a hearing gain. Not in the sense that it magically repairs the physical damage in our inner ears, but in the sense that it increases our sensitivity to the currents of meaning that flow between ourselves and our sounds.

These meanings remain available to us despite our diagnoses of hearing loss and tinnitus. Writers like Stevie Davies discover similarities between different sounds, and thus revitalise our perceptions. Writers like Valeria Luiselli probe our implicit and explicit listening priorities, and encourage us to consider the social forces that affect how we value different sounds. Novels and stories help to diversify the ways in which we relate to sounds as characters in our own narratives, reminding us that we don't always have to think of our hearing through the theme of loss. Other contexts are still available.

Besides the works I have cited in this chapter, there are many other scholars of sound studies who have informed my way of reading novels. Jennifer Lynn Stoever, Nicole Brittingham Furlonge, and Alexander G. Weheliye, for example, have all developed approaches to reading sound that, while not being specifically directed at people with hearing loss, explore the profound and subtle experiences of sound that novels may offer to readers. I believe that attending to sonic experience through reading may have therapeutic benefits that complement the standard treatments for hearing loss and tinnitus. The British Tinnitus Association's website mentions that reading is a helpful activity, but only in the sense that a book may send us to sleep if our tinnitus keeps us awake. Writing is also mentioned as a generally therapeutic creative exercise, but sound is not suggested as a suitable topic. I feel there is an opportunity here: we could offer people with hearing loss and tinnitus the ability to explore sound through language. Sound studies offers us hundreds of ideas that may transform the stories we tell ourselves about our hearing, and reinvigorate our relationship with the audible world.

References

Augoyard, J.-F., & Torgue, H. (2005) *Sonic Experience: A Guide to Everyday Sounds.* Translated by Andrea McCartney & David Paquette. Montreal: McGill-Queen's University Press.
Davies, S. (2018) 'Backpack', in *Arrest Me, For I Have Run Away*, pp. 95–106. Cardigan: Parthian.
Lacey, K. (2013) *Listening Publics: The Politics and Experience of Listening in the Media Age.* Cambridge: Polity.
Luiselli, V. (2020) *Lost Children Archive.* London: 4th Estate.

Messud, C. (2019) 'At the Border of the Novel', review of *Lost Children Archive,* by Valeria Luiselli. *The New York Review of Books*, 21 March.

Mills, M. (2020) 'Testing hearing with speech', in *Testing Hearing: The Making of Modern Aurality*, Tkaczyk, V., Mills, M., & Hui, A. (eds), pp. 23–48. New York: Oxford University Press.

Nancy, J.-L. (2007) *Listening*. Translated by Charlotte Mendell. New York: Fordham University Press.

Napolin, J.B. (2020) *The Fact of Resonance: Modernist Acoustics and Narrative Form*. New York: Fordham University Press.

Pierce, S. (2015) 'Unaccompanied Child Migrants in U.S. Communities, Immigration Court, and Schools', *Migration Policy Institute*, October. Available at www.migrationpolicy.org/research/unaccompanied-child-migrants-us-communities-immigration-court-and-schools (accessed 16 July 2021).

Wong, M.-S. (2018) 'The Thingness of Sound', *Sonic Field*, 11 September. Available at http://sonicfield.org/the-thingness-of-sound-essay-by-mandy-suzanne-wong/ (accessed 16 July 2021).

Wright, D. (1993) *Deafness: An Autobiography*. London: Mandarin Paperbacks.

PART II
Music and Musicology

13
THE SHOW MUST GO ON

Understanding the Effects of Musicianship, Noise Exposure, Cognition, and Ageing on Real-World Hearing Abilities

Samuel Couth

Introduction

Hearing difficulties and tinnitus are common risks associated with occupations where there are high levels and long durations of noise exposure, such as in professional musicians (Sliwinska-Kowalska & Davis 2012). In the context of this chapter, 'noise' refers to loud sounds (i.e. in decibels; dB) which are not necessarily unpleasant or unwanted, as is the case for music. The current permissible occupational noise limit in the UK is 85 dBA for 8 hours' duration, which is reduced by half for each 3 dB increase in noise intensity (Control of Noise at Work Regulations 2005). Recently, Tufts and Skoe (2018) showed that 47% of college musicians exceeded this daily noise exposure limit, compared with just 10% of non-musicians. Changes to legislation have increased hearing protection use and reduced levels of hearing loss in the construction industry over the last 40 years (Rabinowitz et al. 2013), but the music industry lags behind. This is despite the UK music and entertainment sector being subject to the same noise at work regulations as other high-risk industries (Health and Safety Executive 2008).

It has been estimated that between 37% and 58% of classical musicians experience hearing difficulties (Zhao et al. 2010) compared with approximately 18% of the general population (Davis 1989), and approximately 50% of musicians have tinnitus complaints (Jansen et al. 2009) compared to 10% of the general population (Davis 1989). Hearing loss and tinnitus are particularly problematic for musicians because hearing problems affect musical performance skills and limit employment opportunities, as well as impacting on communication and quality of life (Fulford, Ginsborg, & Goldbart 2011). It is surprising, therefore, that despite these increased risks of hearing problems and the potential detriment to career longevity, only 6% of musicians reported consistently using hearing protection (Laitinen 2005), and it may not be until musicians experience irreversible hearing damage that they start to use hearing protection (O'Brien, Ackermann, & Driscoll 2014; Laitinen & Poulsen 2008; Laitinen 2005).

The risk of noise exposure to musicians' hearing may have been underestimated in previous studies because some hearing problems are not obvious using audiometry (the current clinical gold standard). These insidious hearing difficulties have been termed 'hidden hearing loss' (Schaette & McAlpine 2011). Hidden hearing loss describes a loss of synapses between inner hair cells of the cochlea and auditory nerves which transmit electrical signals to the brain (i.e. cochlear

DOI: 10.4324/9781003183624-15

synaptopathy; Kujawa & Liberman, 2009), which could manifest as difficulties with following conversations in a noisy environment (i.e. speech-in-noise perception; Plack, Barker, & Prendergast 2014) and the occurrence of tinnitus (Schaette & McAlpine 2011).

Research groups have attempted to determine the effects of noise exposure on proxy measures of hidden hearing loss, such as speech-in-noise perception (for a review see Le Prell 2019). In particular, musicians have been targeted given that they tend to have high levels of prolonged noise exposure and so may be at high risk of hidden hearing loss. Several research groups have shown abnormal amplitudes (Liberman et al. 2016; Kikidis et al. 2020) and latencies (Skoe and Tufts 2018) of the auditory brainstem response (ABR; an electrophysiological measure of auditory nerve function) in audiometrically normal individuals with high levels of noise exposure, most of whom were musicians, and have been shown to have poorer word recognition in noise performance compared to individuals with low noise exposure (Liberman et al. 2016). Conversely, some studies show no effects of noise exposure on any auditory or speech-in-noise processing tests in audiometrically normal musicians (Yeend et al. 2017), and only a weak-moderate association between noise exposure and electrophysiological measures (Valderrama et al. 2018; Washnik et al. 2020).

In a recent experiment we aimed to assess the effects of both lifetime noise exposure *and* musicianship on electrophysiological *and* perceptual measures of hidden hearing loss, in a single normal hearing participant cohort (Couth et al. 2020). Eighty-five musicians and 52 non-musicians completed a comprehensive test battery to assess proxy measures of hidden hearing loss, including a speech-in-noise processing test, electrophysiological tests, and self-reported tinnitus and hearing in noise difficulties. For each participant, we also obtained a comprehensive measure of lifetime noise exposure, including occupational and recreational activities, using the Noise Exposure Structured Interview (NESI; Guest et al. 2018). In particular, we focussed on early career musicians to determine whether these sub-clinical noise-related effects are detectable even at a relatively young age when interventions to protect hearing longevity may be vital. The data analysis revealed that musicians were more likely to report experience of – and/or more severe – tinnitus and hearing in noise difficulties, but this was not related to the level of lifetime noise exposure. In addition, there were no significant associations between noise exposure and ABR amplitudes and speech-in-noise performance, for both musicians and non-musicians. These findings, therefore, do not support a relationship between noise exposure and so called 'hidden hearing loss' in musicians.

Note, however, that the absence of evidence of noise-induced hidden hearing loss is not the same as evidence of absence. Crucially, there could be a number of explanations for these null findings. In this chapter I will describe a number of key factors which could account for the different ways in which musicians hear – i.e. 'aural diversity' – ranging from enhanced hearing abilities to hearing difficulties in real-world settings (e.g. listening in competing background noise). This could have implications for how we assess musicians' hearing health and ensure career longevity.

Figure 13.1 provides an illustration of a range of factors that could directly and indirectly influence how musicians hear in real-world settings.

The Relationship between Musicianship, Noise Exposure, and Hearing Problems

The hypothesis that we tested in our previous study (Couth et al. 2020) is that, since musicians have higher levels of noise exposure (Figure 13.1 – point 1), this could lead to damage to the auditory pathway (Figure 13.1 – point 2), and thus increase speech-in-noise difficulties and tinnitus (as outlined in the introduction to this chapter; e.g. Liberman et al. 2016). However, as

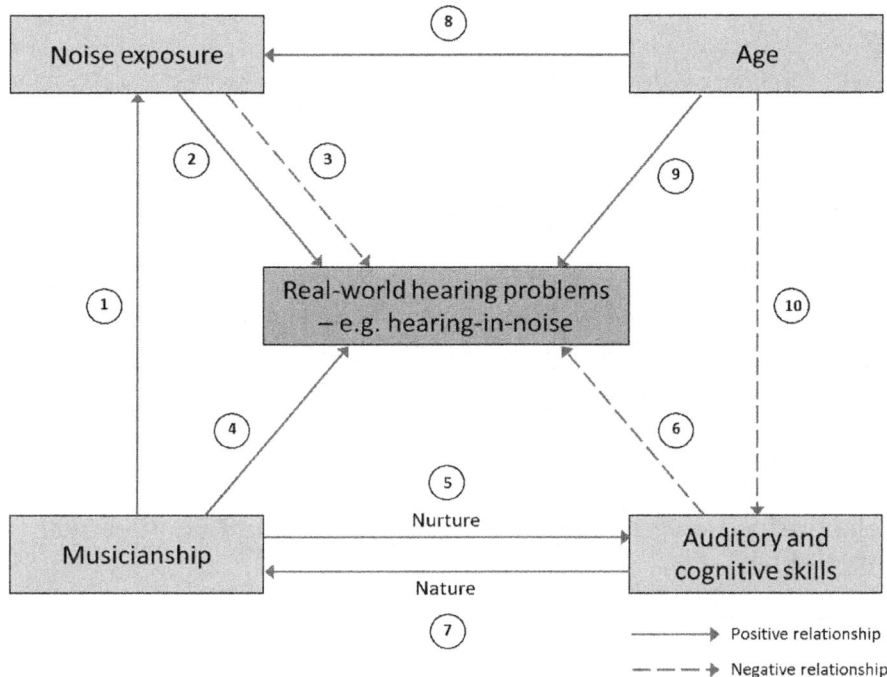

FIGURE 13.1 The complex interaction between musicianship, noise exposure, age and cognition on real-world hearing abilities, such as speech-in-noise processing. See numbers within the text for description of effects

opposed to noise-induced hearing damage, it is possible that mild-to-moderate levels of noise exposure could help to develop a tolerance to high-intensity noise or toughening of the ears, and therefore prevent noise-induced hearing problems (Figure 13.1 – point 3). Miyakita and colleagues (1992) demonstrated that exposure to 70 dB A of music for six hours per day, for nine consecutive days, could reduce the amount of audiometric temporary threshold shift after exposure to a short high-intensity noise (105 dB 1/3 octave band of noise for ten minutes). One possible explanation for this effect is that enhanced efferent (i.e. 'top-down') gain control via the medial olivocochlear system may help to reduce acoustic trauma by inhibiting outer hair cell amplification of the basilar membrane (Bhatt 2017). Alternatively, a recent animal study suggested that pre-exposure to continuous noise at 85 dB SPL may reduce cochlear synaptopathy induced by a high-intensity (106 dB SPL) noise (Fan et al. 2020), which could also be due to enhancement of the medial olivocochlear system (Boero et al. 2018). Taken together, it seems plausible that exposure to some degree of noise may serve to prevent noise-induced hearing damage. In support, there is evidence to suggest that musicians have a stronger medial olivocochlear system compared to non-musicians (Bidelman et al. 2017). The average age that the musicians in our previous study started playing an instrument was seven years old (Couth et al. 2020), and so it is possible that a mechanism to protect hearing from the harmful effects of noise exposure had developed over many years of music noise exposure.

So how can we explain self-reported hearing problems (e.g. tinnitus) in musicians, irrespective of noise exposure and hearing damage (Figure 13.1 – point 4) (Couth et al. 2020)? The simplest account is that musicians rely on intact and precise hearing for their profession and so may be more attentive to – and worried about – noise-induced hearing problems (Zhao et al. 2010). In line with this view, Chesky and colleagues (2009) demonstrated that musicians are more aware of noise-induced hearing problems and have better attitudes to noise exposure and hearing protection than non-musicians (even if those positive attitudes do not translate into hearing protection use). That is not to say that musicians are being overly neurotic about their hearing health, and every hearing complaint should be taken seriously and investigated fully. Electrophysiological and behavioural tests might not be sensitive to detect subtle noise damage, and other tests may be better at establishing noise damage such as acoustic reflex thresholds (Mepani et al. 2018; Wojtczak, Beim, & Oxenham 2017), otoacoustic emissions to assess cochlea outer hair cell function (Hamdan et al. 2008; Job et al. 2009; Couth et al. 2020), and extended high frequency hearing above the normal audiometric range (>8 k Hz; Somma et al. 2008). It is therefore highly recommended that all musicians receive a thorough examination of hearing health using an extensive range of tests on a regular basis, and they should be encouraged to protect their hearing even in these tests do not reveal evidence of hearing damage.

The Relationship between Musicianship, Auditory and Cognitive Skills, and Hearing Abilities

Aside from the theoretical positive effects of music noise exposure on hearing abilities, musical training itself has been shown to be associated with enhanced pitch, timing, and timbre perception (Figure 13.1 – point 5) (Kraus et al. 2009). Musical training promotes neural plasticity throughout the auditory system, even at the subcortical level (i.e. auditory brainstem), through to the primary auditory cortex (Kraus & Chandrasekaran 2010; Sanju & Kumar 2016). It is proposed that enhanced subcortical processing of sounds in musicians is due to top-down feedback from cortical structures via corticofugal pathways (Suga 2008) and/or the medial olivocochlear system (Bidelman et al. 2017). Heightened auditory processing skills could lead to an improvement to listening in real-world environments that rely on similar acoustic features to music perception, such as speech-in-noise perception (Figure 13.1 – point 6) (for reviews see; Kraus & Chandrasekaran 2010; Patel 2014).

In conjunction with enhanced auditory processing skills, cognitive skills may also be exacerbated by musical training. There are numerous studies which advocate enhanced auditory working memory and selective attention in musicians, which may be related to speech-in-noise processing abilities (see Coffey et al. 2017). Returning to our previous experiment (Couth et al. 2020), it is plausible that enhanced auditory and/or cognitive processing skills in musicians could have mitigated the effects of noise exposure on hearing abilities, thus the negative effects of noise exposure on speech-in-noise abilities were cancelled out. Or from a reverse perspective, it has been proposed that noise exposure may suppress the positive association between musical training and speech-in-noise processing abilities (Skoe, Camera, & Tufts 2018).

It is difficult to assume cause and effect between musical training and enhanced auditory/cognitive skills, especially since most studies are cross-sectional and thus only offer a snapshot of musicians' auditory and/or cognitive abilities. Similarly, correlational studies cannot assume a causal relationship between the level of musical training (e.g. years of experience) and auditory/cognitive skills. It is plausible that people who are naturally gifted with enhanced auditory/cognitive processing skills have a predisposition for music and are more likely to pursue musical training (Figure 13.1 – point 7) (Swaminathan & Schellenberg 2018; Mosing et al. 2016; Schellenberg 2015). A small number of longitudinal studies have attempted to examine the direct causal relationship between musical training and speech-in-noise abilities, yet a systematic review revealed few longitudinal studies (4/13) used a high quality research design that adequately examined the causal relationship (e.g. randomised control study), and none of these higher quality designed studies demonstrated a clear benefit of musical training for speech perception (McKay 2021). Further carefully designed longitudinal research studies are required to settle this 'nature vs. nurture' debate for enhanced auditory and cognitive skills in musicians, and to elucidate their relationship with speech-in-noise processing.

The Relationship between Age, Noise Exposure, Cognition, and Hearing Problems

Increasing age is also associated with cumulative levels of noise exposure (Figure 13.1 – point 8) (Lie et al. 2016), which could lead to hearing loss and speech-in-noise deficits. Indeed, ageing and noise exposure are closely linked, and it is difficult to disentangle these effects (Prendergast et al. 2019). Given that the participants included in our previous study (Couth et al. 2020) were relatively young (aged 18–26), lifetime noise exposure levels were relatively low and homogenous, thus the effects of noise exposure on hearing abilities may not have had chance to accumulate or were not observable. Moreover, the musicians in our previous study reported similar levels of lifetime noise exposure to non-musicians, which could be due to the relatively young age of the participants in our study. Both groups were experiencing high intensity recreational noise exposure (e.g. from nightclubs and concerts) within a relatively short life period, which therefore accounted for the majority of their lifetime noise exposure to date, and could explain why we did not detect any differences in hearing function between musicians and non-musicians. It is predicted that lifetime noise exposure may plateau earlier for non-musicians, whereas musicians will continue to experience high levels of noise exposure as they proceed with their careers. Hence it is imperative that musicians protect their hearing at the onset of their musical career in order to maintain hearing longevity long into adulthood.

There is also evidence that ageing is directly related to general declines in hearing function (i.e. presbycusis; Gates and Mills 2005) and has a detrimental impact on speech-in-noise perception (Humes 1996), irrespective of noise exposure (Figure 13.1 – point 9). Sergeyenko and colleagues (2013) demonstrated cochlear synaptopathy in ageing mice that had not been exposed to noise. Additionally, Johannesen and colleagues (2019) showed that decreasing auditory nerve function (i.e. cochlear synaptopathy) is associated with increasing age, but not with increasing noise exposure. Thus, deterioration of hearing abilities may be an unavoidable consequence of ageing, and thus should be considered as a covariate in research studies.

The final factor for consideration is that ageing has a detrimental effect on cognitive abilities (Figure 13.1 – point 10) (Salthouse 2010), which could consequently have a negative effect on speech-in-noise perception. Similar to how musical training may offset noise-induced hearing problems via enhanced auditory and/or cognitive abilities, it has also been proposed that musical training may offset age-related hearing difficulties (Alain et al. 2014). Zendel and Alain (2012) demonstrated that musicians showed less age-related decline in speech-in noise perception compared to audiometrically matched non-musicians, suggesting that musicianship may prevent declines to central auditory processing (i.e. cognitive) rather than the peripheral auditory system. In support, Parbery-Clark and colleagues (2011) showed that older musicians have greater auditory working memory capacity compared to non-musicians, as well as better speech-in-noise performance. Whether musical training affords protection or rehabilitation from age-related cognitive decline and hearing loss is uncertain, where cause and effect cannot be assumed (as per the nature vs nurture debate).

The Show Must Go On

To summarise, hearing function varies between individuals (i.e. 'aural diversity'), which may be due to a range of factors including musicianship, noise exposure, auditory and cognitive function, and ageing. Crucially, these factors are not mutually exclusive and it is likely that hearing abilities, such as speech-in-noise perception, are dependent on a complex interaction of these factors. Accordingly, future research that aims to assess hearing function or dysfunction in musicians should consider these possible factors in the study design. In particular, auditory and cognitive processing skills may act as mediating factors for hearing abilities, which could be masking subtle noise-induced or age-related decline (i.e. hidden hearing loss). Note, however, that these factors may not fully account for hearing status, and there are various other variables that could be considered, such as sex, socioeconomic status, personality, and health and lifestyle factors (e.g. smoking, obesity, cardiovascular disease) (Swaminathan and Schellenberg 2018; Couth et al. 2019; Dawes et al. 2014). It is also vitally important to assess musicians' hearing function throughout the auditory system (from outer- to inner-ear, plus the auditory nerve and brainstem) to identify underlying pathologies that are not detected by standard clinical measures.

In conclusion, further research is essential to understand the time course of noise-induced hearing damage across the lifespan of musicians in order to detect the earliest signs of pathology. This could be beneficial for informing guidelines for regular hearing checks throughout a musicians' career, from initially starting to learn an instrument in childhood, through to their twilight years. In addition, this could have implications for informing intervention design, such as when they should be implemented to be most effective at preventing noise-induced hearing damage. Interventions should focus on increasing the uptake and retention of hearing protection devices, where there is still much room for improvement amongst musicians (Greasley et al. 2018). Ultimately, through further research, we will be able to understand how best to minimise or prevent hearing problems to ensure career longevity and improve general wellbeing for musicians.

Acknowledgements

Samuel Couth's research relating to this chapter was funded by the Colt Foundation and additional support from the Medical Research Council UK (MR/L003589/1) and by the NIHR Manchester Biomedical Research Centre.

References

Alain, C., Benjamin, R.Z., Hutka, S., & Bidelman, G.M. (2014) 'Turning down the noise: The benefit of musical training on the aging auditory brain', *Hearing Research*, Elsevier. https://doi.org/10.1016/j.heares.2013.06.008.

Bhatt, I. (2017) 'Increased medial olivocochlear reflex strength in normal-hearing, noise-exposed humans', Edited by Bernd Sokolowski. *Plos One*, 12(9): e0184036. https://doi.org/10.1371/journal.pone.0184036.

Bidelman, G.M., Schneider, A.D., Heitzmann, V.R., & Bhagat, S.P. (2017) 'Musicianship enhances ipsilateral and contralateral efferent gain control to the cochlea', *Hearing Research*, 344 (February): 275–83. https://doi.org/10.1016/j.heares.2016.12.001.

Boero, L.E., Castagna, V.C., Di Guilmi, M.N., Goutman, J.D., Elgoyhen, A.B., & Gómez-Casati, M.E. (2018) 'Enhancement of the medial olivocochlear system prevents hidden hearing loss', *Journal of Neuroscience*, 38(34): 7440–51. https://doi.org/10.1523/JNEUROSCI.0363-18.2018.

Chesky, K., Pair, M., Lanford, S., & Yoshimura, E. (2009) 'Attitudes of college music students towards noise in youth culture', *Noise and Health*, 11(42): 49. https://doi.org/10.4103/1463-1741.45312.

Coffey, Emily B.J., Mogilever, Nicolette B., & Zatorre, Robert J. (2017) 'Speech-in-noise perception in musicians: A review', *Hearing Research*, 352(September): 49–69. https://doi.org/10.1016/J.HEARES.2017.02.006.

Control of Noise at Work Regulations. (2005) 'The Control of Noise at Work Regulations 2005', www.legislation.gov.uk/uksi/2005/1643/pdfs/uksi_20051643_en.pdf.

Couth, Samuel, Mazlan, Naadia, Moore, David R., Munro, Kevin J., & Dawes, Piers (2019) 'Hearing difficulties and tinnitus in construction, agricultural, music, and finance industries: Contributions of demographic, health, and lifestyle factors', *Trends in Hearing*, 23(January): 233121651988557. https://doi.org/10.1177/2331216519885571.

Couth, Samuel, Prendergast, Garreth, Guest, Hannah, Munro, Kevin J., Moore, David R., Plack, Christopher J., Ginsborg, Jane, & Dawes, Piers (2020) 'Investigating the effects of noise exposure on self-report, behavioral and electrophysiological indices of hearing damage in musicians with normal audiometric thresholds', *Hearing Research*, 395(September): 108021. https://doi.org/10.1016/j.heares.2020.108021.

Davis, A. C. 1989. 'The prevalence of hearing impairment and reported hearing disability among adults in Great Britain', *International Journal of Epidemiology*, 18(4): 911–17. www.ncbi.nlm.nih.gov/pubmed/2621028.

Dawes, Piers, Cruickshanks, Karen J., Moore, David R., Edmondson-Jones, Mark, McCormack, Abby, Fortnum, Heather, & Munro, Kevin J. (2014) 'Cigarette smoking, passive smoking, alcohol consumption, and hearing loss', *Journal of the Association for Research in Otolaryngology*, 15(4): 663–74. https://doi.org/10.1007/s10162-014-0461-0.

Fan, Liqiang, Zhen Zhang, Hui Wang, Chunyan Li, Yazhi Xing, Shankai Yin, Zhengnong Chen, & Jian Wang. (2020) 'Pre-exposure to lower-level noise mitigates cochlear synaptic loss induced by high-level noise', *Frontiers in Systems Neuroscience*, 14 (May). https://doi.org/10.3389/fnsys.2020.00025.

Fulford, Robert, Ginsborg, J., & Goldbart, J. (2011) 'Learning not to listen: The experiences of musicians with hearing impairments', *Music Education Research*, 13(4): 447–64. https://doi.org/10.1080/14613808.2011.632086.

Gates, George A., & Mills, John H. (2005) 'Presbycusis'. In *Lancet*, 366: 1111–20. Elsevier B.V. https://doi.org/10.1016/S0140-6736(05)67423-5.

Greasley, A.E., Fulford, R.J., Pickard, M., & Hamilton, N. (2018) 'Help Musicians UK Hearing Survey: Musicians' hearing and hearing protection', *Psychology of Music*, December, 030573561881223. https://doi.org/10.1177/0305735618812238.

Guest, Hannah, Dewey, Rebecca S., Plack, Christopher J., Couth, Samuel, Prendergast, Garreth, Bakay, Warren, & Hall, Deborah A. (2018) 'The Noise Exposure Structured Interview (NESI), pp. An instrument for the comprehensive estimation of lifetime noise exposure', *Trends in Hearing*, 22: 2331216518803213. https://doi.org/10.1177/2331216518803213.

Hamdan, Abdul-Latif, Abouchacra, Kim S., Zeki Al Hazzouri, A., & Zayton, Georges (2008) 'Transient-evoked otoacoustic emissions in a group of professional singers who have normal pure-tone hearing thresholds', *Ear and Hearing*, 29(3): 360–77. https://doi.org/10.1097/AUD.0b013e31816a0d1e.

Health and Safety Executive. (2008) 'Sound advice: Control of noise at work in music and entertainment', www.hse.gov.uk/pubns/priced/hsg260.pdf.

Humes, L.E. 1996. 'Speech understanding in the elderly', *Journal of the American Academy of Audiology*, 7(3): 161–7. https://europepmc.org/article/med/8780988.

Jansen, E.J.M., Helleman, H.W., Dreschler, W.A., & de Laat, J.A.P.M. (2009) 'Noise induced hearing loss and other hearing complaints among musicians of symphony orchestras', *International Archives of Occupational and Environmental Health*, 82(2): 153–64. https://doi.org/10.1007/s00420-008-0317-1.

Job, A., Raynal, M., Kossowski, M., Studler, M., Ghernaouti, C., Baffioni-Venturi, A., Roux, A., Darolles, C., & Guelorget, A. (2009) 'Otoacoustic detection of risk of early hearing loss in ears with normal audiograms: A 3-year follow-up study', *Hearing Research*, 251(1–2): 10–16. https://doi.org/10.1016/j.heares.2009.02.008.

Johannesen, P.T., Buzo, B.C., & Lopez-Poveda, E.A. (2019) 'Evidence for age-related cochlear synaptopathy in humans unconnected to speech-in-noise intelligibility deficits', *Hearing Research*, 374(March): 35–48. https://doi.org/10.1016/j.heares.2019.01.017.

Kikidis, D., Vardonikolaki, A., Zachou, Z., Razou, A., Pantos, P., & Bibas, A. (2020) 'ABR findings in musicians with normal audiogram and otoacoustic emissions: Evidence of cochlear synaptopathy?' *Hearing, Balance and Communication*, 18(1): 36–45. https://doi.org/10.1080/21695717.2019.1663054.

Kraus, N., & Chandrasekaran, B. (2010) 'Music training for the development of auditory skills', *Nature Reviews Neuroscience*, 11(8): 599–605. https://doi.org/10.1038/nrn2882.

Kraus, N., Skoe, E., Parbery-Clark, A., & Ashley, R. (2009) 'Experience-induced malleability in neural encoding of pitch, timbre, and timing', *Annals of the New York Academy of Sciences*, 1169(July): 543–57. https://doi.org/10.1111/j.1749-6632.2009.04549.x.

Kujawa, S.G., & Liberman, M.C. (2009) 'Adding insult to injury: Cochlear nerve degeneration after noise-induced hearing loss', *Journal of Neuroscience*, 29(45): 14077–85. https://doi.org/10.1523/JNEUROSCI.2845-09.2009.

Laitinen, H. (2005) 'Factors affecting the use of hearing protectors among classical music players', *Noise & Health*, 7(26): 21–9. https://doi.org/10.4103/1463-1741.31643.

Laitinen, H., & Poulsen, T. (2008) 'Questionnaire investigation of musicians' use of hearing protectors, self reported hearing disorders, and their experience of their working environment', *International Journal of Audiology*, 47(4): 160–8. https://doi.org/10.1080/14992020801886770.

Liberman, M.C., Epstein, M.J., Cleveland, S.S., Wang, H., & Maison, S.F. (2016) 'Toward a differential diagnosis of hidden hearing loss in humans', Edited by Manuel S. Malmierca. *Plos One*, 11(9): e0162726. https://doi.org/10.1371/journal.pone.0162726.

Lie, A., Skogstad, M., Johannessen, H.A., Tynes, T., Mehlum, I.S., Nordby, K.-C., Engdahl, B., & Tambs, K. (2016) 'Occupational noise exposure and hearing: a systematic review', *International Archives of Occupational and Environmental Health*, 89(3): 351–72. https://doi.org/10.1007/s00420-015-1083-5.

McKay, C.M. (2021) 'No evidence that music training benefits speech perception in hearing-impaired listeners: A systematic review', *Trends in Hearing*, 25(January): 233121652098567. https://doi.org/10.1177/2331216520985678.

Mepani, A.M., Kirk, S.A., Hancock, K.E., Bennett, K., De Gruttola, V., Liberman, M.C., & Maison, S.F. (2018) 'Middle ear muscle reflex and word recognition in "normal-hearing" adults: Evidence for cochlear synaptopathy?' *Ear and Hearing*, 41(1): 25–38. https://doi.org/10.1097/AUD.0000000000000804.

Miyakita, T., Hellström, P-A., Frimanson, E., & Axelsson, A. (1992) 'Effect of low level acoustic stimulation on temporary threshold shift in young humans', *Hearing Research*, 6(2): 149–55. https://doi.org/10.1016/0378-5955(92)90017-H.

Mosing, M.A., Madison, G., Pedersen, N.L., & Ullén, F. (2016) 'Investigating cognitive transfer within the framework of music practice: Genetic pleiotropy rather than causality', *Developmental Science*, 19(3): 504–12. https://doi.org/10.1111/desc.12306.

O'Brien, I., Ackermann, B.J., & Driscoll, T. (2014) 'Hearing and hearing conservation practices among Australia's professional orchestral musicians', *Noise and Health*, 16(70): 189. https://doi.org/10.4103/1463-1741.134920.

Parbery-Clark, A., Strait, D.L., Anderson, S., Hittner, E., & Kraus, N. (2011) 'Musical experience and the aging auditory system: Implications for cognitive abilities and hearing speech in noise', *PloS One*, 6(5): e18082. https://doi.org/10.1371/journal.pone.0018082.

Patel, A.D. (2014) 'Can nonlinguistic musical training change the way the brain processes speech? The expanded OPERA hypothesis', *Hearing Research*. Elsevier. https://doi.org/10.1016/j.heares.2013.08.011.

Plack, C.J., Barker, D., & Prendergast, G. (2014) 'Perceptual consequences of "hidden" hearing loss', *Trends in Hearing*, 18(October): 233121651455062. https://doi.org/10.1177/2331216514550621.

Prell, C.G. Le (2019) 'Effects of noise exposure on auditory brainstem response and speech-in-noise tasks: A review of the literature', *International Journal of Audiology*, 58(sup1): S3–32. https://doi.org/10.1080/14992027.2018.1534010.

Prendergast, G., Couth, S., Millman, R.E., Guest, H., Kluk, K., Munro, K.J., & Plack, C.J. (2019) 'Effects of age and noise exposure on proxy measures of cochlear synaptopathy', *Trends in Hearing*, 23. https://doi.org/10.1177/2331216519877301.

Rabinowitz, P.M., Galusha, D., Dixon-Ernst, C., Clougherty, J.E., & Neitzel, R.L. (2013) 'The dose–response relationship between in-ear occupational noise exposure and hearing loss', *Occupational and Environmental Medicine*, 70(10): 716–21. https://doi.org/10.1136/oemed-2011-100455.

Salthouse, T.A. (2010) 'Selective review of cognitive aging', *Journal of the International Neuropsychological Society*, 16(5): 754–60. https://doi.org/10.1017/S1355617710000706.

Sanju, H.K., & Kumar, P. (2016) 'Enhanced auditory evoked potentials in musicians: A review of recent findings', *Journal of Otology*, 11(2): 63–72. https://doi.org/10.1016/j.joto.2016.04.002.

Schaette, R., & McAlpine, D. (2011) 'Tinnitus with a normal audiogram: Physiological evidence for hidden hearing loss and computational model', *Journal of Neuroscience*, 31(38): 13452–57. https://doi.org/10.1523/JNEUROSCI.2156-11.2011.

Schellenberg, E.G. (2015) 'Music training and speech perception: A gene-environment interaction', *Annals of the New York Academy of Sciences*, 1337(1): 170–7. https://doi.org/10.1111/nyas.12627.

Sergeyenko, Y., Lall, K., Liberman, M.C., & Kujawa, S.G. (2013) 'Age-related cochlear synaptopathy: An early-onset contributor to auditory functional decline', *Journal of Neuroscience*, 33(34): 13686–94. https://doi.org/10.1523/JNEUROSCI.1783-13.2013.

Skoe, E., Camera, S., & Tufts, J. (2018) 'Noise exposure may diminish the musician advantage for perceiving speech in noise', *Ear and Hearing*, October, 1. https://doi.org/10.1097/AUD.0000000000000665.

Skoe, E., & Tufts, J. (2018) 'Evidence of noise-induced subclinical hearing loss using auditory brainstem responses and objective measures of noise exposure in humans', *Hearing Research*, 361(April): 80–91. https://doi.org/10.1016/j.heares.2018.01.005.

Sliwinska-Kowalska, M., & Davis, A. (2012) 'Noise-induced hearing loss', *Noise and Health*, 14(61), pp. 274–80. https://doi.org/10.4103/1463-1741.104893.

Somma, G., Pietroiusti, A., Magrini, A., Coppeta, L., Ancona, C., Gardi, S., Messina, M., & Bergamaschi, A. (2008) 'Extended high-frequency audiometry and noise induced hearing loss in cement workers', *American Journal of Industrial Medicine*, 51(6): 452–62. https://doi.org/10.1002/ajim.20580.

Suga, N. (2008) 'Role of corticofugal feedback in hearing', *Journal of Comparative Physiology A: Neuroethology, Sensory, Neural, and Behavioral Physiology*. https://doi.org/10.1007/s00359-007-0274-2.

Swaminathan, S., & Schellenberg, E.G. (2018) 'Musical competence is predicted by music training, cognitive abilities, and personality', *Scientific Reports*, 8(1): 9223. https://doi.org/10.1038/s41598-018-27571-2.

Tufts, J.B., & Skoe, E. (2018) 'Examining the noisy life of the college musician: Weeklong noise dosimetry of music and non-music activities', *International Journal of Audiology*, 57(sup1): S20–27. https://doi.org/10.1080/14992027.2017.1405289.

Valderrama, J.T., Beach, E.F., Yeend, I., Sharma, M., Van Dun, B., & Dillon, H. (2018) 'Effects of lifetime noise exposure on the middle-age human auditory brainstem response, tinnitus and speech-in-noise intelligibility', *Hearing Research*, 365 (August): 36–48. https://doi.org/10.1016/j.heares.2018.06.003.

Washnik, N.J., Bhatt, I.S., Phillips, S.L., Tucker, D., & Richter, S. (2020) 'Evaluation of cochlear activity in normal-hearing musicians', *Hearing Research*, 395(September): 108027. https://doi.org/10.1016/j.heares.2020.108027.

Wojtczak, M., Beim, J.A., & Oxenham, A.J. (2017) 'Weak middle-ear-muscle reflex in humans with noise-induced tinnitus and normal hearing may reflect cochlear synaptopathy', *ENeuro* 4(6). https://doi.org/10.1523/ENEURO.0363-17.2017.

Yeend, I., Beach, E.F., Sharma, M., & Dillon, H. (2017) 'The effects of noise exposure and musical training on suprathreshold auditory processing and speech perception in noise', *Hearing Research*, 353(September): 224–36. https://doi.org/10.1016/j.heares.2017.07.006.

Zendel, B.R., & Alain, C. (2012) 'Musicians experience less age-related decline in central auditory processing', *Psychology and Aging*, 27(2): 410–17. https://doi.org/10.1037/a0024816.

Zhao, F., Manchaiah, V.K.C., French, D., & Price, S.M. (2010) 'Music exposure and hearing disorders: An overview', *International Journal of Audiology*, 49(1): 54–64. https://doi.org/10.3109/14992020903202520.

14
DIVERSE MUSIC LISTENING EXPERIENCES
Insights from the Hearing Aids for Music Project

Alinka Greasley

Introduction

There is increasing knowledge in the field of music psychology about how music listening experiences are shaped by listener characteristics such as age and personality (Bonneville-Roussy et al. 2013) and by listening contexts such as being at home, travelling or attending live events (Lamont et al. 2016); however, until recently comparatively little research had focused on how hearing impairments affect music listening. Working with Dr Harriet Crook (an audiologist with special interest in music) and Dr Robert Fulford (a music psychologist with expertise in deaf musicians' performance), we devised a project 'Hearing Aids for Music: Exploring the music listening behaviour of people with hearing impairments',[1] which received funding from the Arts and Humanities Research Council in 2015. The project was a collaboration between the University of Leeds and Sheffield Teaching Hospitals NHS Foundation Trust and its purpose was to explore systematically how levels of hearing impairment and the use of hearing aid technology affect music listening experiences. We conducted a series of survey and interview studies, and collected data from over 1,500 hearing aid users and 100 audiologists (Greasley et al. 2019).

Our findings highlighted similarities in the musical experiences of hearing-impaired listeners, with discernible patterns according to severity of hearing loss. For example, many reported problems with pitch perception, hearing lyrics in music, and distortion, but those with more severe hearing loss were more likely to experience these issues, particularly in live contexts, and were more likely to report difficulties perceiving certain musical styles. However, there were also individual differences within hearing loss category groups. Listeners have unique musical backgrounds, preferences, and auditory needs that shape how they respond to music and what they need from their hearing aid technology. For example, those with musical training were more likely to report frustration with sound quality provided by hearing aids and more likely to explore a range of technological solutions. This chapter provides a narrative account of findings across HAfM studies, detailing broad patterns across the dataset but also focusing in on individual case studies to highlight diversity in music listening experiences. The results provide valuable insights that can be used to manage expectations among hearing-impaired listeners about the types of experiences they may have in musical contexts, and to inform conversations between hearing aid users and audiologists in clinical appointments.

DOI: 10.4324/9781003183624-16

Taking Stock

In our first scoping study (Greasley et al. 2020), we surveyed hearing aid users' experiences of music listening using a short survey distributed in clinic waiting rooms to determine the prevalence of difficulties. The survey asked patients (n = 176) whether they had experienced any problems with music listening, whether they felt this affected their quality of life, whether they had discussed music with their audiologist and if so, whether this had improved their experience. Results showed that around two-thirds of hearing aid users experience issues with music listening, and commonly reported problems included pitch perception difficulties, poor tone quality, difficulties hearing lyrics in songs, and distortion, providing support for existing literature (Moore 2016; Madsen & Moore 2014; Marchand 2019). These problems were often associated with negative psychosocial consequences; many listeners reported experiencing anxiety, frustration, and depression, and some had stopped participating in musical activities as a result. Very few participants reported they had had discussions with their audiologist about music listening and where discussions had taken place, outcomes were mixed with some reporting improvements but many reporting that their listening experiences remained unchanged. Given the key role that music plays in health and wellbeing among the general population (MacDonald et al. 2012), the findings assured us that examining how we can improve experiences for hearing-impaired listeners was essential work.

Asking Practitioners

We then surveyed audiologists (n = 99) about their experiences of discussing music with patients in clinic and their experience in fitting hearing aids for music (Greasley et al. 2020). The audiologists represented varying ages and years of experience, with around half having practised for over ten years. A majority reported that they had discussed music listening in clinic at some point (yes/no response) though the frequency with which audiologists reported having discussions about music in clinic varied, with some reporting that they would ask four out of five patients about music, but others reporting that they would only ask one in five. There was varied confidence in providing advice about music and programming hearing aids for music, and those who had received some form of training (e.g. degree programme, conference talks) and/or who had been practising for longer reported greater confidence. Around half (n = 53) reflected on strategies they would use to improve music listening for patients. The most common strategies employed were disabling adaptive functions for speech (e.g. noise reduction, feedback manager), changes to compression and gain changes (Greasley & Cook 2021), and these suggestions align with advice offered previously by practitioners with expertise in music (Chasin 2010, 2019; Chasin & Hockley 2012). A key finding was that audiologists emphasised that there was no 'one-size-fits-all' approach, and that it was essential to take into account the *individual needs* of the listener. This included asking about the patient's preferred musical genres and listening contexts, and for musicians, what instrument(s) they played and the typical settings in which they performed. In addition, audiologists acknowledged that it often took regular follow-up appointments to adjust the hearing aids for improved music listening and performance. The sustained enquiry and tailoring necessary to address musical needs is challenging within clinical appointments where time is often limited, however evidence from our hearing aid users showed that when a tailored approach is used, this often led to improvements.

In-depth Interviews

The need to take an individual approach, taking into account listeners' diverse needs was borne out in our interview study with hearing aid users, which showed how varied people's listening needs and experiences were even though they had the same diagnosis (e.g. 'mild' or 'moderate' hearing loss). We conducted interviews with 22 hearing aids users, seeking out a roughly equal number of musicians and non-musicians, and levels of hearing impairment to be representative of those in general society. Using the British Society of Audiology criteria for diagnosing hearing loss (BSA 2011), the sample contained those with 'mild' (n = 10), 'moderate' (n = 10), and 'severe'[2] (n = 2) hearing loss (HL). We asked interviewees to reflect on their hearing loss history, musical background (including any musical training), music listening behaviour, hearing aids, any problems experienced in recorded and live settings, and experiences with audiologists. Below, I outline seven case studies to exemplify a range of musical backgrounds and experiences across 'moderate' and 'severe' hearing losses.

Participant A (male, 30 years old, mild HL) has been deaf since birth and wore hearing aids from the age of three, except for a period between the ages of 12–18 years where he reported that he did not wear them for social reasons at school. Participant A listens to music on daily basis, and takes his hearing aids out to listen to music through earphones on the walk to work, though leaves them in when listening to music on the stereo at home. If he wears headphones with his hearing aids, he gets feedback and they are uncomfortable. He mentioned that he had difficulties hearing lyrics with songs but has a work around ('if I want to get to the heart of a song I really like, I will look up the lyrics and listen along and that helps'). His preferred musical styles are rock, acoustic rock, folk, indie rock, any guitar-based music. He is an avid gig goer (acoustic and amplified) and reports that there was a period of five years where he would go to a gig more than once a week. He experiences distortion at live gigs and so takes his hearing aids out, and manages sound levels by moving towards or away from the PA system ('at a quieter gig, I might go further to the front'). If the music is too loud, he wears earplugs to avoid further hearing damage. He plays guitar (self-taught) and reports that his experience is enhanced by having hearing aids in ('it sounds a lot sharper, I can really hear the strings, there's a bit more clarity') and that listening to classical music is better with his hearing aids in ('there's a lot more nuance, you pick up those extra frequencies'). His occupation is a video editor and he reports that he struggles with the mix of audio and speech when watching and editing films, and tries to ensure that the music levels do not interrupt the speech in his own mixes. He takes his hearing aids out in order to wear headphones to do his video editing work and this is a source of frustration ('I'm constantly taking them in and out, in and out, it's annoying'). He would like better technological solutions for his work situation ('this is more of an inconvenience than it should be') but was not aware of what types of solutions are out there.

Participant B (male, 73 years old, mild HL, professional guitarist) started experiencing tinnitus aged 60 and went to have a hearing test which confirmed a hearing loss. He only started wearing hearing aids two years prior to the interview because of his work ('I put it off because I was a professional musician, and musicians are not supposed to wear hearing aids'). He initially got hearing aids fitted, but after negative concert-going experiences ('went to a string quartet concert, it was terrible, the violins in particular were really scraping') sought more advanced solutions. Since having his current hearing aids fitted (top of the range) which have three programs (e.g. general, music, 'zen' program to help with tinnitus) he has had more positive listening experiences. His audiologist encouraged him to bring his guitar into clinic so he could tweak the music program whilst he was playing. He has a volume control which he uses all the time ('I can't stress how important it is… if I'm playing classical guitar, I turn it down… when I go to concerts, I wait for the first loud bit in a Mahler symphony and adjust then so I can ride with the dynamics'). He reports that he listens to Radio 3 at home and that the sound is better with hearing aids. He wears his hearing aids for most classical and jazz concerts ('brass instruments are better with hearing aids, because they thrive on upper frequencies, you get a lot of colour you don't get if you take the hearing aids out, a broader spectrum'); however when he attends jazz bands he takes his hearing aids out as he reports the music is often too loud. He reports occasional distortion when listening to music and switches programs to get slightly different tone quality. He is aware of new Bluetooth technology that changes settings automatically without the need for a remote control, and is looking into this.

Looking across Participant A and B with a mild hearing loss, both report that their experiences of classical music is enhanced by hearing aids because they hear the full spectrum of frequencies, and both report that when they attend loud or amplified gigs they remove their hearing aids. They both play the guitar, and report greater sound clarity when wearing their hearing aids in. However whilst Participant B is content with his hearing aids and remote control to adjust settings, Participant A is frustrated and gave his hearing aids a rating of three out of ten for satisfaction because he experiences feedback if he wears headphones and does not have a music setting at live gigs.

Participant C (female, 73 years old, moderate HL, pianist, singer) experienced sudden hearing loss ten years prior to the interview. She lost hearing in her left ear suddenly, with the right ear unaffected. Despite rigorous testing for more serious underlying conditions (e.g. acoustic neuroma, tumour), no specific explanation could be found for this. She started wearing one hearing aid. Several years later, she experienced further sudden hearing loss in her right ear, which was then worse than the left. She now wears two hearing aids, and over the years has tried different makes and models. She likes to listen to classical, blues, jazz, and dance band. She listens to Radio 3 and goes to gigs at least once a month. Since her hearing loss, she has found it increasingly difficult to listen to music with complex instrumentation ('the best music for my hearing loss is classical chamber music, because there will be two, three, or four voices… orchestral music is hard because I'm not getting all the voices'). She is not able to perceive lyrics in music, and this has had increased her preference for instrumental music, and a need for captions during live concerts. When attending live concerts (mainly chamber ensemble and jazz), she reports some audibility issues ('people will tell you "wasn't that bit good?" and you didn't get it') and pitch perception problems ('I thought the soprano was singing off-pitch, and when everybody applauded I realised she wasn't'). Participant C is a pianist, though no longer plays due to problems identifying whether she is playing the right notes (exemplified when she tries to play duets: 'she can hear what I'm not getting right, but I can't hear what she's not getting right') and the sound that pedalling creates ('using the pedal confuses my hearing aids'). She is a singer, and was singing in a classical choir but reported difficulties with room acoustics ('the one thing that is never properly regulated'), hearing other singers' voices, and hearing the conductor ('it's hard to hear the instructions, and it's hard to hear if you're singing right'). She also reported difficulties talking to people in breaks ('I can't communicate in those big halls, either I went off by myself or I didn't talk to anybody because I couldn't'). She consequently stopped this choir and joined a smaller amateur choir, which she finds easier to perform in and still attends. Whether listening or performing contexts, she emphasised that it was the combination of speech and music that was the main challenge in her listening experiences.

Participant D (male, 47 years old, moderate HL) never had problems with his hearing until he underwent chemotherapy which left him with a moderate hearing loss due to ototoxicity.[3] A window cleaner by trade, he reported that he listened to music everyday ('I listen to music nearly all day, I just love music') and would sing along. His preferred styles are indie, rock, pop, mainly guitar-based music. Since his hearing loss, he has been unable to enjoy music in the way that he did before. The chemotherapy brought on permanent tinnitus (there is some relief when wearing hearing aids), and he experiences pitch distortion which fundamentally affects musical enjoyment ('it's just wobbly, that note is not holding its pitch at all, it's going in and out of tune'). He reports that he is only able to listen for around 15–20 minutes before music sounds out of tune ('my favourite music sounds *horrific*') regardless of what genre he is listening to or whether he is familiar with it, and that his ears get tired after a certain amount of time (which varies). Given that Participant D also reports balance problems, there may be some parallels here with the heightened pitch perception problems experienced by those with Ménière's disease (Hugill, this volume). However, interestingly he does not report problems perceiving lyrics, perhaps because he has been singing along for years and knows all the lyrics to preferred songs. He has a music program fitted on his hearing aids, but reports that this does not provide benefit. Despite the difficulties experienced, he perseveres with music as it's important to him. He listens at work, and continues to attend live gigs even though live concert experiences are often unpleasant and sometimes he has to take his hearing aids out. He maintains a positive mindset ('you just get on with it, you're still vertical aren't you').

Participant E (male, 24 years old, moderate HL) had gradual hearing loss during school years leading to a diagnosis of a rare genetic disorder when he was 19 years old. Whilst his hearing loss is classified as 'moderate' overall, he has severe high frequency loss which he reports 'creates a muddy imbalance sound' and affects his ability to understand speech and perceive lyrics in music. He experiences tinnitus, depending on exposure ('very low ringing after two hours radio show, but it's not painful') and the type of music ('lot of harsh guitars will set tinnitus ringing'). Participant E is highly involved in the music industry. He listens for around 8–10 hours per day, attends 10–15 live gigs a month (pre-pandemic) and is engaged in radio, broadcasting, journalism and DJing at live events. He wore Behind-the-Ear (BTE) hearing aids for several years, but recently started using Completely-in-Canal (CIC) hearing aids which he reported match his lifestyle better as he spends a large percentage of his working day with headphones on, and needed a better solution in live contexts where he was constantly switching between hearing aids and earplugs. Juggling different noise profiles was one of the main reasons he switched ('when I had over the ear hearing aids, I would have to leave clubs after an hour or two, because it was uncomfortable. Now, I'm still very careful about exposure, but I feel the handbrake has been taken off, on what I could or couldn't do'). Participant E describes his current preferences as electronic music, world electronic music, and alternative rock, though he has eclectic tastes overall. In the last two years, he noticed a dramatic reduction in his ability to detect vocals within music and his preferences have shifted as a result. He listens to less rap, hip-hop, and indie ('I can't hang on to narratives in the same way'), gravitating towards ambient and jazz music. He does not experience problems when he is listening to electronic dance music (EDM) with a clear 4/4 beat (and interestingly, loud EDM does not set off his tinnitus). However, to hear properly in nightclubs, he has to have sound levels higher than ideal ('my line of work means that I'm often running things, being on mic, or being behind the booth in a club, I have to sometimes leave them on, and that's when it gets loud, but I have to deal with that'). He mentioned he would often rest his ears, turning his hearing aids off half the time on his daily commute, which he noted, also served as practice in case he ever went fully deaf.

Looking across these individuals with a 'moderate' hearing loss, there are some similarities. Participant C and D experience pitch perception problems which negatively impact their enjoyment of music. Participant C and E experience problems hearing lyrics in songs and have adapted their preferences towards instrumental music. Participant D and E like to listen to as much music as possible, but have to give their ears frequent breaks. However, their different musical backgrounds, preferences, and listening contexts bring unique challenges. Participant C struggles to hear other singers and the conductor in the choir. Participant D finds it difficult to follow melody and guitar lines and is not able to listen for extended periods. Participant E has resolved the problem of taking his hearing aids out to accommodate headphones or earplugs, but has difficulty with amplification levels in nightclubs. What is striking about these listeners is the way in which they are persevering and proactively finding solutions to issues experienced, whether that is seeking out a different choir or campaigning for captions in live events (Participant C), continuing to listen despite pitch distortion (Participant D) or changing hearing aids to fit lifestyle (Participant E). It seems likely that general dispositions, such as openness to experience, resilience, or persistence, may influence outcomes among hearing-impaired listeners, however the role of such factors are yet to be fully explored.

Participant F (male, 74 years, severe HL) had hearing loss and wore hearing aids since he was 30 years old. His hearing was in gradual decline, but chemotherapy seven years ago accelerated this further. He is currently waiting for a cochlear implant (CI). He has a musical background. He was a formally taught pianist, and played the organ in his local chapel. He was highly engaged in listening as well ('well at one time, music was all the time') and reported listening to and performing a wide range of classical and popular styles. Nowadays, he finds it difficult to engage with music ('music comes out as just a noise… a lot of it doesn't make sense'). He noted a gradual decline in his hearing when performing ('I started struggling, you get a singer up there, I found all the higher pitches were missing, the lower ones didn't seem to be any problem, but then it starts going down the ladder') and eventually stopped performing altogether. He no longer plays the piano. Participant F reported that he rarely goes out, but his local village hall puts on community events which he attends two or three times a year, some of which are musical performances. Due to his problems perceiving music, Participant F has taken up photography at these events ('I'm always busy rather than just listening'). He draws on one example of an impersonator who does a regular show ('the problem is he has two big speakers, I'd like to be able to shut these speakers down, if not shut him off all together (laughs), his songs don't come out as they should… it's just noise'). Occasionally Participant F is able to improve his experience of music listening. When he was at the Edinburgh Tattoo, he was able to improve his experience of the drummers and bagpipes using hearing aid settings ('I switched over to the loop system and turned it down a little bit, that gets rid of the harshness of music'). Overall, he has withdrawn from music ('I don't bother much, just now and again'), though he is hoping that if he receives a cochlear implant, he may be able to re-engage with music again.

Participant G (female, 82 years, severe HL) lost hearing in her right ear in her thirties when she had an operation to remove a cyst. She wore one hearing aid and her left ear was unaffected. In her early seventies, she then lost hearing in her left ear suddenly (she had scans and diagnostic tests but the cause was not identified). She was an avid music listener, with a large music collection. She sung in her church choir and in a choral society for 12 years, but had to stop when her hearing got worse ('I used to be part of that, loved it, but that's one of these things I can't do any more'). Now, she is not able to enjoy music listening as she cannot distinguish musical features or perceive lyrics ('it's just not very good at all, I get to about the third or fourth song and switch it off because it drives me mad because I can't tell what they're saying'). Determined to improve her experiences, she has seen a hearing therapist three times to discuss Assistive Listening Devices (ALDs). Her therapist provided her with two different types of wireless microphones to try out at home when listening to CDs ('to see if it was better for me with music, to see if I could hear music clearer'). With the latest streamer she reported improvement with a single male voice, but not with multiple voices ('the first CD I put on was just one voice, sort of ballad, and I said "oh this is marvelous" and then we tried a Boyzone one and I said oh no, no, no, I don't like that'). Participant G goes to see musical theatre occasionally (her friend gets seats at the front so that she is close to the sound source) though she needs captions. Overall, she perseveres with music, though her experiences are rarely positive, and she has reached a level of acceptance ('it's something that I miss, but I'm breathing aren't I?').

Participants F and G used to be fully immersed in music, and music was a key part of their identity, but their hearing loss is now severe/profound and they report it is difficult for them to decipher music at all. Both have accepted that they are unlikely to hear well again (Participant F 'I think we've got to the end of the trail with these [hearing aids] haven't we? My hearing is so bad we can't go much further'; Participant G 'I'd love to improve listening to CDs, but I don't think it'll happen in my lifetime') though both were actively using roger pens to negotiate everyday contexts, and in the case of Participant G, in order to try and improve music listening at home. Participant F is on the waiting list for a cochlear implant. Research evidence shows that whilst melody and timbre perception is still an enduring challenge for CI users (Sorrentino et al. 2020), rhythm perception is retained and tailored musical training can improve music perception (Looi et al. 2016). It does seem that there is a noticeable shift in music perception at the severe/profound threshold. Differences in outcomes between 'mild' and 'moderate' hearing loss on the one hand, and 'severe' and 'profound' hearing loss on the other, have been noted in a recent study (Looi et al. 2019) and was borne out in the large-scale survey we conducted which explored patterns of listening behaviour among a large cohort of hearing-impaired listeners.

National Survey

A central project aim was to establish whether there were patterns in listening experiences which would enable us to give advice tailored by level of hearing loss. We conducted a survey among hearing aid users (n = 1,507) asking them to reflect on their musical engagement and training, preferences and uses of music, hearing and hearing aid technology, experiences of listening to recorded and live music, and discussions with audiologists (Greasley et al. in preparation). Survey questions were translated into British Sign Language (BSL) and around 7% of the sample used the videos. Whilst it is not possible to describe the numerous findings of the study here, group analysis by hearing loss level revealed some broad trends. Whilst there was a generally high level of engagement with music across the sample, those with more severe losses were less likely to be highly engaged, and were more likely to avoid music listening. The sample as a whole had strong preferences for classical, blues, musical theatre, and choral music, which would be expected given the mean age of the sample (60 years) and prior research on age-related trends in preferences (Bonneville-Roussy et al. 2013). However, those with more severe losses were more likely to report difficulties listening to choral, classical, and opera, and less likely to report that instrumentation and harmony were important in their enjoyment of music. Open-ended responses revealed that classical orchestral music in particular, was difficult to listen to for those with more severe losses. There were also differences in experiences in recorded and live settings. In recorded contexts, those with more severe losses were less likely to report that their hearing aids were helpful for hearing lyrics and picking out individual instruments, and were more likely to experience distortion and too much bass. In live contexts, those with more severe hearing loss were less likely to rate hearing aids as helpful for hearing the melody, singer, lyrics, and instruments, and were more likely to experience distortion.

Mapping the Complexities

Findings across these studies present a complex picture. Whilst there are discernible patterns in music listening experiences according to levels of deafness (e.g. mild, moderate, severe, profound), there are considerable individual differences within these groups, shaped by differing musical backgrounds, preferences, and modes and contexts of listening. Uncovering the complexities, facilitated by the mixed-methods approach and large sample size, has provided valuable data for developing advice for hearing aid users and audiologists. Results can be used to inform discussions about listening experiences in different musical contexts and about strategies that could be used to help address any issues arising. For example, difficulties with hearing lyrics was a commonly cited problem for listeners with all levels of hearing loss. Participant A found it helpful to seek out the lyrics and read them whilst listening. Participant C and E were gradually listening to more instrumental music to compensate for reduced enjoyment of music with lyrical content. Participant C attended live events with captions whenever she could. Those with more severe hearing loss are more likely to experience a range of difficulties including problems hearing out musical features (e.g. identifying instruments, hearing harmonies) and difficulties listening to complex styles (e.g. classical orchestral). However, again there are strategies that could help to improve experiences. Participant C reported that she now listens to smaller chamber works due to challenges listening to orchestral works, and has joined a smaller choir due to difficulties hearing herself with a larger chorus (and some of the associated difficulties of hearing conversation and the conductor in a large rehearsal space with poor acoustics). Despite her level of hearing loss (severe/profound borderline) Participant G reported with the use of an Assistive Listening Device, she is able to listen to simple vocal melodies with greater clarity. Using the findings, the HAfM team have developed a series of resources (Crook et al. 2018; Greasley et al. 2018) to help hearing aid users and audiologists navigate the complexities. These include tips for hearing aid users such as engaging in listening practice, how to get the best out of discussions with audiologists, and finding out about ALDs. For audiologists, the guidance focuses on history taking in clinic, useful resources for understanding more about music, and tips for programming hearing aids for music (Greasley & Crook 2021).

Notes

1 *Hearing Aids for Music* project, www.musicandhearingaids.org
2 The two 'severe' were close to 'profound' loss category, as their best ears were 89 and 90 dB.
3 Adverse pharmacological reaction resulting in damage to the inner ear or auditory nerve. See Bisht & Bist (2011).

References

Bisht, M. & Bist, S.S. (2011) 'Ototoxicity: The Hidden Menace', *Indian J Otolaryngol Head Neck Surg.*, Jul; 63(3): 255–9.
Bonneville-Roussy, A., Rentfrow, P.J., Xu, M.K., & Potter, J. (2013) 'Music through the ages: Trends in musical engagement and preferences from adolescence through middle adulthood', *Journal of Personality and Social Psychology*, 105(4): 703–17.

British Society of Audiology (BSA) (2011) *Recommended Procedure. Pure-Tone Air-Conduction and Bone-Conduction Threshold Audiometry with and without Masking.* Berkshire, UK: British Society of Audiology. Available at www.thebsa.org.uk (accessed 16 July 2021).

Chasin, M. (2010) 'Six ways to improve listening to music through hearing aids', *Hearing Journal*, 63(9): 27–30.

Chasin, M. (2019) 'Checklist for optimizing your hearing aids for music'. Available at www.grandpianopassion.com/2019/01/21/chasin-optimize-hearing-aids-music/ (accessed 16 July 2021).

Chasin, M. & Hockley, N.S. (eds) (2012) 'Special issue on music and hearing loss: Preventative and rehabilitative options', *Trends in Amplification*, 16(3): 135–82.

Crook, H., Greasley, A.E., & Beeston, A.V. (2018) *Music counselling and fitting: A guide for audiologists.* Version 1.0, dated 24 September 2018. Available at https://musicandhearingaids.org/resources/ (accessed July 16 2021).

Crook, H., Beeston, A.V., & Greasley, A.E. (2018) *Starting Out with a Music Program: Quickstart Clinic Guide.* Version 1.1, dated 24 September. Available at https://musicandhearingaids.org/resources/ (accessed 16 July 2021).

Greasley, A.E. & Crook, H. (2021) 'Clinical strategies for improving music listening', *ENT & Audiology News*, 30(4), 48–50.

Greasley, A.E., Crook, H., & Fulford, R.J. (2020) 'Music listening and hearing aids: perspectives from audiologists and their patients', *International Journal of Audiology*, 59(9): 694–706.

Greasley, A.E., Crook, H., & Beeston, A.V. (2018) *Music Listening with Hearing Aids.* Version 2.0, dated 24 September. Available at https://musicandhearingaids.org/resources/ (accessed 16 July 2021).

Greasley, A.E., Crook, H., Beeston, A.V., Salter, J.M., Fulford, R.J., & Moore, B.C.J. (in preparation). 'The impact of hearing loss level on listening to music with hearing aids'.

Greasley, A.E., Crook, H., & Beeston, A.V. (2019) Hearing Aids for Music: Findings and recommendations for hearing aid users, audiologists, manufacturers and researchers. Final report of the AHRC-funded Hearing Aids for Music project. Available at www.musicandhearingaids.org (accessed 16 July 2021).

Lamont, A., Greasley, A.E., & Sloboda, J.A. (2016) 'Choosing to hear music: motivation, process, and effect', in S. Hallam, I. Cross, & M. Thaut (eds), *The Oxford Handbook of Music Psychology (2nd Edition)*, pp. 263–84. Oxford: Oxford University Press.

Looi, V., Wong, Y. & Loo, J.H.Y. (2016) 'The effects of training on music perception and appreciation for cochlear implant recipients', *Advances in Otolaryngology*, Article ID 6286514 (26 Jan. 2016). https://doi.org/10.1155/2016/6286514

Looi, V., Rutledge, K., & Prvan, T. (2019) 'Music appreciation of adult hearing aid users and the impact of different levels of hearing loss', *Ear & Hearing*, 40(3): 529–44.

MacDonald, R., Kreutz, G., & Mitchell, L. (2012) *Music, Health, and Wellbeing.* Oxford: Oxford University Press.

Madsen, S.M. & Moore, B.C. (2014) 'Music and hearing aids', *Trends in Hearing*, 18, doi:10.1177/2331216514558271

Marchand, R. (2019) *Hearing aids and music.* Unpublished doctoral thesis, Macquarie University, Sydney, Australia.

Moore, B.C.J. (2016) 'Effects of sound-induced hearing loss and hearing aids on the perception of music', *Journal of the Audio Engineering Society*, 64(3), March. http://dx.doi.org/10.17743/jaes.2015.0081

Sorrentino, F., Gheller, F., Favaretto, N., Franz, L., Stocco, E., Brotto, D., & Bovo, R. (2020) 'Music perception in adult patients with cochlear implant', *Hearing, Balance and Communication*, 18(1): 3–7, doi: 10.1080/21695717.2020.1719787

15
CONSEQUENCES OF MÉNIÈRE'S DISEASE FOR MUSICIANS, THEIR MUSIC-MAKING, HEARING CARE, AND TECHNOLOGIES

Andrew Hugill

Introduction

Ménière's Disease (hereafter *Ménière's*) is a long term, progressive condition affecting the balance and hearing parts of the inner ear. The defining symptoms are acute attacks of vertigo (severe dizziness), fluctuating tinnitus, a feeling of pressure in the ear (aural fullness) and hearing loss. It may affect one ear (unilateral) or both ears (bilateral) and the severity of the symptoms varies greatly between individuals (Lopez-Escamez et al. 2015). It affects roughly 1:1000 of the population and sometimes runs in families. Its cause is unknown and it is incurable, but there are various treatments to relieve symptoms (Paparella 1991; Sajjadi & Papparella 2008; Flint et al. 2014; Patel & Isildak 2016).

There have been many studies of Ménière's and hearing loss (e.g. Lee et al. 1995; Katsarkas 1996; Havia et al. 2004), but few have considered it specifically in relation to music and musicians. The research for this chapter was undertaken partly in response to a letter to the Ménière's Society by Alan Jacques (Jacques 2009) in which he described the 'significant changes' he has experienced, 'which Oliver Sacks in his book *Musicophilia* calls cochlear amusia'. He commented: 'I find it hard to believe that I am alone in this experience, and I certainly think that it is poorly understood by others […]'. Since his experiences parallel the author's own struggles with Ménière's and given the notable lack of published research in this area, the need for the present study was keenly felt (Hugill 2018). This was confirmed during informal discussions at the Ménière's Society's Annual Conference in 2017.

Method

The research was conducted in late 2018/early 2019 and comprised semi-structured interviews with two groups of professional, semi-professional, or amateur musicians. The criteria for inclusion were that the participants should be musically active and have had a diagnosis of either Ménière's or some other form of hearing loss.

Table 15.1 shows the Ménière's Disease Group (MDG), comprising eight musicians with a self-reported medical diagnosis conforming to the Bárány criteria of 'episodes of spontaneous vertigo

TABLE 15.1 Ménière's Disease Group (MDG)

Name	MDG-1	MDG-2	MDG-3	MDG-4	MDG-5	MDG-6	MDG-7	MDG-8
Music	Classical pianist	Classical/band pianist	Musicologist	Violinist/teacher	Singer/songwriter	Harpsichordist/teacher	Pop/rock singer	Jazz pianist
Status	Amateur	Semi-professional	Professional (retired)	Professional	Professional	Professional	Professional	Semi-Professional
Age	71	55	60	53	30	50	30	68
Gender	M	M	M	F	M	F	F	M
Diagnosis (self-reported)	Bilateral Ménière's	Unilateral Ménière's	Unilateral secondary Ménière's	Unilateral Ménière's	Unilateral Ménière's	Unilateral Ménière's	Unilateral 'mild Ménière's-type condition'	
Onset	2005	1979 (1); 2011 (r)	2011	2013	2014	2010	2017	2008/2016
Duration (years)	14	40; 8	8	6	5	9	2	11/3
Hearing loss Description	Severe	Left: profound; Right: normal	Profound deafness in left ear	Low frequency loss in left ear, restored by treatments	Hearing loss has been reduced by drug treatments	Severe in left ear only	Fluctuating (currently none)	Generally mild, but worse in left ear
Other Symptoms	Vertigo, aural fullness, drop attacks	Episodic vertigo with nausea, nerve noise, severe distortion, tone doubling	Severe vertigo, vomiting, sweating, diarrhoea, nystagmus	Pain and fullness in left ear, aversion to sound, distortion	Vertigo	Vertigo, brain fog	Severe vertigo	Vertigo, anxiety

Tinnitus	Sensory	Ringing and/or whooshing, depending on current health.	Subjective/sensory whooshing/occasional throbbing aggravated by painkillers	Subjective/sensory buzzing, ringing, whooshing, ringing and more	Sensory, low ringing	Sensory, mainly low throbbing	Subjective with somatic overlay (ringing, but when hearing is down; a waterfall)	Sensory (high pitched white noise with occasional 2–4 K Hz pitches)
Treatments	Drugs (betahistine, prochlorperazine bendrofluazide)	Endolymphatic sac decompression surgery, drug treatments, dietary/lifestyle modification	No treatments apart from hearing aids, but contemplating a cochlear implant	Multiple treatments, including dietary and lifestyle modifications	Drugs (betahistine, diuretics)	Drugs (betahistine and antidepressants)	Various	Drugs (betahistine, prochlorperazine, syclizine) and lip-reading classes.

usually associated with unilateral fluctuating sensorineural hearing loss, tinnitus and aural fullness' (Lopez-Escamez et al. 2015, 3).

Table 15.2 shows the Other Hearing Difference (OHD) Group, who were chosen to reflect a wide diversity of hearing differences. Their diagnoses were also self-reported, including: three participants with severe or profound deafness from birth or early childhood (one of whom is fitted with cochlear implants); one with a vestibular migraine-like condition which presumably has caused uneven bilateral hearing loss; one with bilateral high frequency loss presumably resulting from head trauma; and one with auditory neuropathy due to autism. The OHD group was selected in order to place Ménière's Disease within a wider context of Aural Diversity (Drever 2017; Hugill 2019). The scientific method was therefore not a comparative study between the two groups, but rather a context-aware analysis of the MDG subset.

The participants were chosen to reflect a wide range of ages. The gender balance was: 8 male and 7 female. The participants come from the following countries: UK (7), USA (3), Australia (2), Canada (1), France (1), Poland (1). The participants work in a wide range of acoustic spaces, including large and small concert halls, professional and home studios, theatres and churches, bars and clubs. They perform to audience sizes ranging from dozens to thousands of people. The participants were identified partly through personal contacts of the author and partly through calls given out in support networks such as 'Musicians4Hearing' (Musicians4Hearing 2019). They were initially contacted via email and given full information about the aims and objectives of the project. They were also asked to complete a factual information sheet and informed consent form before being invited to semi-structured interviews.

During the initial communications, participants were invited to describe their personal and professional histories, focussing in particular on their musical careers, their experiences of hearing loss and any treatments, and their current status. Tables 15.1 and 15.2 summarise these initial responses and reveal both the variability of Ménière's and the diversity of the OHD.

The semi-structured interviews were conducted by the author, either face to face, via video-conferencing or via email, as appropriate to the medical condition or geographical location of the interviewee. Table 15.3 shows the guide used to prompt discussion during the interviews. Where necessary, interviews were automatically transcribed using online software and then verified for accuracy by the author against the original recordings.

The resulting data were analysed using the thematic approach described by (Braun & Clarke 2006). This has much in common with grounded theory (Bryant & Charmaz 2007), but lacks its commitment to theory development as part of the analytical process. The thematic approach was essentially *inductive*, meaning that 'the themes identified are strongly linked to the data themselves' (Braun & Clarke 2006, 12), and *semantic* (i.e. concerned with the explicit meanings of the data). The main benefit of this approach was that it allowed flexibility in generating themes.

Interviews were coded using NVivo software and the resulting nodes were grouped into a thematic map. Word frequency and sentiment analyses were performed to draw out similarities and differences between the two groups. The themes were then reviewed for internal homogeneity and external heterogeneity (Patton 1990) to establish coherent patterns and distinctiveness between them. A further review established the validity of the individual themes in relation to the dataset as a whole. The thematic approach enabled the complicated story of the consequences of Ménière's for musicians to be told in a rigorously analytical yet interestingly vivid way.

TABLE 15.2 Other Hearing Difference Group (OHD).

Name	OHD-1	OHD-2	OHD-3	OHD-4	OHD-5	OHD-6	OHD-7
Music	Sound artist/composer	Bass guitarist	Electroacoustic composer/sound engineer	Academic/performer: early music, non-western music and folk music	Clarinettist/singer	Percussionist composer	Vocalist/voice-over artist
Status	Professional	Amateur (good)	Professional	Professional	Amateur	Professional	Professional
Age	38	40	63	61	32	54	41
Gender	F	F	M	M	F	M	F
Diagnosis (self-reported)	Autism	Genetic hearing loss	MD-like condition (may be vestibular migraine)	Childhood meningitis and subsequent ear infections	Profoundly deaf	Hearing loss presumably caused by traumatic head injury	Hearing loss
Onset	Birth	Birth	2012	Early childhood	Birth	Unclear	Birth
Duration (years)	38	40	7	59	32	c. 15	41
Hearing Loss Description	Objectively normal, but with neurological processing issues	About 50% in both ears, with a cookie bite audiogram (bigger loss in the medium frequencies)	Bilateral (severe in left ear)	Complete loss in left ear. Partial loss in right (about 30% of normal hearing); upper registers generally well perceived, lower register poor	Profound bilateral hearing loss	~50% bilaterally from the top down (virtually no hearing above 2.5k Hz, lower frequencies fairly unchanged)	Severe to profound hearing loss in both ears
Tinnitus/other symptoms	Sensory/somatic, ringing; misophonia and hyperacusis	Sensory, always whooshing with periodic ringing or bell-like sound	Sensory, high-pitched sinus; vertigo	None	Sensory, very high-pitched tinnitus and occasional dizziness	Sensory, ringing, buzzing	
Treatments	Mindfulness training	Hearing aids, mediation, relaxation	Drugs (diuretics and verapamil)	Many over the years. Hearing aids.	Cochlear implants fitted at age 13 and 21	Hearing aids	Hearing aids

TABLE 15.3 Interview guide

- Background
    - How did you get into music?
    - What kind of music and why?
    - What has been your career?
    - How much music do you make nowadays?
    - In what situations do you typically make music?
- Musicianship
    - What do you consider to be the main attributes of musicianship?
    - How important are aural skills and what aural skills?
    - How do you listen? (critically, imaginatively, respectively, etc.)?
    - In what acoustic spaces do you typically work (live, mediated, studio, online etc.)?
    - What technical aspects of music are important for you?
    - What constitutes virtuosity in your field?
    - Who are the leading examples of musicians in your field?
- Hearing loss
    - How has hearing loss and/or tinnitus affected your music-making?
- Other Symptoms
    - [MD only]: How have the other symptoms associated with your Ménière's Disease affected your music-making (aural fullness, vertigo, tinnitus)?
    - [Non MD-only]: Are there any other medical conditions associated with your hearing loss that have affected your music-making, and how?
    - What have been the professional consequences of hearing loss for you?
    - What have been the emotional consequences of hearing loss for you?
- Musical perception
    - How has hearing loss and/or tinnitus affected your perception of: pitch/frequency; harmony/texture; rhythm/beat; dynamics/volume; timbre/spectrum; style/idiom/genre; any other aspects?
- Audiology
    - What have been your experiences with audiology?
    - How would you improve audiology to better reflect your musical situation?
- Hearing aids
    - To what extent do hearing aids currently help your musical life?
    - What would make hearing aids work better in musical situation?

Results

Figure 15.1 shows the thematic map created from the coding of the interview responses. The various sub-themes are grouped around four interconnected main themes: the *medical, personal, musical* and *hearing* consequences of the conditions (whether Ménière's or other). Medical consequences included a range of symptoms and treatments. Personal consequences included effects on careers, emotions, and aspirations. Musical consequences included perception of parameters, musicianship, locations, and tastes. Hearing consequences included care, technologies, listening, differences etc.

Figure 15.2 shows Word Frequency analyses of substantive terms used in the interviews. These revealed some significant differences between the two groups. Certain key words were shared (e.g. hearing, aids, music, sound, people, play/playing, loss, tinnitus), but closer inspection of terms that occur less frequently revealed the MDG's overriding concern with symptomatic issues such as vertigo, diplacusis, hyperacusis, attack(s), and balance. The OHD, by contrast, tended to concentrate less on symptoms and more on musical matters, albeit with some presence of hearing-related terms such as 'cochlear' and 'audiologist'.

Consequences of Ménière's Disease **149**

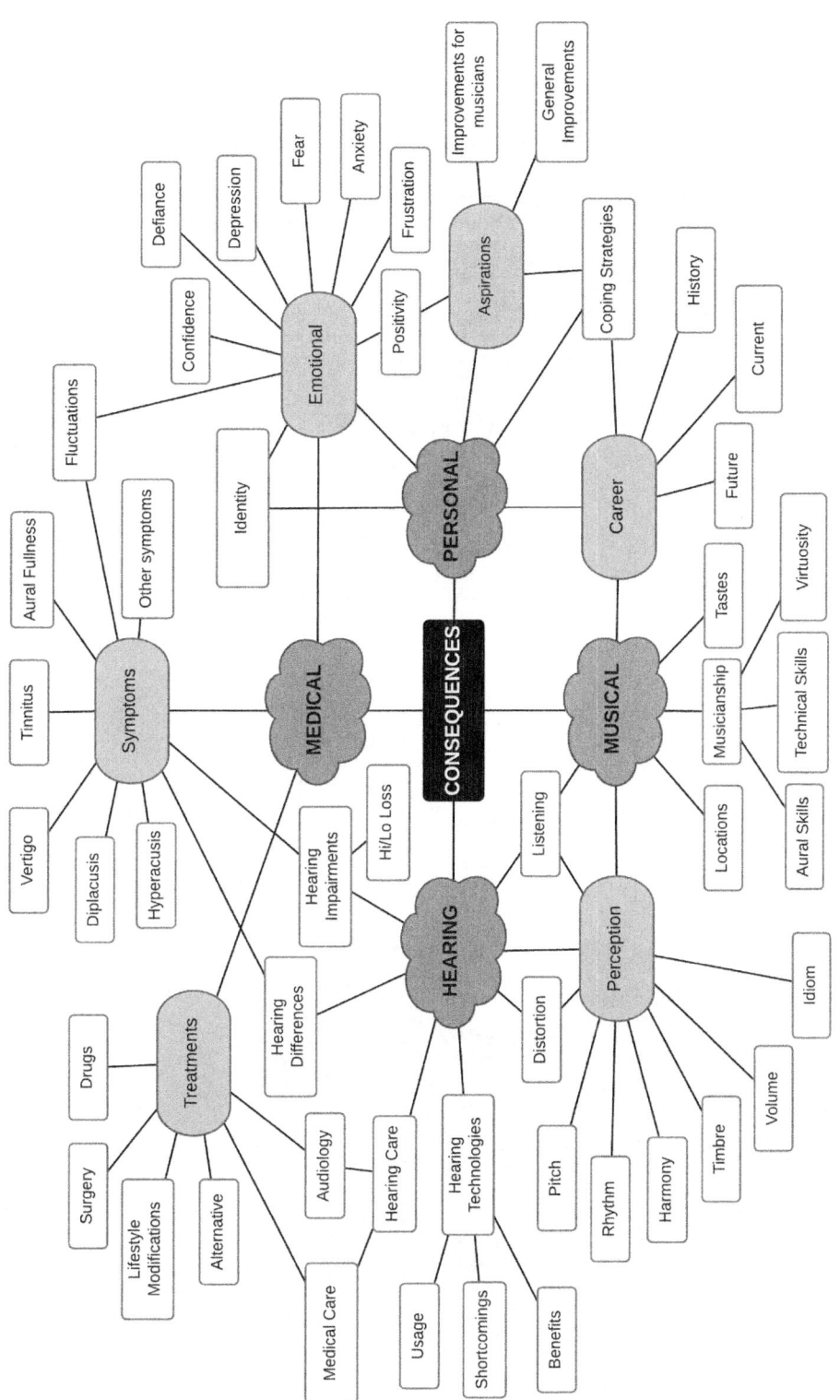

FIGURE 15.1 Thematic map of coded interview responses

FIGURE 15.2 Comparative Word Frequency analysis

To investigate this further, a sentiment analysis of the same data was performed, using the Sentigem API and Rapidminer. This revealed that the MDG's comments were generally less positive and in two cases negative overall. By contrast, the OHD participants, despite their various difficulties, expressed positive sentiments overall. This correlates well with the MDG musicians' descriptions of the unusually tough challenges presented by the unpredictability of Ménière's.

Medical Consequences

The medical consequences comprise an array of common and less well-known symptoms and their treatments. No two Ménière's musicians are exactly alike, as the condition differs a great deal between individuals. For example, it may occur in a single ear (unilateral) or both ears (bilateral) and to varying degrees of intensity over time. However, there were five symptoms reported by all the participants: hearing loss, vertigo, tinnitus, aural fullness, and diplacusis.

Hearing loss was generally unbalanced and severe in the most affected ear. The typical Ménière's hearing profile shows a pronounced loss of low frequencies (the classic 'reverse-slope audiogram'), making this quite different from, say, age-related high-frequency loss. It would fluctuate over time and some participants even reported a temporary return to normal hearing after certain treatments.

Vertigo, while not in itself directly affecting hearing, was widely agreed by the MDG to be the worst symptom of Ménière's:

The vertigo attacks were horrific. I would rather have had, you know, the worst stomach pain you can imagine than being in those attacks, particularly the longer ones which could go on for three and a half hours (MDG-8).

In many cases, vertigo has become less of a problem over time, due either to medical treatments or natural changes such as 'burn out' (gradual cessation of the vertigo effect following destruction of the balance mechanism by the disease), or lifestyle changes. Over time, most of the MDG became more concerned more with hearing loss. Even so, they all agreed that vertigo is a life-changing aspect of the condition that affects everything that follows, including hearing loss. This contrasts sharply with the OHD, only one of whom had ever experienced significant vertigo.

All the MDG experience *tinnitus*, which they mostly characterised as subjective (something only they could hear) and sensory (related to hearing loss or impairment). They were detailed in their descriptions of its triggers, such as caffeine, alcohol, stress, or painkillers. They also observed that an increase in tinnitus usually presages a vertigo attack and, in some cases, the tinnitus goes hand-in-hand with an aversion to sound.

In the OHD group, the only participant who does not experience tinnitus is OHD-5, who was born deaf and is also the only participant fitted with cochlear implants. The causes of tinnitus for the rest of the OHD were much more varied than the MDG, ranging from traumatic head injury to vestibular migraine, from hearing loss to unknown origins dating back to early childhood.

The MDG exhibited some variation in *aural fullness* (an unpleasant sensation of pressure in the ears). MDG-3, for example, has never really noticed fullness, but for MDG-2, 4, and 5, it has been a fundamental aspect of their experience, very painful and challenging, especially when mixed with tinnitus. None of the OHD recorded any aural fullness.

Diplacusis, also known as inter-aural pitch difference, is a phenomenon in which a single auditory stimulus (usually a musical note) is perceived to be made of two separate sounds at different pitches or temporal locations. It is generally regarded as rare amongst musicians with hearing loss (Di Stadio et al. 2018, 9), but is given as an indicator of a differential diagnosis of Ménière's in roughly 50% of cases (Paparella 1991). A major finding of this study is that diplacusis is present in *all* the MDG and *none* of the OHD, with severe consequences for the musicianship of the former. The

MDG participants described the majority of detuned notes as flat (i.e. lower frequency), relative to the in-tune notes. This seems to contradict received wisdom, which suggests that the detuned notes are perceived as sharp. Also, because Ménière's hearing loss is greater in the low register (the reverse-slope audiogram), the tendency is for the fundamentals and lower partials of a given note to disappear, to be replaced by a spectrum of higher partials. These are then subject to the same diplacusis as higher notes, resulting in considerable distortion, which was variously described by the participants as either a difference in pitch or a kind of pitch-doubling effect. Two of the unilateral participants (MDG-4, MDG-8) also commented that the diplacusis can be filtered out by the brain, so that the pitch difference is not generally perceived until headphones are worn. This appears to be a similar phenomenon to listening to a honky-tonk piano, when the brain can hear the intended music despite the acoustic signal being muddied by de-tunings.

Various other Ménière's symptoms included: *Tullio's Phenomenon*, in which dizziness is caused by sudden loud noises (Watson et al. 2000); problems with localisation of sound; 'brain fog' following vertigo attacks; increased photosensitivity; and *hyperacusis* (an increased sensitivity to ordinary sounds or to particular frequencies or timbres). This was a problem for most of the MDG, but by contrast was experienced by only two of the OHD. OHD-6 commented that the amplification of wearing hearing aids can be deafening, while OHD-1 occupies a unique position in the OHD because her difference is not an objectively measurable hearing loss but rather a lifelong neurological condition (autism) that causes an adverse reaction to sound.

Treatments

One major difference between the two groups is the extent of treatments. The MDG have had many different treatments, including dietary and lifestyle modifications (low salt, no caffeine, etc.), stress relief and psychological counselling, allergy treatments, drugs such as betahistine, anti-nausea drugs (e.g. prochlorperazine, cyclizine), diuretics, blood pressure medication, multivitamins, antihistamines, intratympanic injections of steroids or gentamicin, and a range of surgical interventions. The latter can have severe consequences. An endolymphatic sac decompression operation in 1982 resulted in the unexpected complete loss of hearing in the left ear of 19-year-old MDG-2. The effectiveness of the various non-surgical treatments is quite variable, ranging from no effect at all (MDG-8) to restoration of lost hearing (MDG-4). The diversity of treatments and their effects reflects the multi-factorial character of Ménière's, which is more a suite of disorders than a single condition.

For the OHD, by contrast, treatments have consisted mostly of hearing aids with some stress and anxiety management therapies when required. OHD-5 has had cochlear implants fitted.

Most members of both groups have tried therapies for tinnitus, such as: meditation, relaxation techniques, dietary modifications and even drug treatments (antidepressants and diuretics). But the majority in both groups said that hearing aids provide the best relief. The consensus was that, however distressing tinnitus may be, it is something that can be ignored or risen above in time and with practice.

Personal Consequences

Ménière's has irrevocably changed the personal identities of the MDG, both as musicians and human beings. MDG-7 summed up the uncertainties created by fluctuations in the condition thus:

> Oh, it's such a psychological quagmire - it's really hard […] when (my) hearing returns to normal, I don't fit anywhere. I don't fit as disabled. I don't fit as deaf. I don't fit with hearing aids.

Six of the MDG frequently used the words 'fear' or 'terrified'. The three main fears were:

- having a vertigo attack in a difficult situation
- being perceived as incompetent by other musicians (and by themselves)
- worsening of the condition.

The OHD in general were much less fearful. Only OHD-3, whose condition is somewhat similar to Ménière's, confessed to a 'continual fear that the condition will get worse'.

If fear is a triggered response to a threat such as a vertigo attack, then anxiety is the same reaction without the trigger. However, the distinction is also semantic: the MDG often used the word 'fear' to describe their lingering anxieties around the triggered experience, whereas the OHD tended to use 'anxiety' to describe the negative emotional consequences of their generally longer-term conditions. So, for example, whereas MDG-7 described the 'perpetual anxiety at not knowing when and how you're going to be every day', OHD-7 said simply: 'depression and anxiety are a constant with my hearing loss and tinnitus'. Depression was acknowledged by seven of the MDG participants, who required drug treatments or psychotherapy in almost every case. Only two of the OHD mentioned it as a problem, and one of those (OHD-2) has moved past it over time.

Frustration was a common response in both groups to the conditions and especially the limitations they created for musical practice. Lack of confidence was equally widespread. Despite this, almost all the participants displayed both positivity and what MDG-8 called 'defiance' of their conditions. Some have taken an interruption of activity, but all are musically active to some extent. Most have developed coping strategies and some have even used music to re-engage the brain after a vertigo attack.

Musical Consequences

The musical consequences of hearing loss have affected both the careers and the musicianship of participants in both groups. All described how their musical capabilities are conditioned by the characteristics of acoustic spaces. Resonant rooms with high ceilings have led to participants pulling out of rehearsals or performances. Many preferred to work in their own spaces or have built music studios configured to suit their hearing needs. In this respect, there is no difference between the MDG and OHD. Once music-making begins, all participants adapt as best they can.

The participants were asked how they listen: critically (actively analysing what they hear), imaginatively (actively responding to what they hear without analysis) or receptively (passively and uncritically receiving what they hear). The majority described a critical approach to listening that would be expected from such accomplished musicians, but some described different *ways* of listening, such as with the whole body. All stressed the importance of listening to one another, especially in non-notated music-making.

Musical Perceptions

Perception of rhythm is rarely affected in either group, and roughly half the participants experienced difficulties with dynamics (loudness) and musical idiom, but these were spread evenly across the two groups. A distinct picture of the Ménière's musicians emerged from their abilities to detect pitch, harmony, and timbre.

A failure of pitch perception was seen by the majority of participants as the most damaging professionally, especially for musicians who play instruments that require good intonation. All members of the MDG reported problems with this, particularly in lower registers (e.g. 130 Hz and downwards). However, two of the participants were confident that their ability to play in tune or perceive pitch while making music has actually *improved*. In MDG-4's case, this is because the treatments she has undertaken have restored her low frequency hearing. In MDG-8's case, this is because the 'good' ear listens even more closely than before. Despite this, both lacked confidence in their ability to detect pitch accurately. MDG-6 and MDG-2 reported only intermittent or temporary problems, closely linked to diplacusis.

A breakdown in pitch perception can occur at any age. MDG-7, the youngest, gave up performing after being unable to pitch a note in a concert. MDG-1, the oldest, can sing roughly in tune, but is 'generally unable to understand the pitch of what I am hearing'. He attributed this to a long steady decline. The extent of loss of pitching ability seems to be another function of the unpredictability of Ménière's.

Most members of the OHD also experienced pitch perception problems, many in the upper registers where notes tend to blur into one another or disappear altogether. However, OHD-5 and OHD-4, who have both had severe hearing problems since childhood, described being helped by hearing aids or cochlear implants:

> When I got my second [cochlear] implant I realized I could hear very differently the sort of clarinet pitch for the first time.
>
> *(OHD-5)*

> My singing range is that octave below middle C but I'm very aware of the fact that my pitch is very poor down there. And what I instinctively do is just to sing everything up the octave. It's not because I like singing falsetto, although I'm perfectly happy to do it, but it's just that that's where I can pitch it and hearing aids of course help there.
>
> *(OHD-4)*

For the MDG, especially those with bilateral Ménière's, difficulties with perception of *harmony* was marked. Separating individual notes in chords was very challenging. Harmonic combinations sounded like noise, and there was difficulty understanding key changes. A few with unilateral MD were able to adapt their listening somewhat to compensate for the rubbish coming through one ear.

In the OHD, it was the specific nature of the hearing loss that dictated the ability to perceive harmony. Participants with long-term loss, such as OHD-2 and OHD-4, would struggle to hear chord changes. The same was true for OHD-3, who can follow simple harmonic progressions but is lost with more complex chords. OHD-5 preferred simple harmonies, but could recognise intervals such as octaves, thirds, and fifths through their characteristic resonances thanks to the cochlear implants.

The perception of *rhythm* was generally much less of a problem for both groups. In the MDG, only MDG-1 reported rhythmic difficulties, which he related to pitch recognition. In the OHD, OHD-3, and OHD-5 reported issues with anything too polyrhythmic or syncopated, but otherwise rhythmic perception was good.

The MDG found *timbre* more challenging than the OHD. MDG-4 heard flaws in the sound, and three participants reported that they have difficulty identifying instruments. Timbre perceptions vary day-to-day and can also affect pitch perception. 'The timbre of certain sounds can make it difficult for me to hear the pitch when being played in combination with other instruments'

(MDG-2). Several Ménière's participants reporting that diplacusis also distorted timbre as well as pitch.

For the OHD, changes in timbral perception were less of a problem and sometimes even an opportunity. OHD-2 said she 'never used to pay attention to the bass lines when [she] could hear the whole spectrum'. Now she 'pays attention to it, and can really enjoy a song'. OHD-5 commented that 'every single note on the clarinet sounds different and has different qualities produced at a different point of register'. This has become one way in which she can be creative when playing.

Almost everybody struggled with perception of *musical dynamics* (loud/soft). MDG-5 found himself turning up the volume during quiet passages to then find the loud passages too loud. For the majority, coping with the effects of dynamics were mainly a matter of health preservation. MDG-2 treads a fine line between loud and soft, to avoid excessive tinnitus afterwards. MDG-4 wears earplugs and watches how the strings of her violin vibrate to gauge the dynamic level. MDG-7 finds that excessively loud sounds make her balance worse. Many reported physical and psychological consequences of very loud sounds, also affecting perception of timbre. OHD-2 would leap out of her chair if the music was suddenly too loud and found sounds such as harpsichord or recorder annoying. MDG-3 recorded problems with the unpredictable sound of a tuba in particular spaces. MDG-1 found that touch plays an important part in perception of dynamics, and OHD-3 found himself getting irritated by mixes that are too heavy on the higher frequencies.

The interviews explored style or genre. MDG-2 commented:

> I really don't see how my Ménière's experience has affected my music-making with regard to style, idiom, or genre.
>
> *(MDG-2)*

At the other extreme are those whose perception of idiom has been badly affected:

> It's now much more difficult for me to cope with new or difficult music that I've never heard.
>
> *(MDG-1)*

> So louder genres live-wise I would avoid. I think my enjoyment globally of music has decreased. I'm really detached from it comparatively. I just don't get the same kick out of it.
>
> *(MDG-7)*

The perception of idiom seems to have affected participants' musical tastes. MDG-6 described listening to minimalist music (something she had previously enjoyed) as being 'sort of like a like a pneumatic hammer on my head', and MDG-2 nowadays finds himself 'very picky… more drawn to well produced, well planned, and well performed music'. To what extent such shifts in taste might have happened anyway over time is of course unknowable, beyond the obvious observation that everyone's tastes change.

Hearing Consequences

Hearing loss is professionally risky for musicians, because 'the dependence of musicians' success on their full hearing ability multiplies the significance of such disorders' (Pouryaghoub et al. 2017, 34). It is reasonable to assume that musicians are less likely to acknowledge their own hearing loss, and therefore that it is more widespread than is currently recognised, especially in an industry where sustained exposure to loud and intense sounds is commonplace (Chasin 2009). It is the *variability* of Ménière's that presents the greatest challenge:

> After years of variable impairment I am now at a steady bottom!
>
> *(MDG-1)*

> When they tested my ear, my left ear was way different than my other ear, but through my treatment that I've had the last time I had it tested it was back almost back to normal.
>
> *(MDG-4)*

> If I go below 222 Hz, the A below middle C, there's almost nothing now. It was indistinct, but now it's just a sort of buzz.
>
> *(MDG-8)*

All reported distortion when hearing music, whether live or recorded, but it was generally more disturbing for the MDG. MDG-5 described a disturbing physical sensation that vibrates through the whole body, causing a painful 'wobbling' of the eardrum. MDG-4 recalled a strange 'buzzing' from bad quality violins. MDG-2 linked sound distortion to pitch distortion.

In the OHD Group, OHD-3 recounted problems comparing analogue and digital audio quality while mixing and mastering. OHD-6 described 'a flowering of distortion around between 3K and 4K […] now I hear this sort of shadow'. These kinds of phenomena do not seem to be tied to any one kind of hearing loss. In every case, the musicians displayed both an analytical fascination with the distortion and some distress at its consequences.

Hearing Care

All have at some point visited an audiologist. It was clear that there is a difference in expectations between audiologists and musicians. Almost all participants were critical of current audiological practices, citing limitations of the frequency ranges of audiological tests; insufficient consideration given to the quality of sounds within usable hearing range; and a lack of empathy shown by audiologists towards musicians.

Ménière's sufferers often arrived at an audiologist after both they and their doctors have struggled with diagnosis. MDG-7 described the kind of distressing experience that would resonate with many in the MDG:

> It has been so incredibly demoralizing sitting on the floor of emergency under fluorescent lights and an ENT telling you that you're not dizzy, you just need to see a psychiatrist, and just hearing that and knowing that you can't put someone inside your body and make them understand how you're feeling.
>
> *(MDG-7)*

In contrast, the process of audiological care was seen as one by which MDG musicians might be able to take better control of their hearing (and hence lives). As MDG-5 put it:

> I'd almost want my audiologist to be like a producer - to know all the sounds. That would be my dream: to be able to sit with someone who had that vast knowledge of sound and music.
>
> *(MDG-5)*

The frustrations that they experienced were often a result of their realisations of the practical limits on this expectation.

The OHD also expressed some frustrations that audiologists lacked understanding of musicians' needs, but there was some understanding of the challenges facing audiology too:

> I think it's a huge part of the skill of an audiologist being able to debunk those moments when a client has started mustering all the poetic energy that they have, which in the case of some folks is going to be extremely reductive and try to interpret that and turn it into a useful changing calibration.
>
> *(OHD-6)*

Hearing Technologies

In the MDG, only one participant uses hearing aids (HA) when playing or listening to music. This low adoption is mainly because of HA's perceived ineffectiveness in addressing the reverse slope audiogram. However, other problems were also identified: HA can make diplacusis louder and amplify noise; they do not help with directional listening; the general quality of sound is poor; pitch is harder to recognise.

In the OHD group, four use HA when playing or listening to music and three do not. Several recognised that without HA they would be unable to function. There were nevertheless some criticisms. OHD-3 said 'the correction of the HA negates completely the work of the [mixing and mastering] software which flattens the frequency response'. OHD-4 recounted how he still wears the same analogue HA he wore in the 1980s. Despite the lack of support for these aids, he dislikes the way digital aids create an artificial acoustic environment and remove quieter sounds which may the intended objects of focus by the musician. OHD-5 compared the sound quality of HA unfavourably with cochlear implants. OHD-6 described the limitations of his HA quite analytically:

> I discovered it was like listening to a cone filter notched downwards at the crossovers between every single band in the graphic equalizer, which is so utterly useless. Impossible to work with for a musician.
>
> *(OHD-6)*

In non-musical situations, HA adoption in the MDG is higher, with four using them at least some of the time. Five of the OHD use them all the time.

The most common complaint from almost all the participants was that HA are designed for speech and not for music. This echoes recent findings from large-scale quantitative studies (e.g. Greasley et al. 2019). Age-related hearing loss (presbycusis) was never cited as a problem by any of the participants, but one mentioned frustration with his HA because he believed that it *only* addressed presbycusis. The main suggested improvements to HA were a focus on the quality rather than quantity of sound, empowerment of the user through greater control and a better provision for low frequency loss.

Discussion

Ménière's affects a relatively small but significant group within the wider community, with its own distinctive features (Greasley, Hugill, & Jacques 2019). The reverse-slope audiogram is the most immediately apparent difference from other forms of hearing loss. This combines with diplacusis to bring about a disproportionate reduction in the ability to perceive pitch and harmony. In Ménière's, tinnitus varies wildly and this combines with symptoms such as aural fullness to add to the confusion. Vertigo, quite apart from its debilitating aspects, adds fear and anxiety into the mix.

For music-making, this has varying consequences. Some of the MDG participants reported a decline followed by an improvement in musicianship skills as their condition has fluctuated. For others, there has been a continuous decline leading to an almost complete breakdown in ability. Such variability has had inevitably negative consequences for any kind of professional career, something that those in the OHD group who have had very long-term difference have largely overcome. This in turn has affected the sense of personal identity of the MDG and their emotional wellbeing.

The personal commitment of the participants to continued music-making was impressive. Each of them has had to undergo an enormous personal struggle, involving sometimes both physical and psychological pain. They have developed coping strategies that enable them to continue. They also have strong aspirations, both for themselves and for the wider community of hearing-impaired people. Almost all the participants called for more understanding and tolerance of people with hearing loss, improved HA, and better environmental controls on noise levels. MDG-5 and OHD-7 argued for better support groups and networks for musicians with hearing loss. MDG-8 and MDG-4 wanted more education and research into hearing loss. OHD-5 made a passionate plea for aural diversity.

The most common suggestion was that a set of audiology tests for musicians should be developed. While this is not in itself a new idea (Uys & van Dijk 2011), it would be a welcome novelty to the participants. Supra-threshold assessment, while not directly relevant in selecting and fitting amplification, is of great importance to the musicians. Signs of awareness of this need in audiologists would do much to promote a sense of empathy.

Acknowledgements

I would like to pay tribute to the participants who were interviewed for this project. I would also like to thank GN Hearing for their generous funding, and Jennifer Groth for her very helpful critical feedback.

References

Braun, V., & Clarke, V. (2006) 'Using thematic analysis in psychology', *Qualitative Research in Psychology*, 3: 77–101.
Bryant, A., & Charmaz, K. (eds) (2007) *The SAGE Handbook of Grounded Theory*. Los Angeles: Sage.
Chasin, M. (2009) *Hearing Loss in Musicians: Prevention and Management*. San Diego: Plural Publishing.
Di Stadio, A., Dipietro, L., Ricci, G., Della Volpe, A., Minni, A., Greco, A., De Vincentiis, M., & Ralli, M. (2018) 'Hearing loss, tinnitus, hyperacusis, and diplacusis in professional musicians: A systematic review', *Int. J. Environ. Res. Public Health*, 15: 2120.
Drever, J. (2017) 'The case for auraldiversity in acoustic regulations and practice: The hand dryer noise story', *24th International Congress on Sound and Vibration*, London, pp. 1–6.
Flint, P. et al. (2014) *Cummings Otolaryngology*, 6th Edition. Philadelphia: Saunders.
Greasley, A.E., Crook, H., & Beeston, A.V. (2019) 'Hearing aids for music: Findings and recommendations for hearing aid users, audiologists, manufacturers and researchers', final report of the AHRC-funded *Hearing Aids for Music* project. 12 April 2019. Available at www.musicandhearingaids.org/resources (accessed 17 July 2021).

Greasley, A.E., Hugill, A., & Jacques, A. (in preparation). 'Music and Meniere's: insights into music listening and performance through hearing aids'.

Havia, M., Kentala, E., & Pyykkö (2004) 'Hearing loss and tinnitus in Ménière's Disease', *Auris Nasus Larynx*, 29(2): 115–19.

Hugill, A. (2018) 'Composing (my) hearing: some reflections'. Available at https://andrewhugill.com/writings/Composing_hearing.html (accessed 17 July 2021).

Hugill, A. (2019) 'Aural diversity: A journey back to music'. Available at www.auraldiversity.org (accessed 17 July 2021).

Jacques, A (2009) 'Musicophilia' [Letter to the editor]. *Spin*, p. 70.

Katsarkas, A. (1996) 'Hearing loss and vestibular dysfunction in Ménière's disease', *Acta Otolaryngol (Stockh)*, 116: 185–8.

Lee, C.-S., Paparella, M., Margolis, R., & Le, C. (1995) 'Audiological profiles and Meniere's disease', *ENT J*, 74: 527–32.

Lopez-Escamez, J.A., Carey, J., Chung, W.H., Goebel, J.A., Magnusson, M., Mandala, M., Newman-Toker, D.E., Strupp, M., Suzuki, M., Trabalzini, F., & Bisdorff, A., Classification Committee of the Barany S., Japan Society for Equilibrium R., European Academy of Ontology and Neurotology; Equilibrium Committee of the American Academy of Otolaryngology–Head and Neck Surgery; Korean Balance Society. (2015) 'Diagnostic criteria for Ménière's disease'. *J. Vestib. Res.*, 25: 1–7.

Musicians4Hearing (2019) Available at http://musicians4hearing.org (accessed 30 August 2019).

Paparella, M.M. (1991) 'Pathogenesis and pathophysiology of Ménière's disease', *Acta Otolaryngol Suppl.*, 485: 26–35.

Patel, H., & Isildak, H. (2016) 'Ménière's disease: An overview', *Operative Techniques in Otolarygology*, 27: 184–187.

Patton, M.Q. (1990) *Qualitative Evaluation and Research Methods*. Newbury Park, CA: Sage.

Pouryaghoub, G., Mehrdad, R., & Pourhosein, S. (2017) 'Noise-induced hearing loss among professional musicians', *J Occup Health.*, 59(1): 33–7. doi:10.1539/joh.16-0217-OA

Sajjadi, H., & Papparella, M.M. (2008) 'Ménière's disease', *The Lancet*, 372(9636): 406–14.

Uys, M., & van Dijk, C. (2011) 'Development of a music perception test for adult hearing-aid users', *South Afr J Commun Disord*, 58: 19–47.

Watson, S.R.D., Halmagyi, M., & Colebatch, J.G. (2000) 'Vestibular hypersensitivity to sound (Tullio phenomenon)', *Neurology*, 54: 722–8.

16
SOCIALISING AND MUSICKING WITH MILD COGNITIVE IMPAIRMENT

A Case Study from Rural Cornwall

Chris J. H. Cook

Introduction

One of the earliest symptoms of the onset of a dementia is often some kind of change in auditory abilities. Auditory scene analysis (Bregman 1990, 3–9),[1] speech or prosody comprehension, and recognition of environmental sounds are indicative of the kinds of ability that can be affected, and the identification of such changes can potentially be useful in distinguishing between different dementias in diagnosis, as they correlate with the various syndromes (Hardy et al. 2016). People with Lewy body diseases such as Parkinson's disease or dementia with Lewy bodies, for example, may experience sound detection issues such as auditory hallucinations (Golden & Josephs 2015, 3794)[2] while people with behavioural-variant frontotemporal dementia may become inattentive or averse to environmental sounds and music (Hardy et al. 2346–7). Alzheimer's dementia, meanwhile, can make it difficult for people to locate, distinguish between, and keep track of sound sources in noisy environments. It can also lead to hyperacusis: an increased sensitivity to sound resulting in a lower threshold of sound pain. It is on this general phenotype, or group of symptoms, that I shall focus here, as Trevor – a key interlocutor in my doctoral research with whom I worked to compose a piece of sonic ethnography exploring his sound world and changing listening abilities – has a diagnosis of mild cognitive impairment (MCI).

MCI is not technically considered to be a type of dementia as it does not affect multiple domains of cognition, nor does it have such a similarly extensive impact on a person's day-to-day life (Knopman & Peterson 2014, 1453). It is, however, most commonly caused by underlying Alzheimer's disease and greatly increases the likelihood of later receiving a dementia diagnosis. It also correlates with auditory disorientation (auditory scene analysis issues) and hyperacusis, similarly to Alzheimer's dementia (Idrizbegovic et al. 2011, 250). These are factors that impact on Trevor's quality of life and, in particular, his social life, as he is an amateur musician playing the descant recorder in an early music ensemble, amongst various other musical pursuits.[3]

Unsurprisingly, the overwhelming majority of discussions of the auditory symptoms of dementias are to be found in neurological literature, where they are a topic of increasing clinical interest (Hardy et al. 2016, 2339). But as we shall see, the ways in which such symptoms play out in individual lives can have multiple social impacts ranging from the insidious to the acute, and thus warrant closer sociological investigation. The auditory aspects of these illnesses touch upon wider themes of disability, acoustic ecology, ethnomusicology, and of course, aural diversity. I have previously argued for the ethical and epistemological merits of taking a dialogic and practice-based approach to such research, as well as outlined some of the challenges and imbalances thereof, in relation to the year or so I intermittently spent conducting fieldwork with Trevor (Cook 2021). But I did not discuss the ways in which Trevor's auditory abilities might work to subvert or support his personhood, and this is a crucial aspect to consider in understanding how such abilities can further mediate people's relationships to their physical and social environments if they develop a dementia.

Person-Centred Care and Acoustic Habitus

Personhood is an important concept in contemporary dementia care practice, with Tom Kitwood's *Dementia Reconsidered: The Person Comes First* considered a foundational text (Kitwood 1997). Prior philosophies of selfhood in Alzheimer's dementia had maintained that, because new experiences are not generally retained, the person's sense of being and thus selfhood were disrupted in a process of 'unbecoming' (Fontana & Smith 1989). Kitwood advocated instead for praxis emphasising 'personhood': an explicitly relational conception of selfhood which is grounded in feelings and relationships (Kitwood, 80–93). Interconnection, interdependence, and intersubjectivity are essential to Kitwood's description of personhood, meaning that it can be bestowed by others and supported through recognition and validation in conversations or activities acknowledging relationships, emotions, identity, reflection, and creativity. With further theorisation emphasising the situatedness of a person over time through, for example, embodiment, emplacement, and habitus,[4] the selfhood of people with dementia is considered to require the support of a person's agentive potential (Hughes 2001; Kontos 2005; Baldwin & Capstick 2007). And although such efforts are seldom sufficiently resourced, dementia care praxis now routinely aims to take a 'person-centred' approach, focussing on how individuals with a dementia can be empowered by caregivers through references to their self-identity and sociality prior to their dementia.

Acoustic ecology and sound studies literatures are replete with examples of people's embodiment, connection, socialisation, emplacement, immersion, enculturation, and enskilment (and sometimes their inversions) through sound (Sterne 2012). The effects of dementias on auditory abilities could foreseeably touch upon any of these processes. In one study, for example, an avid birdwatcher with semantic dementia (another syndrome caused by frontotemporal lobe degeneration) had become notably less able to recognise bird calls or names but could still visually recognise the birds relatively well (Muhammed et al. 2018). He was able to identify birds' size and migratory behaviour characteristics from the calls but was less able to identify whether they were wetland dwellers or not, leading the researchers to speculate that those categories of his avian auditory knowledge that could be inferred from the sound (e.g. size) or recalled through episodic memories (e.g. the seasonality of previous sightings) enabled him to recognise sounds, but other more arbitrary associations (e.g. names and habitat knowledge) were affected in line with his syndrome's usual phenotype. As a birder of 30 years' experience, one could imagine the various species, places, soundscapes, and social groups he was familiar with from his practice might all be resources for supporting personhood in his case, were these various kinds of relations brought into his care through conversations or reminiscence materials.

In a frequently concurrent area of auditory impairment, there are some obvious similarities here to the account given of a highly particular way in which naturalist Richard Mabey was affected by the progression of presbycusis (Mabey 2005, 155–8). Unable to hear blackcaps and swifts, as well as parts of warbler calls to such an extent that he did not recognise them, Mabey assumed that the biodiversity of his local area was declining. Years after the disappearances, however, he overcame a disdain for enhancing technologies and tried listening again with a directional microphone and headphones, discovering that not only were the expected species still present in the environment, but that further sonic and thus ecological detail was now detectable to him. Mabey's presbycusis had negatively inflected his relationship with his local environment as a result of his intersecting contextual knowledge of climate change.

The mixes of specialised and tacit sonic knowledges over time in these two examples provide some insight into the ways in which soundscapes and individual acoustic habitus (or, when shared by a community, acoustemology) (Feld 2003) might be implicated in how someone's personhood is affected by illness through sound. As the precise symptoms and trajectories of illness amongst people with any kind of dementia are highly specific to each individual – one of the primary factors that motivated moves towards person-centred approaches in dementia care – it follows that the effects of a dementia on someone's everyday listening will be similarly variable.

Trevor's Social Auditory Space: Wednesday Wanderers

Living alone in St Just, a small town near Penzance in west Cornwall, a large part of Trevor's social life derives from his membership of two dementia-friendly activity groups organised by the Sensory Trust. This is a charity based in St Austell which provides accessible, nature-based activities for children with disabilities, people with autism, people with dementia, and carers. It was in one of their dementia-friendly activity groups, the 'Wednesday Wanderers' walking group, that I first met Trevor.

The Wednesday Wanderers meet every Wednesday fortnight in the broad locality of St Ives, where this particular group is based (the Sensory Trust runs several others serving different areas across Cornwall). Each session consists of a walk in a scenic location, which must be reachable with a car and have had a risk assessment of the route to be taken carried out by the charity beforehand. The walk is either followed by a visit to a local cafe or includes a stop for tea somewhere along the route. The group comprises between five and ten beneficiaries accompanied by a similar number of family carers and volunteers trained by the charity. There tends to also be a mix of newer and older members, with some – including Trevor – having participated in the group for over five years. Important social support relationships are formed through the group, with many interactions also taking place outside of their official meetings. During the COVID-19 lockdowns, the Sensory Trust organised telephone calls amongst its group members in an attempt to provide a continuation of these crucial support networks.

Trevor's Barriers to Wednesday Wanderers Participation

Within the various scenarios of the Wednesday Wanderers' activity outlined above, several impacts of Trevor's auditory symptoms on his participation are notable. The cafe visits, for instance, present him with two major challenges. Firstly, the visits are often to relatively small establishments, such as one I attended in the back of a village Post Office. The whooshing of the coffee maker, scraping of chairs on the floor, clattering of crockery, and various simultaneous conversations happening amongst members of the group made for a very complex and dynamic acoustic environment, or auditory scene. The close proximity of the various sound sources within the splashily reverberant space meant that I struggled to hear what people were saying at times; the difficulty of understanding speech within this challenging auditory scene was compounded for Trevor. He has a degree of presbycusis, meaning that a higher cognitive load is required to decode the information sought from the relatively reduced sound components detectable by him. As the greatest risk factor for the more common types of dementia is age, this comorbidity frequently intersects with the impairments of auditory scene analysis that can occur with Alzheimer's disease (Golden et al. 2015, 700). The acoustic environment of the small cafe was also quite loud, with the number of people attending the group resulting in both more simultaneous conversations and a relative increase in incidental noise from the cafe's functioning. Trevor's hyperacusis caused him to seek out a slightly quieter spot at the end of the table and to pull his sweater hood over his head. I observed that he did not seem able to engage in conversations during this part of the session to the same extent that he was on the walk immediately prior.

Of course, when a Wednesday Wanderers session involves a tea stop en route rather than a cafe visit, this part of proceedings takes place outside. Participants are spaced a little more widely, usually on some combination of public benches and a few folding chairs which the volunteers carry for the occasion. Should these chairs scrape on the ground, the sound is not reflected to any great extent, while the insulated flask used for the beverages does not produce a wide, loud noise spectrum in regular use as do espresso machines. Cardboard cups are also provided, eliminating clattering. This all makes for a more accessible acoustic environment for someone with auditory scene analysis impairments, as foreground sounds (such as speech that one is trying to listen to) are more audible with reduced background sound levels and fewer competing sounds to disambiguate them from. The greater signal-to-noise ratio of this auditory scene also has an effect on group sociality in that fewer simultaneous conversations tend to happen: one is less likely to end up talking only to those most proximate when it is possible to hear people who are further away, so more of the group is able participate in a conversation. For Trevor in particular, the preferability of outdoor tea stops is heightened due to impaired vision. He is registered with the Royal National Institute of Blind People as severely sight impaired and cannot rely on being able to lipread indoors. The decision to take tea en route is, of course, necessarily informed by a wider range of factors than just the auditory scene. The group will still walk in light rain, for example, but stopping outside for too long could quickly lead to beneficiaries becoming uncomfortably cold. Even if the general awareness across the group of particular challenges posed by auditory impairments was higher, the accessibility of the auditory physical and social spaces of the sessions would continue to require a balancing of multiple concerns. There is no simple solution beyond increasing awareness to ensure that auditory accessibility is critically considered in group plans.

Another issue Trevor mentioned relates to his difficulty with navigating social conventions around loudness in the car journeys to and from the walks. Transport for those who need it is provided in collaboration with local networks of volunteer drivers. The drivers play an important role in facilitating beneficiaries' participation in the group, and thus in the maintenance of support networks. Keenly aware of this role and the good intentions of volunteers, Trevor sometimes finds himself being reluctant to ask for the radio to be turned down. In fact, as multiple members may travel in the same vehicle, the range of sound sensitivities therein has, as Trevor described it, produced situations where some want the radio turned up while he would rather it was turned down. As awareness of presbycusis is at a higher level amongst the general population, the kind of default level set by the driver is likely to be too high for Trevor. He pointed out, though, that mentioning this could come across as confrontational or ungrateful, unless he were to try to explain his different experiencing of loudness and thus derail whatever conversation was taking place in the car.

Meanwhile, Trevor has also had difficulty participating in the lockdown-necessitated telephone calls that have characterised the recent life of the group. As a result of his particular combination of auditory symptoms, Trevor has a notable aversion to telephone use. Telephone phobia is more commonly associated with anxiety issues and speech impediments (Marshall 1994, 30), but it is not surprising that Trevor highlighted it given the nature of speech-in-noise comprehension impairments that can be caused by Alzheimer's disease. One specific auditory impairment underlying this broader category of impairment is a change in the ability to perceive very short gaps or silences in continuous signals, making it hard to hear separations between words being spoken (Hardy et al. 2016, 2344, 2349). By design, signal bandwidth is relatively narrow in telephone systems to allow more calls to be transmitted simultaneously on the same line. Combined with the often-suboptimal signal-to-noise ratio of Trevor's landline; the acousmatic condition of telephonic listening; Trevor's presbycusis; and the risk of sound pain due to his hyperacusic threshold shift should he not hear something – causing it to be repeated louder – telephone use has accumulated negative connotations for Trevor. This has further mediated his relationship with the group at precisely the time where people everywhere have needed to proactively find ways to maintain their social interactivity.

Trevor's Musicking

Alongside his participation in the Sensory Trust groups, Trevor's other main source of social interaction relates to musical practice. His musicking – Christopher Small's term referring to any kind of engagement with music (Small 1998) – largely consists of rehearsals with an early music ensemble, as well as other, more solitary musical activities, such as listening to recordings and undertaking instrumental practice. The first time I spoke to Trevor, at a session with the Wednesday Wanderers on the King George V Memorial Walk in Hayle in 2018, our conversation took in various forms of musicking: the instruments we had played previously, our experiences of music education, our tastes in music, and the early music ensemble he has played in for over a decade. The ensemble is named 'Western Wynd', after the sixteenth-century *cantus firmus* of masses by Taverner, among others. Now primarily a recorder duo in which Trevor plays the descant recorder, the ensemble once included a relatively wide and variable array of instruments such as bass viol and crumhorn, until previous members either moved or passed away. Trevor had at times played the violin (his first instrument) and cor anglais (probably his favourite instrument) in the ensemble, in addition to the recorder.

The most basic cognitive issues that affect Trevor have been changes in his abilities to form topographical memories and to retain some short-term memories. While the combined impairments of vision and both spatial and short-term memory have necessitated increased planning whenever he needs to travel, they have also forced him to develop a highly particular strategy with regards to musical performance. When approaching a repeat sign in a score, Trevor often cannot remember whether the section has already been repeated (meaning that the repeat sign is ignored with the musician instead continuing on to the next bar). In one of several instances where his listening struck me as being particularly discerning, he thus starts listening out for indications in the other musicians' performances that they are on the second iteration of a section already: a slightly exaggerated rallentando (decreasing pace) or diminuendo (decreasing level), for example. Trevor's long-standing abilities as a musician in picking up such expressive cues enable him to work around his uncertainty of short-term memory in this situation. The strategy is more effective when he is playing with musicians he has played with for longer, as he has become more familiar with their performance styles with increasing experience.

Trevor's Barriers to Music Participation

With the narrowing of opportunities for social interaction that resulted from Western Wynd's reduction to a duo, Trevor tried joining a community recorder ensemble in Helston. This one was not as conveniently located, requiring two bus changes to reach the house where they rehearsed.

As a community-oriented group emphasising a participatory rather than presentational musical practice (Turino 2008), the number of players who would be present each week was not known beforehand. On those occasions when more than three or four players were present, the sound levels became too loud for Trevor to manage. The amount of time and expense involved in attending the group, which Trevor otherwise enjoyed as he got on well with the people and liked the repertoire, meant that he stopped participating due to his hyperacusis.

Over the course of my time with Trevor, it became apparent that the specific timbres and sonorities of many musical instruments could each pose challenges for him in different ways. It became increasingly painful for him to play the violin early on in his illness, due largely to the relatively short distance between the sound holes and the player's ears. Sounds which are loud, bright, and high-pitched in general are problematic; he referred especially to the particular kind of excitable, whistle-register scream produced by toddlers as being a sound that can result in both a headache and feelings of nauseousness for him, with the nauseousness returning in waves of decreasing severity when he involuntarily remembers the sound over the coming hours. Another instance of this distinctive pattern of recurring distress in recalling an earlier sensory impression was several years earlier, as part of a pre-rehearsal warm up, when a trombonist played a note as loudly as possible. Trevor recalled that it was a note around the middle of the instrument's range and lasted only for a second or so, but the sensation of searing pain was immediate and quickly followed by a bout of nausea with an ongoing headache. Later, when he mentioned how the loud note had been painful and caused him to feel sick, others present thought he was overreacting or being dramatic. Again, a low general awareness of hyperacusis – a term which Trevor himself did not know at the time – amongst a social group meant that the need for some accommodation of his hearing profile went unrecognised.

Conclusion

It is not surprising that musicians might pride themselves on their sensory acuity as listeners: listening skills are honed over years of experience in practice, participation, and performance. Trevor, for instance, can discern which of the local piano tuners has tuned the piano in a church hall when he performs there, as he has played in many local churches over the years. A similar ability is also evident in his disdain for the Foley sound of bedsheets in *The Archers* radio drama, which sound more like plastic bags to him than cotton sheets. Trevor's acuity with regard to sounds that he cares about – sounds that relate to his self-identity as a musician, a radio drama aficionado, and a Wednesday Wanderer, for instance – came across to me as an important aspect of his personhood. This may be partly why Trevor was evidently keen to point out to me how he finds low awareness of hyperacusis and auditory disorientation in his social environment so demoralising.

As Suzel Reily and Katherine Brucher state, '[m]usicking ... is an effective technology of interactivity that is used throughout the world in mediating people's relations to their localities, shaping their commitments to the locality and to the people with whom they interact within it' (Reily and Brucher 2018, 2). Trevor's issues around sound intensity and intelligibility in speech and music sounds demonstrate that disability is a result of interactions between bodies and environments, be they physical or social.

Acknowledgements

I would like to thank Trevor Synge-Perrin for all his time and insights in contributing to this research. Thanks also to the Wednesday Wanderers and Ellie Robinson-Carter of the Sensory Trust for making me feel welcome, and to CHASE-AHRC/Goldsmiths for funding the research.

Notes

1 'Auditory scene analysis' is a cognitive process in which the complex mixture of all sounds arriving at the ears is deconstructed into the various discrete sound sources (or 'auditory streams') that a hearing person perceives.
2 Muffled, rustling-type sounds and choral music are commonly reported, with comorbid hearing impairments increasing the reporting of musical hallucinations originating from earlier in life, e.g. children's songs and school hymns.
3 To be sure, Trevor's hyperacusis does not seem to be a result of hair-cell recruitment, which can result in similar outcomes. Recruitment issues are usually a result of presbycusis and occur when sound frequencies are not detected due to damaged hair cells, leading others to raise their voices so that the person will hear them. Above a certain amplitude, the membrane below the hair cells distorts such that nearby hair cells are activated, making the sound suddenly both detectable and very loud. Trevor did not recognise this characteristic 'jump' in loudness when I described it to him, nor did he appear to react in such a manner when we encountered conditions where it might have occurred.
4 'Habitus' is sociologist Pierre Bourdieu's term describing those accumulated ways of perceiving, gesturing, holding oneself, and the like, that people pick up through experience and through which they can demonstrate insider status.

References

Baldwin, C., & Capstick, A. (2007) 'Personhood: Critical commentary', in Baldwin, C. & Capstick, A. (eds), *Tom Kitwood on Dementia: A Reader and Critical Commentary*, pp. 173–87. Maidenhead: Open University Press.
Bregman, A.S. (1990) *Auditory Scene Analysis: The Perceptual Organization of Sound*. Cambridge, MA: MIT Press.
Cook, C.J.H. (2021) '*Trevurr*: A Dialogic Composition on Dementia, Auraldiversity, and Companion Listening', *Organised Sound*, 26(2): 230–39.
Feld, S. (2003) 'A rainforest acoustemology', in Bull, M. & Back, L. (eds), *The Auditory Culture Reader*, pp. 223–40. Oxford: Berg.
Fontana, A., & Smith, R.W. (1989) 'Alzheimer's disease victims: The 'unbecoming' of self and the normalization of competence', *Sociological Perspectives*, 32(1): pp. 35–46.
Golden, E.C., & Josephs, K.A. (2015) 'Minds on replay: Musical hallucinations and their relationship to neurological disease', *Brain*, 138(12): 3793–3802.
Golden, H.L., Agustus, J.L., Goll, J.C., Downey, L.E., Mummery, C.J., Schott, J.M., Crutch, S.J., & Warren, J.D. (2015) 'Functional neuroanatomy of auditory scene analysis in Alzheimer's disease', *NeuroImage: Clinical*, 7: 699–708.
Hardy, C.J.D., Marshall, C.R., Golden, H.L., Clark, C.N., Mummery, C.J., Griffiths, T.D., Bamiou, D.-E., & Warren, J.D. (2016) 'Hearing and dementia', *Journal of Neurology*, 263(11): 2339–54.
Hughes, J.C. (2001) 'Views of the person with dementia', *Journal of Medical Ethics*, 27(2): 86–91.
Idrizbegovic, E., Hederstierna, C., Dahlquist, M., Nordström, C.K., Jelic, V., & Rosenhall, U. (2011) 'Central auditory function in early Alzheimer's disease and in mild cognitive impairment', *Age and Ageing*, 40(20): 249–54.
Kitwood, T. (1997) *Dementia Reconsidered: The Person Comes First*. Maidenhead: Open University Press.
Knopman, D.S., & Peterson, R.C. (2014) 'Mild cognitive impairment and mild dementia: A clinical perspective', *Mayo Clinic Proceedings*, 89(10): 1452–9.
Kontos, P.C. (2005) 'Embodied selfhood in Alzheimer's disease: Rethinking person-centred care', *Dementia*, 4(4): 553–70.
Mabey, R. (2005) *Nature Cure*. London: Chatto & Windus.
Marshall, J.R. (1994) *Social Phobia: From Shyness to Stage Fright*. New York: Basic Books.
Muhammed, L., Hardy, C.J.D., Russell, L.L., Marshall, C.R., Clark, C.N., Bond, R.L., Warrington, E.K., & Warren, J.D. (2018) 'Agnosia for bird calls', *Neuropsychologia*, 113: 61–7.

Reily, S.A., & Brucher, K. (2018) 'Local Musicking: An Introduction', in Reily, S.A. & Brucher, K. (eds), *The Routledge Companion to the Study of Local Musicking*, pp. 1–12. Abingdon: Routledge.

Small, C. (1998) *Musicking: The Meanings of Performing and Listening.* Middletown, CN: Wesleyan University Press.

Sterne, J. (2012) 'Sonic imaginations', in Sterne, J. (ed.), *The Sound Studies Reader*, pp. 1–18. Abingdon: Routledge.

Turino, T. (2008) *Music as Social Life: The Politics of Participation.* Chicago: University of Chicago Press.

17

THOMAS MACE

A Hearing-Impaired Musician and Musical Thinker in the Seventeenth Century

Matthew Spring

Introduction

Age related hearing loss is a normal part of the human condition and for musicians, both today and in the past, the problem of maintaining a musical life in the face of increasing auditory impairment is all too familiar. Up until Beethoven's well documented career we know relatively little about the practical response musicians made to hearing loss; the subject by its very nature being taboo for those hoping to maintain a successful professional practice.[1] In the past a career as a performer was often the preserve of the young, in some cases the very young; and musicians who continued to perform into old age were relatively uncommon. All too often deafness could be the first step on the road to destitution and bankruptcy. The precarious position of elderly musicians found a response in the setting up of 'The Royal Society of Musicians' which was founded in 1738 as the quaintly titled 'Fund for decay'd musicians', with Handel as a founder member and major benefactor.[2] This chapter explores the ways that hearing loss affected the thinking on music of one particular seventeenth-century English lutenist, Thomas Mace (c. 1613–1706), and the practical steps he took to continue his professional life. I discuss how Mace was an inspiration to me as a fellow deaf lutenist and further consider why Mace could be important to us today in his response to disability, and the lessons we can learn from his experience.

Thomas Mace's book *Musick's Monument* (1676) is perhaps the most important English source of solo lute music after 1640 and contains other music for viol and theorbo.[3] Apart from the music it contains it is also one the most important books on many aspects of musical practice from the seventeenth century. As well as being a lute and viol player Mace was an active teacher and singing man at Trinity College Cambridge from 1635 to his death in 1706. Crucially he experienced hearing loss around or after middle age yet managed to continue his musical life as a player, singer and teacher. In response Mace modified his instrument to help him hear, designed an acoustical performing chamber to maximise the sound potential of an enclosed space, and invented new instruments. Interestingly Mace never liked loudness for its own sake but always strived for an equality of sound that would allow all parts from highest to the lowest to be heard with clarity; and thought about instruments and spaces that could best achieve this.

I had not heard of Mace until I studied the lute with Diana Poulton in the years 1977–9. She was a compelling and interesting musician in her own right, had been taught by Arnold

Dolmetsch, and has been the subject of a recent biography (Abbott 2013). She lent me her copy of *Musick's Monument* and, as I read the book, I quickly became aware that Mace had suffered a considerable loss of hearing by the time he was preparing his book, but that he had not been deterred and had sought his own solutions to his situation. As a fellow lute payer and one that had experienced considerable hearing loss in early childhood I was particularly drawn by Mace's writings and life experiences. Like Mace I have managed a career as a teacher, performer, and writer on music. Mace has been an example and an inspiration to me in showing that deafness need not preclude a life in music, and alternative approaches can be sought and found.

Mace and Disability

Well known to lutenists and to some extent viol players, Mace's importance as a polemicist and writer on practical music-making and on 'affect' in music is often overlooked. Above all Mace argued for 'expression and expressivity' in performance and not for instrumental music played 'in a pure and uninflected way' characteristic of much contemporary performance of seventeenth-century music (Hancock 2011, 1). Mace's jovial and optimistic written style, and his gift for multiple adjectives, hides the increasingly difficult circumstances of his middle and old age. In his first publication, a pamphlet on how to improve the road system in England in the 1670s, titled *Profit Conveniencey and Pleasure to the whole Nation, being a short rational discourse lately presented to his majesty concerning the high ways of England (1675)*, Mace included an epistle to the King with the following revealing passage:

> I am no courtier, know not how to Mode,
> But bluntly this contrive for public good.
> And though I'm well-nigh Deaf and well-nigh
> Blind; (Mace 1675).

This is the only reference in all of Mace's works to his loss of sight. References to his loss of hearing are more common and he touches upon in *Musick's Monument* when explaining his Lute-Dyphone (Mace 1966a, 203). Certainly, hearing problems would have made his duties as a lay clerk of Trinity College difficult in the extreme. On 17 April 1706 a singing man's place was made void by 'Mr Mace' at Trinity College, and there is no suggestion that this was anyone other than Mace (Tilmouth & Spring 2013). Thus, it would seem that he kept his place, at least in name, until his death. Probably he was able to continue his singing for a time despite his loss, but for how long is not known and it is possible that he may have had to employ a deputy.

Nothing is heard from Mace after 1676 until 1690 when an ad appeared in London which included the following:

> Men say the times are strange; 'tis True
> 'Cause many strange things hap to be;
> Let it not then seem strange to you,
> To here one strange thing more to see.

In Devereaux Court, next the Grecian Coffee House, at the Temple Back-gate, There is a Deaf Person Teacheth Musick to Perfection; who by reason of his great age v. 77 is come to Town, with his whole stock of rich musical furniture and instruments and books to put off, to whomsoever delights in such choice things; for he hath nothing light or vain, but all substantial and solid music.

(GB-Lbl Harley 5396, no. 386, fo. 129v)

There follows a list of articles for sale including an organ, a pair of viols, his pedal-harpsichord, a single harpsichord, a double-lute (Mace's Dyphone), several other lutes, viols, and theorboes, and a large collection of music and books including unsold copies of *Musick's Monument*, which he is prepared to dispose of cheaply. Crucially it seems that Mace had continued his musical life as far as teaching was concerned, at least until 1690. Mace stayed only four months in London and in 1698 he published his last pamphlet *Riddles, Mervels and Rarities or A New way of Health, from an Old Man's Experience* (Cambridge) (Mace 1698). This pamphlet is partly an advert for his 'English Priest's Powder' and does not touch upon his deafness though it gives advice on many aspects of health and wellbeing and the part music can play in this.

Mace and Trinity College

Mace was probably born around 1613 and lived to the advanced age of 93. He started learning the lute in 1621 at the age of eight and at 13 he was singing in the chapel of Trinity College, Cambridge. Mace's uncle was already a lay clerk at Trinity from 1627 and this family connection with the College is likely to have been his *entrée* to the chapel. He claims to have served at Trinity for 50 years at the time of his writing *Musick's Monument*, and his portrait gives his age as 63 at the time of publication in 1676 (Mace 1966a, 25 and reverse of the title page). Yet, as noted above, Mace remained in his job despite his hearing loss until his death in c. 1706 (Jacquot 1966). It seems that he served his entire career at Trinity College, which if we include his time as a chorister, would span a remarkable 80 years, though there was at last one gap due to the Civil War (Payne 1987, 140).

Mace was one of six lay clerks working with four priests, ten choristers, and a choir master who also served as the organist for the choir (ibid., 128). In 1639 Mace migrated from singing counter tenor to tenor. He also taught singing, the viol, and the lute while in Cambridge and was doing so as early as 1647 when he taught John Worthington, fellow of Emmanuel College singing and the viol (Jacquot 1966, xxix). Mace married and had a family. He taught his son John the lute through his book in 1671, and he must have had a teaching practice as he refers frequently in *Musick's Monument* to his 'scholars' on the lute (Jacquot 1966, xxix). Mace did leave Cambridge during the Civil War and was in York where he remained with his family during the siege of the city in 1644. He witnessed the destruction of the Anglican choral tradition during and after the war years and saw its revival under Charles II at the restoration. For most of his life Mace was a Cambridge fixture as a singer, teacher, and player. He was interested in all forms of music but had clear and decided views on the theory and practice of music, and an unforgettable written style with which to express himself.

Musick's Monument

The 1676 book is a distillation of Mace's life's work as a musician teacher, practitioner, and thinker. It is divided into three parts: the first on Cathedral Music; the second a tutor of the lute; the third on the viol and music in general. The first part is sub-divided into sections on 'Parochial Music' and 'Cathedral Music' and is aimed at raising the standards of church music at all levels across the country. Mace is always practical and suggests approaches to improving singing when expertise and resources are minimal or non-existent. The second and largest part, subtitled 'The Lute Made Easy', is a complete handbook for learning the instrument without a teacher, and includes important information on practical matters such as stringing, fretting, removing the lute's belly, along with a guide for the complete beginner working systematically through the basis of technique. It is replete with eight complete suites in tablature, plus a number of preliminary exercises, that total 58 pieces in all. The third part gives instruction on the viol but also is the most informative on Mace's musical thinking as regards musical rhetoric and expression. It is also the section that reveals the most about his own hearing and his thoughts on how best to hear and experience music. The book ends with 'Musick's Mystical and Contemplative Part' in which music is a means of connecting with the divine: '*All things, (what e're) in Nature, are Thus Rounded, Thus* Mystically Limited, *and* Bounded; *Some* Harmonize *in* Diapasons Deep. *Others again. more* lofty Circles *Keep*' (Mace 1966a, 269).

Mace's *Musick's Monument* is a highly idiocyncratic book, full of anecdotes, marginalia, asides, and was printed using a wide variety of type sizes and faces; and large and sometimes bizarre recourse to italic script. It had with several distinct purposes and is aimed at several rather different audiences. Certainly, he intended to generate income from his *Monument*. He announced in the 'Advertisement concerning the Value and Price of the Book' (up to 10 August 1767) that the reduced subscriber's price of 12 shillings would be held out for a further three months as clearly pre-sales had not gone well and it had cost him dear to produce ('My unexpected Great Charge') (Mace 1966b). He may have been attempting to change careers in the face of his impending further hearing loss and to advertise the value of his musical innovations so that he might begin to sell them for profit. He wished to reform and advance the state of sacred music in England after the destruction of the war and commonwealth periods. Mace is seen as a musical conservative who wished to defend the musical culture of the past and revive aspects of it that he saw disappearing, such as viol consort music and the dying art of the lute. However, there are aspects of his thinking and ideas that were innovatory and forward looking. Above all Mace wanted to pass on his lifetime's experience of his art to posterity. He makes the point that so often past masters did not divulge their knowledge so that their art died with them.

In all this Mace was disappointed and the book made little impression at time. There were still unsold copies in the 1690s and his list of subscribers were in the main limited to his connections in Cambridge and York. The book certainly failed in Mace's desire to revive the lute as lute playing in Britain after 1670 had few followers, unlike on the continent (Spring 2001, 430). One reason may have been that the form of lute he favoured (the 12-course lute) and his preferred tuning (French Flat) were archaic by 1676 and that this limited the appeal of the book.

Mace's Response Hearing Loss – The Lute Dyphone

The most significant insight into Mace's response to his increasing auditory impairment lies in his invention of the Lute-Dyphone. This rather comic and strange instrument he devised himself to help him hear and thus continue as a player. It is a 'double-lute' (Mace 1966a, 203–6). Two lutes joined end to end, with two sets of strings and two heads. One end is tuned and pegged like an English theorbo and the other like a 'French lute'. He subtitles the instrument the 'lute of fifty strings'. Mace invented it and made it 'with his own hands' in the year 1672. He says:

> The *Occasion of Its Production*, was *My Necessity*: viz. *My Great Defect in Hearing*; adjoining with *My Unsatiable Love and Desire after the Lute*; It being an *Instrument so Soft*; and *Past my Reach of Hearing*, I did Imagine, it was possible to *Contrive a Louder Lute,* than ever any yet had been; whereupon after divers *Crafts,* and *Contrivances*, I pitch'd upon *This Order*; the which has (in

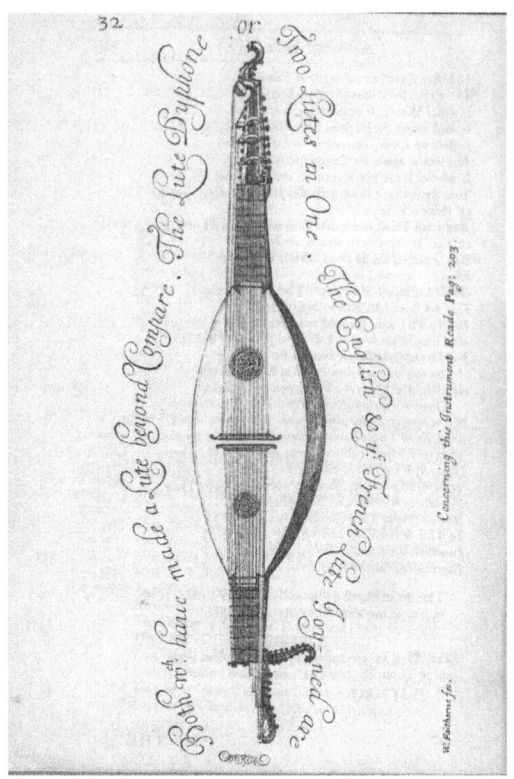

FIGURE 17.1 The Lute Dyphone from Thomas Mace's *Musick's Monument* (p. 32)

> *Great Degree*) answered my *Expectation*; it being absolutely the *Lustiest* or *Loudest Lute that I ever yet heard*; for although I cannot hear the least *Twang* of any other *Lute*, when I *Play* upon *It*; yet I can hear *This, in a very Good Measure*; yet not so *Loud*, as to *Distinguish Every Thing I Play*, without the *Help of My Teeth*; which when I lay *Close to the Edge of It*, (*There*, where the *Lace is Fixed*) I hear *All I Play Distinctly*; so that *It* is to Me (*I Thank God*) *One of the Principal Refreshments, and Contentments I Enjoy in This World*; ….
>
> (Mace 1966a, 203)

The idea that he used his teeth as a means of hearing is interesting as teeth are fixed into the skull and allow the vibrations of music to travel to the cochlea through the bone structures in the head, without the need for the middle ear mechanism to function, and effectively he was using his teeth like a bone-anchored hearing aid.

Mace mentions that when you play one of the lute's ends, the strings of the other 'Unite in Harmonical Sounds'. One end of the lute is tuned like a theorbo (g', d', a', f) for the four upper courses) and the other as a French Lute with a tuning that has an open chord on the upper strings (g', d', b, g).

> The *Majestic Theorboe*, either for *Voice, Organ* or *Consort* etc. and The *High Improved French Lute* for *Airy*, and *Spruce, Single* or *Double Lessons*; and is also a *Most Admirable Consort Instrument*, where They know how to make the *Right Use of It*, and not to suffer It to be *Over-Top'd* with *Squaling-Scoulding-Fiddles*; but to be *Equally Heard* with the *Rest* …
>
> (Mace 1966a, 204)

Inequality of Parts

Mace's dislike of the violin is apparent throughout the book. He finds their sound disagreeable and much prefers the gentler timbres of the viol and lute. Above all he abhors the fact that the music becoming popular after the Restoration placed ever more emphasis on the upper part or parts, to the detriment of the concept of equality of parts that was at the heart of consort music in pre-commonwealth Britain. He makes the point that there needed to be many more bass instruments than treble to balance the sound – yet contemporary practice had it the other way around with treble instruments outnumbering bass. He says:

> For, what is more *Reasonable* that if an *Artist* upon the *Composition* of a *Piece of Music* (suppose) of 3, 4, 5, 6, or more *Parts*; (but hold there; the *Moads* has cut off most of the *Great Numbers*: Well I'le say 3 or 4 (yet most commonly 2 *Parts*) suppose what Number you will;) I say is it not *Reasonable* yea *Necessarily Reasonable*, *That all Those parts should be Equally Heard?* Sire it cannot *Reasonably be Deny'd*.
>
> Then what *Injury* must it needs be to have *Such Things* Played upon *Instruments, Unequally Suited*, or *Unevenly Numbred*? viz. *One Small Weak-Sounding Bass Viol* and 2 or 3 *Violins*; where-as one (in *Reason*) would think, that *One Violin* would bear up *Sufficiently* against 2 or 3 *Common-Sounding-Basses*: especially such as you shall *Generally* meet with, in their *Ordinary Consorts*.

This is a very *Common Piece of inconsiderate Practice*, at *This Day* (Mace 1966a, 233).

Here Mace is railing against the new fashion for trio-sonatas with violins as against consorts with equal parts and such as those using viols.

Mace and Acoustical Space

Another manifestation of Mace's acoustical awareness, conditioned no doubt by his hearing disorder, though he does not say so explicitly, is his concern with optimising musical space and sound diffusion within that space. When discussing posture in playing the lute Mace advised the use of a table to lean the lute against. This can free the left hand, help to secure the lute in place, but also allows the table to act as a resonator and amplifier for the lute as its vibrations carry straight into the table's edge (Mace 1966a, 71).[4]

In the *Monument* Mace discusses his design for a table organ to be placed in a dedicated music room. The organ is to be built into the table with eight desk places also built into it (with one of the eight desks for the organist). The idea is that the organ's sound would be equally diffused among and envelop the players, and thus hold the group together.

> The *Organ* standing in the midst, must needs be of a more certain and stead use to *Those Performers*, that if it stood at a *Distance*; They all *Equally Receiving* the same *Benefit* no one more than another; whereas according to the constant *Standing* of *Upright Organs* (at a *Distance* from the *Table*, and much *Company* usually *Crowding* between the *Organ* and *Table of Performers*) some of the *Those Performers*, who sit farthest off, are often at a loss, for want of *Hearing* the *Organ*, so *Distinctly* as they should, which is a *Great Inconvenience*. And if it be so to the *Performers*, it must needs be alike *Inconvenient*, or more, to *Those Auditors*, who sit far from the *Organ*.
>
> (Mace 1966a, 242)

FIGURE 17.2 Thomas Mace's Table/Organ, *Musick's Monument* (p. 243)

Most ambitious of Mace's ideas is that of a music room designed solely with the performance and clear audibility of musical sound in mind. Writing in the 1670s when there was no such thing as a dedicated music space his thinking is much before its time. Mace's room has a table in the centre for the performers, and organs and other instruments in the corners. The auditors are to be places in 12 distinct galleries each of which is raised up and reached by four sets of stairs.

He says:

> The *Room* It Self to be *Arch'd*; as also the 4 *Middle Galleries* (at least) if not *All Twelve*. And *Built* one *Story* from the *Ground*, both for *Advantage* of *Sound*, and also to avoid the *Moisture* of the *Earth*, which is very bad, both for *Instruments* and *Strings*.
>
> The Room would be *One Step Higher*, that the *Galleries*, in the *Floor*, the better to conveigh the *Sound* to the *Auditors*.
>
> (Mace 1966a, 240)

The galleries are intended to hold up to 200 people in the round. An important point is that 'The musick will be Equal to all alike'. Mace says 'It cannot be easily *Imagin'd*, what a *Wonderful Advantage* such a *Contrivance* must needs be, for the *Exact*, and *Distinct Hearing* of *Musick*; without doubt far beyond all that ever has yet been used' (Mace, 241). There would double doors in each of the four walls and the music room would be one story higher than the auditors' galleries to better 'conveigh the *Sound* to the *Auditors*' (Mace, 240). A great advantage would that 'The *Room* being *Thus Clear*, and *Free from Company*, all *Inconveniences* of *Talking*, *Crowding*, *Sweating* and *Blustering*, etc. are taken away' (Mace, 240). Here Mace may be touching on the common 'cocktail party' problem of following one sound though human hubbub.

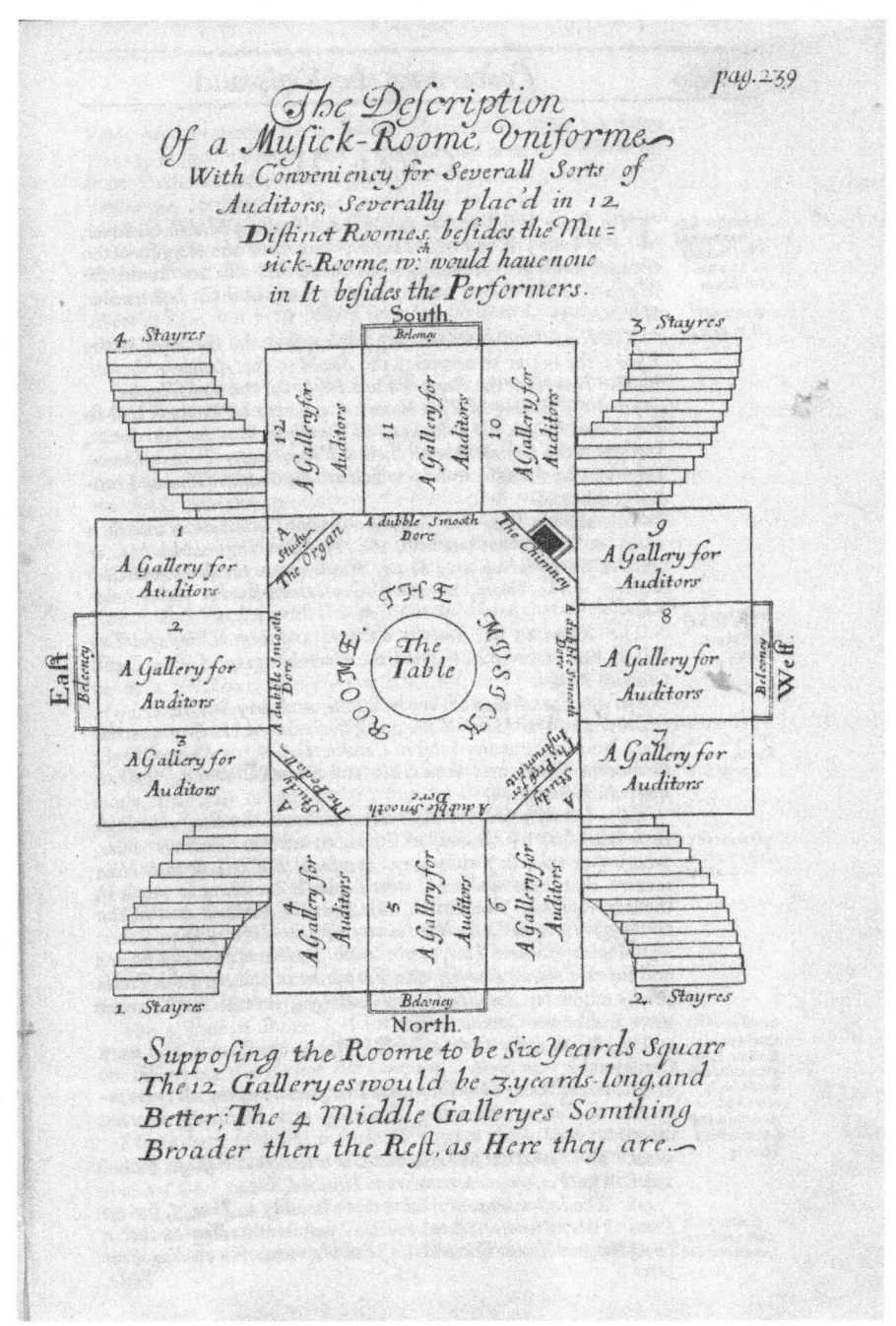

FIGURE 17.3 Thomas Mace's Music Room, *Musick's Monument* (p. 239)

Expression, 'Humour' and 'Mood'

It is clear that Mace's own auditory impairment contributed considerably to all his thinking on music. He is concerned with space and audibility. While he is not against loudness in itself, indeed uses the word 'lusty' a lot as a positive term, he is always at pains to emphasise that sounds should be equitable in their distribution and all pitch ranges should be equally present (Mace, 203). In many places he decries 'scalding violins' which crowd out all other instruments. He is scornful of the guitar which he regards as '*a bit of the Old lute*' (Mace, 237). He speaks of violin ayres as 'rather fit to make a Man's *Ears Glow*, and his *Brains full of Frisks,* etc. than to *Season, and Sober his Mind, or Elevate his Affection* to *Goodness*' (Mace, 236). His concern is more with nuance, variety in tone, dynamics, and speed, and with mood, which collectively he refers to as 'humour'.

His lute pieces are unusual in that he asks not only for different levels of loudness and softness but also gives more idiosyncratic directions to 'sob', and 'crackle', gestures which he describes in some detail (Mace, 270). In some pieces he gives almost programmatic explanations of the 'humouring' he expects and in this he sheds much light on what must be one of the least understood aspects of music of this period (Mace; see also Hancock 2011, 6–8). In his example pieces there are pause marks, dynamics, plentiful ornaments all of which are explained in detail (Mace, 171).[5] Discussion of how to add interest and variety at such a micro-level is unusual in seventeenth-century music and contradicts the idea held by many today that early music should be performed in an unadorned 'straight' and unemotive way.

Conclusion: The Relevance of Mace Today

The relevance of Mace's experience today is that he did not give up on music in the face of advancing hearing loss but looked for and found ways around it, while recognising the difficulties it presented. He made modifications to his instrument and thought hard about how to improve the audition of music for all people. When or how he lost his hearing, we do not know. As he gives no clear reason the assumption is that it was age-related. Somehow, he did not lose his job. Most interesting to me is his overarching concern for equality of sound – that the listener needs to be able to hear the collective of parts. He objects to one part being so loud as to obscure others – particularly lower parts. My own hearing profile has exactly this problem in that I do not hear sounds much below middle c and need to construct low notes from the overtones they produce. This is particularly difficult with pure tones that rely heavily on the fundamentals. Hearing aids are limited in that they tend to simply amplify the loudest sound and hearing quieter sounds through the louder sounds is much more difficult for a deaf person using hearing aids than someone with good hearing.

Notes

1 There is considerable literature written about Beethoven's deafness. For a recent article see Saccenti (2011).
2 For the history of The Royal Society of Musicians see www.rsmgb.org/history/
3 Mace 1966a (Modern facsimile edition as volume I of Musick's Monument, CNRS editions Paris, 1966. Volume II contains the transcriptions and context). For biographies of Mace, see: Thackeray (1951); Watson (1908–09); Narve (2010). For musical culture, see: Jacquot (1973). For lute and instrumental performance practices, see: Pulver (1937); Gill (1950); Adam (2003).
4 Thomas Robinson in *Schoole of Musick* (1604) also recommended this positioning of the lute for best results.
5 See 'My Mistress' for all these added features.

References

Abbott, T. (2013) *Diana Poulton, the Lady with the Lute*. Norwich: Smokehouse Press.

Adam, P. (2003) 'Thomas Mace: Musick's monument—a seventeenth-century instruction manual', *Polyfonia*, 2 (spring): 91–107.

Gill, D. (1950) 'The Lute and Musick's Monument', *The Galpin Society Journal*, 3 (March): 9–11.

Hancock, W. (2011) 'Thomas Mace and a sense of 'humour': The case for expression in seventeenth-century English Instrumental Music', *The Lute*, 51: 1–19.

Jacquot, J. (1966) *Musick's Monument*, II, CNRS, 'Mace et la vie universitaire a Cambridge'.

Jacquot, J. (1973) 'Thomas Mace and the musical life of his era', in Gnepler, G. (ed.), *Festschrift für Ernst Hermann Meyer zum sechzigsten Geburtstag*, pp. 215–222. Leipzig: Dt. Verlag f. Musik.

Mace, T. (1966a) *Musick's Monument* (London, 1676). Modern facsimile edition as volume I of Musick's Monument, CNRS editions Paris, 1966. Volume II contains the transcriptions and context.

Mace, T. (1966b) *Musick's Monument*. 'Advertisement concerning the Value and Price of the Book', unpaginated advertisement inserted before p. 1.

Mace, T. (1675) *Profit, Conveniency and Pleasure*. London.

Mace, T. (1698) *Riddles, Mervels and Rarities or A New way of Health, from an Old Man's Experience*. Cambridge. Full text available at https://quod.lib.umich.edu/e/eebo2/A88936.0001.001?view=toc (accessed 17 July 2021).

Narvey, B. (2010) 'The man of the monument: Thomas Mace', *Lute News*, 95: 8–15

Payne, I. (1987) 'Instrumental music at Trinity College, Cambridge, c. 1594–c. 1615: Archival and bibliographical evidence', *Music & Letters*, 68(2).

Pulver, J. (1937) 'The English theorists. XV Thomas Mace', *The Musical Times*, 78: 601–4.

Saccenti, E. (2011) 'Beethoven's deafness and his three styles', *British Medical Journal*, 343, d7589. Available at https://doi.org/10.1136/bmj.d7589 (accessed 17 July 2021).

Spring, M. (2001) *The Lute in Britain*. Oxford: Oxford University Press.

Thackeray, R.M. (1951) 'Thomas Mace', *The Musical Times*, 92: 306–7.

Tilmouth, M., & Spring, M. (2013) 'Mace, Thomas', *Grove Music Online, Oxford Music Online*. Oxford: Oxford University Press. Available at www.oxfordmusiconline.com.proxycu.wrlc.org/subscriber/article/grove/music/17320 (accessed 19 January 2013).

Watson, H. (1908–1909) 'Thomas Mace, the man: The book: And the instruments', *Proceedings of the Royal Musical Association*, 35: 87–107.

18

DO YOU HEAR WHAT I HEAR?

Some Creative Approaches to Sharing and Simulating Diverse Hearing

John D'Arcy

Introduction

In its early stages, the *Do You Hear What I Hear* project explores how aural diversity might be explored with audiences through technology-assisted interactive experiences. The project aims to incorporate augmented-reality audio within participatory performance in an exploration of a spectrum of aurality. It is hoped that these performances might help audiences better understand diverse sensory experiences and come to question preconceptions of normalcy in hearing.

This chapter documents the development of *Do You Hear What I Hear* through three initial pilot activities carried out at public events and conferences between 2018 and 2020 and the audio processing software used in these. Some participant feedback is shared, along with ideas for development of future activities.

Context

Jonathan Sterne points to the otological 'normalism' pervasive throughout societal discourse on human hearing that reaches across various fields in science and technology (Sterne 2015). Addressing the interdisciplinary field in which he situates himself, Sterne proposes that 'sound studies – but also many forms of politics – begins with hearing the hearing of others' (Sterne 2015, 66). I find this phrase to be a valuable provocation for the activities of *Do You Hear What I Hear*, to find ways of better understanding diverse modes of hearing through the act of listening.

Aural representations of sensory difference are commonplace in media and arts where sound design interprets a specific character's hearing perspective. Altman (1992) terms this technique 'point-of-audition' sound (POA). Audiences are accustomed to the sonic tropes of 'shellshock silence' and 'cinematic tinnitus' often associated with negative experiences of pain and trauma. However, a recent episode of the BBC's hospital drama *Casualty*, 'Jade's World', attempts to present a more rounded representation of sensory difference. This production involved Deaf representation in the writing and direction team and carefully designed POA sound based on recurring deaf character Jade's sensory experience (Ward et al. 2020).

Elsewhere, audio processing for hearing loss simulation (HLS) and cochlear implant (CI) simulation is deployed in audiological research in trials amongst a broad base of participants. Simulations are also used in the design of hearing aid and CI products (to broaden participant testing pools) and in the marketing of these products (typically to illustrate the 'need' for a device).

HLS is also adopted in sensory awareness training in the realm of healthcare and education. While these activities aim to improve positive attitudes towards sensory difference, some forms of 'simulation' training have come under criticism. French (2013) proposes that simulation exercises may create a sense of individualisation and medicalisation, which may ultimately convey misleading information and cultivate negative attitudes towards disability. French calls for 'disability equality training' approaches based on dialogue around broader societal issues of inclusion and representation.

My first work with the sounds of sensory diversity was as the sound designer for the theatre piece *The Unheard* (2017). I consulted with the playwright Vanessa Haynes to accompany her autobiographical narrative about hearing loss, tinnitus, and hearing aid usage with aural representations using audio signal processing and sound synthesis. The audience heard these aural representations via manipulation of both pre-recorded sounds and the performer's voice live on stage. At different times these were heard via surrounding loudspeakers and individually assigned headphones.

In a survey conducted with the audience of *The Unheard*, some listeners drew links between the experience and experiences in their own lives ('my father wears a hearing aid and I found it very useful and effective to have a first-person experience'). Others investigated their preconceptions ('I reflected on the assumptions I make about other people's sensory abilities'). Some felt prompted to address their everyday recognition of sensory diversity ('be more patient', 'more aware', 'show empathy', 'be more tolerant and understanding').

Perhaps the most exciting responses (1) alluded to assumptions of the 'normal hearing' community: 'I assumed I knew what hearing impairment was… I was wrong'; and (2) considered how technologically-mediated listening experiences might challenge these assumptions and understandings: 'I feel like I have learned more from this immersive theatre experience than I have from written and verbal communication alone'. Responses like these helped encourage me to develop *Do You Hear What I Hear* to explore how aural diversity might be shared through mediated listening experiences.

The Initial Activities of *Do You Hear What I Hear*

Do You Hear What I Hear would adopt two key considerations of *The Unheard*: (1) real-time manipulation of audio to convey varying modes of hearing; and (2) the use of individual headphones for audience members. *Do You Hear What I Hear* would introduce additional considerations: (3) audience mobility; (4) dialogue with the audience; (5) mediation of audience voices; (6) audience control of audio settings. It is hoped that through these strategies, the project might create affective experiences and stimulate meaningful conversation around aural diversity whilst avoiding the pitfalls of simulation discussed earlier.

Below, these six key considerations of the project are discussed concerning the three initial activities involving three versions of a bespoke smartphone application:

i. *Ways of Hearing* app developed for a workshop at the Sonic Arts Research Centre, Belfast.
ii. *Do You Hear What I Hear v1* app update for exhibition activities at Belfast City Council's Summer of Music programme 2018, various conferences in 2019 (TaPRA, Irish Sound Science & Technology Association and Aural Diversity) and NI Science Festival in 2020.
iii. *Do You Hear What I Hear v2* app update for remote facilitation at Urban-Related Sensorium 2020.

Real-time Manipulation of Audio to Convey Varying Ways of Hearing

Developing from the aural representation of Hayne's hearing loss and tinnitus in *The Unheard*, it was hoped that the activities of *Do You Hear What I Hear* might convey a larger palette of aural diversity, including hyperacusis, CI listening, and others. The aural representations or simulations of hearing adopted in audiology research, sensory awareness training and media demonstrate various approaches. Some aim for physiological or phenomenological realism. Others adopt artistic impressions or interpretations. The initial activities of *Do You Hear What I Hear* would adopt an approach broadly based on physiological or technological aspects of specific ways of hearing but not modelled on specific individuals (e.g. audiograms, CI settings). This approach would involve audio processing to interpret some aspects of a particular sensory difference rather than claiming a 'realistic' simulation to avoid the feeling of individualisation and medicalisation sometimes critiqued in simulation experiences.

The first app, *Ways of Hearing*, featured two modes: a multiband compressor conveying age-related hearing loss and a noise vocoder interpreting the audio processing of a CI. A variety of techniques are commonly deployed in HLS (Mourgela 2019 provides a useful summary of these). Due to the audio processing capabilities of the smartphone application, it was decided that the multiband compressor would serve as a good impression of commonplace differences in dynamic range and spectrum filtering (EQ). The noise vocoder employed to mimic the filterbank stage of a CI's audio processing. Since this implementation, a recent study suggests that the traditional noise vocoder approach to CI hearing simulation may be significantly improved by combining various spectral filtering methods (Dorman et al. 2020). Similar techniques may improve future iterations of *Do You Hear What I Hear* if deemed most appropriate to represent CI hearing realistically.

The subsequent app update *Do You Hear What I Hear v1* added additional audio settings aiming to decentralise further the assumed normalcy of the listener's own hearing. One of these was influenced by Matt Green's animal hearing exploration project *Ears of Others* (2015). This used an amplified notch in high frequency sounds to create an interpretation of animal hearing and start a conversation around high-frequency sensitivity among humans with conditions such as hyperacusis. Another two additional audio settings, 'hypothetical ears', hinted at future technological hearing augmentations. One of these tuned a resonant filter bank into bell-like musical chords, while the other used a modulating stereo delay creating pitch-shifting echoes across two ears.

The third app, *Do You Hear What I Hear v2*, added a 'drone selector' that allowed one of four additional signals to be added to the audio mix. These additional signals were a selection of sine wave tones and filter noise based on varying descriptions of tinnitus (Kaltenbach 2011).

Listener responses, both verbally during the activities and in feedback surveys completed afterwards, demonstrated a keen interest and curiosity in the variety of audio settings. Whilst listening, audiences showed signs of concentration and contemplation, often articulating their interpretations of sonic characteristics. While many listeners made aesthetic judgements of individual audio settings, the broad reaction to the variety of settings was promising:

> "I guess I assumed my hearing was 'normal', but I now appreciate that there are many different ways of hearing."
>
> "What a variety of different ways of hearing there exists and how difficult it is to imagine another person's aural perspective."

Individual Headphones for Audience Members

In *The Unheard*, individual headphones gave listeners a close-up experience of the live audio processes conveying Hayne's hearing loss and tinnitus. Headphones have been used extensively in theatre and audio art to explore embodiment, immersion, and intersensory perception (Klich 2017). Particularly influential on *The Unheard* were the intimate sound stage of *Reassembled Slightly Askew* (2015) and the sharing of another's perspective in *The Encounter* (2015).

The initial activities of *Do You Hear What I Hear* rather more closely echo Peter Ablinger's headphone-based interactive sound artwork *Kopfhörer* (1999), where listeners hear their surroundings through microphones mounted on their headphones. The individual link between the headphones and live microphone feed would be central in heightening embodiment and immersion whilst exploring the audio settings of the *Do You Hear What I Hear* apps.

The headphones used in initial activities were chosen for their balance of cost, audio quality and relatively strong noise isolation (-35 dB) to help block out external sounds blending with the audio received from the app. Nevertheless, loud sounds would still cause a noticeable bleed through the headphones, reducing the intended clarity of the app audio.

An important observation during testing was the potential for audio feedback caused by the proximity of the microphone to the headphones when headphone speakers were exposed (i.e. not worn on the head). This was prevented by keeping volume levels low during setup and including an introductory warning about high volume levels.

Audience Mobility

A key consideration of *Do You Hear What I Hear* was audience mobility. Mobile works as a subset of headphone theatre and sound art raise the same questions around immersion and embodiment whilst inviting a physical exploration of an environment. In site-specific/promenade theatre, elements of narrative and soundtrack augment everyday spaces, asking us to experience these environments in new ways (Barton 2012). Whilst prominent artists such as Janet Cardiff and Lundhal & Seitl use pre-recorded narrative and soundscapes, the initial activities *Do You Hear What I Hear* would aim to incorporate the live audio feed of the in situ aural surroundings.

Smartphones with inbuilt microphones were used, affording portability and ease of app prototyping. MobMuPlat was chosen as a wrapper for the PureData audio programming platform, allowing distribution to Android and iOS devices. The portable smartphone set up in the initial activities of *Do You Hear What I Hear* allowed the audience to hear the sounds of their surrounding environment through the varying audio settings of the app, helping frame the discussion around aural diversity within everyday environmental listening.

Dialogue with the Audience

The initial activities of *Do You Hear What I Hear* were centred around a dialogue between the audience and a facilitator so that the different audio settings could be given context within a discussion of aural diversity. It was hoped that this interaction would encourage critical engagement with one's own hearing and consideration of broader implications such as equality and inclusion.

During the initial activities, the discussion and listening process was preceded by some questions on the audience survey sheet, hoping to prime the audience for a critical reflection on sound and hearing. Questions included:

- 'What are your favourite sounds?' (most respondents chose music, water and birds)
- 'What are your least favourite sounds?' (most respondents chose loud, high-frequency sounds, or a particular instance of voice or speech)
- 'What would you change about your hearing' had a wide variety of answers, including 'nothing', 'better', 'clearer', 'sensitivity', 'less chaos', 'less background', 'less crowds', 'hear distance', 'less damage', 'remove tinnitus', 'turn on/off', 'echolocation, and 'would have mood music in the background all the time'.

The first workshop, *Ways of Hearing (2018)*, was held as a one-hour group session for 15 participants in a three-part structure:

1. Introduction (including overviews of hearing loss and CI hearing, a guide to the mobile listening activity, the functionality of the *Ways of Hearing* app)
2. Mobile listening activity (vocalisation and listening using the *Ways of Hearing* app, carried out in the building's auditorium, hallways/staircases and outdoors)
3. Reflective conversation amongst the participants

Following the *Ways of Hearing* workshop, a shorter 20-minute activity was designed with the aim of embedding reflective conversation into the listening activity, and working with smaller groups of five to allow more one to one engagement with the facilitator. Here, the *Do You Hear What I Hear* v1 app was used, with listeners gathered around a table (indoor or outdoor depending on venue) and carried out listening activities while conversing with the facilitator. The activity was structured to demonstrate the different audio settings of the app one by one. A narrative device ('trying on someone else's ears') was used, with a name given to each audio setting: *Jean* (HLS); *Charlie* (boosted high frequencies); *Rory* (noise vocoder); *Elliot* (harmonious filterbank); and *Morgan* (stereo echoes). The introduction made clear that these 'ears' were not realistic simulations or replications but rather creative interpretations and impressions of aural diversity.

Each audio setting presented an opportunity to discuss a different aspect of hearing and sound while allowing individuals to share relevant anecdotes about their hearing and that of friends and family. Whilst exploring the HLS (*Jean*), the audience was introduced to the frequency spectrum, dynamic range, and how sensitivity typically changes with age. The noise vocoder (*Rory*) was an opportunity to discuss the technologies of CI and introduce the cultural debates around it. This setting also impeded speech recognition for some listeners, introducing a consideration of how some ways of hearing may impact the cognitive load of everyday verbal communication. The final two 'hypothetical ears' *Elliot* and *Morgan* started a speculative conversation about how we might use technology to change our hearing for aesthetic or functional reasons. Hopefully, these conversations reposition hearing technologies not just as 'cures' or 'treatments' but rather, as He et al. (2014) suggests, signposts on a continuum of individual differences.

The *Do You Hear What I Hear v2* app update was developed specifically for remote facilitation at the online conference Urban-Related Sensorium in 2020. This version of the activity incorporated the information and questions previously delivered by the facilitator as onscreen instructions in a step-by-step guide through audio settings and a series of listening and sound-making activities. Creating this app helped refine the core components of the dialogue with the audience as a concise text, and positive audience feedback was encouraging for further development of a downloadable interactive app. However, it is hard to gauge how listeners interpret the audio settings and information around sensory differences without in-person dialogue.

Mediation of Audience Voices

The activities of *Do You Hear What I Hear* invite listeners to speak, sing, and produce a variety of noises into the microphone and hear these directly through theapp's audio processing. Many representations of hearing in media and HLS are heard on pre-recorded audio. However, some projects such as Ablinger's *Kopfhörer* (1999), with live sound mediated through microphones mounted on headphones, allow the listener to join the sound scene and interact with the system. In *Do You Hear What I Hear,* it is hoped that the listener hearing their vocalisations through the audio settings will create more significant engagement with the sonic experience and ultimately the discussion around aural diversity.

The audience was invited at various points during the activity to speak directly into their smartphone microphone. Typically, audiences showed some initial trepidation around vocalising aloud. Many individuals whispered, spoke quietly, or mumbled at first. In these instances, the facilitator actively encouraged louder vocalisation, and as the activity progressed, most individuals confidently spoke into the microphone. In audience feedback, some respondents indicated their favourite part of the activity was 'hearing my own voice'.

The use of smartphones allowed audience members to quickly move their handsets to angle the inbuilt microphone towards their mouth or the other group members. This was particularly popular for audience members participating in the activity as a pair or a group. In audience feedback, some respondents indicated this was their favourite part of the activity ('laughing with my mum and brother').

Perhaps the most interesting audio settings for users to explore with their voices were the 'hypothetical ears'. Whilst listening through *Elliot*, individuals made percussive noises such as clapping and tapping to hear the musical response of the resonant filterbank. The *Morgan* settings seemed to inspire extended use of one's voice in two ways. Firstly, the echo of the voice heard whilst trying to continue speaking prompted a sense of self-talk monologue, with moments of confusion and weighty cognitive load (a phenomenon demonstrated beautifully in Nancy Holt and Richard Serra's video *Boomerang* (1974). Secondly, the changing vocal pitch caused by the modulating echo time created a sense of wonder, curiosity, and alienation as listeners conversed with their own low and high echoes. Several individuals alluded to gender stereotypes, raising conversations around the physiology of the voice and one's perception of their own voice.

Audience Control of Audio Settings

It is hoped that the ability to control audio settings within the *Do You Hear What I Hear* apps will help listeners better understand the underlying audio processing effects and ultimately engage more deeply with the conversations around diverse ways of hearing. Some HLS demonstrate one or two pre-set audio settings. However, others like 3D Tune-in's *Online Toolkit* web app offer many adjustments to explore sonic effects (e.g. 'level of hearing loss', 'frequency smearing', and 'temporal distortion'.

Looking to the realm of augmented-reality audio apps, many give the user intricate control over settings that manipulate the processing of the live microphone signal. Reality Jockey's *RJDJ* (2008) used the smartphone's touchscreen, gyroscope and GPS as input controls for audio effects parameters such as delay and filtering to alter the listener's soundscape in what they called 'reactive music'. The app's successor *Hear – Advanced Listening* (2016) took some of the live audio processing ideas of *RJDJ* but presented these as a set of 'filters' with specific functional or aesthetic effects designed for specified listening scenarios: 'Talk', 'Sleep', 'Office', 'Relax', 'Happy',

'Super Hearing'. The Hear One earbuds (2017) led a wave of wireless earbuds with built-in controllable audio effects such as noise and hum reduction, speech enhancement, and reverb. Other manufacturers followed suit with features such as hearing profile EQ matching and increasingly intelligent background noise control, potentially turning many mobile devices into DIY hearing aids.

The initial *Ways of Hearing* app had two core settings (HLS and noise vocoder). However, the individual parameters of these were pre-set. The *Do You Hear What I Hear* v1 app introduced a rectangular draw pad in the centre of the screen that allowed users to control some audio settings, tapping and dragging along an up-down, left-right XY axis.

During the activities, listeners were invited to adjust the controls and describe how the sounds were changing. Following these responses, the facilitator would explain the key aspects of audio manipulation and how they might relate to the listener's perception. In the *Hear – Advanced Listening* app, the controls for audio processing often have abstract names (e.g. 'Time Scramble' and 'Unhumanize') and affect multiple parameters with one control slider, concealing the underlying audio effects from the listener. While this might be beneficial to the simplistic user experience of this app, *Do You Hear What I Hear* aims to share an understanding of sound, so audio effects are explained in detail where possible. The exploration of control seems to be an engaging aspect of the activity for some listeners ('I liked to switch between the ears and play around with different sounds').

Potential Developments for *Do You Hear What I Hear*

Overall, the initial activities of *Do You Hear What I Hear* received an enthusiastic response from audiences. Comments in feedback surveys used descriptors 'fun', 'great', 'different', 'weird', 'scary', 'cool', and 'important'. Some responses indicated evocative experiences; for example, 'it made me much more aware and observant of how sound can change how you feel things, even how you see or concentrate'. Some critical areas for potential developments have been identified based on audience feedback and reflection on the initial activities.

Diverse Collaborators and Audiences

Acknowledging my position as hearing 'normally' within mainstream hearing culture, the strength of *Do You Hear What I Hear* will depend on quality collaboration with diverse ears (artists, researchers, technologists, and facilitators) who may inform and participate in future activities. The initial activities of *Do You Hear What I Hear* were designed for delivery via verbal communication, and only three of over two hundred total audience members wore hearing modifying technologies. Future iterations should consider how the activities might reach and be accessible for broader audiences of diverse hearing.

Hardware and Software

The initial apps have audio latency longer than the 5–6ms tolerated in hearing aids (Stone et al. 2008). Future iterations should consider alternatives to the smartphone to optimise low latency mobile audio processing. The attenuation of exterior sound offered by the headphones currently used could also be improved with more substantial physical sound isolation and noise-cancellation software. There is potential to create a binaural experience with headphone-mounted microphones and consideration of spatial audio perception. The audio settings of the app may also be refined to convey additional aspects of sensory difference.

Interaction and Engagement

Thus far, activities have used dialogue with a facilitator to guide listening and interaction. Some responses to audience surveys suggested the app be released for public download. However, there are currently concerns that the app's audio controls might simply be used as audio effects or be misinterpreted without facilitation and dialogue.

Future developments could introduce new engagement strategies such as narrative storytelling or game-like scenarios to guide the audience through their experience: interaction with other audience members, exploration of space, critical listening strategies, and audio device control. There may also be opportunities for improvised vocalisation, linking to my ongoing participative performance practice as the director of Belfast City Choir and HIVE Choir. This may allow for more diverse, non-semantic ways of giving voice. Narrative, gameplay, and increased vocalisation adopted in future activities might help encourage more individual reflection on aural diversity and foster personal advocacy for inclusion and equality amidst prevalent hearing normalcy.

Summary

Let us return to Sterne's proposal that the field of sound studies 'begins with hearing the hearing of others' (Sterne 2015, 66). The core premise of *Do You Hear What I Hear* is that strategies are drawn from the diverse disciplines of sound art, theatre, HLS, and disability studies to create interactive performances that share the hearing experiences of diverse listeners. The activities of *Do You Hear What I Hear* aim to create thought-provoking and memorable moments, hopefully giving rise to broader conversations and critique around dominant societal structures that frame some ways of hearing as 'normal'. Moreover, perhaps in hearing 'through someone else's ears', we might learn more about our own.

References

Ablinger, P. (1999) *Kopfhörer*. https://ablinger.mur.at/hoerstuecke.html
Altman, R. (1992) 'Sound space', in Altman, R. (ed.), *Sound Theory, Sound Practice*. New York: Routledge.
Barton, B., & Windeyer, R. (2012) 'Immersive negotiations: Binaural perspectives on site-specific sound'. In Birch, A. & Tompkins, J. (eds), *Performing Site-Specific Theatre*. London: Palgrave Macmillan.
Dorman, M F., Cook Natale, Sarah, Baxter, Leslie, Zeitler, Daniel M., Carlson, Matthew L., Lorens, Artur, Skarzynski, Henryk, Peters, Jeroen P.M., Torres, Jennifer H., & Noble, Jack H. (2020) 'Approximations to the voice of a cochlear implant: Explorations with single-sided deaf listeners', *Trends in Hearing*, 24: 1–12.
French, S. (2013) 'Introduction'. In Swain, J., French, S., Barnes, C., & Thomas, C. (eds), *Disabling Barriers – Enabling Environments*. London: Sage.
He, S., Grose, J., Teagle, H., Woodard, J., Park, L., Hatch, D., Roush, P., & Buchman, C. (2014) 'Acoustically evoked auditory change complex in children with auditory neuropathy spectrum disorder: A potential objective tool for identifying cochlear implant candidates', *Ear and Hearing*, 36.
Holt, N., & Serra, R. (1974) *Boomerang*. New York: Museum of Modern Art.
Kaltenbach, J.A. (2011) 'Tinnitus: Models and mechanisms', *Hearing Research*, 276(1): 52–60.
Klich, R. (2017) 'Amplifying sensory spaces: The in- and out-puts of headphone theatre', *Contemporary Theatre Review*, 27(3): 366–78.

Mourgela, A., Agus, T., & Reiss, J.D. (2019) 'Perceptually motivated hearing loss simulation for audio mixing reference', paper presented at *147th Audio Engineering Society International Convention*.

Sterne, J. (2015) 'Hearing', in Novak, D., & Sakakeeny, M. (eds). *Keywords in Sound*. London: Duke University Press.

Stone, M.A., Moore, B.C., Meisenbacher, K., & Derleth, R.P. (2008) 'Tolerable hearing aid delays. V. Estimation of limits for open canal fittings', *Ear Hear*, 29(4): 601–17.

Ward, L., Reynolds, J., & Paradis, M. (2020) 'Creating Jade's world', *BBC*. Available at www.bbc.co.uk/rd/blog/2020-07-casualty-jade-hearing-loss-aid-binaural (accessed 1 June 2021).

19
SIGN IN HUMAN–SOUND INTERACTION

Balandino Di Donato

Introduction

Interactivity is a theme widely explored in the field of Sonic Interaction Design (SID) by placing sound at the centre of the design (Rocchesso et al. 2008). This field of research reflects on several aspects of sonic interaction such as perceptual, cognitive and emotional, product sound design, auditory display, and sonification. SID aims to explore *'ways in which sound can be used to convey information, meaning, and aesthetics and emotional qualities in an interactive context'* (Franinović & Serafin, 2013). Whilst SID has previously highlighted the sonic aspects, here is outlined the idea of Human–Sound Interaction (HSI), which focuses on the investigation of human factors in interaction with sound (Di Donato et al. 2020). In this work, we focused on the perception of sonic affordances and the bodily actions that they evoke, considering our capabilities to perceive them. The term affordance was first used by Gibson (1966), and its principles rely on the possible action that each object evokes based on the characteristics of the objects and the capabilities of the subjects (Gibson 1979). As in the work of Godøy et al. (2006), Godøy (2010), and Tanaka et al. (2012), sonic affordances are here intended as sound features that evoke a certain bodily action.

This body of work on musical affordances and embodiment of music drove the creation of new technologies for the control of audio-visual processes through body movements that might have a meaningful result in a music context. This work resulted in creating MyoSpat (Di Donato et al. 2017). MyoSpat is an interactive audio-visual system that enables processing sound through gestural interaction. Precisely, a musician can process live audio in input and lighting projections through arm and hand movements tracked using Inertial Measurement Unit sensors and electromyography (EMG). MyoSpat was used by E. Turner to compose and perform *The Wood and the Water* (2017) and *Start Cluster* by Devaney (2017).

In the first piece, Turner uses Sign Language as part of her performance. These aspects were later studied in the context of Aural Diversity (see the following section), the study of sound and music that addresses the full range of human hearing types and what it means for the design of musical instruments (Hugill, 2019).

Gaver (1991) separates affordances into four categories upon the capability of being perceived: (i) *correct rejections* when there is no affordance and it is not perceived; (ii) *perceived*, the affordance is present and perceived; (iii) *hidden*, the affordance is present but it is not perceived; and (iv) *false*

DOI: 10.4324/9781003183624-21

FIGURE 19.1 Eleonor Turner playing *The Wood and The Water* using MyoSpat

affordances, when an affordance is perceived but does not exist. The discovery of these affordances and the subsequent interactions are driven by a continuous action-perception loop (Svanæs, 2000). This plays an even more important role when considering the diverse spectrum of human abilities to perceive them. In the context of musical affordances, none of the works mentioned above focused on aural diversity, and how others' hearing profile (otologically normal, hearing impaired, and D/deaf) can impact the perception of musical affordances. The HSI project aims to bridge this gap.

The following sections of this chapter will focus on the piece *The Wood and the Water,* and the role that Sign Language can take in the design of musical instruments and interaction with them. This second section will briefly introduce signed music performance and some of the issues on this topic. Finally, the conclusion and future directions of this work are presented.

The Wood and the Water by Eleanor Turner

The Wood and the Water, for harp and electronics, is composed by Eleanor Turner using MyoSpat. The piece represents the primary output of the HarpCI project (Di Donato et al. 2020). The performer elaborates the auditory and visual feedback through hand gestures. Such elaborations make herself and the audience explore the acoustic space and sounds living in it as tangible.

With this piece, Turner aimed to express and communicate some of her personal experiences through an original type of musical poetry. The first step was writing down the foundation poem on paper to establish what she wished to express. Then, using British Sign Language (BSL), it evolved into a more descriptive and expressive poem that she could sing and play on the harp. The simplest musical gestures in the piece are BSL signs that begin on the harp with the plucking of the strings to create the sound and are completed away from the strings. In fact, they often continue for a long time away from the strings and even away from the instrument – above, around, behind, underneath and on the side of the harp, enabled by the MyoSpat sound spatialisation and delay. Aside from those exact signs that create the poem, the music sets the scene of walking through a forest, hearing the feet crunching through the leaves, atmospheric sounds coming from all around and being alone with one's thoughts. A connecting musical motif takes us further on our walk through the forest; a break from the signed poem and complex electronic effects. The most intense moment in the piece uses spatialisation together with the gesture-controlled effects and the signed poem; all brought about by the discovery of a pool of water calling for Turner's honest, personal reflection. The rhythmical spoken word and music passage that follows is Turner's impassioned response to this challenge and is dense with electronic effects and the complexity of words and music angrily spilling out all over each other.

The Wood and the Water has been recorded in studio and performed in different music festivals and conferences, such as Audio Mostly 2017 and Shanghai's Electronic Music Week 2017 (recordings of these performances are available at https://balandinodidonato.com/). During rehearsal and performances, it was observed that the role of sign language was not only to communicate the lyrics to an aurally diverse audience, but to blend the gestural interaction with audio-visual processes. With this performance, Turner and I scratched the surface of the potential to adopt Sign Language as means of interaction with an interactive system as well as the audience. In the HarpCI project, the interaction with MyoSpat was designed to support the instrumental technique and inadvertently sign language. The HSI project aims to extend this intuition and explore the use of sign language for interaction design with interfaces for musical expression.

Signed Music and Human–Sound Interaction

Painting, literature, dance, literature, and music are art forms that are seen as unique to the human experience. However, communities sometimes redefine these art forms for their ability to produce them or appreciate them. In the case of music, deafness is often considered a debilitating condition (Cripps et al. 2017). Music, as known to the hearing community, is formed of an organisation of sound that precludes deaf people from any meaningful involvement in its creative practice. Sign Language was born as a means of communication for d/Deaf people. In relation to music, it was initially used to interpret lyrics only. In more recent years, a growing number of Sign Language literate and deaf communities have taken advantage of it as a means to create and appreciate music. This gave life to what is now called signed music and new category of artists: deaf performers (Cripps et al. in press). This artform is becoming increasingly widespread and recognised by institutions, such as the Royal Conservatoire of Scotland, which opened a BA course in British Sign Language and English (Royal Conservatoire of Scotland 2021). Sign Language performances were mainly for a d/Deaf audience or highly Sign Language literate. In the last two decades, Sign Language performed music has become popular on online video streaming platforms.

The community of music Sign Language interpreters recognised this issue and are constantly finding ways to build a language, or Sign Language 'dialects' that are able to communicate also played music. In her talk on enhancing music through Sign Language, the deaf artist Sun Kim (2015) talks about how movement is equal to sound in deaf culture. She says: 'How is it that I understand sound? Well, I watch how people behave and respond to sound. You people are my loudspeakers, and amplify sound. I learn and mirror that behaviour. At the same time, I've learnt that I create sound, and I've seen how people respond to me. […] In deaf culture, movement is equal to sound.' She then continues explaining how sound can be experienced visually, through touch or as an idea. As a note cannot be fully captured and expressed on paper, the same holds true for a concept in American Sign Language (ASL). Music and ASL are both highly spatial and inflected. As subtle changes in the instrumental technique of a musician, so a small difference in performing a sign can affect its entire meaning. In a study reviewing the work of two deaf people, Cripps et al. (2017) highlight how signed music constitutes a new and unique form of performance art, maintaining common elements with both Sign Language and music. The amount of Sign Language performed music is growing and growing. For example, YouTube channels of Timm (2006), Signmark (2009), T.L. Forsberg (2015), and Sean Forbes (2006). In recent years we started to see this artform appear in mainstream channels. For example, Dexterity (2017)'s performance of Queen's *Bohemian Rhapsody* at the TEDxSydney, or the several performances of ASL interpreted music pioneer Gallego (2021). Different music artists are working towards making music accessible to deaf people by releasing videos featuring the use of Sign Language. Examples are *You Need Me, I Don't Need You* by Sheeran (2011), *Pride* by American Authors (2016) and McCartney's (2012)*My Valentine Featuring Natalie Portman and Johnny Depp.*

In her article analysing the relationship between Sign Language and Music, Maler (2013) highlights several issues that the popularity of these videos poses, such as the cultural appropriation of the Deaf culture by the hearing community, and the debate on hearing people using Sign Language to 'show off'. At the same time, signed-music performance can also have a positive impact on Deaf cultural heritage. Signed music can be a catalyser for freeing Deaf communities from oppressive historical processes and disseminate knowledge of this artistic practice (Morêdo Pereira 2021). With awareness surrounding cultural issues, the HSI project to bridges research on signed-music performance with the field of interaction design and the making of digital musical instruments.

After an analysis of different song-signing video, in her conclusions, Maler writes,

> Deaf music provides analysts with a unique opportunity to investigate how people of all different hearing abilities perceive and interact with music in order to interpret and create it with their hands and bodies.
>
> *(Maler 2013)*

She then continues saying 'the analogical aspects of sign language and gesture correlate particularly well with the analogical resources of music, while the more symbolic aspects of sign language help us parse meaning with greater ease than if the signer's movements were purely dance. This special property of song signing presents an opening for further analysis in the fields of disability studies, musical embodiment, and music perception.'

In reference to my work, these quotations give rise to the following questions: how can we build instruments and design interactions with them, such that they are meaningful to an aurally diverse audience? What framework/s can we adopt to quantitatively and qualitatively evaluate the relationship between Sign Language gestures and the music, here intended as both lyrics and instrumental parts?

To study sonic affordances perceived by Sign Language translators and gestures enacted to communicate music and lyrics to d/Deaf people, a large data-set that includes motion and sound features of Sign Language performed music is being created (Di Donato 2021). This data set, currently under development, is a collection of raw quantitative data, computed higher-level features and qualitative analysis conducted through coding of visual and audio data (Saldana 2021). The modelling of this data will then be the foundation of knowledge for designing new instruments performable by signed-music performers. This approach presents a series of limitations, and future work will also build around these. For example, as highlighted by the deaf dancer Yan Liu in (Canadian Cultural Society of the Deaf YouTube 2016), signed music should be considered an artform in itself. As opposed to conventional poetry, where we have words for which signs are well defined, in music, 'signs themselves, the way they move, they create music'. Another open question remains the difference between different signed music genres. Like music, we have classical, popular, electronic, rock, and other genres, which are influenced by the cultures in which music is composed. The same happens for signed music; performers are influenced by their cultural background and the spoken sign language. In reference to my work, how digital musical instruments can support the music creation process considering the diversity of signs? Future work aims to answer these questions and contribute to the literature on signed-music performance.

Conclusions

This chapter presented the initial developments of the Human–Sound Interaction project in the context of Aural Diversity. In this scenario, HSI aims to bring music-making and experience to anyone, regardless of their hearing profile. The interaction with musical instruments and the audience is fundamental in both the making and performing music; this is a vital element for musicians and the public. Including Sign Language in the interaction design of musical instruments can make music more accessible to both music makers and the audience. *The Wood and the Water* was the first step in this direction. Importantly, this performance demonstrated the feasibility of blending instrumental music performance with Sign Language. Here technologies to be created could play a significant role. New technologies can welcome anyone to create and experience music, regardless of their ability to act and experience the world around us.

References

American Authors (2016) *Pride*. Available at https://youtu.be/7bAaN-LCcHI (accessed April 2021).

Canadian Cultural Society of the Deaf YouTube (2016) *Signed Music Rhythm of the Heart HD*. Available at https://youtu.be/FLazgI_phNQ (accessed December 2021).

Cripps, J., Rosenblum, E., Small, A., & Supalla, S. (2017) 'A case study on signed music: The emergence of an inter-performance art', *Liminalities: A Journal of Performance Studies*, 13(2): 1–24.

Cripps, J., Small, A., Rosenblum, E., Supalla, S.J., Whyte, A.K., & Cripps, J.S. (in press) *Signed Music and the Deaf Community. Culture, Deafness & Music: Disability Studies and a Path to Social Justice*. In A. Cruz (ed.), *Culture, Deafness & Music: Disability Studies and a Path to Social Justice*. Rotterdam, NL: Sense Publishers.

Devaney, K. (2017) *Star Cluster*. Availabe at https://youtu.be/9ToP33Ki2SE (accessed 9 April 2021).

Dexterity, A. (2017) *Queen's Bohemian Rhapsody Performed in Sign Language*. Available at https://youtu.be/1E0VdL9UqtM (accessed April 2021).

Di Donato, B. (2021) *HSI-data*. Available at https://github.com/balandinodidonato/HSI-data (accessed April 2021).

Di Donato, B., Dewey, C., & Michailidis, T. (2020) 'Human-Sound Interaction Towards human-centred cross-modal interaction with sound', *Proceedings of the 7th International Conference on Movement and Computing*. New Jersey, USA: Association for Computing Machinery.

Di Donato, B., Dooley, J., & Coccioli, L. (2020) 'HarpCI, empowering performers to control and transform harp sounds in live performance', *Contemporary Music Review*, 36(6): 667–686.

Di Donato, B., Dooley, J., Hockman, J., Bullock, J., & Hall, S. (2017) 'MyoSpat: a hand-gesture controlled system for sound and light projections manipulation', *Proceedings of the International Computer Music Conference (Shanghai, China)*, pp. 335–40.

Forbes, S. (2006) *Sean Forbes*. Available at www.youtube.com/user/seanforbes/ (accessed 9 April 2021).

Forsberg, T.L. (2015) *TL Forsberg*. Available at www.youtube.com/channel/UCrEGub-Em6dT-UJm901S GXQ (accessed April 2021).

Franinović, K., & Serafin, S. (2013) *Sonic Interaction Design*. Cambridge, MA: MIT Press.

Gallego, A. (2021) *Amberg Productions*. Available at www.ambergproductions.com/ (accessed April 2021).

Gaver, W. (1991) 'Technology affordances', *Proceedings of the SIGCHI Conference on Human Factors in Computing Systems*, New Orleans, LA: Association for Computing Machinery, pp. 79–84.

Gibson, J.J. (1966) *The Senses Considered as Perceptual Systems*. Boston: Houghton Mifflin.

Gibson, J.J. (1979) 'The theory of affordances', *The Ecological Approach to Visual Perception*, pp. 119–37.

Godøy, R. (2010) 'Gestural affordances of musical sound', in Godøy, R., *Musical Gestures: Sound, Movement, and Meaning*, pp. 115–37. New York: Routledge.

Godøy, R., Haga, E., & Jensenius, A. (2006) 'Exploring music-related gestures by sound-tracing: A preliminary study', *Proceedings of the 2nd International Symposium on Gesture Interfaces for Multimedia Systems, Leeds, United Kingdom*, pp. 27–33.

Hugill, A. (2019) 'Aural diversity'. Available at https://auraldiversity.org/ (accessed 12 April 2021).

Maler, A. (2013) 'Songs for hands: Analyzing interactions of sign language and music', *MTO: A Journal of the Society of Music Theory*, 19(1). Available at: https://mtosmt.org/issues/mto.13.19.1/mto.13.19.1.maler.html (accessed August 2021).

McCartney, P. (2012) *My Valentine*. Available at https://youtu.be/f4dzzv81X9w (accessed April 2021).

Morêdo Pereira, J. (2021) *Deaf on Stage: The Cultural Impact of Performing Signed Songs*. London: University College London (UCL).

Rocchesso, D., Serafin, S., Behrendt, F., Bernardini, N., Bresin, R., Eckel, G., …Visell, Y. (2008) 'Sonic interaction design: Sound, information and experience', *CHI '08 Extended Abstracts on Human Factors in Computing Systems*, pp. 3969–3972.

Royal Conservatoire of Scotland (2021) 'BA Performance in British Sign Language and English' Available at www.rcs.ac.uk/courses/ba-performance/ (accessed 12 April 2021).

Saldana, J. (2021) *The Coding Manual for Qualitative Researchers*. London: SAGE Publications.

Sheeran, E. (2011) *You Need Me, I Don't Need You*. Available at https://youtu.be/ZXvzzTICvJs (accessed April 2021).

Signmark (2009) *Signmark*. Available at www.youtube.com/user/signmarkprod (accessed April 2021).

Sun Kim, C. (2015) *The Enchanting Music of Sign Language*. Available at www.ted.com/talks/christine_sun_kim_the_enchanting_music_of_sign_language (accessed March 2021).

Svanæs, D. (2000) *Understanding Interactivity: Steps to a Phenomenology of Human-Computer Interaction*. Norway: Norges teknisk-naturvitenskapelige universitet.

Tanaka, A., Altavilla, A., & Spowage, N. (2012) 'Gestural musical affordances', *Proceedings of the 9th International Conference on Sound and Music Computing*, Copenhangen, Denmark. Available at https://research.gold.ac.uk/id/eprint/14647/1/Gestural_Musical_Affordances.pdf (accessed August 2021).

Timm, R. (2006) *Rosa Lee Timm*. Available at www.youtube.com/channel/UCWDxkkg2vNvH0MsAxp3Z f_Q (accessed April 2021).

20
THE AURAL DIVERSITY CONCERTS
Multimodal Performance to an Aurally Diverse Audience

Duncan Chapman

> *The leaves crisping like when you walk on them*
> *all we could hear was dad snoring so we recorded it*
> *children shouting and cars starting up*
> *Nature sounds or deep inside the ocean .... sounds*
> *I like.... a Lambo engine*
> *aaah rustling noise of money*
> *the sound of fresh snow*
> *chopping sounds*
> *(Favourite sounds from a group at*
> *Beauchamp College, Leicester)*

The First Concert: The Old Barn, Kelston Roundhill, 6 July 2019

On a beautiful Saturday in the summer of 2019, groups of people made their way up Kelston Roundhill between Bristol and Bath to The Old Barn. The doors to the building were wide open, with a long table set up outside for food later and straw bales placed on the hill for people to sit and listen. The audience for the two performances were free to move between the inside and outside, they could listen on wireless headphones, they could lie on a specially made vibrating floor and feel the sound through their bones, they could even listen to the performance whilst swinging on a giant swing strung in the trees outside. As the performance unfolded we were presented with a sequence of old and new music that moved from the folksongs of Matthew Spring via the jazz clarinet of Ruth Mallalieu to the physical experience of vibration in Sam Sturtivants vibrating floor installation and the detailed and strange sounds of Andrew Hugill's 'Diplacusis Piano'.[1]

Rarely is it possible to experience such a wide range of music in the course of one event. Even more rarely (outside of therapeutic situations) does it happen that the music we were listening to was created specifically for those with a wide range of hearing and, importantly for the Aural Diversity project, *by* a group of composers and performers who were themselves aurally divergent.

There were two performances that afternoon. After the 2:30 performance there was time to meet, eat, and talk with the performers and share our experiences of what we had just listened to.

All of the performances had simultaneous British Sign Language translation of spoken introductions / texts and several were accompanied by visual projections. Included in the programme was information about the specific details of the hearing profiles of the composers and performers. Also added to each piece was a description, duration and listening suggestions, e.g:

> *Sanitary Tones*
> by John L. Drever c.10 minutes
> Instrumentation: Vocal sounds
> Description:
> Hand-dryer recordings voiced and transformed. Performers are spaced around the performance space. A pre-recorded track is mixed with the live voices. Medium loudness to quiet. No sudden bursts. The performers will phonate gently.
> Listening suggestions:
> Unmediated in all spaces, and via streaming.

Kelston Barn on a beautiful Saturday afternoon was for me a magical experience. I had travelled there from a frenzied week in London running music workshops in special schools and had camped in a tent on a small campsite down the hill. My day had consisted of breakfast in a wood followed by a refreshing swim in the river followed by the concert then a long journey home.

FIGURE 20.1 Listening outside with wireless headphones (Kelston Barn summer 2019)

Photo: © Miguel Angel Aranda de Toro (used with permission.)

Aside from my curiosity and interest in the work of composers and performers some of whom I had known for many years, my main reason for attending the first concert was because I had been asked to curate the second one. The second concert would inevitably be very different to this experience. Not all performances can have the perfect location, weather, and timing. I came away with a number of key questions:

1. What was missing?
2. How do we create an environment for listening that is truly inclusive of those with diverse hearing?
3. How could I engage with a wider range of creators of work and what were the appropriate collaborative strategies for this to work?
4. How to deliver coherence? How to make an event that celebrates diversity in listening and content yet still feels like 'one' thing rather than a 'pick and mix' type of 'relaxed' concert that I know wouldn't work well for the demographic of the audience, composers, and performers?
5. How should the next concert be presented? How long should each section be and what modes of listening could be used?
6. What parts of the Kelston concert are 'portable' and could be carried forward to Leicester in November?

FIGURE 20.2 Listening inside (Kelston Barn, summer 2019)

Photo: © Miguel Angel Aranda de Toro (used with permission.)

The Second Concert: Attenborough Arts Centre, Leicester, 30 November 2019

The second Aural Diversity Concert took place at the Attenborough Arts Centre on 30 November 2019. It formed part of the first Aural Diversity conference at the University of Leicester. The Attenborough Arts Centre is on the university campus and is specifically focussed on working with disabled artists and communities. It has a number of spaces, including: a gallery, artists' studios, and a performance space. Leicester in November is very different to Kelston in July. It was not going to be possible to have the wonderful mixture of inside and outside listening that characterised the first concert, so a different strategy was needed. So I planned to use many of the available spaces in the Centre.

I decided to include several of the pieces that had been specially created for the first concert, but also to add new pieces made in collaboration with a group of local people with diverse hearing. One of the things that I felt was missing from the first concert was engagement with more people as creators of work. Previous experience working with widely different groups of participants on music and sound-art projects led me to want to explore the notions of Aural Diversity with a wider range of people. After a number of dead-ends, I made contact with two distinct groups of potential participants. One was a small group of adult artists and musicians who had experienced profound changes to their hearing. I was very interested to find out how this had influenced the music and art that they make. The other group comprised young people at the Hearing Support Centre at Beauchamp College in Leicester. They all wore cochlear implants. To find out more about how their hearing affected their perception of sound and music, I asked both groups the same questions:

- What is your favourite sound in the world that isn't a piece of music or 'musical instrument'?
- Are there any sounds that you particularly identify with as belonging to where you live?
- Are there any sounds that you are keen on that you don't think other people like?
- Are there any sounds you miss as your hearing has changed?
- Are there any sounds you would want others to hear that they might not have come across?

Here are some of the responses from the group at Beauchamp College:

> *The leaves crisping like when you walk on them*
> *all we could hear was dad snoring so we recorded it*
> *children shouting and cars starting up*
> *Nature sounds or deep inside the ocean .... sounds*
> *I like.... a Lambo engine*
> *aaah rustling noise of money*
> *the sound of fresh snow*
> *chopping sounds*
> *yeah I can't hear my cat purring*
> *with the dogs claws scattering on the floor*
> *my cat purring*
> *It's annoying and it sometimes distracts me*
> *It's a mixture of humming and singing*
> *relaxing*

birds singing

if I like stroke him I can feel him

annoying my mum with saying 'relax dude' and annoying my dad with making a loud whooooo noise

Making splashing noises

The kettle heating up

listening to a car engine

my dad snoring

I like scraping my nails on the back of my phone case…. and my dad hates it

Total silence …. when I take my hearing off

And from the adults:

> *I know that i can't trust my hearing because the hearing aid they've got some built in circuitry that can ….it can kind of vary things ….then again it took me a long time to get the experts to switch those circuits off but then i'm left with quite a bit of feedback some times so it's all so much more … volatile I suppose I can't really rely on what i'm hearing but have to take a chance and have to sort of let go of being precious about getting sounds right.*
>
> *(Simon)*

> *Erm yeah, so there's the bells of Leicester cathedral and when I first moved to Leicester I was on the 6th floor of a block of flats and you could hear them from quite far away and the they tended to 'warbledness' of just what you could vaguely recognise as bells but that happened every Thursday and I could always hear it and it was a big part of the new soundscape of where I lived when I first moved here so yeah the bells of Leicester.*
>
> *(Tim)*

This information became critical in my composition of a new piece, entitled *From the Station to the University*. The duration of this piece was the length of time it takes to walk from Leicester Railway Station to the University of Leicester. I wanted to give audience members and conference attendees a glimpse of the sound of the city as perceived by the groups of people with diverse hearing. The piece was designed for headphone listening.

One of the most successful aspects of the audience experience of the first concert was being able to move about, from inside to outside the building. This was obviously not going to be possible at the Leicester concert so I had to devise a different structure to the event.

One driver for the new structure was the needs of Andrew Hugill's *Diplacusis Piano* piece. In the first concert, this was presented as a live performance with real-time spectrogram projections. But the piece had developed and expanded to include many more sections, and was now 30 minutes long and presented entirely on video. After discussing how this could be presented in ways that were accessible to a wide audience and in the context of the event, we decided to alternate live performances with two sound installations: *Thirty Minutes for Diplacusis Piano* (to be screened in the large space) and Sam Sturtivant's *Sensonic* for vibrating floors (which would play in one of the art studios). The instructions to the audience therefore read as follows:

> *This concert will have three sections of live performance which will be interspersed with sections where the audience will be free to roam between different spaces experiencing the music as an installation in a diverse range of ways. Feel free to move to a different listening position / method in between pieces. In*

> the sections between the live performances (Installation sections) there will be different things happening in different spaces, these will be repeated so you are able to hear everything if you wish OR listen to the same thing twice. Also in the Installation sections we will be streaming a 'tinnitus relief' soundtrack on one of the headphone channels so you will be able to listen to this if you would like to have a listening break.
>
> All the music in the concert will be streamed live to wireless headphones so you can listen in the Hall, Cafe area, Gallery and also in Studio 3 upstairs where you will also be able to experience the music via a vibrating floor and low level audio playback.[2]

The second concert was, in my view, very successful in the way that it engaged with an audience of general public alongside experts and specialists who had come to the Aural Diversity conference taking place at the University. We had imagined that we would have to 'model' the behaviour of moving between pieces and sections but at the event the audience naturally flowed from one space to another. Having a bit more time and a dedicated space meant that the vibrating floor installation had a good environment for people to spend time in and some audience members spent the whole evening lying on the floor.

We were also able to make more use of the wireless headphone system so that there was a tinnitus relief channel available which some folk used in the cafe space to take a break from the live music. As with the first concert the BSL translation worked well and also was used in some of the pieces where texts were heard, this was a bit of a challenge for the interpreters as in one piece the texts would come in different orders in each performance. However, there was a real sense of collaboration with Elizabeth Oliver and Donna West, the BSL interpreters.

Critical Reflections

Reflecting on his experience of the first concert, John L. Drever describes the experience of using his lived experience of the problems with hand-dryer noise to create a piece which manages to combine raising awareness of a problem with something that is engaging and beautiful to listen to. This is music created 'from the inside' by someone who does not have what might be termed 'auraltypical' hearing. He writes:

> Exhale: airstreams channelled from the lungs, setting the vocal cords in the larynx into vibrational movement and onwards through the resonant vocal tract, the resulting soundwaves project out across the audience. This vocal soundscape comprises the full spectrum of sound from noise to pure tone: sonorous vocalic (vowel sounds) drones with distinct pitch and fluctuating formants; gentle trilling ululations; narrow bandwidth white noise of sibilance; the pure tones of whistling; percussive glottal and labial articulations. Noise counterbalancing pitch. The contrasting qualities of voice indicate a diverse ensemble of ages and gender. No one voice dominates, implying attentive listening, as well as sound-making is at play. There is not one spatial focus; the performance event is dispersed, voices are not spatially fixed but a combination of stasis and motion, hence everyone is in the best seat. Transitory moments of density give way to spatiality. There is a fluidity between the auditory perception of an individual utterance (i.e. an auditory event) among the chorus of voices and the physical position of the individual utterings (i.e. sound source), as the direct acoustic voice and its electroacoustically mediated partner is broadcast via surround sound PA, combine and diverge. There is a lull in the texture. A three-note melody sings out and is passed around; an echolalic imitation with each performer versioning the theme. It is unrushed, expiration

seems to be dictating the length of each call, ineluctably linked to lung capacity. Some calls keep the energy and pitch consistent, some letting it ebb and flow acknowledging the natural cycle of breathing, as the tones rise and fall.

(John Drever, reflections on Sanitary Tones: Ayre #3 [Kelston])

These reflections are informed by the audience listening conventions in operation at the Aural Diversity concerts:

- Listen anywhere, anytime
- Decide how to listen before each piece
- Move about quietly but freely
- No applause – use 'flappy hands'
- Be careful with any object that might make a noise
- Respect the hearing needs of others

There are also some open suggestions about how one might listen:

- Co-located, unmediated, acoustic
- In a break-out space, or outside
- Streaming to hearing aids (via Bluetooth)
- Streaming to user-controlled headphones (available to all)
- On the vibrating floor, created by Luke Woodbury
- Watching BSL and/or video interpretations when available
- Another method designed by yourself

In recent years there have been many controversies around audience behaviour in concerts. An article in the *Daily Telegraph*, for example, declared: 'Audiences at the Proms are ignorant of the correct time to clap and need educating to avoid spoiling the music for others.' (Allen 2009). It seems significant to me that the Aural Diversity conventions are called 'conventions' rather than 'rules'. They represent a much gentler call for empathy and understanding, rather than a new set of rules to be obeyed at risk of being ejected or publicly shamed. Instead of assuming that the audience is somehow 'ignorant' of how to behave and need 'educating' to somehow do the 'right' thing, they are asked to simply be considerate. All of the composers and performers in the concert are coming from a lived experience of diverse hearing and therefore I would argue that the 'expertise' lies within the group.

There is also a profound difference between the Aural Diversity experiences and those of 'relaxed' concerts. The word 'relaxation' is subject to more than one interpretation. On the one hand, the UK radio station *Classic FM* proudly proclaims that its *Classic FM – Relax More* CD compilation contains 'the most relaxing Classical music'. On the other hand, so called 'relaxed' concerts have become quite common in recent years. These will typically consist of short items, often joined together with a narrative, and performed in a conventional concert venue, but with the audience lights left on and people given permission to move about and talk as they like. These are often promoted as being 'autism friendly' and 'accessible' to a wide range of audiences.

Both of these are in a different world to the Aural Diversity concerts. The first treats music as a soporific warm blanket to ease away the stress of the world, while the second can be a bombardment of rapidly changing over-stimulation that is alienating to many of the audiences it is aimed at and completely inappropriate to those with tinnitus, hyperacusis or deafness. An Aural Diversity concert offers a way for those who might be otherwise be excluded to participate, to have a voice and create work for both those with assumed 'auraltypical' hearing, and those with diverse hearing profiles.

In 2020, the Covid pandemic brought conventional concerts and performances to a sudden stop. Suddenly there were empty concert halls, theatres and gig venues. Organisations realised that they would have to try and find new ways to continue and there was a huge surge of activity in which the likes of symphony orchestras and opera companies talked in the media about 'taking their work online'. For some of us working at the 'edges' of music and performance there was more than a bit of *déja vu* about this. Telematic performance has been a feature of experimental musicking for some years, but has until recently not been something that is considered as an option by mainstream cultural organisations (Oliveros 2007; Szigetvari 2009). 2020 has changed much of the landscape and is has become apparent that 'taking our work online' involves much more than simply putting a camera in front of it and broadcasting the output to Youtube.

For many disabled musicians the start of the Covid lockdown was a 'welcome to my world' moment. Many disabled artists have had to develop their work in isolation anyway and have become experts at managing the technologies necessary for this to be successful. Adrian Lee, a composer, musician and guitarist who is also blind commented:

> As a working musician I found the 2020 pandemic afforded an opportunity to focus on how low-cost remote network technology might afford a solution to a lack of live musical and social contact. The pandemic has produced a situation where many disabled people, including disabled musicians, might observe that the general restrictions on employment and personal mobility have presented a situation which is already familiar to them. Virtually the entire population is now in the same boat as disabled friends and colleagues in the sense of being denied access to a wide range of professional and social musical activities. A disabled person might be tempted to observe, with a touch of irony, 'welcome to my world' but to take the matter a little more seriously, perhaps this represents an opportunity for society at large to learn from the ingenuity and resilience which disabled people bring to their daily life and work. When I go to my music studio to play, I can now rehearse record and play live concerts with anyone in the world who I might connect with. With one simple levelling action we have overcome one fundamental barrier to participation both professionally and socially.

There can be considerable advantages to remote collaboration. For people who have hearing loss, tinnitus, diplacusis, or hyperacusis this can mean that: volume can be controlled to suit, as can the balance between the ears; EQ can be adjusted to suit specific hearing needs; and there is no chance of startling disturbance from other audience members (no sudden clapping or random noises). This level of control over the listening situation could provide a model for diverse listening.

Conclusion

By creating concerts that are specifically designed to embrace and welcome those with diverse hearing the Aural Diversity project has started on a journey of making music and sonic art that reflects the diversity of hearing as something with tremendous creative potential. For many of the people who came to the Aural Diversity concerts a 'normal' concert is inaccessible. This is not because music is something that they cannot enjoy, but because the context of the conventional performance can be stressful and unpredictable. Giving the choice to listen simultaneously in multiple ways and to change the mode of listening to suit the situation gives audience the control to have an experience that is tailored to their specific needs. Changing the context of the listening environment changes who can be in the room.

Many technologies, such as live captioning, audio description, sign language interpretation on screen, and hearing loops in venues, have been developed as tools for access. These are important and vital tools but there are also creative possibilities that embracing different ways of listening can bring to all audiences and creators. Shifting the focus from the interpretation of existing works to the creation of original work brings a whole world of possibilities and (as with the experience of the composers and performers in these concerts) facilitates the continuing artistic careers of those who would otherwise have to abandon music completely as their hearing changes.

'Mainstream' musical organisations have much to learn from the experience of these concerts. At a time when, post-pandemic, many are exploring hybrid ways of working, there is a wider interest in including things like live streaming as part of their 'normal' activities. This raises many possibilities, for example:

- Using the technology of live streaming to allow users to control their own listening experience in terms of volume, EQ, balance and compression. This does not only apply to remote listeners. Many of these things can be done with portable devices.
- Following on from the model of the Aural Diversity concerts: having performances that include the options for listening in and out of the hall. This does happen in some 'relaxed' events but, as mentioned earlier, these are hardly ideal for the audiences that came to our concerts. It is quite normal these days to have surtitles, audio description or BSL interpretation, it could be equally possible to allow for different modes of listening.
- Commissioning work that is specifically designed to embrace diverse hearing profiles.
- Giving information in publicity and programmes that allows potential audiences to be able to make informed choices about what might be suitable for them to attend.
- Thinking about the flow of concert programmes from an aural diversity perspective, considering issues such as balance between periods of sound and breaks, levels of intensity and activity, the character of the music, and so on.

Acknowledgements

Thanks to Prof. Andrew Hugill and Prof. John L. Drever for inviting me to be involved in the project. To Balandino Di Donato and Dr Simon Atkinson for valuable technical and musical support. Tracey Coates, Specialist Teacher for Hearing Impaired Children. Adrian Lee, Simon Le Boggit, and Tim Baker for insight into their worlds and to the composers and performers in the concerts. Thanks also to Courtenay Johnson for administration.

Notes

1 The full programme is available at https://auraldiversity.org/concert1.html (accessed 16 July 2021).
2 The full programme is available at https://auraldiversity.org/concert2.html (accessed 16 July 2021).

References

Allen, N. (2009) 'Proms audiences shouldn't clap so much, says expert', *The Daily Telegraph*. Available at www.telegraph.co.uk/culture/5826377/Proms-audiences-shouldnt-clap-so-much-says-expert.html

Oliveros (2007) 'From telephone to high-speed internet: A brief history of my tele-musical performances', *Leonardo Music Journal*, 19. Online supplement available at https://ccrma.stanford.edu/groups/soundwire/publications/papers/chafeLMJ19-2009.pdf

Szigetvari, V. (2009) 'Making new waves in the global village'. Available at www.makingnewwaves.hu/mnw2009/about_en.html

21
MUSIC-MAKING IN AURALLY DIVERSE COMMUNITIES
An Artist Statement

Jay Afrisando

I am a composer and sound artist. As of this writing, my hearing condition is 'normal'. I believe I can, more or less, hear things most people can 'normally' hear, like birds, low hiss, distant airplanes flying over my head, rustling leaves, and conversations in the middle of a party. Within the sonic arts community, I also believe that I can perceive things people can 'normally' detect, like pitches, rhythm, timbre, texture, dynamics, and gestures in space.

I had considered these capabilities typical standards until in 2018 when I wondered 'do deaf people enjoy music?' My 'mainstream' view was that sound is, at once, the essential ingredient in music and a barrier for deaf people. The more I researched deafness, hearing, disability, and accessibility, the more I realised my assumptions were invalid, partial, and unjust. There is no such thing as a single, fixed condition of hearing and deafness. This notion of typicality has been advanced, creating inconspicuous standards within the sound industry, the sonic arts, and sonic education. Consequently, these sonic systems have marginalised those who do not meet the standardised or expected perception.

My interest in the intersection of arts and diverse bodies, especially diverse hearing profiles, started realisation. I have since become concerned with the musical experiences of aurally diverse listeners, and they have shaped my works and artistic direction henceforth.

Multisensory and Multimedia

My first work specifically addressing this new concern is the 2019 extended version of 'The (Real) Laptop Music :))'. This two-channel audiovisual piece emerged from a question regarding the laptop as a 'musical instrument': is it to be used mainly to operate sonic software or as a source of sound? This audiovisual piece displays the visuals of my laptop being hit, tapped, touched, scratched, and pressed by my hands. The audio directly corresponds with the visuals, with all the sound being percussive.

This piece was originally composed in 2017 without taking aural diversity into consideration. However, I had a unique sensory experience when the piece was about to be premiered at the New York City Electroacoustic Music Festival-International Computer Music Conference 2019.

The piece was diffused to a six-channel loudspeaker system within a small space and projected onto a screen via a projector. During the soundcheck when the overall loudness was being adjusted, I sensed the middle to low frequencies with my whole body. It felt like my skin and body became a big membrane and resonator. Suddenly I was enjoying that moment which, for a while, made me forget to pay attention to the sound and visuals.

I know I had certainly had this kind of tactile experience in the past, from sensing my own heartbeat to witnessing a 5.6 Richter scale earthquake in my hometown of Yogyakarta, Indonesia. I know these experiences do not sound special to other people. However, for a hearing person like me, consciously experiencing the sound using sensory faculties beyond the ear and making a critical observation made me realise that sound and vibration are actually no different. They come from the same acoustical energy. It is a matter of which part of the body perceives the energy that brings the different sensations. My own experience has become an embodied knowledge beyond any theoretical research.

This experience brought me to a major revision of 'The (Real) Laptop Music :))'. The second version of the piece emphasises an objective and a presentation mode intended for aurally diverse audiences, including but not limited to deaf people, cochlear implant and hearing aid users, and 'normal' hearing listeners. During the Aural Diversity Conference 2019, my piece was diffused to a four-channel loudspeaker system with moderate loudness that accommodated people with hyperacusis and presbycusis. I also prepared balloons for audiences who wanted to feel the vibration propagated from the loudspeakers on their hands or other body parts. Moreover, I provided a programme note, revised from the original, to accommodate those who wanted to know what to expect during the presentation.

After the performance, I was delighted to know that some in the audience, including deaf persons, cochlear implant and hearing aid users, persons with cochlear amusia, persons with tinnitus, and persons with Ménière's disease, found the piece enjoyable. I was also elated to know that some autistic listeners found the small details in the piece engaging, some others found the piece's visuals memorable, and some 'normal' hearing audiences found the piece mesmerising.

To me, being appreciated by aurally diverse audiences has revealed that musical experiences do not only rely on aural perception but also visual and tactile modes. I believe, as long as I communicate and deliver an interesting and convincing experience, it does not matter whether the music is less or even no longer sonic.

Visually Listening and Music in the Mind

'The (Real) Laptop Music :))' led me to my next compositional journey, *[SOUNDSCAPTION]*. *[SOUNDSCAPTION]* is a series of digital no-audio video works aimed to trigger sonic imagery, which plays an important part in active listening. Exhibiting a variety of soundscapes through video footage, this series explores captions – an element of accessibility that benefits not only deaf and hard-of-hearing people but also hearing persons – to describe 'the sound'. This work offers the opposite of an acousmatic experience. While in acousmatic listening we experience sound without seeing its source, in *[SOUNDSCAPTION]* we listen by seeing an object without perceiving its sound. This work investigates 'visually listening' as an aspect that aurally diverse listeners may have in common.

The ideas for *[SOUNDSCAPTION]* arose from my own experience during my self-quarantine due to the COVID-19 pandemic. As the world was forced by the virus and people were mandated by local and national authorities to stay at home, the pandemic era – especially the first three months – saw the emergence of online platforms like never before.

As soon as typically offline interactions were required to go online, new problems appeared. Responding to hearing content-creators, many aurally diverse people expressed concerns that the contents they were viewing and/or listening to were inaccessible. During this time, I witnessed a rise in modes of accessibility such as captions, alt-text, sign language, and audio descriptions promoted by anyone, regardless of ability, who cared about access. 'Caption your video!' was one expression I mostly saw on my social media timeline.

At the same time, the pandemic also affected me personally. I mostly stayed at home, and although I am a person who likes such privacy, I experienced stress and anxiety that led to sensory fatigue. I became exhausted from listening to any audio sources from my laptop and smartphone, as they led to my becoming sensory-overloaded.

This condition induced me to watch online videos mostly with the audio muted, which was surprisingly enjoyable. Nearly everything I watched was muted, even music videos. I attempted to comprehend how watching muted videos made a difference; it surely did. Some videos triggered my sonic imagination, while others did not. Sometimes I turned up the volume on some videos just to check the actual sound. My sonic imagination did not always match reality. Nonetheless, it was interesting to feel a divergent perception towards those audiovisual sources. Having this experience, I argue that a compelling musical experience may occur in mind without direct sonic stimuli.

I manifested this experience in a creative artwork by making a no-audio video series. Inspired by the recent ascendancy of accessibility during the COVID-19 pandemic, I employed open captions to drive viewers' sonic imagination. Instead of using a standard captioning method, I devised my own captioning style using REAPER software, exploring placements and the opacity that make its appearance more visually dynamic, providing imagined sonic experiences beyond using the static text approach. The captions were is applied to various video footage from my archive to make a compelling visual presentation.

[SOUNDSCAPTION] attempts to find a similarity in the act of listening between people with different hearing profiles. The exploration of visual perception to create an imagined aurality provides an aesthetic experience that may resonate with both Deaf and hearing cultures.

This experiment has resulted in three videos: '[SOUNDSCAPTION: Soundwalk]' (2020), '[SOUNDSCAPTION: Self-quarantine]' (2021), and '[SOUNDSCAPTION: Applause]' (2021). This series will be augmented with additional videos.

The Impact of Aural Diversity on Communities, Creativity, and Beyond

'The (Real) Laptop Music :))' and *[SOUNDSCAPTION]* series are my humble efforts to reduce my implicit bias as a typically hearing person, which may otherwise unintentionally harm people with different hearing conditions, and to invite society to question our fixed assumptions regarding hearing, listening, and the notion of auditory-centricity in sonic arts and our daily lives. I do not deny that sound is a basic component of music and listening. However, reality suggests that factors, including non-sonic stimuli and our body, shape aural and musical experiences. My embodied experiences, observations of diverse hearing conditions, and interactions with aurally diverse audiences have showed that sonic arts are multisensory phenomena that include aural, visual, and tactile modes.

Through my works that address aural diversity, I hope to promote more inclusive arts, providing accessible experiences to aurally diverse people. By promoting multisensory values, I also aspire to contribute to abolishing audism – a system that advocates the superiority of typical hearing and speech (Humphries 1977, 12) – in composition and invite those who are adept in other sonic-related fields, including but not limited to music education, musicology, music psychology, and phenomenology of listening, to do the same.

As an artist living in aurally diverse communities, I also see myself as responsible for helping shape society. In my view, acknowledging aural diversity in part acknowledges the reality that our bodies have limitations in perceiving the quality and quantity standards devised by typical hearing people. I attempt to make an artistic effort that embraces both the realist model (Siebers 2008, 53–69) and the social model of disability (Linton 1998), acknowledging both how a body meets barriers in an environment and how access can be established. I deem it significant to create lasting inclusive and accessible arts ecosystems.

Embracing aural diversity in my works has significantly shifted my aesthetics in a direction that takes my target audiences into account. It has consciously shifted my compositional thinking towards a listener-first paradigm that influences my artistic decisions, including instrumentation and methodology. Consequently, I have rerouted my creativity towards working with various media. The use of multimedia to target different aural, visual, and tactile sensory modes of expression in the sonic arts is indeed nothing new. However, emphasising aurally diverse listeners has expanded my aesthetics possibilities.

It is worth noting that understanding different hearing profiles takes immense effort. I had to learn not only different cultures, like Deaf cultures, and audiological terms and concepts but also complex interactions between the social and the medical views of disability. I have realised that it is not only about making a piece that specifically targets certain bodily conditions, but also considering cultural and even moral aspects. I argue we should avoid making an artwork that creates another oppression and discrimination towards other sensory modes, positioning typical bodies as being superior. It is not as easy as it sounds, and this is certainly a lifetime learning process for me both as an artist and an individual.

An aural diversity emphasis foregrounds the listener as an important determinant of music-making and musical experience. It further accentuates music as a diversely embodied phenomenon rather than a static, fixed object. The same stimulus – be it the acoustical energy that is audible and tactile or the radiant energy that is visible – will certainly be perceived differently from one perceiver to another, depending on one's bodily condition. Contemplating all the facets of aural diversity will create more diverse conceptions of music-making that may lead to a broader theorisation of sonic arts and listening.

References

Humphries, T. (1977) *Communicating Across Cultures (Deaf/Hearing) and Language Learning*, Ph.D. Dissertation, Union Graduate School, Cincinnati, OH.
Linton, S. (1998) *Claiming Disability: Knowledge and Identity*. New York: New York University Press.
Siebers, T. (2008) *Disability Theory*. Michigan: University of Michigan Press. doi:10.3998/mpub.309723.

22
ATTENTION REFRAMED

A Personal Account of Hearing Loss as a Catalyst for Intermedia Practice

Simon Allen

Experimental Beginnings

If every sound bears a message, wherever the impulse of a sound can be detected its message exists in some form. Listening to music, the degree of comprehension required to receive these messages is most relaxed. Free from the interpretive specifics of speech, music invites subjectivity – and for hearing impairment such as my own, making music is an accessible activity. This access I enjoy as a professional, is largely the result of working in the context of experimental arts, whose community finds a deal of motivation in dismantling tradition. My training as a 'classical' musician – inevitably ingrained – is now stripped back to what is essential; what remains are the parts that still function with hearing loss. Investigating new methods to communicate music whilst hearing through an 'impaired' system, is now a large part of my work.

Navigating a music career with hearing loss, the message of each sound is accompanied by an interrogation of the accuracy of what is heard. This questioning is most persistent when dealing with well-known musical colours for which there are predetermined expectations; employing or receiving these sounds are processes that accentuate feelings of skills under test. Alongside these known colours is another world of novel sounds developed through careful experiment or playfulness that find merit in uniqueness unencumbered by universal standards. Some novel discoveries can be built into new experimental instruments – others are unstable in execution, difficult to revisit, existing specific to a momentary set of conditions. In working with new sounds, that persistent questioning of the veracity of what is heard, is turned from a tiring reflex into an enjoyable investigative muscle, and my own musical language these are the sounds that dominate.

During formal music training my hearing was as ordinary as my peers. At the time my hearing changed around 30 years ago, I was learning to listen with finer detail, especially to sounds marginal enough to be largely unnoticed, and spent much of my time playing with physical materials in search of a new sonic palette. In retrospect, the timing of hearing loss with that developing will to listen so intricately, was partially driven by a preference for controlled listening environments. At the same time, I was moving away from working as an orchestral percussionist towards smaller groups where contemporary music finds economic viability; a shift in artistic interest precipitated by needing a work environment where speech comprehension was easier.

Today my listening feels more acute than before hearing loss. The progressive slip of hearing ability is not running parallel with that of listening, which now has enhanced intention and is spent wisely. With or without the assistance of technology – and like many others with hearing loss – I hear all the musical attributes of pitch, rhythm, colour, moment, spatial arrangement, and the measurement of time. I feel no inhibitors to the exercise of musical ideas – only factors that shape their individuality. Changed hearing brings heightened sensitivity that exposes itself differently according to the type of work – I can hear minute changes in volume and mix in the studio by increments of less than a decibel; I detect low frequencies that others strain to hear and feel acutely aware of difference tones. The usual description of these sensitivities would be – high frequency loss that progresses from around 800 Hz upwards with attendant hyperacusis and tinnitus; most sounds above 2kHz registering as hiss. Whilst a hearing curve of this shape would have been given no place in the music for which I first trained, it has proved less hindrance to finding a creative place in the world of experimental and improvised music.

Experimental music and the novel inventions of improvisation feed upon the curiosity and adaptability of performers, embracing idiosyncratic skills as fresh possibilities. Consequently, their making environment already has a neurodiverse population – a state seldom talked about. Acceptance of difference within this community is surely a natural function of experimental practices for which the relevance of uniform training is in constant question. Creative agency is so valued that many experimental musicians choose to self-identify more broadly as artists; a new sense of self, well fitted to an arena where ideas about music are disseminated through diverse communicative means. Texts, graphics and images as alternatives in addition to traditional music notation are amongst the creative stimuli used to refresh the depth and variety of outcomes. Musical suggestion often appears in conceptual form with a strong sense of invitation. Instructional poetry – written, drawn, sculptural, moving or static – each means of communication also offers a different quality of accessibility for the interpreter.

The wider accessibility of these tools is also attractive for artists seeking an introduction to sonic practices, enabling them to explore audio elements as they would any other new material. Many artists active within and in association with experimental music have no experience or need of formal music training; their qualification is their engagement with listening – a developable skill, distinct from hearing. Although this is an ideal area for deaf musicians to exercise ideas, deafness within this community is rarely apparent.

Aspiring to or finding an educational path to my current position would have been hard, if hearing loss had preceded my musical education. Thankfully attitudes are improving with advocacy, guidelines are refining and research into neurodiversity within many fields stimulated. Enacting change in a fuller sense towards achieving inclusive educational and professional environments, is still limited by social attitudes towards difference. The gatekeepers requiring sensitisation are not only policy makers but also those found at home in the family, where aspirations develop according to options that are apparent. It follows that all developments in research must aim to be highly visible and find testing ground that is as widely relevant as possible; a requirement well partnered with the experimental arts.

Accessible Practice

In 2012 I was commissioned by Arts Council England to compose and direct a large-scale multimedia work for the Cultural Olympiad as part of the Unlimited festival. The resulting 80 minute composition *Resonance at the Still Point of Change* for five instrumentalists, two singers and narrator, featured multiple moving images, projected text, audio description and onscreen lighting. The work aimed to be inclusive in ways that heightened the subjective response of each audience member; a composition structured to offer many alternative routes through the narrative. In the case of text elements, for example – an idea verbalised at a given point, could appear as visual text elsewhere, dislocated across time. Different media layers also contained moments exclusive to hearing whilst absent to sight, and vice versa. Employing similar compositional approaches on a smaller scale in 2019 for the first Aural Diversity concerts and conference, *Map Fragments* and *Aerosol (after Cornell)* are works incorporating sign language with images, on screen text and music. Accepting that I am unable to read British Sign Language, these latter experiments investigated how I could script for BSL whilst allowing it greater independence. The strategy for this was to invite the signer to repeat words or phrases freely according to their meaning or physicality, drawing out a stronger sense of poetic choreography from within the movement language of signing. As with the interplay of media in my earlier work, the dislocation between projected and signed text explores the textures of non-synchronous counterpoint. Few would be able to read all these components simultaneously, and as composer and writer, I too was unable to understand every sign of the BSL interpreter. Taking a playful approach to BSL in this way is important to maximising its creative potential beyond interpretation.

Similarly, onscreen text was revealed rhythmically in phrases relating to music, and words as objects were floated onto specific parts of images. Unlike subtitling or simple interpretation these layers are not added solely to accommodate the needs of a section of audience members. Each of the component parts in this expanded counterpoint is a means for artistic expression as rich as any other – and is made using technology easily available in arts education settings at many levels. Structuring these works is a process of achieving balance between layers of media; singly, or in any combination they must to produce a satisfying version of the composition, whilst avoiding overstatement in the whole. In rehearsal, music notation, mappings, text instructions, images, creative notes, and conversation are the stimuli for creative musical action – there is no single overarching 'full score' documenting the complete work.

I find the experience of making this kind of work compels me to revisit old questions relating to the place of music notation as the backbone of 'Western art music', and its effect upon the development of music studies. What is a score? What can constitute a score? How well understood are the positive and negative aspects of formal music training? How do these questions relate to diversity in the workplace? All these questions have a relationship with issues of access for both audience and performers. They are answered through experimentation, by making new work. Experimental music making is continually expanding and within the growing community of makers, neurodiversity has a strong presence. This is something we are yet to become fully aware of.

23

LOST AND FOUND

A Pianist's Hearing Journey

David Holzman

My musical talents were evident early and I started taking piano lessons at the age of five. In the fifth grade, a virus destroyed 90% of hearing in my left ear. I tried to ignore the loss, but eventually had to come to terms with my handicap.

One ear meant sounds were weaker, reached me less immediately and, most important, made it hard to distinguish voices (words or music) in a polyphony of sounds. My right ear was perfect. I heard pitches and harmonies easily but was rarely confronted with complex music.

That began to change when I entered Chatham Square Music School in 1962. I began studying chamber music. When I was told that I was too loud and that I was not fully in sync with my partners, I had to take notice. It was the faintest beginning of my efforts to use my eyes to recognise cues from my partners, my body to impart cues, and my brain and body to achieve dynamic balance.

When I entered Mannes College of Music, I began to focus upon twentieth-century music with its complexities of harmony, rhythm, counterpoint, and touch. My teacher, Paul Jacobs, helped me to achieve autonomy of hands (Messiaen was a major help) and later of individual fingers.

I finally discovered the most serious pianistic damage created by no left ear-my left hand was, without my knowing it, too loud for my right hand. I gradually recognised the need to tilt my body (and my mind) towards the right side so my left hand was less heavy. Some years later, I began to realise that voicing complex chords, even when arpeggiated, required the same tilt towards the top to allow the top note of a chord to stand out, especially as it was so often the melodic line. This involved finger, wrist, arm, and mind to 'hear' a properly balanced chord, whether top voice or inner voice.

It was always a bit of a guessing game, as my ear would not confirm that the sound I wanted was indeed what was actually the result. For the past year, with paired Cochlear Implants (CI) and Hearing Aids (HA), my ears indeed hear what I do and so they finally lead the way.

This constant challenge created a very basic dilemma. I trusted my fingers more than my ear. When a thumb had to make awkward motions such as moving from a white key to a black key I would not know whether my tone was affected; or if an inner finger would rub an adjacent note I would not know whether the note was heard. Efforts to find magic fingering was a great addition to my pianism but was often unnecessary. Now my hearing largely captures reality and solutions of fingering and pedalling are usually simpler.

Lost and Found: A Pianist's Hearing Journey **211**

Soon after graduating, I began an active career in New York's new music scene, premiering hundreds of works, both solo and chamber.

More Loss

In my mid-forties, I was practising for an upcoming CD. I took a ride on my bike to relax. I forgot my helmet and equally dangerous, I was using new medication for epilepsy. I paid the price as I had a seizure while riding, fell on my right ear and lost much of my hearing in that ear. A hearing aid helped for speech but not music. Playing with others was close to impossible. For many years my chamber career was gone. I felt deep emotional wounds which I tried to hide. I slowly confronted these and have largely overcome them decades later.

Luckily, there were projects which needed completion, most notably CDs of the piano music of Donald Martino. The extraordinary efforts to complete these CDs not only kept me active but proved a blessing as both the composer and the producer, Joel Gordon, gave me both the musical and emotional help to openly confront my loss and to grow.

The central work to be recording was the legendary *Pianissimo*. As the score shows (Figure 23.1) even a pianist with two perfect ears would have trouble hearing the correct pitches and then

FIGURE 23.1 Part of the score of *Pianissimo* by Donald Martino, with David Holzman's markings
Reproduced with kind permission of Lora Martino.

transforming them into music. It was a challenge, but I found many means to 'hear' the score and ultimately make it compelling listening.

My first tool was RHYTHMIC MEMORY. I remember using it to master the devilish rhythms of Milton Babbitt's *Partitions*. It meant subdividing beats and playing individual notes as upbeats or afterbeats-triplets, quintuplets etc. Practising was a progression from very slow to faster in which gradually sub-beats disappear, larger beats take over, and ultimately pure rhythms are in my mind and body. The slow efforts ineffably brought pitch recognition into awareness.

VISUAL MEMORY: I realised that both seeing and imagining black and white patterns on the keyboard made it easier to reach for distant notes and, more, to feel complex chords in my fingers. This led to KEYBOARD AWARENESS where finger, wrist and arm can reach notes and chords throughout the keyboard with whatever tilt or combination of inside/outside is called for, i.e. thinking ahead. This led to TRUE HEARING both in mind and eventually ear for even the most complex lines and chords.

Two years later, I completed another CD which featured Schoenberg's op. 11 piano pieces. This brought back my studies with Paul Jacobs and his help with touch and color. Visual symbols such as slurs, staccatos and ghost-like runs all required special motions, shapes and tensions in fingers, wrist, and arm (Figure 23.2). This digital choreography led to a widening of my sensitivity to colour and expressive playing.

After a few slow years, my career and spirit were brought back when I was asked to record a collection of works by Stefan Wolpe for Bridge Records in celebration of his Centennial. I revered his music, and jumped at the opportunity to show myself at my best. I did so, not only by using the learning tools described above (Figure 23.3) but by making my handicaps strengths. I gave myself all the time needed, reduced seizure medications to retain full sharpness, and worked in what I can only describe as a pure environment.

I am virtually alone with my piano. No noise indoors except an occasional phone which I often confuse with piano if I hear it at all. Outdoors, even with open windows, virtually a void. It was close to timeless. Slow hands separate and hands together work was an intense and satisfying chunk of my day. A seizure occasionally came at the end of a day's work as if a validation of my efforts. With one ear, I heard a clear pitch even if distant. Charles Rosen wrote about the physical joy of touching the keys. That was certainly present for me.

The cd received much acclaim and was the first of five during the decade. All of them featured challenging masterpieces which I loved. All were successful in part because of the purity of the experience – intensity, acceptance, and pleasure.

By the last of the CDs the purity was damaged. My audiologist introduced a music program for my HA. Sadly, the program was meant for casual listeners, not concert pianists. The amplification created a harsh and artificial sound which made focus harder. What was worst was that the irregular strength of frequencies which I heard due to my grade B ear was amplified. I was utterly confused about what was causing these jarring changes from one note to another – my piano or my fingers. This had been an issue for a long time but now was too much to bear. It was two years later that a doctor finally described this as the result of a Grade-B ear. Now, with the CI, these disparities are targeted by 'mapping' and have largely disappeared. I left this doctor and began looking for a real solution where sound was normal, clear, and musical. I could not go back to deafness nor stay with ugliness.

FIGURE 23.2 Arnold Schoenberg *Drei Klavierstücke*, Op. 11, Nr. 1. First page with David Holzman's annotations

Reproduced by arrangement with Universal Edition A. G. Wien.

FIGURE 23.3 First page of *First Piece, Battle Piece* by Stefan Wolpe, with David Holzman's annotations

Found

A new doctor urged me to try a cochlear implant. She led me to NYU Cochlear Center where it was determined that I was indeed eligible for a CI. I received one along with a Resound HA. This was six years ago and it has been a slow and difficult process, but one which is reaching the ending I had hoped for.

Receiving the implant was indeed a thrill. But the first stages were similar to all experiences with hearing aids, namely getting used to new sounds. What was unique was hearing, however poorly, out of two ears.

While hearing speech was a fairly steady progression, music was slower. Hearing one or two shadowy pitches came after a month, but beeps and buzzes dominated for more than a year. At first, volume was kept low on CI for comfort and to let me hear music. After a year, a new audiologist told me that my hearing in left ear would not improve enough unless volume was higher. She was correct. Despite the torture of year 2, I began to hear more notes of fairly clear pitches. The CI pitches were almost a semitone higher than my right ear, which made playing torment, but by the third year, my brain seemed to be modifying the disparity and playing became less of an effort. However, I still hear unfamiliar music a half step too high which causes confusion.

There was a continual expansion of pitch recognition and equal strength between ears, often moving me to tears. Complex counterpoint (still more in playing than listening) began to be a multi-dimensional experience. A Bach fugue or a work of new music came through as never before.

I now began to hear more high treble and the sounds sustained longer. I didn't need to focus on left hand as much. Thus, feeling two hands as one unity was becoming natural. I also realised that the CI, when given a precise strength could modify the metallic sounds of the HA. Thus, at piano, CI would be minimal strength (10) and HA moderate (40) and mellowness was the result.

All this was documented by my CD of the music of John McDonald. In early 2017, I was still complaining during recording about the disparity between devices. Six months later, I was much more comfortable. John wrote pieces describing each mood. 'The Berceuse to Play with Two Devices' ends with long sustained high G's, which was a metaphor for my advance.

But unity was still a long journey. In late 2019, the CI gained so much power that my left ear dominated my hearing-a surreal experience after sixty years of deafness. I was soon fitted with a new processor for the CI and a Resound Quattro, the most advanced HA. This would allow for 'pairing' where my smartphone connects via streaming my HA and my CI as one. Thus all sounds are more unified. After a few months, progress was great towards achieving this unity for much though still not all of a working day.

I had been taken aback by the increased power of all sounds, from telephone rings to car honks to piano. It was hard to believe that a normal musician heard such loud sounds with ease. I had volume programs for CI, including a low one for piano. But by the fourth year, I became more accepting of power and now, nearly six years in, I do not use program 3 for piano. I am finally hearing loud sounds as part of my musical vocabulary – and enjoying it! Still, pitches are not fully clear and thick chromatic chords cause trouble. That is my major hope for yet a newer Resound which I am awaiting.

Coda

I am beginning to feel as though I am returning to that 'zone of purity' I experienced before. Sounds seldom disturb me and the occasional intrusion of a confusing noise elicits a smile and no more. Became of the pandemic, I have time to spend on the few things that matter – people and piano. I found a work which challenges and inspires me – Beethoven's *Diabelli Variations* – and I have spent many hours slowly mastering it. Balances and counterpoint came close to naturally even as the challenges are great. My personality is involved after months of pure labour. I listen to Schubert's three-dimensional songs and *Quintet* with love and tears. I'm a perfectionist, so I will seek even more advances. My thanks to Resound, Cochlear, my doctors and my friends for their help.

24
COMPOSING WITH HEARING DIFFERENCES

Andrew Hugill

Composing with hearing differences (in my case, severe hearing loss, balance disorder, and autism) presents many challenges. It also raises a key question: who is the music *for*? If I work *with* my differences, then what emerges is a kind of music that represents me but may present barriers to wider enjoyment or comprehension. If I *ignore* my differences, then the music that emerges may be successful but fails to express any aspect of my true self. It is definitively out of reach to me.

I have tried to address these questions through my recent composition. To understand how I have done so requires first a discussion of the differences themselves and their consequences for me.

Hearing

For the first 50 years of my life, I barely gave my hearing any consideration. Like most musicians, I took it for granted, accepting what I now realise were its extraordinary characteristics as standard. I had musician friends with severe or profound hearing loss and I admired their ability to overcome those challenges. I knew about Beethoven's hearing loss, of course, and I was aware of prominent deaf musicians such as Evelyn Glennie. I had a kind of half-baked heroic narrative that I attached to such people, although I cannot pretend that I gave it much thought. I composed, performed, and taught music in the same way as the vast majority of people do, giving scant attention to hearing.

All that began to change in 2007, when I experienced my first severe vertigo attack. I was in my studio composing, when suddenly the world began to spin violently around me. The feeling passed after several minutes, but its force was quite shocking. Over the next couple of years, the episodes of vertigo steadily increased in frequency, duration, and intensity. Along with the vertigo came tinnitus (a ringing in the ears), a sense of aural fullness (a pressure in the ear) and, to my great alarm, creeping loss of hearing in my right ear. The hearing loss seemed to affect bass frequencies most. I began to lose contact with the bottom register of the piano.

In 2009, this was diagnosed as Ménière's Disease. It started out as unilateral (only affecting the right ear) but soon became bilateral (affecting both ears, albeit unevenly). As well as constant balance problems which, at their height, were giving me three vertigo attacks per week, each lasting

3–5 hours and accompanied by constant vomiting, my hearing rapidly deteriorated. I reached a point of severe hearing loss in the right ear and somewhat less severe in the left, with constant fluctuating tinnitus in both ears. I was given gentamicin injections directly into the inner ear which, after a few months, gave me relief from the vertigo. This was in effect a chemical labyrinthectomy (surgical removal of the inner ear balance and hearing mechanism), and I now balance using my eyes. I fall over in the dark.

Another phenomenon entered the picture. As well as having lost the ability to hear low pitches, I now realised that when a single note was played, I would hear two different notes, one out of tune with the other. This is called diplacusis, and it is very common in Ménière's. Most people don't notice it, but for musicians it is very troublesome. I began to find that even simple music would turn into a kind of microtonal mush very quickly. Also, it combined with the tinnitus to make listening to music for longer than a few minutes intolerable. Knowing that I could not hear music properly diminished the pleasure it gave me. I stopped attending concerts. I did much less composing, too. The thing that had been my primary motivation in life was drifting away. I switched careers, to work more in digital technology and academic leadership. But I kept all this a secret, known only to a few friends, until 2017.

Autism

In 2018, at the age of 60, I was professionally identified as autistic. I was extremely sceptical about this possibility at first. But over about a year and after a lot of research, it became obvious to me that it was true. The psychologist's diagnosis, when it came, was not a surprise. There are many aspects to receiving a late diagnosis like this (and, by the way, I prefer the term 'professional identification' to 'diagnosis', since autism is not an illness or a disease, but rather just a neurological difference that is present from birth). This chapter will not concern itself with most of them, but only with the implications for my hearing.

Ever since childhood, I had listened in an autistic way. How could I do otherwise? Bill Davies' chapter in this volume summarises what that means. For me, there were several facets. Firstly, I had a kind of extreme sensitivity to sound and would hear details others would miss. This applied whether the sounds were musical or not. So, for example, I would hear the overtones in piano chords very clearly and often listen to those first and foremost. I would also listen to fridges or motorways and try to notate them. Or I would focus on the detail in an orchestral work, often missing the bigger picture. The second characteristic was synaesthesia. I always associated certain sounds with certain colours and vice-versa, and this would sometimes merge into taste too. I found myself drawn to composers who had similar experiences, such as Scriabin and Messiaen. However, I never took it too seriously, because it seemed vague and unscientific, too hard to pin down. It was just 'one of those things' that I mostly ignored. Finally, I would hear small sounds, such as electricity running through cables or light bulbs. These kinds of super-detailed environmental sounds occupied a big presence in my listening, so much so that I would have to work hard to drown them out in comparison to the sounds I was *supposed* to be listening to.

Now, the extraordinary thing about all of this is that, until my autism identification, *I just assumed everybody else heard in the same way!* Post-identification, I now know that my hearing was always unusual, which explains so much about the way I have understood music. Being able to listen in those ways was beneficial in certain musical situations but could also be a problem in day-to-day life.

The distortions caused by Ménière's have naturally affected my autistic listening too. The past few years have been a process of coming to terms with the consequences of this. I have used technology a great deal. For example, my marvellous GNResound hearing aids have really helped to offset some of the worst effects and enabled me to appreciate music again to some extent, while my noise-cancelling headphones shield me against the kind of sounds that typically disturb an autistic person. I quite often use the two in combination with a Minimic – a small wearable device which streams directly to my hearing aids – so that I can block out surrounding noise in crowded environments while being able to maintain a conversation with someone. These are survival strategies that help me get through everyday situations.

Composition

How may one create something beautiful in response to such challenging hearing conditions? Finding my way back to composition since the onset of Ménière's has been extremely difficult. I have had to rethink my whole approach and find ways of working that I can tolerate and even enjoy. It has taken roughly ten years to get here, and I thank autism a lot for that, because my determination to get up each day and follow certain routines is a kind of autistic bloody-mindedness that will not take 'no' for an answer.

Throughout the ten years, I did not entirely give up composing, but the work I produced was frequently unfinished. I have struggled to develop a consistent approach to composition which responded creatively to these new challenges. There were two conflicting possibilities:

1. Revert to writing dots on paper in the classical way. The advantage of this was that I knew how things *ought* to sound. I can still audiate (hear music in my head when reading a printed score). The music I hear when I do this is a memory of music heard earlier in life. I developed score-reading skills at a young age. The ability has not left me, but imaginary music is not music! I would never be able to hear the music I wrote this way, except in my imagination.
2. Continue to work directly with sound (as I have increasingly done throughout my career) but try to find new ways of doing that. The advantage of this was that it would give me a way to engage with music fully. The disadvantage was that it was very difficult and even painful to achieve.

In the end, I have tended to go down the second path, although I do still sometimes produce music notation as well. There have been three recent works that I would like to describe, to give a sense of what this means in practice: *Thirty Minutes* for diplacusis piano; *Kelston Birdsong*; and *Spectrum Sounds*.

Thirty Minutes for Diplacusis Piano

Marcel Duchamp wrote in the *Box of 1914* 'one can look at seeing; one cannot hear hearing'. This composition, or rather collection of compositions, resists that statement by creating a new digital instrument – the diplacusis piano – that reproduces something of what I hear when a normal piano is played.

The work consists of 30 pieces for diplacusis piano. Each piece lasts around one minute and they may be played in any order, and for as long as required. They may be experienced either as audio-only or video. The brevity of the compositions reflects the enormous difficulty of composing for and listening to this instrument.

The project began with a systematic attempt to map the discrepancies in hearing between my two ears. First, I played a piano note at a given frequency (rounded to a whole number), checking

TABLE 24.1 Andrew Hugill's diplacusis

Note	Frequency in Hz (rounded)	Left Ear Difference (Hz)	Left Ear Perception (Hz)	Right Ear Perception (Hz)	Right Ear Difference (Hz)
F♯2/Gb2	92	-1	91	86	-6
G2	98	-2	96	95	-3
G♯2/Ab2	103	-1	102	100	-2
A2	110		110	104	-6
A♯2/Bb2	116	-2	114	110	-4
B2	123		123	117	-7
C3	131		131	125	-5
C♯3/Db3	138		138	132	-6
D3	147		147	140	-7
D♯3/Eb3	156		156	151	-4
E3	165		165	151	-11
F3	174		174	168	-6
F♯3/Gb3	185		185	180	-5
G3	196		196	194	-4
G♯3/Ab3	207		207	204	-3
A3	220		220	212	-8
A♯3/Bb3	233		233	229	-2
B3	247	-1	245	240	-7
C4	261	-2	259	251	-10

with a fine pitch meter that the tuning was correct before proceeding. I then blocked my right ear and sang the note I heard, checking against the pitch meter. The left ear (my 'good' ear) gives generally very accurate pitch, with a few slight deviations towards the lower and upper ends of my singing range. I then blocked my left ear and performed the same exercise using my right. Table 24.1 shows the pitches, and the differences. Pitch was not the only difference: for example, the perceived amplitude was considerably softer from 138 Hz downwards and fell away steadily. This captures my diplacusis as it was in 2017. My hearing has continued to deteriorate a little bit since then, but on the whole has stabilised, so the model holds up reasonably well five years later.

What we can see quite clearly from this is that my diplacusis is active at all frequencies, but also variable. For some pitches, it is more than a semitone. For others, rather less. I hear these two pitches combined, with the out-of-tune one being softer than the in-tune.

To go beyond my singing range required refence to my audiogram, from which it was clear that the hearing in my right ear is a lot worse than my left ear. The left ear has normal hearing (above 10 dB) in the region between 1500 Hz and 4000 Hz, which is my useful in speech situations, but there is quite a lot of hearing loss around that just the same. Nevertheless, my pitch perception in that ear is tolerable. As is typical with Ménière's, the lower frequencies are the ones that have disappeared the most.

Working with this information took many months of struggle. I could no longer rely on my singing voice to help me understand my own pitch perception, because the rest of the piano keyboard is simply out of range. To make matters worse, every time I tried it was like working in a hall of endlessly reflecting mirrors. I would listen to my diplacusis with my diplacusis. It was very uncomfortable and very tiring. I therefore worked on trying to understand my own hearing by feeling my way through trial and error. Several key features gradually emerged:

1. There is an octave between F♯5 (~698 Hz) and F♯6 (~1397 Hz) where there is no diplacusis at all.
2. In the range above that, the diplacusis gradually reappears, getting worse as it gets higher.
3. The range from C4 (~261 Hz) down to F2 (~87 Hz) is affected by unpredictable amounts of diplacusis.
4. Below E2 (~82 Hz) this unpredictable diplacusis effect continues, but now a new phenomenon enters, presumably resulting from the general loss in low frequency hearing. The fundamental frequencies of each note and then the first and second partials, gradually disappear, leaving a thudding sound and a collection of higher overtone frequencies. This complex spectrum is then subject to precisely the same diplacusis that affects the higher register, resulting in a perceptible shift in spectrum but no discernible change in pitch.

Given the difficulties of translating the above into any kind of instrument, I eventually had to seek help. I worked with Craig Vear from De Montfort University, using his ears to help me understand how the notes unfolded over time. The diplacusis piano is not really a piano at all, despite having piano sounds as its raw material. If I play a common chord, or attempt to play some classical piano music, all one hears is an out-of-tune piano. It's a bit like a honky-tonk but worse – some kind of abandoned instrument. Interestingly, the brain filters out the 'rubbish' from the signal and quickly the out-of-tune-ness recedes. To avoid sounding like I'm just trying to write piano music for a bad instrument, I had to find a new way of thinking about composing for this diplacusis piano.

The method I developed used a rolling spectrogram display to understand the behaviour of the overtones. I was then able to chain these together to make viable sequences based on overtones alone. The spectrograms themselves became a kind of digital score, enabling me compose musical sequences that made some sense of my hearing differences. To hear and see these, please visit https://andrewhugill.com/music/thirtyminutes

The first performance on the Diplacusis Piano was given by myself at the Old Barn, Kelston Roundhill, near Bath, UK, on 6 July 2019, as part of the 'Aural Diversity' concert. I had composed an extended piece lasting ten minutes and played it with the spectrogram rolling across screen in real time. Two things emerged from this experience: the piece itself lacked shape due to the challenging nature of the material and it was extremely tiring both to play and to listen to. Reflecting on this led me to the short forms of the *Thirty Minutes*, which even include a silent movement to give the ears a forced rest. This version was performed as an installation during the second 'Aural Diversity' concert at the Attenborough Arts Centre, University of Leicester, on 30 November 2019.

Kelston Birdsong

This piece comprises a selection of recordings of birds typically found at Kelston Roundhill near Bath, interspersed with human calls and responses performed by a mixed flexible ensemble on a range of instruments. The piece is written for an aurally diverse group of musicians. The idea is that the birdsongs are categorised according to frequency range/audibility and then allocated to each musician based on their hearing profile. When a musician hears one of 'their' birds, they play a call from a call sheet. When the other musicians hear that call, they answer with a response from a response sheet. Each call/response set is written in such a way as to be most audible to the calling musician. The idea of this piece was to theatricalise the act of listening in a way which demonstrated the hearing characteristics of each individual. This was music consciously written for others, not just myself, and that sought to accommodate a range of hearing types.

Spectrum Sounds

This collection of seven short pieces was commissioned by the BBC in 2021 as part of its 'Culture in Quarantine' series aimed at disabled and/or neurodivergent artists. The music draws on the kind of autistic listening described above: heightened sensitivity to patterns or details that others do not always notice; the ability to decompose music or soundscape into its constituent parts; and the synaesthetic association of colours with certain musical and non-musical sounds. So the 'spectrum' in the title is both the colour spectrum and the autistic spectrum. Each piece is very different in character and written for a different solo instrument. Nearly all the musicians I worked with were neurologically or aurally divergent.

The pieces also continue to examine my own hearing characteristics. One piece, for example, entitled *Verdigrade,* combines a normal piano with the diplacusis piano to give an idea of the creeping distortion of diplacusis. Another, entitled *A Robin in the Snow* (for solo violin), tells a little story of how my hearing is opened out by a robin's song in winter. For the 'orange' piece I worked with Anya Ustaszewski to create music that was pleasant to both our ears. This meant creating original sounds to which she responded on the flute, and then mixing and combining those into a mutually agreeable piece (given her hyperacusis and misophonia and my array of hearing issues). Also, for the first time, I employed a hearing assistant, Simon Atkinson, who was able to help with the mixing and mastering process when that became too challenging for my ears.

As well as the music itself, I have created evocative transcriptions for each piece. These are visual versions, designed to convey the music to those who cannot hear or who would rather listen in a different way. They adopt an array of approaches, but are essentially movies combining text, imagery, spectrographical and other parametric information, and music notation.

25
COMPOSING 'WEIRD' MUSIC

Anya Ustaszewski

Legally, I am not normal. This was the reason my local Environmental Health department gave to refuse to intervene when I was in agony during the early hours of one morning, due to repeated explosions of fireworks nearby.

I experience hyperacusis and misophonia. Busy public spaces are often unbearable unless I wear high attenuation earplugs. Bonfire night causes me days of pain. Every time an emergency services vehicle passes, I clamp my hands to my ears to reduce the sensory input, enduring the hurtful stares of passing members of the public as I do so.

I live in constant fear of the next auditory onslaught.

Perhaps as a result of this, I have been fascinated by music for as long as I can remember. I still, perhaps adorably or embarrassingly, have one of the first ever cassettes I owned, 'Chipmunk Rock'.

My mother says she remembers me making up songs as a young child, with pretty melodies but dreadful lyrics.

When, aged nine, I asked the Deputy Headmaster of my primary school if I could have piano lessons, I was met with an aggressive reprimand as my lack of piano ownership or access meant it was deemed a stupid request. A couple of weeks later, he approached me and asked if I was still interested in learning an instrument, listing the available options. I chose the flute.

This began a period of ten years of lessons, exams, up to seven ensemble rehearsals each week and participating in at least nine performances a year. It was wonderful. I was so dedicated to my musical studies that if I was deemed to have misbehaved, my mother would punish me with a temporary ban on my flute practice. I was bewildered when I learned that most other students despised music practice and often only bothered after persistent nagging from their parents.

Some things were different for me compared to my musical peers. I could not tune my flute. The act of producing a sound while listening to another sound and trying to compare the two was so overwhelming and utterly confusing to me. I relied on my fellow flautists to tell me when I was flat or sharp. The problem persists to this day and I feel a great deal of shame about this.

When listening to any piece of music, I seemed to be able to 'zoom in' on certain instrumental sections' parts of the overall work more quickly and easily than others in my music classes. I loved listening to how different parts of any ensemble piece would interweave. Music just made sense to me in a way that much else of life did not.

DOI: 10.4324/9781003183624-27

Despite my enjoyment of composing, I didn't start to take it seriously until the final two years of my time at university. Previously, I had composed pieces limited to whichever style and structure teachers advised was needed to succeed in my studies. It hadn't occurred to me that composing the music I felt and wanted could ever be acceptable. My university tutors helped me feel safe to discover my voice and encouraged me to express myself.

The bedroom door of the flat my friend was renting back in the early 2000s made the most beautiful unsticking sound. I suspect this was caused by part of the material which was meant to make it draught proof, or even delay a fire's progress, having deteriorated to the extent that it might well have represented a hazard to her. After a few futile attempts to capture this sound, due to my Attention Deficit Hyperactivity Disorder meaning I forgot repeatedly to bring all of the required equipment, when I was finally able to record samples, I didn't stop there. Her washing machine door made a slightly muffled clicking sound. There were metallic sounds from ornaments decorating her room. There was the spray bottle of water she used to dampen clothes while ironing. There was the sound of her bike as she wheeled it indoors to its storage place.

I went home and spent the next few days going through the numerous samples and developing my compositional ideas. This culminated in what is still one of the pieces I enjoy most, 'nmo20', composed for my friend as a birthday gift.

I first read about the Social Model of Disability while waiting for the diagnostic assessment at which I was confirmed to be autistic.

I often consider how this relates to hyperacusis and misophonia. Responses I've received when disclosing my hearing quirks to others, or when in situations which have led me to display traits of these, have ranged from eye rolling and tuts, telling me that I should just learn to accept that some settings are loud (which is essentially to say that I should shut up and just endure the pain) to wishes that a cure will one day be found.

An enduring memory for me is a public meeting in 2010, regarding disability access plans for the 2012 Olympics and Paralympics, at which the representative from the organising body detailed the various measures to be put in place to facilitate accessibility. These included, quite rightly, British Sign Language interpretation and subtitling. When I asked about provision for those who had highly sensitive hearing, such as the option of booths similar to those used by commentators, I was aggressively told that there was no intent to create a reduced-volume space for those who could not endure noise without pain and that such people would have to accept that noise was simply a fact of the event. Anyone who couldn't tolerate noise could either use a one of the quiet rooms provided on some of the sites, thus missing the sporting events, or stay at home and watch the televised coverage.

I have come across similar stances with the vast majority of organisations I've contacted over the years. For some reason, hyperacusis and misophonia are seen as wilful, immature overreactions rather than differences which, without understanding and accessibility adjustments, can be profoundly disabling.

Access needs certainly can clash, for example a high-contrast, bright colour scheme can be helpful to some individuals with sight difficulties whereas, for someone like me with autism-related visual sensitivities and Mears-Irlen Syndrome, such schemes are excruciatingly painful. I do not consider clashing access needs an acceptable excuse for failing to cater for, or even care about, certain differences while making concerted efforts to deliver adjustments for others.

Noticing sounds that others do not, while sometimes resulting in receiving insults from those who refuse to believe that sounds imperceptible to them can be quite distinct to someone with hyperacute hearing, has had a profound effect on my life.

As my interest in finding my own style of composing grew, I realised that I could harness the results of my hyperacute hearing to inform my work. I became aware that where others might hear a sound, recognise and identify it and then think nothing further of it, I would find myself fixating on certain sounds, wanting to hear them over and over again and imagining the artistic possibilities.

Throughout the last two years of my university education, I alternated between borrowing field recorders to collect samples of sounds from 'everyday' objects and sitting in front of my laptop working through these collections and building pieces.

In my work, I seek to explore and creative possibilities of sounds and to use my music to express and communicate my sensory world to others.

Perhaps due to being autistic, I can become fixated upon certain sounds. At present, I'm obsessed with metallic sounds and have been for some years. This has led to interesting conversations with scrap metal workers, builders and scaffolders in which I explain briefly that I compose 'weird music' in the hope that they will allow me to take a few items of their work materials. So far, I've been met with combinations of smiles and odd looks, but despite my anxiety, I am becoming more comfortable with these responses.

Through my music, I feel I can communicate my emotions, ideas, and intentions authentically. I can say what I truly mean. As with all expression, some will respond to it positively, some negatively and some with indifference.

The world will always hurt. The barrage of noise, seemingly increasing loudness and the unpredictability of the auditory environment, continue to cause me excruciating pain and at times debilitating fear.

I wouldn't ever want my hearing to change. The beauty of certain sounds, the joy in discovering new ways to explore, express and communicate far outweigh the pain.

I hope that wider society will become more receptive to and understanding of aural diversity, both to create a more accessible and inclusive culture and to enable anyone, with any type of hearing, to be able to find their own kind of auditory joy.

INDEX

Note: Page numbers in **bold** indicate tables; those in *italics* indicate figures.

3D Tune-in 183

Ablinger, P., *Kopfhörer* 181, 183
absolute hearing threshold 60
absolute pitch 93
acousmatic listening 204
acoustemology 162
acoustic habitus 161, 162
acoustic privacy 46
acoustics 1, 6
acoustic shock 21
Adams, R. 3
adolescents 19
affordances: cochlear implants 74; deafblindness 64, 65, 67, 69, 70; sign in Human–Sound Interaction 187–8, 190
Afrisando, J.: 'The (Real) Laptop Music :))' 203–4, 205; *[SOUNDSCAPTION]* 204–5
age factors: dementia 163; Ménière's Disease 146, 154; musicians 129; music preferences 140; *see also* children; older people
ageing process 129, 130
age-related hearing loss *see* presbycusis
Alain, C. 129
Allen, S.: *Map Fragments and Aerosol (after Cornell)* 209; *Resonance at the Still Point of Change* 208–9
Altman, R. 178
alt-text 205
Alzheimer's disease 160; hand dryer noise 49; selfhood 161; speech comprehension 164; *see also* dementia
Amazon, Alexa 58
American Academy of Paediatrics 29

American Authors, *Pride* 190
American Sign Language (ASL) 190
anatomy: clinical perspective 14; foetal 30
animal hearing 1; *Ears of Others* project 180
anxiety: Ménière's Disease 153, 158; tinnitus 84
aphasia 58
Apple, Siri 58
artificial intelligence (AI) 4; cochlear implants 78; idealised ear 58
Asperger Syndrome 90
Assistive Listening Devices (ALDs) 139–40, 141
Atkinson, S. 222
Attenborough Arts Centre Aural Diversity Concert 196–200, 221
attention: auditory processing model 92; autism 94, 96, 97, 98; musicians 128; writing 114
attention deficit (hyperactivity) disorder 43, 224
audio description: COVID-19 pandemic 205; deafblindness 67; live music 201
audiology: clinical perspective 13–14, 16; hearing aid users and music listening 134, 135, 141; Ménière's Disease in musicians 156–7, 158; tests 116
audio-phonation 52
auditory hallucinations 20–1, 160, 166n2
auditory normate 55–62; design and systematically distorted communication 57–9; idealised sonic citizen 55; legislation 59–61; lived experiences 56; social relational model of sonic exclusion 56–7; social (re)production 61; template 56; *see also* auraltypicality
auditory processing: autism 92–4, 98; disorders (APD) 17, 20; model 91–2, *91*

auditory scene analysis 166n1; Alzheimer's disease 163; mild cognitive impairment 160, 162, 163
auditory skills, musicians 128–9, 130
augmented reality audio 178, 183–4
Augoyard, J.-F. 116, 117, 118
aural diversity: clinical perspective 13–22; nature of 1–5; paradigm shift 10
Aural Diversity Concerts 193–201; first 51, 193–5, *194*, *195*, 196, 197, 221; second 196–200, 221
Aural Diversity project 4–5
aural fullness 151, 158, 217
auraltypicality 1, 3; auditory processing model 91–2, *91*; hand dryer noise 42–3; musicology 9; *see also* auditory normate
auscultation 3
autism 90–8; Afrisando's 'The (Real) Laptop Music :))' 204; anecdotal reports 94–7; auditory processing 92–4; autism hour 59; composing with 217–22, 224; hand dryer noise 45, 49–50; hyperacusis 90, 93, 95, 97, 98, 152, 218; Ménière's Disease 152; neurodiversity 42–3; relaxed concerts 199
automatic writing 83, 85–6, 87, 88n4
autophony 82, 83
average hearing thresholds (AHT) 60

Babbitt, M., *Partitions* 212
Babypod 30
Back, L. 2–3
Barnett, S. 65, 67
Bauman, H.-D.L. 3
BBC: *Casualty* 178; Culture in Quarantine series 222
Beckett, S., *The Unnameable* 119
Beethoven, L. van: *Diabelli Variations* 216; hearing loss 9, 168, 217; *Heiligenstadt Testament* 9
behavioural-variant frontotemporal dementia 160
Belfast City Choir 185
big data, and cochlear implants 80
bipolar disorder 57
Blacking, J. 8
Blackman, L. 82, 84
Bog Standard 43
Bohm, D. 83
Bourdieu, P. 166n4
brain injuries 58
Braun, V. 146
British Film Institute 56
British Sign Language (BSL) 201; Aural Diversity Concerts 194, 198, 199; experimental music 209; Olympics and Paralympics 224; Turner's *The Wood and the Water* 189
British Society of Audiology (BSA) 136
British Standards: ISO 226:2003 2, 60; ISO 3744: 2010 47; ISO 12913-1: 2014 6, 7
British Tinnitus Association 121
Brucher, K. 165

built environment: auditory normate 58–9, 60–1; clinical perspective 22; toilet facilities 43
Butt, J. 9

captioning: Afrisando's *[SOUNDSCAPTION]* 204–5; experimental music 209; hearing aid users and music listening 137, 139, 140, 141; live music 201; Olympics and Paralympics 224
Cardiff, J. 181
Casualty 178
cerebral palsy 49
Chapman, D., *From the Station to the University* 197
Chesky, K. 128
Chevallier, C. 93
children: autism 93, 94; hand dryer noise 44–5, *45*; hyperacusis 19; ISO 226: 2003 2; musicians 127; premature birth 28; tinnitus 18
Chion, M. 52, 66
cholesteatoma 13
Clarke, E. 2
Clarke, V. 146
Classic FM 199
clinical perspective 13–22; anatomy, physiology, and functionality 14–16, *15*; diversity, impairment, or loss? 21–2; hearing disorders 17–21; hearing well 16–17
closed-captioning *see* captioning
cochlea: clinical perspective 14–22; foetal 30, 31
cochlear amusia 204
cochlear implants (CI) 4; Afrisando's 'The (Real) Laptop Music :))' 204; Aural Diversity Concerts 196; clinical perspective 13–14, 17, 18, 20; *Do You Hear What I Hear* project 180, 182; electrodogram 78; Ménière's Disease 152, 154, 157; music listening 139, 140; pianist's experience 210, 212, 215; simulation 178–9; as soundscape arranger 73–80
Cochlear Limited 73, 80
cochlear synaptopathy 125–6, 127, 129
cognitive impairment: mild 160–5; *see also* Alzheimer's disease
cognitive skills: ageing process 129; musicians 128–9, 130
composers: in aurally diverse communities 203–6; experimental music 207–9; with hearing differences 217–22; 'weird' music 223–5
concerts *see* live music
congenital deafness 14, 17, 21
Correfocs 101–10; burning, drumming, and relating to space 107–8; emotions in fire and drums 106–7; fire, devils, and clothing 104–5; history and name 102–4; place and senses 101–2; senses and protective gear 105–6, **106**, **107**
Corrigan, D. 64, 71
Costanza-Chock, S. 70
COVID-19 pandemic: Afrisando's *[SOUNDSCAPTION]* 204; *Correfoc* research 102, 108; hand washing practice 43; live music

200, 201; lockdowns and telephone calls 162, 163–4; lockdowns and tinnitus 84; positives 216
Crary, J. 68–9
Cripps, J. 190
Crompton, C.J. 94
Crook, H. 134
Csikszentmihalyi, M. 97

Daughtry, J.M. 44
David, A.L. 38
Davies, S., 'Backpack' 115, 118, 121
Davis, L.J. 56
Dawson, G. 94
d/Deaf people 3; Afrisando's 'The (Real) Laptop Music :))' 204; Beethoven 9, 168, 217; built environment 58; clinical perspective 14, 16, 17, 21; congenital deafness 14, 17, 21; Dickinson's poetry 112–14; enjoyment of music 203; experimental music 208; Glennie 9, 217; hearing aid users and music listening 136; legislation 61; lived experience 112–14; Mace 168–76; music-making 203, 204, 206; point-of-audition sound 178; relaxed concerts 199; signed music 189–91; single-sided deafness 18; social relational model of sonic exclusion 57; temporal norms 59; visual events as sound 116; see also hearing loss
d/Deaf Studies 3
deafblindness 64–71; Mace 169
decibels 2; hand dryers 47–8; occupational noise limit 125
deep listening 66, 67
Dembe, A. 50
dementia 160–5; with Lewy bodies 160; see also Alzheimer's disease
DeNora, T. 74
depression 153
Descartes, R. 39, 68
Devaney, K. *Star Cluster* 187
Dexterity 190
Dickinson, J., *Alphabetula* 112–14
diplacusis: clinical perspective 20; composing with 218–22, **220**; dysharmonia 20; Ménière's Disease 151–2, 154, 155, 157, 158; monoralis 20; in musicians 8; piano 219–21; remote collaboration 200
Disability Studies 3, 56–7
Dodge, M. 74
Dolmetsch, A. 169
Do You Hear What I Hear project 178–85; context 178–9; initial activities 179–84; potential developments 184–5
Drever, J.L.: Aural Diversity project 4; *Litany of the Hand Dryers* 51; *Sanitary Tones: Ayre #1 [Airblade]* 51; *Sanitary Tones: Ayre #2 [Dan Dryer]* 51; *Sanitary Tones: Ayre #3 [Kelston]* 51–2, 194, 198–9
drumming, *Correfocs* 101–10
Duchamp, M., *Box of 1914* 219
dyslexia 43

Dyson, J. 45–6
dyspraxia 43

earplugs: *Correfocs* 105, 108–9; hearing aid users and music listening 136, 138, 139; hyperacusis and misophonia 223; Ménière's Disease 155
Ears of Others project 180
ear worms 20
echo, *Do You Hear What I Hear* project 183
Edwards, T. 69
elderly people *see* older people
Encounter, The 181
Engelen, H. 52
environmental noise: foetal hearing 32, 33, 37; Ménière's Disease 158; *see also* hand dryers
epilepsy 211, 212
ergo-audition 52
Ettinger, B.L. 39

Fairnie, J. 94
fiction 115–21
Findlay-Walsh, I. 70
fire, *Correfocs* 101–10
Five Village Soundscapes project 75
FJDJ app 183
Fletcher, H. 2
Fletcher–Munson curves *see* ISO 226: 2003
flow 97, 98
foetal hearing 27–39; auditory environment 27, 29–39; auditory stress in neonatal wards 28–9; computational modelling 37–8, *38*; experimentation 37; filter 32–5, *34–5*; Sonic Womb Orrb 35–7, *36*; ultrasound images of ear *31*
Forbes, S. 190
Forsberg, T.L. 190
Franinović, K. 187
French, S. 179
frequency perception 1–2; deafblindness 69
frontotemporal dementia 160
Fryer, L. 64, 67–8, 70
Fulford, R. 134
Fuller, M. 68
functional hearing loss 21
Furlonge, N.B. 121

Gallego, A. 190
Garland-Thomson, R. 56, 68
Gaver, W. 187
Gélat, P. 37
gender factors: acoustic privacy 46; *Do You Hear What I Hear* project 183; Ménière's Disease in musicians 146
Gibson, J.J. 187
GIFT-Surg 38
gigs *see* live music
Glennie, E. 9, 217
Godøy, R. 187
Goodman, S. 55, 57, 69

Gordon, J. 211
Greed, C. 43, 50
Green, M. 180

Habermas, J. 57
hallucinations, auditory 20–1, 160, 166n2
Hamraie, A. 56, 58
hand dryers 42–53; acoustic privacy 46, 47, 48; acoustic testing 47–8, 49; audio-phonation 52; auraltypical world 42–3; Drever's *Sanitary Tones* 51–2, 194, 198–9; findings 50–2; hand washing practice 43; infant hearing 44–5, 45; noise and power 45–6; social survey 49–50; sound design 52; subgroups in toilet research 43; toilet acoustics 48–9
Handel, G.F. 168
hand washing practice 43
haptification 69
Haraway, D. 75, 114
harmony perception, in Ménière's Disease 153, 154, 158
HarpCI project 188, 189
Harrington, L. 113
Hart, E., *Sounds of the Unborn* 29
Haynes, V., *The Unheard* 179, 180, 181
He, S. 182
headphones: Ablinger's *Kopfhörer* 181, 183; Aural Diversity Concerts 193, 194, 197, 198; Chapman's *From the Station to the University* 197; *Do You Hear What I Hear* project 179, 181, 184; hearing aid users and music listening 136, 137, 138, 139; noise-cancelling 219; *The Unheard* 181
Hear – Advanced Listening app 183–4
hearing aids 4; Afrisando's 'The (Real) Laptop Music :))' 204; audio latency 184; augmented reality audio apps 184; Beethoven 9; clinical perspective 16, 17–18, 20; cochlear implants comparison 76–7; hand dryer noise 49; hearing loss simulation 179; limitations 176; Ménière's Disease 152, 154, 157, 158, 219; music listening 134–41; pianist's experience 210, 211, 212, 215; speech of user 76; *The Unheard* 179
Hearing Aids for Music project 134–41
Hearing Landscape Critically conference (2015) 4
hearing loops 201
hearing loss: age-related *see* presbycusis; as catalyst for intermedia practice 207–9; clinical perspective 13, 15, 17–18, 21; composing with 217–22; *Correfocs* 109; *Do You Hear What I Hear* project 182; hand dryer noise 46, 53; hidden 125–6, 130; lived experience 116, 176, 207–22; Ménière's Disease 143, **144**, 146, 151, 152, 155–8; musicians 8, 125–9, 210–16; music listening 134–41; noise-induced (NIHL) 18; reading and sound, relationship between 117, 121; remote collaboration 200; simulation (HLS) 178–9, 180, 182, 183, 184; *The Unheard* 179, 180, 181; unilateral 18; *see also* d/Deaf people; deafblindness

hearing protection: musicians 125–6, 128, 129, 130; *see also* earplugs
Hear One earbuds 184
Henriques, J. 33, *36*, 65, 66
hidden hearing loss 125–6, 130
high-speed hand dryers *see* hand dryers
HIVE Choir 185
Holt, N., *Boomerang* (with R. Serra) 183
Holzman, D. 4
Howe, F. 85
Hughes, B. 59
Hugill, A.: Aural Diversity Concert 4, 51, 219; *Kelston Birdsong* 219, 221; *A Robin in the Snow* 222; *Spectrum Sounds* 219, 222; *Thirty Minutes for Diplacusis Piano* 193, 197, 219–21; *Verdigrade* 222
Human–Sound Interaction (HSI), sign in 187–91; signed music 189–91; Turner's *The Wood and the Water* 188–9
Hume, D. 68
hyperacusis: Afrisando's 'The (Real) Laptop Music :))' 204; Alzheimer's disease 160; autism 90, 93, 95, 97, 98, 152, 218; clinical perspective 19, 21; composing 'weird' music 223–5; *Do You Hear What I Hear* project 180; hand dryer noise 49, 53; Hugill's *Spectrum Sounds* 222; Ménière's Disease 152; mild cognitive impairment 160, 163, 164, 165, 166n3; musicians 8, 208; pain 19, 223, 224, 225; relaxed concerts 199; remote collaboration 200; temporal norms 59

Ihde, D. 76
imagination: deafblindness 66–8; reading and sound, relationship between 116
Impey, A. 66
incubators for premature babies 27, 28–9, 38
Intelligent Facility Solutions 47, 51
inter-aural pitch difference *see* diplacusis
interior design *see* built environment
International Symbol of Access 60
Irigaray, L. 39
ISO 226: 2003 2, 60
ISO 3744: 2010 47
ISO 12913-1: 2014 6, 7

Jacobs, P. 210, 212
Jacques, A. 143
Jauniaux, E. *36*
Johannesen, P.T. 129
Joyce, J., *Ulysses* 119

Kafer, A. 68
Kanngieser, A. 56
Kassabian, A. 2
Kelston Roundhill Aural Diversity Concert 193–5, *194*, *195*, 196, 197, 221
Khalfa, S. 93
Kingma, E. 39
Kitchin, R. 74

Kitwood, T. 161
Krznaric, R. 53
Kuppers, P. 68
Kyle, J. 67

Lacey, K. 115
Latour, B. 79
learning disabilities: auditory normate template 56; autism 90; voice-first computing 58
Lee, A. 200
legislation 59–61
Leman, M. 66
Lewis, M.: *How in the World Do We Know?* 68; *No Such Thing as Empty Space* 67–8, 69
listening walks 74–6
Liu, Y. 191
live music: hearing aid users 136–7, 138, 140–1; online 200, 201; relaxed concerts 199; *see also* Aural Diversity Concerts
Locke, J. 68
Lopez-Teijon, M. 30
loudness: Afrisando's 'The (Real) Laptop Music :))' 204; autism 93, 98; *Correfocs* 105, 108, 109; Mace 168, 176; Ménière's Disease 153, 155; mild cognitive impairment 163, 165; musicians 125; and power 44, 45–6, 48–9, 50, 51; sensitivity *see* hyperacusis
Luiselli, V., *Lost Children Archive* 115, 117–21
Lundhal & Seitl 181
Lute-Dyphone 169, 171–2, *172*
lyric perception, hearing aid users 134, 135, 136, 138, 139, 140–1

Mabey, R. 161–2
Mace, T. 168–76; disability 169–70; Lute-Dyphone 169, 171–2, *172*; *Musick's Monument* 168–76, *172, 174, 175*; relevance today 176; Trinity College Cambridge 168, 169, 170
machine listening 1, 4, 79
Mahabharata 28
Maisieres, A.T. de *36*
Maler, A. 190
malingering 21
Mallalieu, R. 193
Mampe, B. 28
Martino, D. 211; *Pianissimo* 211–12, *211*
Mathé, I.D. and Y., *Sounds of the Unborn* 29
Mauldin, L. 80
McCartney, P., *My Valentine* 190
McCormack, L. 35
McCormack, M., *Solar Bones* 119
McDonald, J. 215
McEwan, I., *Nutshell* 28
McLeod, D., *Intimate Karaoke, Live at Uterine Concert Hall* 30
Mears-Irlen Syndrome 224
medial olivocochlear system 127, 128
Melbourne, A. 38

Ménière's Disease: Afrisando's 'The (Real) Laptop Music :))' 204; Aural Diversity project 4; composing with 217–22; hand dryer noise 49; hearing care 156–7; hearing consequences 155–6; hearing technologies 157; medical consequences 151–2; musical consequences 153; musical perceptions 153–5; musicians 143–58, **144–5**, *149–50*; personal consequences 153; pitch perception 138; treatments 152
Ménière's Society 143
Mercè, la 103
Mermod, A. 35
Messiaen, O. 210, 218
Messud, C. 118
middle ear muscles 20, 21
middle ear myoclonus (MEM) 20
mild cognitive impairment (MCI) 160–5
Mills, M. 77, 116
Milton, D.E.M. 94
mindfulness 14
Minimic 219
misophonia: clinical perspective 19–20; composing 'weird' music 223–5; hand dryer noise 53; Hugill's *Spectrum Sounds* 222
Miyakita, T. 127
Moe, A.M. 113–14
Mottron, L. 93
Mufti, N. 38
Mullender, R. 3
Murray, J. 3
musical dynamics 155
musical hallucinations 20–1
musicians: age, noise exposure, cognition, and hearing problems 125–30, *127*; COVID-19 pandemic 200; experimental 207–9; hearing aids 136–7, 139; hyperacusis and misophonia 223–5; Mace 168–76; Ménière's Disease 143–58, **144–5**, *149–50*, 217–18; mild cognitive impairment 160, 164–5; pianist's hearing journey 210–16
Musiek, F.E. 60
MyoSpat 187

Nancy, J.-L. 116
Napolin, J.B. 117
National Autistic Society 59
neonates 27, 28–9, 30, 31–2
neurodiversity 42–3; experimental music 208, 209; Hugill's *Spectrum Sounds* 222
neurotypicality 42
Nightingale, F. 43
nociception, *Correfocs* 106, 108, 109
noise: autism 93, 95; environmental *see* environmental noise; occupational noise limit 125; and power, hand dryers 44, 45–6, 48–9, 50, 51; sensitivity *see* hyperacusis; volume *see* loudness
noise-cancelling headphones 219
Noise Exposure Structured Interview (NESI) 126
noise-induced hearing loss (NIHL) 18

noise vocoders: *Do You Hear What I Hear* project 180, 182; *Ways of Hearing* app 184
Norman, K. 2
normate *see* auditory normate
normate-time 68

older people: age-related hearing loss *see* presbycusis; musicians 129, 168
Oliver, E. 198
Oliveros, P. 2, 66
Olympics 224
Online Toolkit app 183
OptimUS 37
Orrb Technologies 35
otoacoustic emissions (OAE) 16, 17, 18
Otohimes 46, *47*, *48*
otology 13–14
ototoxicity 138

pain: *Correfocs* 108, 109–10; hyperacusis 19, 223, 224, 225; mild cognitive impairment 165
Paralympics 224
Parbery-Clark, A. 129
parcopresis 46
Parker, T. 56
Parkinson's disease 160
paruresis 46
Pascal scale 2
Paterson, K. 59
patient reported outcome measures (PROMs) 13
Pavlicevic, M. 66
Pavlov, I. 14
Penner, B. 43
perceptual capacity, autism 94
permanent threshold shift (PTS) 18
personhood, mild cognitive impairment 161, 165
Philips Design 52
physiology 14
pianist's hearing journey 210–16
pitch difference, inter-aural *see* diplacusis
pitch perception: autism 93, 98; composing with hearing differences 220; hearing aid users 134, 137, 138, 139, 158; hearing loss 212, 215; Ménière's Disease 138, 153–4, 155, 157, 158
Plato 38–9
poetry 112–14
point-of-audition (POA) sound 178
post-traumatic stress disorder (PTSD) 49
Poulton, D. 168–9
Pouryaghoub, G. 155
power and noise, hand dryers 44, 45–6, 48–9, 50, 51
prediction, auditory processing model 92
pregnancy *see* foetal hearing
premature babies 27, 28–9, 30, 31–2
presbycusis: Afrisando's 'The (Real) Laptop Music :))' 204; clinical perspective 15, 17–18; *Do You Hear What I Hear* project 180; Mace 168–76; Ménière's Disease 157; mild cognitive impairment 162, 163, 164; musicians 129, 168; progression 161–2; recruitment issues 166n3
privacy, acoustic 46
prosody comprehension: autism 93–4, 98; mild cognitive impairment 160
prosthetic technologies *see* cochlear implants; hearing aids
pure tone audiometry (PTA) 16, 17

Queen, *Bohemian Rhapsody* 190
quiet hours 59

reading and sound, relationship between 115–21
Reality Jockey 183
Reassembled Slightly Askew 181
recruitment 17
Reily, S.A. 165
Reiss, B. 3
Remington, A. 94
reverberation 118
rhythm perception, Ménière's Disease 153, 154
Rice, T. 3
Robinson, T. 176n4
roger pens 140
Rosen, C. 212
Royal Conservatoire of Scotland 189
Royal Society of Musicians 168
Rychtáriková, R. 60

Saariketo, M. 77
Sacks, O. 143
Sahley, T.L. 60
Schaeffer, P. 2, 66
Schafer, R.M. 6, 45, 48–9, 74
Schoenberg, A., op. 11: 212; *Drei Klavierstücke 213*
schools 60
Schubert, F. 216
Scott, D. 32–3
Scriabin, A. 218
selfhood, mild cognitive impairment 161, 165
semantic dementia 161
Sense 64–71
sensitivity to sound *see* hyperacusis
Sensory Trust 162–4
Serafin, S. 187
Sergeyenko, Y. 129
Serlin, D. 3
Serra, R., *Boomerang* (with N. Holt) 183
Sheeran, E., *You Need Me, I Don't Need You* 190
shellshock silence 178
sign language: Aural Diversity Concerts 194, 198, 199; clinical perspective 17; COVID-19 pandemic 205; deafblindness 69; experimental music 209; Human–Sound Interaction 187–91; live music 201; Olympics and Paralympics 224
Signmark 190
Silberman, S. 43
simulated hearing loss 178–9, 180, 182, 183, 184

single-sided deafness (SSD) 18
Siri 58
Skinner, J. 114
Skoe, E. 125
sleep 68–9
Sloterdijk, P. 39
Small, C. 164
Smalley, D. 2, 66
social anxiety 57
social media, and autism 94–5
social model of disability 5, 57, 206, 224
social relational model of sonic exclusion 56–7
Solomons, L. 83, 85–6, 87
sonic experience 116–21
Sonic Inclusion project 56
Sonic Interaction Design (SID) 187
sonic objects 118, 120
Sonic Womb project 27–8, 30–8
soundscapes 5–7; autism 95, 95–7, 98; cochlear implant as soundscape arranger 73–80; *Correfocs* 101; mild cognitive impairment 162; womb 29–30
Southworth, M. 5
spatial hearing 76
speech comprehension: Alzheimer's disease 163–4; hearing loss 207; mild cognitive impairment 160
speech perception: audiology tests 116; auditory processing disorders 20; auditory processing model 92; autism 93–4, 95, 98; cochlear implants 76, 77; deafblindness 69; *Do You Hear What I Hear* project 182, 183; frequency perception 2; hand dryer noise 46; hearing aid users 76, 135, 136, 138; hearing loss 210, 211, 215; Ménière's Disease 157; mild cognitive impairment 163; mother's 28, 29, 30–1, 36; musicians 126, 128–30; presbycusis 17; single-sided deafness 18; textual hearing aids 115
Spring, M. 193
Springer Handbook of Auditory Research 2
stammer 57
stapedius muscle 20
Stein, G. 83, 85–6, 87, 88n4
Sterne, J. 3, 69, 75, 178, 185
stethoscopes 3
Stockhausen, K. 46
Stoever, J.L. 55, 121
Sturtivant, S. 193; *Sensonic* 197, 198
Subpac 64
subtitles *see* captioning
Sun Kim, C. 189–90
superior semicircular canal dehiscence 82, 83, 84, 85, 88
surtitles *see* captioning
synaesthesia 218, 222

Tadoma 69
Tanaka, A. 187

telephones: mild cognitive impairment 162, 163–4; norms 116
temporary threshold shift (TTS) 18
tensor tympani muscle 20, 21
tensor tympani syndrome 20
textual hearing aids 115–21
theory of mind 93–4
Thom, J. 61
Thomas, M., 'Extreme Rambling' 61
Thompson, E. 6
Thompson, M. 30, 82
timbre perception, Ménière's Disease 153, 154–5
Timm, R. 190
tinnitus: Afrisando's 'The (Real) Laptop Music :))' 204; Aural Diversity Concerts 198; Aural Diversity project 4; cinematic 178; clinical perspective 14, 18–19, 21; composing with 217–22; *Correfocs* 109; *Do You Hear What I Hear* project 180, 182; hand dryer noise 53; hearing aid users and music listening 136, 138; lived experience 82–8, 116, 217–22; Ménière's Disease 143, **145**, 151, 152, 155, 158; musicians 8, 125–9, 208; reading and sound, relationship between 117, 121; relaxed concerts 199; remote collaboration 200; *The Unheard* 179, 180, 181
Tinnitus, Auditory Knowledge and the Arts project 82
Tlalim, T., *Tonotopia* 4
Tomatis, A.A. 2, 39, 52, 53
Torgue, H. 116, 117, 118
Tourette's Syndrome 61
Truax, B. 2, 6, 60, 66, 75
Tsing, A.L. 83, 87, 88
Tufts, J.B. 125
Tullio's Phenomenon 152
Turner, E., *The Wood and the Water* 187, *188*, 188–9, 191

underwater listening 33
Unheard, The 179, 180, 181
unilateral hearing loss 18
Unlimited festival 208
Urban-Related Sensorium conference 182
Ustaszewski, A. 49, 222; 'nmo20' 224

vaginal speakers 30
Van de Cruys, S. 94
Vear, C. 221
Vella de Gràcia, La 102, *103*, *104*
vertigo: composing with 217–22; Ménière's Disease 143, 151, 152, 153, 158; tinnitus 84
vestibular schwannoma 13
visual impairment: colour schemes 224; hand dryer noise 49; Mace 169; mild cognitive impairment 163; social relational model of sonic exclusion 57; *see also* deafblindness
Voegelin, S. 66, 67, 70
voice-first computing 58

Wallace, R. 9
Ways of Hearing: app 179, 180, 182, 184; workshop 182
wearable technology 80
Weheliye, A.G. 121
Weinberg, M.S. 46
'weird' music, composing 223–5
West, D. 198
Westerkamp, H. 50; *Kit Beach Sound Walk* 50
Wet Sounds 33
wheelchair users 59
Whitman, W. 113

Will, B. 83, 85
Williams, C.J. 46
Wolpe, S. 212; *First Piece, Battle Piece 214*
womb as auditory environment 27, 29–39
Wong, M.-S. 120
World Health Organization (WHO) 32
World Soundscape Project 75
Wright, D. 116, 120
Wylie, J. 114

Zendel, B.R. 129
Zhang, M. 98

Printed in Dunstable, United Kingdom